DEVILS AND REBELS

Devils and Rebels

THE MAKING OF HAWTHORNE'S DAMNED POLITICS

Larry J. Reynolds

THE UNIVERSITY OF MICHIGAN PRESS

ANN ARBOR

Contents

debtedness to Nina Baym, Millicent Bell, Sacvan Bercovitch, Lawrence Buell, Bell Chevigny, Samuel Coale, Phyllis Cole, Monika Elbert, Teresa Goddu, Len Gougeon, Gordon Hutner, Buford Jones, Robert Levine, Deshae Lott, Richard Millington, Joel Myerson, Frederick Newberry, Leland Person, Sandra Petrulionis, Joel Pfister, Jeffrey Steele, and Susan Williams.

I owe a special debt to two friends and Hawthorne specialists, Brenda Wineapple and Thomas Mitchell, who read early portions of this study. I thank them for their expert commentary. I'm also grateful to the anonymous readers for the University of Michigan Press for their detailed responses. The fine editors Jana Argersinger and Albert J. von Frank helped me improve a portion of this study, published as the article "The Challenge of Cultural Relativity: The Case of Hawthorne," *ESQ: A Journal of the American Renaissance* 49 (2003): 129–47. Another portion appeared as the essay " 'Strangely Ajar with the Human Race': Hawthorne, Slavery, and the Question of Moral Responsibility," in *Hawthorne and the Real: Bicentennial Essays,* ed. Millicent Bell (Columbus: Ohio State University Press, 2005), 40–69. I am grateful to the anonymous readers of that volume for their commentary.

For generously sharing with me useful information and documents over the years, I wish to thank Amy Earhart, Robert Gross, Julie Hall, Jan Little, Melinda Ponder, and Magnus Ullén. Three of my colleagues have been generous enough to read the entire book in manuscript and to suggest needed revisions: I'm deeply grateful to my current department head, Jimmie Killingsworth, for his timely and helpful reading; to my good friend Dennis Berthold, for his expert reading and helpful responses, given week after week following our racquetball games; and to my wife, Susan Egenolf, for her insightful reading, penetrating questions, and warm support. To Susan and our children, Charlotte and Logan, I also extend heartfelt gratitude for their joy, love, and patience.

Note on the Texts

Throughout this study, I have used *The Centenary Edition of the Works of Nathaniel Hawthorne*, ed. William Charvat et al., 23 vols. (Columbus: Ohio State University Press, 1962–97). This edition is cited parenthetically in the text by volume and page number. The titles of the volumes are as follows:

Vol. 1: *The Scarlet Letter* (1962)
Vol. 2: *The House of the Seven Gables* (1965)
Vol. 3: *"The Blithedale Romance" and "Fanshawe"* (1964)
Vol. 4: *The Marble Faun: or, The Romance of Monte Beni* (1968)
Vol. 5: *Our Old Home: A Series of English Sketches* (1970)
Vol. 6: *True Stories from History and Biography* (1972)
Vol. 7: *"A Wonder Book" and "Tanglewood Tales"* (1972)
Vol. 8: *The American Notebooks* (1972)
Vol. 9: *Twice-Told Tales* (1974)
Vol. 10: *Mosses from an Old Manse* (1974)
Vol. 11: *The Snow Image, and Uncollected Tales* (1974)
Vol. 12: *The American Claimant Manuscripts* (1977)
Vol. 13: *The Elixir of Life Manuscripts* (1977)
Vol. 14: *The French and Italian Notebooks* (1980)
Vol. 15: *The Letters, 1813–1843* (1984)

ation with the unpopular presidency of Franklin Pierce (whom Thoreau called the "Devil")[1] and his subsequent lack of partisanship during the Civil War alienated him from his Concord neighbors, his Peabody relatives, and leading abolitionists, a number of whom damned him as inhumane and heartless. This moralistic approach to Hawthorne's politics persists into the present day, and he continues to be charged with the sins of blindness, cowardice, and escapism.[2] Because he shared the racism of his white middle-class society, this feature of his vision, rather than his political independence (or "perversity," as Emerson called it), has become the focus of recent judgments directed at him.[3]

The opprobrium cast on Hawthorne, past and present, illuminates not merely the difficulties faced by a public intellectual of imagination and thoughtfulness during times of political strife but also the need to develop a more comprehensive approach to the literary history of the American Renaissance, an approach less indebted to the discourse of New England righteousness and more attentive to perspectives and values beyond that region. Let me hasten to say I have no quarrel with judging an author with respect to one's own present set of moral and political values (how can one do otherwise?); however, to be fair, scholars need to recognize and allow for the cultural relativity of such values. Hawthorne's racism is a case in point—it was invisible to other white citizens in his time, though glaringly wrong in ours.

The challenge of understanding the nature and development of Hawthorne's political views is complicated by the highly charged partisan environment in which he lived and the strong centripetal force it exerted and continues to exert on every would-be independent observer, making detachment seem morally untenable. Moreover, the main issues that stirred passions and colored judgments in his times—slavery, women's rights, tyranny, revolution, violence, war—still maintain their power to affect us. Because of my own politics, I have no desire to defend Hawthorne's "brooding conservatism," as James Mellow calls it, or his repugnant racism, which Brenda Wineapple has acutely highlighted;[4] nevertheless, I believe that to do justice to the depth, complexity, and even progressiveness of Hawthorne's political views, it is necessary to place them in a larger context than antebellum New England reform and to examine them from Hawthorne's perspective, as part of his own historically and internationally informed—albeit still partial—imagined world. I recognize the main ethical question raised by such a task:

put on his pacifism by current events and the aggressiveness of his fellow New Englanders. Despite his marginalization and temporary militancy, however, Hawthorne remained constant to his political principles, resisting the hostile currents of thought around him, though well aware of the accusations of treason and immorality leveled at him by friends, family, and one part of himself.

Introduction:
The Damnation of Hawthorne's Politics

I was at that time devoting myself to the cause of emancipation, and was daily hearing from some of our anti-slavery rank and file sharp words concerning Hawthorne, but never for a moment did I have any such feeling towards him. . . . He had not the flexibility of principle displayed by so many in those days. He thus had no party,—then nearly equivalent to having no country.

  —Moncure Daniel Conway, *Life of Nathaniel Hawthorne*

We should be sorry to cast a doubt on the Peaceable Man's loyalty, but he will allow us to say that we consider him premature in his kindly feelings towards traitors, and sympathizers with treason. . . . There are some degrees of absurdity that put Reason herself into a rage, and affect us like an intolerable crime—which this Rebellion is, into the bargain.

  —Editor's (Hawthorne's) note, "Chiefly about War-Matters"

In the midst of the Civil War, Nathaniel Hawthorne wrote his friend Horatio Bridge, thanking him "for a shaded map of Negrodom, which you sent me a little while ago. What a terrible amount of trouble and expense, in washing that sheet white!—and, after all, I am afraid we shall only variegate it with blood and dirt" (18:428). The map Hawthorne refers to most likely resembled the *Moral Map of U.S.* (see figure 1), which Northern abolitionists had used to illustrate the white moral purity of the free states compared to the black evil of the Southern slave states. The map's linking the putative color of slaves with the evils of slavery was an injustice so ingrained in the American political unconscious that it remained invisible, even to abolitionists. Embedded within Hawthorne's comments on the map are two features of his political thought that would earn him condemnation in his own times and ours. The first is his skepticism, called by one of his English critics "the most immoral kind of political fatalism."[1] The second is his racism (implicit in the term "Negrodom"), which has become more noticeable and objectionable with each passing year.

Hawthorne's skepticism about purifying the country by eliminating slavery arose not from any proslavery sentiments (he detested slavery, calling it a "foul scurf" [23:431] on the South) but, rather, from his deep-seated belief that attempts to rid a village, region, or nation of evil could produce results just the opposite of those desired, especially if the means used were violent. As a student of history and lifelong observer of human nature, he considered almost all people and causes irrevocably "variegated," a mixture of moral qualities resistant to purification and cleansing. In such tales as "The Birth-Mark" (1843) and "Earth's Holocaust" (1844), he made this point explicitly, and it also informed his attitude toward the abolitionist movement. In 1857, he insisted, in response to an abolitionist pamphlet by his sister-in-law Elizabeth Peabody that "[v]engeance and beneficence are things that God claims for Himself. His instruments have no consciousness of His purpose; if they imagine they have, it is a pretty sure token that they are *not* His instruments. The good of others, like our own happiness, is not to be attained by direct effort, but incidentally" (18:116). In "Chiefly about War-Matters," Hawthorne speaks of the Civil War in the same terms: "No human effort, on a grand scale, has ever yet resulted according to the purpose of its projectors. The advantages are always incidental. Man's accidents are God's purposes. We miss the good we sought, and do the good we little cared for" (23:431).

Because of this conviction, Hawthorne found himself during the 1850s and 1860s more and more at odds with his New England contemporaries, who professed to have direct access to a "higher law," or the will of God. Appeals to this "law" became frequent among abolitionists after the publication of Senator Frederick Seward's speech before Congress on March 11, 1850, attacking the bill for the Compromise of 1850 and arguing that there was "a higher law than the Constitution."[2] In their defense of John Brown, the tran-

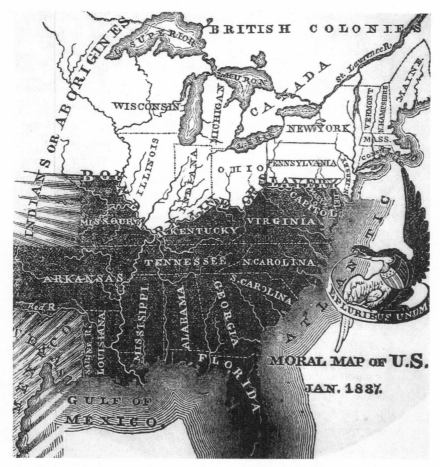

Moral Map of U.S. Frontispiece of *The Legion of Liberty! And Force of Truth,*
2nd ed (New York: American Anti-Slavery Society, 1843).

scendentalists Thoreau and Emerson referred to this "higher law" as well.
Following Hawthorne's death in 1864, Emerson lamented in his journal that
his Concord neighbor had "removed" himself "by the indignation his perverse politics & unfortunate friendship for that paltry Franklin Pierce
awaked,—though it rather moved pity for Hawthorne, & the assured belief
that he would outlive it, & come right at last."[3] Obviously, the "right" position Emerson referred to was his own, and it carried heavy moral weight. In

fact, a sense of moral superiority circulated in the Concord community with regard to Hawthorne for many years after his death. In 1886, Philip R. Ammidon commented, "I remember with what concern I once heard a resident of Concord, a man not unknown in the world of letters, speak of certain evils likely to result from 'Hawthorne's fall.' " The "fall" referred to Hawthorne's "effort in behalf of his old college comrade and life-long friend [Pierce], that was supposed to imply a state of moral declension fitly indicated by the sinister word."[4] Such an assessment surely added to the sense of isolation Hawthorne experienced during his final years.

The most hostile criticism Hawthorne received during his lifetime came in response to his public comments on the Civil War in "Chiefly about War-Matters." The essay originated in Hawthorne's attempt to penetrate the patriotic propaganda surrounding him, and as he began the essay, he explained, "I gave myself up to reading newspapers and listening to the click of the telegraph, like other people; until, after a great many months of such pastime, it grew so abominably irksome that I determined to look a little more closely at matters, with my own eyes" (23:404). As it did for Walt Whitman, the closer look led to compassion for those soldiers victimized by the war. Hawthorne had visited a Union prison house in Virginia, the old engine house that was John Brown's fort. He later described the rebel soldiers he saw there as "simple, bumpkin-like fellows, dressed in homespun clothes, with faces singularly vacant of meaning," adding, "It is my belief that not a single bumpkin of them all . . . had the remotest comprehension of what they had been fighting for, or how they had deserved to be shut up in that dreary hole" (23:429). Elsewhere in the essay, he expressed skepticism about the war effort and disdain for John Brown. Not surprisingly, he was consequently denounced as unpatriotic and slandered as treasonous. William Lloyd Garrison's *Liberator* called the essay "flippant and heartless" and accused the author of writing "automatically, as though his veins were bloodless!" Hawthorne's suggestion that the rebel soldier be allowed "an honorable burial in the soil he fights for" outraged the *Liberator:* "[W]hat claim have these traitors to any sympathy or apology beyond what is due to the worst felons of the human race? To talk of 'an honorable burial' for such, is to confound all moral distinctions."[5] Conway, in his biography of Hawthorne, came close to blaming him for the war itself. His reasoning was that Franklin Pierce was a political unknown until Hawthorne's campaign biography brought him to national attention and got him elected president; Pierce's subsequent weakness allowed the slavocracy to repeal the Missouri Compromise and precipitate "Bleeding Kansas," which "made the war inevitable."[6] Even Whitman, late in life, recalled of Hawthorne, "What a devil of a Copperhead he was! I always more or less despise the Copperheads, irrespective of who they are."[7]

The charge that Hawthorne was a "Copperhead" (i.e., a Northerner who supported the South) lacks validity, as does the assertion that he sympathized with slavery or slaveholders. Throughout his adult life, Hawthorne held extremely loyal sectional sympathies, and he considered the South unworthy of the Union. Until the early 1850s, he remained a loyal member of the Democratic Party, which had strong Southern membership. Yet deep divisions emerged within the party in 1848, and whereas Franklin Pierce had Southern friends and sympathized with the Southern view of states' rights, Hawthorne did not. Thus the Fugitive Slave Law of 1850 drove him into the camp of the Free-Soil Party (dedicated to prohibiting slavery in the new territory acquired from Mexico), as it did many other Northern Democrats, including Whitman and former president Martin Van Buren (the Free-Soil candidate for president in 1848). Whereas Pierce supported the Compromise of 1850 because his greatest loyalty was to the Union, Hawthorne longed for the day New England could exist independent of the slaveholding South. During the Civil War, his outlook coincided with that of his friend Charles Sumner, the famous Free-Soil and later Republican senator who helped him secure his appointment as consul to Liverpool. On February 13, 1862, Hawthorne told his friend Horatio Bridge that Pierce "is bigoted to the Union, and sees nothing but ruin without it; whereas, I, (if we can only put the boundary far enough south) should not much regret an ultimate separation" (18:428).

Even before the war began, Hawthorne wrote his publisher William Ticknor that perhaps "I shall have a new Romance ready by the time New-England becomes a separate nation—a consummation I rather hope for than otherwise" (18:363). Like many of his contemporaries, Hawthorne observed the growing sectionalism of the 1850s, caused by slavery and by the industrialization in the North and the increase in wealth, population, and power that accompanied it, all of which evoked a sense of paranoia and hostility in the South.[8] At the end of 1854, Hawthorne wrote his friend Bridge from England that the United States seemed "so convulsed with party-spirit" that "it looks to me as if there were an actual fissure between the North and South, which may widen and deepen into a gulf anon" (17:294). When civil war finally broke out, Hawthorne wanted the North to go its separate way, yet he rejected the binary thinking that reduced the war to a matter of good and evil, patriotism and treason. On March 8, 1863, he informed the Englishman Henry Bright, "The war-party here do not look upon me as a reliably loyal man, and, in fact, I have been publicly accused of treasonable sympathies;— whereas, I sympathize with nobody and approve of nothing; and if I have any wishes on the subject, it is that New England might be a nation by itself" (18:543).

Later in 1863, Hawthorne sparked even deeper political animosity by dedicating his collection of essays on England, *Our Old Home,* to Pierce, whom New Englanders blamed for colluding with proponents of slavery. In 1863, Pierce was declared a traitor in the press when he spoke out against the Lincoln administration and when a letter of his was discovered by Union troops in the home of Jefferson Davis after Davis had fled. Thus, when Hawthorne's *Our Old Home* appeared several months later, with a prefatory dedication to Pierce, guilt by association dogged him. Hawthorne knew how impolitic the dedication would be but wished to acknowledge his gratitude and respect for Pierce. As he expected, the gesture brought more righteous indignation his way. A notice in *Harper's Weekly* found the "tone of doubt and indifference" toward the Civil War repellent, like that of "the most charming companion who should prove to have no objection to infanticide."[9] Emerson vented his disgust by cutting the dedication from his complimentary copy of the book, and Harriet Beecher Stowe, in a November 1863 letter to Hawthorne's publishers, Ticknor and Fields, inquired, "Do tell me if our friend Hawthorne praises that arch-traitor Pierce in his preface and your loyal firm publishes it. I never read the preface and, have not yet seen the book, but they say so here, and I can scarcely believe it of you, if I can of him. I regret that I went to see him last summer. What! patronize such a traitor to our faces! I can scarce believe it."[10]

Because Hawthorne's death, occurring in 1864, came during the war, a number of the contemporary memorial reviews of his career addressed his recent politics. George William Curtis, a Northern Democrat, who had been a friend of Hawthorne's at Brook Farm and later Concord, found himself struggling to suppress his outrage at Hawthorne's lack of partisan fervor. His *North American Review* essay on Hawthorne's works begins by citing

Hawthorne's great-grandfather's infamous role in the Salem witch trials and dramatizing the judge's treatment of Goodwife Corey, exclaiming, "What a piteous picture of the awful Colonial Inquisition and the village Torquemade! What a grim portrait of an ancestor to hang in your memory, and to trace your kindred to!" Referring to Hawthorne's Salem origins, Curtis asserts, "The old witch-hanging city had no weirder product than this dark-haired son." After characterizing Hawthorne as hard, cold, and perverse, Curtis claims that "the high tides of collective emotion among his fellows left him dry and untouched." Curtis credits Massachusetts with the Puritan righteousness needed to contend with the corrupt South—"the moral and physical tenacity which is wrestling with the Rebellion was toughened among these flinty and forbidding rocks"—and he judges that in *The Scarlet Letter,* "there seems to be wanting a deep, complete, sympathetic appreciation of the fine moral heroism, the spiritual grandeur, which overhung that gloomy life." Curtis saw such heroism and grandeur as invigorating the Union—a sight, he claims, Hawthorne missed: "[H]is own times and their people and their affairs were just as shadowy to him as those of any of his stories." Thus Curtis argues that we must ask of Hawthorne, "Is he human? Is he a man?"[11]

Another Concord neighbor who disdained Hawthorne for his politics was Franklin Sanborn, teacher of the Emerson, Hawthorne, and Alcott children and one of the "Secret Six" who sponsored John Brown's Harpers Ferry raid. In his book *Hawthorne and His Friends: Reminiscence and Tribute* (1908), Sanborn claims that when Hawthorne returned from England, he was "less shy, more accustomed to meet his fellow mortals gracefully,—but, too, less simple and agreeable in his intimate manners and general character." Sanborn attaches guilt by association to Hawthorne by pointing out that in the summer of 1863, he "sat on the platform at Concord, New Hampshire, at the bench of his friend Pierce, . . . and listened to the almost treasonable speech of Pierce against the war."[12] (Pierce faulted the Lincoln administration for exercising "unconstitutional, arbitrary, irresponsible power.")[13] As for the Civil War itself, Sanborn claims that Hawthorne "hardly reflected upon the situation" and that his "Chiefly about War-Matters" was incoherent: "it puzzled both the friends and foes of human liberty."[14]

Both Sanborn and Curtis, prolific writers and memoirists, exerted a strong influence on twentieth-century scholarship, not just because of their firsthand knowledge of the major New England authors, but also because of their system of values and beliefs, which appealed to the literary historians who emerged from the region in the years that followed. (As is well known, the American literary tradition has been dominated for the most part by the New England literary tradition.) For twentieth-century scholars, Hawthorne served as a foil in discussions of his more activist contemporaries. For example, Merle Curti, in his *The Growth of American Thought* (1943), observes that during the Civil War, "Almost all the leading men of light and learning exemplified ardent patriotism," yet Hawthorne, "already near the end of his road, was numbed by the national catastrophe."[15] George Frederickson, in his study of antebellum Northern intellectuals, *The Inner Civil War* (1965), dismisses Hawthorne, saying, "he was the only notable writer or thinker who took a detached and critical view of the Union cause. Elsewhere in the intellectual community, there was nothing but the most fervent devotion to the Northern effort."[16]

Among Hawthorne's more recent biographers, condescension and disapproval predominate. In James R. Mellow's *Nathaniel Hawthorne in His Times* (1980), Hawthorne is said to respond to the political scene with "comic perversity,"[17] while for Edwin H. Miller, in *Salem Is My Dwelling Place* (1991), Hawthorne's "familiar ambivalence afforded him a kind of cowardly protection and freedom from commitment."[18] Brenda Wineapple's *Hawthorne: A Life* (2003) uses Hawthorne's racism as a major motif and asserts that "he identified with the southern white slaveholder" to some extent and defended "passivity and inaction, the one a psychological state, the other a political one, and both of them consistent with the proslavery argument."[19] In important critical studies linking Hawthorne's romances to his politics, disapproval likewise reigns. Jonathan Arac's "The Politics of *The Scarlet Letter*" (1986) demonstrates the ways in which Hawthorne's *The Life of Franklin Pierce* and *The Scarlet Letter* both argue against radical "convulsive action," and Arac dismisses Hawthorne's view of slavery as "a fantasy of evanescence."[20] Sacvan Bercovitch, in *The Rites of Assent* (1993), finds Hawthorne "ideologically fixated, like some Ahab of compromise," whose resistance to change "drained him of crucial intellectual and moral resources."[21]

In the wake of such studies, even more indignant judgments emerged. The most severe appeared in a 1994 essay by Eric Cheyfitz, who charges

Hawthorne with "immoral political passivity" and a "simply reprehensible stand on the slavery issue." Cheyfitz finds that Hawthorne's views "mark, at best, a shocking lack of conviction on his part, a glib hypocrisy, no matter how 'representative' they may be of the mainstream politics of his time." As for Hawthorne's comments on abolitionism, they are "the easy remarks of a comfortable, middle-class, white, Protestant male who feels no need to envision forms of transformative social action in a time of crisis."[22] In a 2001 essay, "Hawthorne and the Slavery Question," Jean Fagan Yellin judges Hawthorne according to the moral standards she associates with the abolitionists, charging him with a "failure" to analyze his "racial responses" at a time "when other white New Englanders were painfully examining their responses to slavery and race, making moral judgments on these issues, and acting on their judgments." For her, Emerson's example puts Hawthorne's to shame: "If Emerson's efforts to confront his moral responsibility anticipate the efforts of a later generation adequately to respond to the Holocaust, Hawthorne presents a stark contrast. . . . In Emersonian terms, he apparently never could stop dodging and obliterating."[23] In an otherwise sympathetic study of Hawthorne published in 2005, Clark Davis cites "the moral failings of [Hawthorne's] pro-Unionist, Democratic politics," which he sees as at odds with the ethical content of Hawthorne's fiction. Davis finds it "simple enough" to register the "obvious callousness, lack of imagination, and deplorable quietism" of Hawthorne's perspective on slavery, which "offers little more than an excuse for doing nothing about anything, a distrust of action so complete that it advocates a sort of paralysis."[24]

The moral indignation directed at Hawthorne and his politics comprises only a small portion of the vast critical commentary devoted to his works over the last century and a half, almost all of it positive and focused on his art—that is, his themes, sources, symbols, irony, narrative techniques, and so on. Nevertheless, in this age of ideological critique, Hawthorne's politics have attained prominence and are often used as a key to his works. Moreover, he himself encouraged such an approach. As Richard Brodhead has observed, "few American writers of the nineteenth century so consistently take the political as the scene for their life and work as Hawthorne does."[25] Brodhead, who has provided one of the most useful studies of Hawthorne politics to date, finds that for Hawthorne, "the political is a mode of engagement that generates plural and incompatible outlooks, each with the power, at certain moments, to compel understanding and to initiate action, and each with the power to make the other appear delusory." Hawthorne's "peculiarity," Brodhead claims, is "that when he embraces one of these outlooks the effect is typically to make it dissolve, indeed to replace it with its opposite."[26] In his well-known analysis of *The Scarlet Letter*, Sacvan Bercovitch recognizes Hawthorne's "strategy of pluralism" and, like Brodhead, attributes it to a desire to dissolve conflict. With the Compromise of 1850 in mind, Bercovitch sees a "mystifying sense of multiplicity" in *The Scarlet Letter* and asserts that "Hawthorne's point is to intrigue us with notions of conflict in order to dispense them."[27]

While Hawthorne surely preferred peace to conflict, tolerance to intolerance, he certainly did not lack the courage to take a stand or to endure opposition. He preferred to do so, however, after viewing controversial issues from a number of perspectives and avoiding the rashness and reductiveness of binary thinking. Such an approach indeed obviates quick and bold action, yet it does not necessarily dissolve opposition; moreover, it has the advantage of revealing the various facets of an issue that, like a three-dimensional object, looks different depending on where you stand to view it. Hawthorne's approach to political issues, in other words, was not unlike his approach to the Gothic cathedrals that so fascinated him. With regard to both, he sought a better sense of the whole through sustained study from multiple perspectives. At the beginning of the Civil War, for example, he accurately informed his English friend Francis Bennoch that we "have gone to war, and we seem to have little, or, at least, a very misty idea of what we are fighting for. It depends upon the speaker, and that, again, depends upon the section of the country in which his sympathies are enlisted. The Southern man will say, We fight for state rights, liberty, and independence. The middle and Western states-man will avow that he fights for the Union; whilst our Northern and Eastern man will swear that, from the beginning, his only idea was liberty to the Blacks, and the annihilation of slavery. All are thoroughly in earnest, and all pray for the blessing of Heaven to rest upon the enterprise" (18:387).

At the heart of Hawthorne's most thoughtful political vision, then, is circumspection, the willingness and tendency to entertain multiple points of view. In *The Scarlet Letter*, the famous chapter "Another View of Hester" provides the reader with an account of how both the Puritan community and Hester shifted their perspectives and arrived at deeper understandings of one another. This shift has widely been discussed as fictional narrative technique, yet when it comes to Hawthorne's politics, his insistence on "another view" has seldom received critical attention. Brook Thomas, for example, who has provided a brilliant analysis of the richness of Hester's citizenship, expresses the standard interpretation of Hawthorne's *The Life of Franklin Pierce* when he laments the "political quietism of the sort that Hawthorne succumbed to in the 1850s when he argued that slavery would wither and die of its own accord."[28]

Thomas's assertion, which few would disagree with, is based on a misreading, for Hawthorne made no such argument. What he actually wrote puts this idea forward as "another view" and "probably as wise a one" as that of the abolitionists, who were calling for immediate emancipation, heedless of consequences (23:352). As Richard Hofstadter has pointed out, the abolitionists did not have a clear "conception of how the slave was to be freed nor how an illiterate, landless, and habitually dependent people were to become free and self-sufficient citizens in the hostile environment of the white South."[29] "Abolition was a question of right, not expediency," declared William Lloyd Garrison, "and if slaves have a right to their freedom, it ought to be given them, regardless of the consequences."[30] Hawthorne, however, invariably considered alternatives and consequences. In fact, most of his major works focus obsessively on consequences. Thus, when addressing political issues and problems, he pondered future developments. In May 1861, a month after the Civil War began, he wrote to his friend Bridge,

> I don't quite understand what we are fighting for, or what definite result can be expected. If we pummel the South ever so hard, they will love us none the better for it; and even if we subjugate them, our next step should be to cut them adrift. If we are fighting for the annihilation of slavery, to be sure, it may be a wise object, and offers a tangible result, and the only one which is consistent with a future Union between North and South. A continuance of the war would soon make this plain to us; and we should see the expediency of preparing our black brethren for future citizenship by allowing them to fight for their own liberties, and educating them through heroic influences. (18:381)

Through such considerations, Hawthorne supported the militia act then being passed by the Thirty-seventh Congress, empowering the president to enroll "persons of African descent" as soldiers, which Lincoln finally decided to do more than six months later.[31]

Hawthorne's habitual assumption of the perspectives of different persons (essential to the craft of fiction writing, which engaged none of his famous Concord contemporaries) and his exposure to the views of those in other times and places enabled him often to rise above partisan propaganda and excitement, which he detested. His goal, which he chose not to defend, was to arrive at a wider and deeper understanding than that prevalent among political partisans. His wife, Sophia, understood and appreciated this trait in her husband. In the spring of 1862, while he was in Washington, D.C., she wrote to him, "I could wish thou mightest be President through this crisis, and show the world what can be done by using two eyes, and turning each thing upside down and inside out, before judging and acting. I should not wonder if thy great presence in Washington might affect the moral air and work good."[32] In his own mind, Hawthorne tried to be as open as possible to views beyond those exclusive to New England, even if uncertainty and doubt thereby came into the picture. Henry James, in a powerful insight, defended Hawthorne's "Chiefly about War-Matters" by calling it an "interesting . . . example of the way an imaginative man judges current events—trying to see the other side as well as his own, to feel what his adversary feels, and present his view of the case."[33] What James appreciates here is Hawthorne's informed and thoughtful approach to dealing with one's enemies.

Given the final disdain directed at Hawthorne's politics at his death, one might assume he drifted away from the perspectives of his friends and family, yet his estrangement from his New England contemporaries arose not from changes in his politics but, rather, from changes in theirs, especially their turn to violence. A remarkable consistency runs through his life, making him cling both to his early political principles and to friends he made as a young man. This study will focus on the principles, but his relations with several friends deserve mention, if only to illustrate the nature of his steadfastness.

His college classmate Horatio Bridge was an early patron of Hawthorne's, helping him launch his career by guaranteeing the publishers of *Twice-Told Tales* (1837) against loss. Almost twenty years later, Hawthorne, though never financially secure himself, extended Bridge a sizable loan, telling his publisher William Ticknor to "let him have the money as long as he wants it, even should it be till the day of doom" (17:507). Similarly, when his longtime improvident friend John O'Sullivan found himself in desperate financial straits in 1854, Hawthorne, who had suffered from O'Sullivan's financial incompetence, wrote Ticknor, "I have determined to buy some real estate in New York; not that I want it, but because I must either buy this property [of O'Sullivan's], or lend $3000 to O'Sullivan, who never would be able to pay me"(17:289). In a letter to Ticknor of January 19, 1855, Hawthorne explained, "when the friend of half my lifetime asks me to assist him, and when I have perfect confidence in his honor, what is to be done? Shall I prove myself to be one of those persons who have every quality desirable in friendship, except that they invariably fail you at the pinch? I don't think I can do that" (17:303). Finally, in dealings with his longtime friend Franklin Pierce, another college friend, Hawthorne extended moral support, not only during Pierce's successful presidential campaign, but even when his career and reputation plummeted and almost everyone in the North considered him a traitor. In the midst of the Civil War, Elizabeth Peabody warned Hawthorne not to dedicate *Our Old Home* to Pierce, given his disrepute, but Hawthorne rebuffed her, declaring, "There is a certain steadfastness and integrity with regard to a man's own nature . . . which seems to me more sacred and valuable than the faculty of adapting one's self to new ideas, however true they may turn out to be. The Dedication can hurt nobody but my book and myself" (18:590).

This particular feature of Hawthorne's value system—his loyalty and steadfastness—accounts in part not only for his marginalization within New England near the end of his life but also for his uniquely complex understanding of America's revolutionary past, particularly his appreciation for the loyalist point of view, even though he found it deeply flawed. In *The Whole History of Grandfather's Chair,* when the boy Charley declares that all the Tories should have been tarred and feathered, Grandfather asks him, "Can you not respect that principle of loyalty, which made the royalists give up country, friends, fortune, everything, rather than be false to their king?" (6:177–78). As an independent, contemplative, and serious student of history, Hawthorne not only respected such a "principle of loyalty" but also tried his best to live by it.

CHAPTER 1

Revolution and Warfare

A revolution, or anything, that interrupts social order, may afford opportunities for the individual display of eminent virtue; but, its effects are pernicious to general morality.

　　—Hawthorne, "Old News"

In truth, the whole system of a people crowing over its military triumphs had far better be dispensed with, both on account of the ill-blood that it helps to keep fermenting among the nations, and because it operates as an accumulative inducement to future generations to aim at a kind of glory, the gain of which has generally proved more ruinous than its loss.

　　—Hawthorne, *Our Old Home*

Hawthorne possessed a constitutional aversion to abrupt change, in whatever form it came—personal, social, political. Although he appreciated the vitality evident in mass transformative action, it also evoked his anxiety and resistance, especially when it involved crowds and mobs. His preference for quiet thought over bold action, for diplomacy over conflict—which critics have lamented in relation to his politics at midcentury and seen as yoking *The Scarlet Letter* (1850) to the Compromise of 1850 and to *The Life of Franklin Pierce* (1852)[1]—became an unapologetic part of his system of values when he was quite young. This chapter will examine its development and features.

Stability and Reason

In a poem from Hawthorne's youth, titled "Moderate Views" and dated February 13, 1817 (when he was twelve!), he writes, "With passions unruffled untainted by pride / By reason my life let me square" (23:3). As early as *Fanshawe* (1828), his first published work, written in his early twenties, Hawthorne posits the power of repose and stability, especially in the face of impassioned activity. One of his male protagonists, Edward Walcott, reveals his immaturity by getting violently drunk and accepting the challenge to a duel from the accomplished villain Butler. The duel never occurs, but Walcott's more self-possessed fellow student Fanshawe triumphs over Butler (who has kidnapped the beautiful Ellen Langton), not through violent action, but by standing steady at the top of a cliff as Butler, trying to reach him, slips and falls to his death. In an overwrought scene that doubtless contributed to Hawthorne's decision to conceal his authorship of the novel,[2] he writes that Fanshawe's "limbs seemed to grow firm and strong, and he stood on the edge of the precipice, prepared for the death-struggle which would follow the success of his enemy's attempt. But that attempt was not successful. When within a few feet of the summit, the adventurer grasped at a twig, too slenderly rooted to sustain his weight. It gave way in his hand, and he fell backward down the precipice. . . . With all the passions of hell alive in his heart, he had met the fate that he intended for Fanshawe" (3:451). As Nina Baym has pointed out, Fanshawe's goodness is "entirely interior—a matter of thought, feeling, and sensibility."[3] Butler's evil, by comparison, is exterior and violent, and it flows from "the passions of hell alive in his heart." Stability, whether physical or emotional, thus signifies goodness in the fictional world of *Fanshawe*.

For Hawthorne, strong feelings not under the control of the intellect posed a grave threat not only to individuals but also to societies and nations. Like Edmund Burke, he came to disdain radical action and to imagine revolution and warfare in terms of a breakdown in the familial order—murder of the father, distress for mother and children. In 1840, Hawthorne described Burke as "one of the wisest men and greatest orators that ever the world produced" (6:176), and one finds a consistent Burkean conservatism underlying Hawthorne's settings, symbols, and themes. Time and again in Hawthorne's tales and novels, individuals and mobs engage in forms of symbolic emasculation, portrayed as savage or demonic. A major psychological source of this recurrent fictional trauma was most likely the radical change that occurred in Hawthorne's own life after his father, a sea captain, died of yellow fever in Surinam when Hawthorne was four years old. This event seems to have encouraged Hawthorne to think of himself as a dispossessed aristocrat of sorts, with a vague claim to English nobility.

One need not subscribe to Frederick Crews' theory that Hawthorne suffered from unresolved filial hatred to believe that after he, his sisters, and his mother had to move in with her Manning relatives to survive, the boy experienced a sense of upheaval and victimization that stayed with him throughout his life.[4] Austin Warren astutely put it long ago, "His family had been eminent and powerful; they had lost their eminence and their power, but they retained their pride—their sense of a position in society traditionally (and, as they supposed, by right) theirs, but which was not conceded them, and which, lacking the means to sustain, they practically yielded."[5] In his influential Freudian study, Crews claims that "to the anxiety of all unappreciated writers Hawthorne added the snobbish nostalgia of the disinherited son; his research into Salem history provided him with a rival identity to that of the ineffectual, impecunious, careerless young man surrounded by mercantile *nouveaux-riches.*"[6] As Hawthorne came to maturity, writing became the primary means he used to assert his superiority to his more active and privileged contemporaries. He was well aware that his powers of observation and composition set him apart from and above almost everyone he knew, but he had the grace to scorn his achievements, as evidenced by the false modesty of his prefaces.

Despite his preference for poets over warriors, Hawthorne, as a youth, admired Andrew Jackson, who became his political hero. Broadly speaking, the Jacksonians' major appeal came from Jackson's heroic image and a populist rhetoric that celebrated egalitarianism, minimal government, and the virtues of the common man. Not until the 1840s did the Democratic Party, under the leadership of George Bancroft, have much purchase in Massachusetts. According to Elizabeth Hawthorne, when General Jackson visited Salem in 1833, her brother "walked out to the boundary of the town to meet him, not to speak to him, only to look at him; and found only a few men and boys collected, not enough, without the assistance that he rendered, to welcome the General with a good cheer."[7] Jackson's successful opposition to the newly rich New England Whigs, who were so dominant in Boston, provided one reason Hawthorne responded so positively to him, and Jackson's personality provided another. Fearless, proud, willful, Jackson seemed to stand for principles of equality and self-reliance that Hawthorne claimed as his own. The Jackson we now know as the shady land speculator, unprincipled slaveholder, ruthless military leader, and unlawful destroyer of Indian life and culture was not Hawthorne's Jackson; his was the mythic folk hero, the great Democrat, the champion of the common man.[8] In his biography of Franklin Pierce, Hawthorne calls Jackson's administration "the most splendid and powerful that ever adorned the annals of our country" (23:287), and as T. Walter Herbert has observed, "Jackson embodied for Hawthorne the heroic manhood that made sense of his secluded life."[9] In his *French and Italian Notebooks,* Hawthorne calls Jackson "the greatest man we ever had; and his native strength, as well of intellect as character, compelled every man to be his tool that came within his reach; and the cunninger the individual might be, it served only to make him the sharper tool" (14:367). Hawthorne clearly appreciated Jackson's political acuity, a trait he himself came to possess in no small measure, as his political appointments attest.

Hawthorne's youthful Jacksonianism explains his surprising affinity for various working-class people—farmers, teamsters, boatmen, stage folks—many of whom he met on his excursions through New England and upstate New York in the 1830s. This affinity, however, did not keep him from identifying with a number of his more refined fictional characters when they were assailed by their social inferiors (Hester being the most obvious example), and even those characters (e.g., the Pyncheons) who suffer from the "absurd delusion of family importance" (2:19) receive the benefit of his nostalgia for a lost aristocratic past, even if he has to wrench a plot to provide it.[10] F. O. Matthiessen, in his classic *American Renaissance,* first observed that "a peculiar kind of social understanding made Hawthorne hold to both the contrasting terms of this paradox of being at once a democrat and a conservative."[11] Hawthorne's joke in "The Custom-House" about having been beheaded by bloodthirsty Whigs reveals a deep-seated anxiety about revolutionary violence,[12] and his notorious outburst about the "d——d mob of scribbling women" (17:304) also suggests an aristocratic sense of persecution. Like Burke, Hawthorne empathized with the royal family. In a letter to his fiancée, Sophia Peabody, in 1840, he told her about a nightmare of his: "Dearest, thou didst not come into my dreams, last night; but, on the contrary, I was engaged in assisting the escape of Louis XVI and Marie Antoinette from Paris, during the French revolution. And sometimes, by an unaccountable metamorphosis, it seemed as if my mother and sisters were in the place of the King and Queen" (15:427–28). The king and queen were subsequently decapitated of course. In the fall of 1849, after the death of his actual mother and his own firing, or "decapitation," Hawthorne refreshed his memory of the 1789 French Revolution by reading Alphonse de Lamartine's *History of the Girondins* (1847), which had just inspired the 1848 revolution in France and the tragic "Bloody June Days" that followed. At the same time, he started writing *The Scarlet Letter,* using a scaffold as his central setting.[13] After Hawthorne's death, James Russell Lowell defended Hawthorne's patriotism but admitted, "There were certain things and certain men with whom his essentially aristocratic nature could not sympathize."[14]

Transformative Political Violence

As Hawthorne was growing up, calls for a national literature permeated the U.S. intellectual scene, and as he began his writing career, he responded to these calls by studying New England history intently, from the early Puritan settlements to the outbreak of the American Revolution. Cotton Mather's *Magnalia Christi Americana* (1702), Daniel Neal's *The History of the Puritans* (1816–17), and John Winthrop's *History of New England from 1630–1649* (1825–26) were just a few of the many historical works he checked out of the Salem Athenaeum during his apprentice years. A number of his early tales treat political tensions in the colonies, and he uses these tensions to dramatize various psychological and moral struggles that his fictional characters undergo. The fact that his own paternal ancestors played prominent roles in colonial history piqued his interest, but given his aversion to violent conflict, he chose to question America's various military successes in ways none of his contemporaries did. Progress, especially when achieved through warfare, was a concept he viewed with suspicion, and this dark take on his nation complemented his view of his fellow man, with both contributing to the "great power of blackness" that his fellow pessimist Melville admired.[15]

A number of Hawthorne scholars—most notably Michael Colacurcio,

Michael Davitt Bell, and Frederick Newberry—have shown that Hawthorne participated in the effort to create a national literature using features of New England history popular with the romantic historians and historical romancers of the 1820s and 1830s. Unlike most of his contemporaries, Hawthorne subjected this history to close scrutiny and viewed with deep irony the prevailing myth about the progress of America from colony to nation. As Newberry astutely puts it, "Patriotic interpretations of seventeenth-century Puritanism and its typological extension to the Revolutionary War are simply too well made, the logic entirely too reductive and the coherence altogether too tight. As a serious historian/artist, Hawthorne recognized that the historical record was more complex than popular ideology would have it."[16] I would add that Hawthorne's sympathies flowed toward those victimized by political violence, rather than those who emerged victorious from it. For him, unlike many of his countrymen then and now, favorable political ends failed to justify violent political means. Only in historical retrospect could the "old footprints of war," such as fortifications and battlefields, achieve some value, by serving as "picturesque memorials of an epoch of terror and suffering" and teaching children to be "less prodigal than their fathers in sacrificing good institutions to passionate impulses and impracticable theories" (23:418–19).

As Hawthorne drew on his readings in seventeenth- and eighteenth-century American history, he developed the strong pacifism that served as the foundation of his political thought. Although this pacifism wavered at times—for example, as the Civil War began, he, like everyone else, was "breathing slaughter" (18:422)—it nevertheless served as the basic and consistent principle by which he implicitly judged the actions of individuals and nations. In his early works, this pacifism can be seen in his accounts of the persecution of Others (including Indians, Quakers, and witches) and of mobs rioting in opposition to established authorities. He explicitly voiced his philosophy with regard to historical narrative in his preface to his children's textbook *Peter Parley's Universal History on the Basis of Geography* (1837), where he warns his reader,

> As you lift the curtain of the past, mankind seem from age to age engaged
> in constant strife, battle and bloodshed. The master spirits generally stand
> forth as guided only by ambition and superior to other men in wickedness

as in power. . . . It is necessary that history should be known, that we may learn the character and capacity of man; but in telling of the vices and crimes that soil the pages of the past, I have taken advantage of every convenient occasion, to excite hatred of injustice, violence and falsehood, and promote a love of truth, equity and benevolence. (23:266)

One of his first and most striking early attempts to excite hatred of violence appears in "The Gray Champion" (1835), which juxtaposes the appearance of one of the regicides of Charles I in Hadley, Massachusetts, in 1675 with the revolt in Boston in 1689 against the government of Sir Edmund Andros.[17] While the story has been read as a celebration of the spirit of the American Revolution, anticipated by the Puritans, it is also filled with irony directed at the Puritans themselves, whom the "Gray Champion," with his "stern composure," restrains as much as he does the redcoats of the Governor's Guard. The crowd of Puritans, gathered in King-street to challenge the governor and his bloodthirsty mercenary soldiers, features "the veterans of King Philips's war, who had burnt villages and slaughtered young and old, with pious fierceness, while the godly souls throughout the land were helping them with prayer" (9:11). When the regicide suddenly appears, confronts the marching troops, and cries "Stand!" he emboldens the crowd, who also confront "the soldiers, not wholly without arms, and ready to convert the very stones of the street into deadly weapons" (9:16). Andros and his men then "commence a slow and guarded retreat" (9:17). Yet neither the Puritans nor "the group of despotic rulers" nor even the threatening regicide himself ("back, lest I foretell the scaffold!") gain as much implicit approval in the story as the peaceful resolution of the conflict.[18] The regicide's success, in other words, lies in his courage to stand his ground and defy force rather than employ it.

In "My Kinsman, Major Molineux" (1831), Hawthorne dramatizes an alternative ending to a similar conflict that occurs some seventy-five years later. In the story, the "inflammation of the popular mind" (11:209) in the mid-seventeenth century causes angry colonists to torture and perhaps murder the royal governor, Robin's kinsman.[19] The youth Robin, fresh from the country, is affected by political contagion in the town when he encounters the mob that is carrying his kinsman out of town, tarred and feathered: "a bewildering excitement began to seize upon his mind; the preceding adventures of the night, the unexpected appearance of the crowd, the torches, the confused din, and the hush that followed, the spectre of his kinsman reviled by that great multitude, all this, and more than all, a perception of tremendous ridicule in the whole scene, affected him with a sort of mental inebriety" (11:229). Robin reacts with manic laughter, joining in the "senseless uproar" of the mob, which moves on, "like fiends that throng in mockery round some dead potentate, mighty no more, but majestic still in his agony" (11:230). By thus participating in "the foul disgrace of a head grown gray in honor," Robin reveals a weakness of character that earlier ironic references to his "shrewness" anticipate, and though he may yet "rise in the world," as his new gentleman friend suggests at the end of the tale, the violence inflicted on Robin's kinsman threatens to stain that rise with guilt.

The metamorphosis that occurs in "My Kinsman," from innocent youth to almost savage adult, anticipates similar transformations that occur in Hawthorne's subsequent works due to the "contagion," "infection," or "fever" of the hour—as he often terms it, to suggest its virulence. Peter Shaw has argued that Hawthorne's treatment of the American Revolution can be read as the adolescent coming-of-age ritual rooted in folklore, which anticipates Freud's description of scapegoat king rituals in *Totem and Taboo* (1913).[20] While Hawthorne indeed envisioned revolution as an initiation rite of sorts, a transformative experience that alters the subsequent lives of those who engage in it, the alteration frequently involves the fall into sin and guilt. This point can perhaps best be illustrated by turning to a story that long fascinated him, about an innocent youth turned savage killer during the American Revolution. This story, based in fact, serves as a primary source for one of his late unfinished romances, "Septimius Felton." But he first mentions it in "The Old Manse" preface, where he recalls hearing it from James Russell Lowell.

Hawthorne and his new bride, Sophia, moved to the Old Manse in Concord in July 1842, knowing it had close ties to the Revolutionary War, because within view from an upper window was the hill on which the Concord militia stood to confront the British troops who had come to Concord to confiscate weapons being stored by the populace. The American Revolution began on April 19, 1775, at the nearby site of the Old North Bridge, with the firing of the shot "heard round the world," as Emerson put it in his poem "Concord Fight."[21] Two British soldiers were killed that day, and in "The Old Manse," Hawthorne relates the following, attributing it to Lowell:

> A youth, in the service of the clergyman, happened to be chopping wood, that April morning, at the back door of the Manse; and when the noise of battle rang from side to side of the bridge, he hastened across the intervening field, to see what might be going forward. . . . The tradition says that the lad now left his task, and hurried to the battle-field, with the axe still in his hand. The British had by this time retreated—the Americans were in pursuit—and the late scene of strife was thus deserted by both parties. Two soldiers lay on the ground; one was a corpse; but, as the young New-Englander drew nigh, the other Briton raised himself painfully upon his hands and knees, and gave a ghastly stare into his face. The boy—it must have been a nervous impulse, without purpose, without thought, and betokening a sensitive and impressible nature, rather than a hardened one—the boy uplifted his axe, and dealt the wounded soldier a fierce and fatal blow upon the head. . . . Oftentimes, as an intellectual and moral exercise, I have sought to follow that poor youth through his subsequent career, and observe how his soul was tortured by the blood-stain, contracted, as it had been, before the long custom of war had robbed human life of its sanctity, and while it still seemed murderous to slay a brother man. (10:9–10)

Embedded in the last sentence of this account is Hawthorne's ironic critique of the dehumanizing and desensitizing effects of war, directed at his own nation and its brutish citizens.

The story stuck with him. Some twenty years later, in the midst of the Civil War, Hawthorne, now living at the Wayside, was visited by the young English journalist Edward Dicey, to whom Hawthorne told the story once more. In Dicey's version of this retelling, "some British soldiers, returning to carry off the wounded, found their comrade with his head split in two, and raised the cry that the Americans scalped the dead,"[22] a detail that may have contributed to Hawthorne's decision to endow his protagonist in "Septimius" with Indian blood. Dicey's account provides the information that the boy grew to be a very old man and that "the thought that he had killed a wounded man in cold blood haunted him to his grave."[23] The motive for his act, according to Dicey, was fear and self-defense, whereas in Hawthorne's earlier version, the boy acts "without purpose, without thought." What usurps purpose and thought, of course, is the surrounding circumstances, the impassioned events that have just transpired, the exchange of shots at the Old North Bridge. (The boy, whose name was Ammi White, was known to be slow-witted.)[24]

In both versions, related twenty years apart, one can discern three persistent and profound ideas that underlie Hawthorne's political thought and that infuse his fiction: first, that under the influence of political excitement, an innocent, peaceful youth can transform into a savage adult; second, that political unrest and open warfare rob human life of its sanctity and make brutal murder seem justified and inevitable; and third, that a burden of guilt arises from politically inspired violence, even when the cause seems righteous at the time. Political unrest, as well as witchcraft hysteria, fell into the category of the "contagion" of the hour, generating what Hawthorne often describes as a "stream" or "river" into which one leaps, almost against one's will. This development controls the climax of "My Kinsman" and constitutes a key scene in *The House of the Seven Gables,* as the enfeebled Clifford experiences a similar pull when a political procession marches by beneath his balcony. The drums, fifes, banners, and crowd of people generate a noisy spectacle that he beholds "not in its atoms, but in its aggregate—as a mighty river of life, massive in its tide, and black with mystery" (2:165). Excited, he becomes "a wild, haggard figure, his gray locks floating in the wind . . . ; a lonely being, estranged from his race, but now feeling himself man again, by virtue of the irrepressible instinct that possessed him" (2:166). On the verge of leaping from the balcony into the crowd, he is restrained by his horrified sister Hepzibah and cousin Phoebe.

Goodman Brown, the eponymous hero of "Young Goodman Brown," experiences a similar transformative excitement during his journey into the forest, which may be a dream. From the depth of a "black mass of cloud" that is "sweeping swiftly northward," he hears, "a confused and doubtful sound of voices," including that of his wife, Faith. Maddened with despair and laughing manically, he rushes forward, "the chief horror of the scene" (10:83), drawn to the clearing where the "great multitude" has converged to participate in a witches' Sabbath presided over by "a dark figure," presumably the devil. To enhance the savage nature of the scene, Hawthorne scatters among the Puritans "Indian priests, or powwows, who had often scared their native forest with more hideous incantations than any known to English witchcraft" (10:85). Thus Brown, like Robin and Clifford, becomes deranged by the group behavior surrounding him and is drawn into it by the desire to alleviate his sense of confusion and estrangement. His resolve to "stand firm against the devil" (10:82) proves inadequate, and he instead flies through the forest to join his fellows.

In one of his last written works, "Chiefly about War-Matters," Hawthorne ponders the slaughter taking place during the Civil War and wonders whether his nation will ever be able to resist the impulse to kill others for a cause, under the influence of martial stimuli.

> Will the time ever come again, in America, when we may live half-a-score of years, without once seeing the likeness of a soldier, except it be in the festal march of a company on its summer-tour? Not in this generation, I fear, nor in the next, nor till the millennium; and even that blessed epoch, as the prophecies seem to intimate, will advance to the sound of drum and trumpet. (23:406)

For a nation at war, such detached and ironic speculations can seem hostile and treasonous.

Racialized Violence and Doubling

Hawthorne understood that the demonization of one's enemies often constituted the cultural justification for inflicting violence on them. In "My Kinsman, Major Molineux," the leader of the revolutionary mob appears as a satanic figure, with his face painted half red and half black. By "his fierce and variegated countenance," he "appeared like war personified" (11:227). With this personification, Hawthorne taps into the cultural imaginary of his day, infused with images of racialized violence and terror. ("Wild figures in the Indian dress" [11:227–28] follow in the train of the "fierce and variegated" leader.) As the crowd scenes in his works reveal, Hawthorne exploited for effect the demonic symbolism of dark racial Others (both "red" and "black"), yet he also interrogated the mirroring effects of these Others, drawing on his knowledge of American history. He learned, for example, that with the first

English settlers, fears of Indian attacks and black uprisings dominated the racial fantasies (and nightmares) of whites in America, who regarded Indians as devil worshipers, their shamans as witches.

In the colonies, the terms *black* and *Indian* were used interchangeably. During a Hartford witchcraft case in 1662, for example, a witness testified to seeing the accused in the woods with "two black creatures like two Indians but taller"; and during the Salem examinations of 1692, Sarah Osborne described a nightmarish encounter with "a thing like an indian all black."[25] As Mary Beth Norton has pointed out, "the association among Indians, black men, and the devil would have been unremarkable to anyone in the Salem Village meetinghouse."[26] The same would apply to other colonists throughout America, as Negro slaves joined Indians as objects of fear and terror. In 1690, a rumor spread through the Massachusetts Bay Colony that two Jersey men, Isaac Morrill and George Mousher, were encouraging slaves to "goe for Canada and Joyne with the French against the English and So come downe with the French and Indians upon the backside of the country and destroy all the English and Save none but only the Negro and Indian Servants and . . . the French would come with vessels and lay at the harbours that none Should escape."[27] In colonial New York, fears of a slave revolt in 1712 led to the death sentence for twenty-seven local Negro slaves. Six of the condemned committed suicide, and as colonial governor Robert Hunter reported to London investors, "twenty one were executed, one being a woman with child, her execution by that meanes suspended, some were burnt others hanged, one broke on the wheele, and one hung a live in chains in the town, so that there has been the most exemplary punishment inflicted that could be possibly thought of."[28] In 1741, in New York City, fear of a slave insurrection led to general hysteria among the white population; as a consequence, 143 blacks were arrested, 18 were hanged, 11 were burned alive at the stake, and 70 were banished from the colony.[29]

Such gruesome "exemplary" punishments in the eastern colonies were matched on the western frontier, where encounters with Indians provoked similar white anxiety, reaction, and cruelty. Hawthorne's introduction to "Roger Malvin's Burial," which mentions "Lovell's Fight" of 1725, coyly claims, "Imagination, by casting certain circumstances judiciously into the shade, may see much to admire in the heroism of a little band, who gave battle to twice their number in the heart of the enemy's country" (10:337). Readers can easily miss the irony of the "certain circumstances" one must ignore in order to admire the "heroism" of Lovell's band, but as Colacurcio has pointed out, Captain Lovell's troops were bounty hunters who began their scalp-hunting expedition by killing a party of Indians in their sleep. The tragic death of young Cyrus Bourne in the story can thus be read not only as expiation of Reuben Bourne's personal guilt but also, as Colacurcio puts it, as "a prophecy of some bloody purgation from national guilt."[30] By participating in savage acts as an Indian fighter, as well as by concealing his desertion of Roger, Reuben acquires a heavy moral burden that he shares with his nation.

Hawthorne had an aversion to violence and believed that attempts to destroy evil could have a doubling effect, transforming the hater into the hated. He thus placed himself in opposition to his Indian-hating countrymen throughout his career. He claimed to "abhor an Indian story" (10:429). Yet in the *American Magazine of Useful and Entertaining Knowledge,* which he edited for six months in 1836, he wrote an account of the famous Indian raid on the Duston home in Haverhill, Massachusetts, on March 15, 1697. He took the details of the account from Cotton Mather's *Magnalia Christi Americana,* which praises Hannah Duston for killing her Indian captors (a family of two men, three women, and seven children). After a forced journey of many days and some 150 miles, Hannah and two other captives bashed in the heads of ten of the Indians as they slept, scalped them, and made their way back to a white settlement with the scalps, all supposedly with the help of God. As Mather tells it, "their *Indian* Master sometimes when he saw them dejected would say unto them, *What need you Trouble your self? If your God will have you delivered, you shall be so!* And it seems our God would have it so to be."[31]

In Hawthorne's retelling, Hannah receives no such praise, only condemnation, as she transforms into a savage herself. "Oh, the children!" he writes, lamenting, "Their skins are red; yet spare them, Hannah Duston, spare those seven little ones, for the sake of the seven that have fed at your own breast." But, of course, she does not. Calling her "this awful woman," and a "raging tigress," Hawthorne then relates,

The work being finished, Mrs. Duston laid hold of the long black hair of the warriors, and the women, and the children, and took all their ten

scalps, and left the island, which bears her name to this very day. According to our notion, it should be accursed, for her sake. Would that the
bloody old hag had been drowned in crossing Contocook river, or that
she had sunk over head and ears in a swamp, and been buried, till sum-
moned forth to confront her victims at the Day of Judgment; or that she
had gone astray and been starved to death in the forest, and nothing ever
seen of her again, save her skeleton, with the ten scalps twisted round it
for a girdle! But, on the contrary, she and her companions came safe
home, and received the bounty on the dead Indians, besides liberal presents from private gentlemen, and fifty pounds from the Governour of
Maryland.[32]

Hawthorne's article represents hackwork of sorts, and his condemnation of
Duston seems excessive. Nevertheless, the article reveals the extent to which
his pacifism extended to Native Americans and thus set him apart from other
historians. He did not accept righteous violence or murderous revenge as
justifiable behavior, though he was willing for fate, chance, or providence to
mete out such justice, if it chose. His nonsectarian religious sentiments were
more influenced by the New Testament than the Old, a point this study will
return to in chapter 6.

The *Democratic Review* and "Legends of the Province House"

In 1837, Hawthorne received a letter of invitation from an aggressive young
editor named John O'Sullivan, asking him to contribute to a new venture,
The United States Magazine and Democratic Review. He agreed, and the first
stories he submitted, a framed set of four titled "Legends of the Province
House," focus on the American Revolution and display the subtle irony with
which Hawthorne had come to regard the political behavior of both loyalists
and rebels during the period of the royal governors. O'Sullivan's interests
were both cultural and political, and in his introduction to the first issue of
October 1837, he claims that his new magazine seeks to remedy "the anti-
democratic character of our literature" by "vindicating the true glory and
greatness of the democratic principle, by infusing it into our literature, and
by rallying the mind of the nation from the state of torpor and even of de-
moralization in which so large a proportion of it is sunk."[33] Hawthorne
found the *Democratic Review* congenial and subsequently published twenty-

five stories in its pages. He and O'Sullivan shared a number of political principles, including a commitment to pacifism, and they became good friends (the Hawthornes chose O'Sullivan to be the godfather of their first child, Una).[34]

Despite their friendship, Hawthorne did not, as some scholars have suggested, tailor his stories to O'Sullivan's political agenda as set out in his editorial pieces, which urged American expansionism, the annexation of Texas, and neutrality on slavery.[35] Hawthorne was both too independent and too penetrating in his political vision to do so. Moreover, the invitation O'Sullivan extended to Hawthorne and others who wrote for the *Democratic Review* was made on literary and financial grounds, not political ones, which is why authors having an array of political positions—including Bryant, Lowell, Poe, Thoreau, Simms, Whitman, and Whittier—appeared in the magazine during O'Sullivan's editorship (1841–46). As a result of such contributors, the *Democratic Review* became one of the foremost literary periodicals of the nineteenth century.

As for its politics, the *Democratic Review*, while founded with the encouragement of President Van Buren and later aligned with the Van Buren wing of the Democratic Party, sought to achieve a wide audience in both the North and the South. In the July–August 1845 issue, O'Sullivan focused on the issue of the annexation of Texas, declaring, "In respect to the institution of slavery itself, we have not designed, in what has been said above, to express any judgment of its merits or demerits, *pro* or *con*. National in its character and aims, this Review abstains from the discussion of a topic pregnant with embarrassment and danger—intricate and double-sided—exciting and embittering—and necessarily excluded from a work circulating equally in the South as in the North." Claiming that annexation is "a question with which slavery had nothing to do," O'Sullivan points out, accurately, that "opinions were and are greatly divided, both at the North and South, as to the influence to be exerted by it on Slavery and the Slave States." As for expansionism, O'Sullivan vigorously promoted it with his famous pronouncement that there can be no doubt "of our manifest destiny to overspread the continent allotted by Providence for the free development of our yearly multiplying millions."[36] Because O'Sullivan was a pacifist, however, he supported annexation only "*if it should be carried into effect in a proper manner.*"[37] He believed Texas could be purchased from Mexico and that this would speed the end of slavery in the United States by providing an outlet for that institution in Mexico and Central America.[38]

Although Hawthorne claimed O'Sullivan as a friend and sought his support for political patronage, he was well aware of his faults, especially his financial and political recklessness and his lack of penetrating thought.[39] Hawthorne's "Legends of the Province House," published in the *Democratic Review* in 1838–39, can be seen as expressing his own unique combination of democratic and conservative sensibilities. He both supports the American colonists in their efforts to challenge British imperial rule and sympathizes with those British loyalists victimized by colonial crowds and mobs. The first three of the legends in the series treat key events during the American Revolution supposedly told to the narrator by an elderly gentleman, Mr. Bela Tiffany, who is fond of good liquor and lives in the current-day Province House, which has been turned into a hotel. As he relates Tiffany's tales, the narrator claims that he himself has made "changes as seemed conducive to the reader's profit and delight" (9:243), and so Hawthorne filters his own political views through two layers of narrative. In the fourth legend, titled "Old Esther Dudley," he alters one of these layers by attributing the story to an old loyalist, who joins Tiffany and the narrator in the barroom. "The sentiment and tone of the affair," the narrator declares, "may have undergone some slight, or perchance more than slight metamorphosis, in its transmission to the reader through the medium of a thorough-going democrat" (9:291). Ironically, this "Legend" is the least democratic of the four, and its title character, Esther Dudley, proves a more sympathetic figure than Howe, Hutchinson, or Lady Eleanore, all of whom proudly disdain the colonial "rabble" and suffer humiliation as an apparent result.

By means of multiple perspectives, Hawthorne conveys his sense of the complexity of American revolutionary history, which such historians as George Bancroft chose to elide in their more patriotic and nationalistic accounts.[40] Hawthorne indicts the duplicity, pretensions, and pride of individual representatives of the British aristocracy yet does not deny their humanity or their difficulty in coping with a world in turmoil. In "Howe's Masquerade," General William Howe, proud commander of the British army in America, is tricked into witnessing a ghostly procession of Puritan and royal governors, which prophecies Howe's retreat in the face of Washington's army, then laying siege to the city. By staging his masquerade ball,

Howe seeks "to hide the distress and danger of the period" (9:243), but Hawthorne, by showing the colonists putting on an alternative masquerade, unmasks Howe's true feelings. Outraged at the pleasure that Colonel Joliffe, a Whig "now too old to take an active part in the contest" (9:244), shows at Howe's discomfiture, Howe threatens him "fiercely, though with a quivering lip," thus betraying his fear. In response, the colonel tells him, "The empire of Britain, in this ancient province, is at its last gasp to-night;—almost while I speak, it is a dead corpse;—and, methinks the shadows of the old governors are fit mourners at its funeral!" (9:254). As the tale ends, Howe departs with a "gesture of rage and sorrow" (9:253), as the besieging army of Washington moves to a nearer height above the town, thus anticipating the shift in political power soon to ensue.

In "Edward Randolph's Portrait," British arrogance and power again receive a jolt, even though the protagonist, Lieutenant-Governor Thomas Hutchinson, is a native of Boston. In the course of the tale, he decides to allow royal troops to occupy Castle William and Boston itself, thus setting the stage for conflict between an occupying army and a rebellious people. Hutchinson's favorite niece, Alice Vane, warns him against this decision by referring to the curse suffered by Edward Randolph, who obtained the repeal of the first provincial charter and thus became the "arch enemy" of the people of New England. Randolph's portrait, hanging in the Province House, shows the torment he later suffered, and Alice tells her uncle that "when the rulers feel themselves irresponsible, it were well that they should be reminded of the awful weight of a People's curse" (9:262). To her and to the officers in attendance, Hutchinson proudly replies, "The king is my master, and England is my country! Upheld by their armed strength, I set my foot upon the rabble, and defy them!" (9:266). They soon defy him, however, and violence breaks out. In his dying hour, "far over the ocean," Hutchinson, "gasped for breath, and complained that he was choking with the blood of the Boston Massacre" (9:269).

If "Edward Randolph's Portrait" indicts British arrogance, it does not simultaneously applaud mob spirit, and the same is true of the third legend, "Lady Eleanore's Mantle." The title character demonstrates an aristocratic pride that seems to lead to her undoing, yet the exaggerated quality of this tale undercuts its obvious political thrust. One thus suspects that Hawthorne wished his more alert readers to question the explicit moral put in the mouth of Lady Eleanore as she suffers from smallpox: "The curse of Heaven hath stricken me, because I would not call man my brother, nor woman sister. I wrapt myself in PRIDE as in a MANTLE, and scorned the sympathies of nature; and therefore has nature made this wretched body the medium of a dreadful sympathy" (9:287). Though the tale suggests that Eleanore deserves her fate, the colonists she disdains seem no more admirable in their behavior. When she arrives in Boston and steps from her coach onto the back of her kneeling lowbred would-be lover, the rejected and mad Jervase Helwyse, the crowd of people "were so smitten with her beauty, and so essential did pride seem to the existence of such a creature, that they gave a simultaneous acclamation of applause" (9:276). Later, when she and her mantle seem the source of the smallpox, their admiration turns to rage.

> The people raved against the Lady Eleanore, and cried out that her pride and scorn had evoked a fiend, and that, between them both, this monstrous evil had been born. At times, their rage and despair took the semblance of grinning mirth; and whenever the red flag of the pestilence was hoisted over another, and yet another door, they clapt their hands and shouted through the streets, in bitter mockery, "Behold a new triumph for the Lady Eleanore!" (9:284)

Even Jervase Helwyse, a "youth of no birth or fortune" (9:276), does not garner the reader's sympathy, because when he visits Eleanore's bed chamber, he maliciously gloats over her fall into sickness and disfigurement, shaking "his finger at the wretched girl" and displaying "insane merriment" (9:287). Later that night, as a man of the people, he leads a colonial mob in a procession that ends with the burning of Eleanore in effigy, which seems to end the plague she supposedly brought upon them. Hawthorne thus uses the tale to vivify the metaphor of political "contagion," making it the equal of aristocratic pride in its virulence.

The last legend, the story of Esther Dudley, although told "through the medium of a thorough-going democrat," again reveals a sympathy and respect for persons independent of their class or political loyalties, for the royalist Esther, who remains behind in the Province House after Sir William Howe and all other British officials leave, appears as a harmless and kind old soul. As "a representative of the decayed past" (9:294), she has long depended on the king for food and shelter after her family's fall into poverty.

After the rebels win the Revolution, she dwells "year after year, in the Province-House, still reverencing all that others had flung aside, still faithful to her King, who, so long as the venerable dame yet held her post, might be said to retain one true subject in New England, and one spot of the empire that had been wrested from him" (9:296). When the new Republican governor, John Hancock, finally arrives to take possession of the Province House, he makes a speech affirming the superiority of American democracy over British royalty.

> "Alas, venerable lady!" said Governor Hancock, lending her his support with all the reverence that a courtier would have shown to a queen. "Your life has been prolonged until the world has changed around you. You have treasured up all that time has rendered worthless—the principles, feelings, manners, modes of being and acting—and you are a symbol of the past. And I, and these around me—we represent a new race of men—living no longer in the past, scarcely in the present—but projecting our lives forward into the future. Ceasing to model ourselves on ancestral superstitions, it is our faith and principle to press onward, onward!" "Yet," continued he, turning to his attendants, "let us reverence for the last time, the stately and gorgeous prejudices of the tottering Past!" (9:301)

Within moments of the speech, Esther dies on the steps of the Province House, but Hancock remains unfazed, claiming, "She hath done her office!" and adding, "We will follow her reverently to the tomb of her ancestors; and then, my fellow-citizens, onward—onward! We are no longer children of the Past!" (9:302).

Given the self-aggrandizing posturing of Hancock, it is rather obvious that Hawthorne intends some irony here. Though Hancock offers an exaggerated version of the expansionist rhetoric found in some of O'Sullivan's *Democratic Review* pieces, his vision should not be confused with Hawthorne's more qualified and skeptical one. Moreover, Hawthorne elsewhere reveals his reservations about Hancock. In "A Book of Autographs," Hawthorne reports that an associate called Hancock a man "without a head or heart." Yet Hawthorne defends using Hancock as "a majestic figure," rather than "a real personage," because "the pages of history would be half unpeopled, if all such characters were banished from it" (11:367). In "Legends of the Province House," a few individual characters, such as Alice Vane and Dr. Clarke, who calmly step forward to speak on behalf of the people's rights, appear best to represent Hawthorne's politics and counter the more defiant and impassioned representatives of both British imperialism and colonial insurgency.[41]

Early Pacifism: *The Whole History of Grandfather's Chair*

Because Hawthorne's perspective on the American Revolution as found in "Legends of the Province House" is so layered and hidden from view, critics have disagreed about the politics at work within the work. A more transparent window opening on Hawthorne's political thought is provided by a group of candid children's stories, written about the same time. His three-part book *The Whole History of Grandfather's Chair* (1841) is a little-studied but most profoundly political work, in which the author's pacifism and aversion to violence stand clearly unveiled. Given his young audience, Hawthorne abandoned his usual irony and granted his kindhearted narrator, Grandfather, a penetrating vision in accord with his own. As Grandfather informs his young audience about major events in the country, from the founding of the Massachusetts Bay Colony through the beginning of the American Revolution, he critiques the colonists and their leaders and avoids offering the conventional filiopietistic pap. His young auditors voice the multiple responses that Hawthorne often attributes to the interpreters he uses in his romances, when controversial issues are under consideration.

Four children gather around periodically to hear Grandfather's stories.[42] The most fully developed child character is Laurence, a bright, thoughtful twelve-year-old who listens carefully and reacts with mature dismay to Grandfather's stories of the violence done to the Indians, the Quakers, the Acadians, and even the Tories. His nine-year-old brother, Charley, "a bold, brisk, restless little fellow" (6:11), acts as Laurence's foil and delights in the stories of warfare, showing no sympathy for victims or losers. After hearing of the suffering of the Acadians at the hands of English who drove them from their homes, for example, Charlie cries, "It was their own fault. . . . Why did not they fight for the country where they were born?" (6:129). As for the Tories, he wishes they had all been "tarred and feathered every man of them!" (6:177).

The boys' cousin, ten-year-old Clara, and their little sister, five-year-old Alice, venture fewer opinions than the boys and react with tears and sadness to Grandfather's accounts of death and suffering, which he often ameliorates for their benefit. When Clara asks if there were slaves in the colonies, for example, Grandfather responds with selective accuracy.

> Yes, black slaves and white. . . . Our ancestors not only bought negroes from Africa, but Indians from South America, and white people from Ireland. These last were sold, not for life, but for a certain number of years, in order to pay the expenses of their voyage across the Atlantic. Nothing was more common than to see a lot of likely Irish girls, advertised for sale in the newspapers. As for the little negro babies, they were offered to be given away, like young kittens. (6:109)

Charley jokes about Alice trading her doll for such a real baby, while Clara makes no reply to the explanation, which certainly seems offensive to today's reader. Apparently Hawthorne thought that Grandfather's child auditor would take it kindly and that his own readers would find it amusing. In his telling of the Boston Massacre, though, Grandfather makes Alice cry, and she becomes an ethical agent on the topic of war. As Grandfather concludes his account of the Boston Massacre, "the violent sobs of little Alice" interrupt him, and Hawthorne explains,

> In his earnestness, he had neglected to soften down the narrative, so that it might not terrify the heart of this unworldly infant. Since Grandfather began the history of our chair, little Alice had listened to many tales of war. But, probably, the idea had never really impressed itself upon her mind, that men have shed the blood of their fellow-creatures. And now that this idea was forcibly presented to her, it affected the sweet child with bewilderment and horror. (6:170)

As Hawthorne was writing *Grandfather's Chair* during 1840–41, the country was electing General William Henry Harrison president of the United States. Harrison had earned fame as an Indian fighter in the Old Northwest and as governor of the Indiana Territory, where he defeated the forces of Tecumseh at the Battle of Tippecanoe in 1811. The Whigs chose Harrison as their presidential candidate (over the logical choice, Henry

Clay), because of his popularity as a war hero and his unknown positions on divisive contemporary issues, especially slavery. The Whigs fashioned no party platform for the election but got out the vote for Harrison and his running mate, John Tyler, by orchestrating the famous "Log Cabin and Hard Cider" campaign, which featured music, parades, torchlight processions, lots of hard cider, and the memorable slogan "Tippecanoe and Tyler, too." Taking a page from the Democrats' smearing of John Quincy Adams in the 1828 campaign, the Whigs caricatured the incumbent Democratic president Martin Van Buren as an aristocratic Eastern snob. Although a Democratic governor was elected in Massachusetts (by one vote), the Whigs won the presidential election, causing Hawthorne to resign his post as measurer at the Boston customhouse, a job he detested anyway.

General Harrison and the Whigs' demagoguery provide the political background to Hawthorne's *Grandfather's Chair*, which emphasizes the bogus popularity of war heroes and the susceptibility of the masses to warmongering. In part two of the book, titled "Famous Old People," Hawthorne has Grandfather awaken to an "approaching uproar" that "grew loud and high": "There was the music of drum, fife, and bugle, intermixed with shouts, seemingly of boyish voices, and the clatter and tramp of innumerable feet upon the pavement. Glancing at the darkened windows, Grandfather could see the glare of torches, and lanterns on the tops of poles, borne onward through the tumult" (6:86). At first, Grandfather mistakes the uproar for an imaginary scene from the colonial past, but young Laurence tells him, "It is a procession of the boys of Boston, in honor of Old Tippecanoe, . . . and Charley has run away to join them." Hawthorne's narrative then reads: "'Ah, well!' said Grandfather, smiling, 'Boys are the same in every generation—always aping their fathers—always taking a mimic interest in grown men's affairs" (6:87). Although Hawthorne chooses not to venture any opinion about the popularity of "Old Tippecanoe," the entire dialogue diminishes the honor accorded him.[43] After Grandfather and Laurence discuss the possibility that the schoolboys during the time of the French and Indian War had snowball fights in imitation of the combatants, Grandfather asserts, "Yes; the great game of war is easily shown to be ridiculous. . . . And would not this [snowball fighting] be as reasonable a mode of settling national disputes, as if swords, bayonets, tomahawks, bullets, and cannon-balls, were the instruments of warfare?" (6:87–88). In his later writings, Hawthorne would continue to characterize war as the activity of immature persons and nations.

Grandfather's commentary on the treatment of Indians by the early American colonists critiques not only General Harrison's reputation (though Jackson, whom Hawthorne admired, earned his fame in similar fashion) but all Indian hating. Grandfather tells how "for nearly half a century after the arrival of the English, the red men showed themselves generally inclined to peace and amity. They often made submission, when they might have made successful war" (6:42). The English settlers, he says, stole the Indian's land, attacked and killed them "without any very evident necessity for so doing" (6:43), and "talked of making the Indians their servants, as if God had destined them for perpetual bondage to the more powerful white man" (6:47). Such offensive religious and racialist arguments still held public sway, as Hawthorne well knew, and in a passage startling for its progressive thought, he has Grandfather tell the children,

> I have sometimes doubted whether there was more than a single man, among our forefathers, who realized that an Indian possesses a mind, and a heart, and an immortal soul. That single man was John Eliot. All the rest of the early settlers seemed to think that the Indians were an inferior race of beings, whom the Creator had merely allowed to keep possession of this beautiful country, till the white men should be in want of it. (6:43)

This critique of the early settlers' attitudes speaks to a controversial contemporaneous political issue, as Hawthorne surely intended. Under the Indian removal policies of the Jackson and Van Buren administrations, the U.S. government was displacing seventy thousand Indians from their lands east of the Mississippi, to satisfy the demands of white land seekers. On October 1, 1838, the first group of Cherokees were driven on a march westward on what became known as the Trail of Tears. A reporter from Maine riding with the Cherokees recorded, "The sick and feeble were carried in wagons. . . . a great many ride on horseback and multitudes go on foot—even aged females, apparently ready to drop into the grave, were traveling with heavy burdens attached to the back—on the sometimes frozen ground, and sometimes muddy streets, with no covering for their feet except what nature had given them. . . . We learned from the inhabitants on the road where the Indians passed, they buried fourteen or fifteen at every stopping place."[44] A full-blooded

Cherokee recorded the journey through Missouri: "Women cry and make sad wails. Children cry and many men cry, and all look sad when friends die, but they say nothing and just put heads down and keep on go towards West. Many days pass and people die very much."[45] In contrast to such suffering, in December 1838, President Van Buren told Congress, "It affords sincere pleasure to apprise the Congress of the entire removal of the Cherokee Nation of Indians to their new homes west of the Mississippi. The measures authorized by Congress at its last session have had the happiest effects."[46] Eight months earlier, Emerson had accurately warned Van Buren, "You, sir, will bring down that renowned chair in which you sit into infamy if your seal is set to this instrument of perfidy; and the name of this nation, hitherto the sweet omen of religion and liberty, will stink to the world."[47]

Despite Hawthorne's admiration for Jackson, he apparently agreed with Emerson and rejected the notion that Indians deserved to be driven from their lands.[48] He presents as one of the most heroic figures in *Grandfather's Chair* the Puritan minister John Eliot, who established schools among the Indians, learned their language, and taught them to read and to pray, behavior that is now seen as tainted with imperialism yet was admirable in Hawthorne's eyes. Eliot's labors translating the Bible into the Indian tongue receive a chapter-length discussion, and he is said to complete the task after the "community of red people, whom Mr. Eliot had begun to civilize," vanished during King Philip's War (6:50). Grandfather tells how Eliot "resisted both the craft of the politician, and the fierceness of the warrior," both of whom insisted that "the only method of dealing with the red men was to meet them with the sword drawn, and the musket presented" (6:47). Instead, Eliot

> sat writing in the great chair, when the pleasant summer breeze came in through his open casement; and also when the fire of forest logs sent up its blaze and smoke, through the broad stone chimney, into the wintry air. Before the earliest bird sang, in the morning, the apostle's lamp was kindled; and, at mid-night, his weary head was not yet upon its pillow. And at length, leaning back in the great chair, he could say to himself, with a holy triumph—"The work is finished!" (6:48)

As a fellow writer, Hawthorne could surely appreciate Eliot's efforts. He records that Eliot's "disinterested zeal for his brother's good" elevates him above all his fellow Puritans, in Grandfather's view, especially those engaged in warfare. When Charley asks about King Philip's War, Grandfather impatiently replies, "I have no time to spare in talking about battles," and when Charley persists by asking who the captain of the English was, he is told, "Their most noted captain was Benjamin Church—a very famous warrior. . . . But I assure you, Charley, that neither Captain Church, nor any of the officers and soldiers who fought in King Philip's war, did any thing a thousandth part so glorious, as Mr. Eliot did, when he translated the Bible for the Indians" (6:50). In *The Blithedale Romance,* Hawthorne again pays tribute to Eliot, in a vision Coverdale has at the rock called "Eliot's Pulpit," where he imagines seeing "the holy Apostle of the Indians, with the sunlight flickering down upon him through the leaves, and glorifying his figure as with the half-perceptible glow of a transfiguration" (3:119). Eliot clearly represented all that Hawthorne most admired about the inspired and dedicated intellectual, and he served as Hawthorne's political exemplar.

A year before he died, Hawthorne, in *Our Old Home* (1863), revisited the issue of military glory, while describing a visit to the great hall in Chelsea Hospital, London, filled with "trophies of battles fought and won in every quarter of the world."

> [I]n truth, the whole system of a people crowing over its military triumphs had far better be dispensed with, both on account of the ill-blood that it helps to keep fermenting among the nations, and because it operates as an accumulative inducement to future generations to aim at a kind of glory, the gain of which has generally proved more ruinous than its loss. I heartily wish that every trophy of victory might crumble away, and that every reminiscence or tradition of a hero, from the beginning of the world to this day, could pass out of all men's memories at once and forever. (5:257)

As for who deserves to be remembered, Hawthorne turns in *Our Old Home* to the figure of the poet, who makes the past "intelligibly noble and sublime to our comprehension." He asserts that "it is not the statesman, the warrior, or the monarch that survives, but the despised poet whom they may have fed with their crumbs" (5:267). Thus, argues Hawthorne, "the helmet and war-saddle of Henry the Fifth, worn at Azincourt and now suspended above his tomb, are memorable objects, but more for Shakespere's sake than the victor's own" (5:268). Hawthorne's comments in this late work of nonfiction confirm the lack of irony with which he presented Grandfather's views some twenty years previously. Although Hawthorne was too modest to ever compare himself to such writers as John Eliot or Shakespeare, he nevertheless looked to them as the most admirable contributors to civilization, occupying a station far above political leaders and warriors or even the combination of the two.

In the second part of *Grandfather's Chair,* following a brief mention of the witchcraft hysteria, "the saddest and most humiliating passage in our history" (6:79), Hawthorne focuses on events surrounding the seventeenth-century conflict between England and France in the New World and indicts the warmongering of many colonial leaders. Grandfather maintains his pacifism as he tells of the failed attempt to conquer Canada with Cotton Mather's blessing, in 1711, after an English fleet arrived and "there was now nothing but warlike bustle in the streets of Boston. The drum and fife, the rattle of arms, and the shouts of boys, were heard from morning till night." The recruiting completed, a fleet with seven thousand English soldiers and New England colonists set sail on a voyage that Grandfather explains was to become a tragedy: "In a few weeks, tidings were received, that eight or nine of the vessels had been wrecked in the St. Lawrence, and that above a thousand drowned soldiers had been washed ashore, on the banks of that mighty river." Thus is underscored the senseless waste of this unaccomplished mission. Grandfather's commentary on this military effort laments that "the old moral and religious character of New England was in danger of being utterly lost." To this, Laurence remarks, "How glorious it would have been, . . . if our forefathers could have kept the country unspotted with blood!" "Yes," replies Grandfather, "but there was a stern, warlike spirit in them from the beginning. They seem never to have thought of questioning either the morality or piety of war" (6:96). Obviously, Hawthorne wishes the young readers of his children's book to engage in such questioning.

The horrible effects of war on those who stay at home becomes a topic Hawthorne raises as Grandfather tells about a 1744 military expedition planned by the new governor of Massachusetts, William Shirley, who sent soldiers to attack the French at Louisbourg, "a fortified city, on the Island of Cape Breton, near Nova Scotia" (6:113). Although the siege of the city succeeded, many colonists died. When Laurence asks, "did the country gain any real good by the conquest of Louisbourg?" he is told that the English parliament sent about a million dollars of gold and copper coins to repay the colonists. Grandfather asks, "Was not this a pretty liberal reward?" to which Laurence replies, "The mothers of the young men, who were killed at the siege of Louisbourg, would not have thought it so." Grandfather then agrees: "every warlike achievement involves an amount of physical and moral evil, for which all the gold in the Spanish mines would not be the slightest recompense" (6:118). As an afterthought, he weakly asks the children to consider that the siege prepared the colonists "for the great contest of the revolution." "In that point of view," he adds, "the valor of our forefathers was its own reward" (6:119)—a sentiment lacking conviction as well as logic.

Hawthorne's pacifism remains consistent in *Grandfather's Chair*, even as the colonists change their religion and causes. In part 3, "Liberty Tree," he calls into question the violence of the rebel colonists as he had that of the earlier Puritan leaders. "The Hutchinson Mob" (1841) describes an attack on Lieutenant Governor Hutchinson's house by angry colonists in 1765, responding to the Stamp Act. As the story opens, the mob was "growing fiercer and fiercer, and seemed ready even to set the town on fire, for the sake of burning the king's friends out of house and home" (6:155). Hutchinson's daughter alerts her father that the rioters are coming "as wild as so many tigers," yet we learn "[h]e was an old lawyer; and he could not realize that the people would do anything so utterly lawless as to assault him in his peaceful home" (6:157). But they do enter, like an "enraged wild beast" and a "tempestuous flood," and they destroy tables, hearths, volumes of his library, family portraits, and mirrors. At the end of the account, Grandfather tells the children that this "was a most unjustifiable act. . . . But we must not decide against the justice of the people's cause, merely because an excited mob was guilty of outrageous violence" (6:159). However, the imagery of this violence, rather than its justification, predominates in the telling.

The same holds true when Grandfather next relates events surrounding the Boston Massacre, provoking Laurence to observe, "The Revolution . . . was not such a calm, majestic movement as I supposed. I do not love to hear of mobs and broils in the street. These things were unworthy of the people, when they had such a great object to accomplish" (6:171). In "The Tory's Farewell," Hawthorne's sympathy for those displaced by the Revolution becomes clear and makes explicit those values dramatized in "My Kinsman,

Major Molineaux." As old Chief Justice Oliver sadly departs the Province House, he is greeted with scorn by the colonists: "all hereditary reverence for birth and rank was gone. The inhabitants shouted in derision, when they saw the venerable form of the old chief justice. . . . 'See the old tory!' cried the people, with bitter laughter. 'He is taking his last look at us. Let him show his white wig among us an hour hence, and we'll give him a coat of tar and feathers!' " (6:194). The old man weeps, and Hawthorne conveys his thoughts: " 'They curse me—they invoke all kinds of evil on my head!' thought he, in the midst of his tears. 'But, if they could read my heart, they would know that I love New England well. Heaven bless her, and bring her again under the rule of our gracious king! A blessing, too, on these poor, misguided people!' " (6:195). The sympathy Hawthorne extends here is intended not to deny the positive good effected by the Revolution but, rather, to remind his readers that those who opposed the Revolution did so with perspectives and feelings that deserved understanding and respect.[49]

Revolution and Slavery

As discussed earlier, Hawthorne well understood the symbolic role of dark racial Others in American history. His knowledge stemmed not only from the history of warfare between New England colonists and Native Americans but also from the French Revolution and the slave rebellions it inspired in the Americas. Throughout Hawthorne's youth, the words *Santo Domingo* (the English name used to refer to the French colony of Saint-Domingue, later named Haiti) conjured up images of black men murdering unsuspecting women and children in the middle of the night. As Eric Sundquist has pointed out, Santo Domingo became a "primary point of reference for both proslavery and antislavery forces in the United States."[50] For the abolitionists, Santo Domingo served as a warning to slave owners of what would happen if they refused to abandon their "peculiar" institution. For slavery apologists, the horrors of Santo Domingo were the direct result of abolitionist ideas and activities, which had to be suppressed for the safety of all. To a certain extent, the threat and fears had a basis in fact.

Recent studies have explained the rage and cruelty that attended the revolt of the slaves of Saint-Domingue by focusing on the appalling cruelty inflicted on them before their uprising.[51] Jeremy Popkin has pointed out that "half the slaves in 1790 were survivors of the fearful Middle Passage, and the plantation owners of Saint-Domingue had a reputation for particularly brutal behavior."[52] Joan Dayan has described a notorious example of such behavior in the case of Seigneur Nicolas Jejeune, a coffee planter known for his sadism. In March 1788, Jejeune was charged with killing four of his slaves and torturing two others, women whose feet, legs, and elbows he roasted. As Jejeune was awaiting trial, the women were found in irons on his plantation with their limbs already rotting, and they soon died. Jejeune defended himself at his trial by claiming,

> The wretched state of the negro naturally makes him detest us. It is only by force and violence that we subjugate him; he must nourish in his heart an implacable hatred, and if he does not commit against us every evil that he could, it is only because his will is enchained by terror; so, if we do not weigh down his chains proportionate to the dangers that we risk with him, if we draw out his hatred from its state of numbness, what can stop him from trying to break these chains?[53]

Jejeune was acquitted by the French Superior Council at Le Cap, and the fourteen slaves who had reported him to the court were punished. As Dayan concludes, "in just three years, the slaves, whose courage he had foreseen, revolted."[54]

One ardent proslavery account of the Haitian Revolution describes it as a time when "blood flowed in torrents; lust and violation were made things of custom; and the population lost almost the traits which distinguish humanity from the brute."[55] Why? From the Southern perspective, the incitement of abolitionists was to blame. The first insurrection in Saint-Domingue was led by Vincent Ogé, a free mulatto who had participated in the Paris discussions of the French Antislavery Society (Société des Amis des Noirs) and, after the fall of the Bastille, had gone to England, where he received money from the leading English abolitionist Thomas Clarkson. Ogé sailed to Charleston, where he bought arms and arrived back in Saint-Domingue in the fall of 1790, to lead a revolt of some three hundred mulattoes, which was put down by fifteen hundred white militia and black volunteers. Ironically, Ogé had no intention of freeing the black slaves; he sought only equal rights for his own class, the mulattoes, *gens de couleurs.*

After his capture, Ogé and his fellow rebel Jean-Baptiste Chavannes were gruesomely executed by the French authorities, but one result of his insurrection was a series of nocturnal meetings among slave leaders in the summer of 1791, resulting in the massive slave revolt beginning the night of August 22. Various published accounts of the revolution stress its horrors, and in his best-selling history of 1801, Bryan Edwards, a British planter-observer, focuses on such dramatic scenes as a white baby held aloft on a stake, white women raped on the corpses of their husbands, and the torture of Madame Séjourné.[56] By the beginning of 1792, countless plantations had been destroyed, and chaos had overtaken the island. In the years that followed, the political situation became exceptionally complex and brutal, as the slaves, mulattoes, and whites—Spanish, French, and British—vied for control of the island.

The most famous leader of the Haitian Revolution was the black ex-slave Toussaint Louverture, who, by the beginning of 1793, had emerged as a brilliant military commander, fighting first with the Spanish, then switching his allegiance to the French and driving the British from the island. Claiming loyalty to France, but asserting his independent authority, Toussaint conquered Spanish Santo Domingo in the east, put down a mulatto uprising in the west and the south, and took control of all of Hispaniola in 1801, restoring peace and order. On orders from Napoleon, who sought to reestablish slavery in France's West Indian colonies, Toussaint was betrayed, arrested, deported, and imprisoned in a French dungeon, where he died in 1803. The black general who assumed his place after Toussaint's arrest became a satanic figure to many observers and confirmed many prejudices about blacks, slave and free. Jean Jacques Dessalines, with help from the yellow fever, defeated the French forces on the island and completed the revolution by methodically massacring all the white colonists who remained.[57]

Although the United States severed its ties with Haiti, black slaves throughout the Americas were inspired by its example. After all, here, in the words of C. L. R. James, was "the only successful slave revolt in history, and the odds it had to overcome is evidence of the magnitude of the interests that were involved. The transformation of slaves, trembling in hundreds before a single white man, into a people able to organize themselves and defeat the most powerful European nations of their day, is one of the great epics of revolutionary struggle and achievement."[58] In 1822, when Denmark Vesey led his abortive slave revolt in South Carolina, his followers testified that he had been inspired by the example of the slaves of Saint-Domingue.[59] Similarly, in 1812, José Antonio Aponte conspired to lead a slave insurrection in Cuba, promising his followers assistance from Haiti. As Matt D. Childs has observed, the Haitian rebellion had lasting impact on Cuba: it "brought to fruition dreams of wealth and extravagance for Cuban planters, but also their nightmares of an apocalyptic demise at the hands of the same slaves who filled their bank accounts. For slaves, the success of the Haitian Revolution resulted in expanding the living nightmare of human bondage throughout the island, while it encouraged many slaves to put into action their risky dreams of ending slavery through rebellion."[60] During the first decades of the nineteenth century, Cuban officials and planters remained anxious about a Haitian-style revolt, and indeed, images of Haiti, as Childs points out, reappeared in the La Escalera slave conspiracy of 1844.[61]

Hawthorne learned much of what he knew about slavery in the West Indies from reading Sophia Peabody's *Cuba Journal*, a series of letters Sophia (born in 1809) wrote to her mother over her eighteen-month stay during 1833–35 on the sugar plantation of the Morrell family in western Cuba. Wealthy, cultured, and of Spanish blood, the Morrells had fled Santo Domingo during the Haitian Revolution and had successfully reestablished themselves in Cuba, in the region set aside by the Spanish government for refugee planters. During Sophia's stay, the Morrells' extensive plantations employed hundreds of slaves, including nine house slaves in the hacienda where Sophia lived. Her reform-minded sister Mary, who accompanied her to Cuba, was appalled by the slavery she witnessed, but Sophia focused on the beauty of the landscape and its therapeutic effects on her previously ill health. As Sophia's biographer, Patricia Valenti, has pointed out, Sophia remained detached "from the political turmoil amid which she lived for a year and a half."[62] She admired General Miguel Tacón, described by Valenti as "perhaps the most brutal and repressive agent of the Spanish monarchy" in Cuba.[63] Sophia seems to have fallen in love with the dashing Don Fernando de Zayes, whose family, located on a coffee plantation two miles away, was one of the richest and most cultured in Cuba. Together, she and Don Fernando enjoyed the leisure activities slave plantation life made possible: they read and discussed books, played chess, danced the waltz, and went horseback riding through the lush and beautiful countryside.

Despite Sophia's attempt to keep slavery and the threat of slave revolt out of sight in the *Cuba Journal,* at times they surface. In one of her letters, for example, she describes a morning ride and the enjoyment of the "sublimity & beauty" of the earth and sky, until she passes "a flock of negroes."

> Those who had caps on pulled them off—some stretched out their arms—
> & most of them commended me to GOD in this majestic & beautiful lan-
> guage, which gives an association of refinement to all who utter it. They
> are quite acquainted with me because I so often ride & I suppose the poor
> creatures enjoy my greetings—for I always throw into my manner &
> voice the greatest possible kindness I can command. But their appearance
> broke upon my spell of enchantment rather painfully—slavery in the very
> dawn of the new light upon the new earth-! the light that was coming for
> all—but came not to them.[64]

On another occasion, Sophia encounters a man on horseback with a slave walking before him in chains. "It was such a revolting sight," she relates, "that the aspect of our thoughts was changed at once, & we concluded that we would give up all the charms of this Paradise rather than be subjected to such shocks."[65] Although obviously self-involved in her letters, Sophia does not totally ignore the dangers surrounding her. During one visit to a sugar plantation owned by her host, she writes,

> On this estate there is no judgment used in the management, and the mis-
> erable wretches are badly treated and have no holiday from one end of
> the year to another. Oh such objects as some of them were. It made my
> heart sick to look at them. One with his fierce eye and brow, and brawny
> black and blue limbs looked like the very spirit of evil; yet even he was
> courteous, and when I attempted to get a crust of the sugar, moved away
> the impediments with a promptitude that wrung my heart a great deal
> more than if he had flung the burning fluid in my face. He looked like the
> untamable *obliged* to *appear* tame.[66]

When he read Sophia's *Cuba Journal,* apparently during his solitary jour-
ney in the late summer of 1838, Hawthorne copied out some eleven items in his own notebook and soon found himself in love with its author. One of his entries, so consonant with his central political idea, reads: "Dolorita, daugh-

ter of Feliciana—Grief, the daughter of Felicity" (23:197). In her journal, Sophia identifies Feliciana as a domestic slave on the Morrell plantation and Dolorita as her daughter, who, Sophia writes, "is well named, for such a doleful ditty she keeps up from morning till night could not be surpassed by the abstract principle of woe."[67] Hawthorne also used the *Cuba Journal* as a source for "Edward Randolph's Portrait," discussed earlier, which treats a volatile political situation analogous to that the *Cuba Journal* tries to repress. Alice Vane, modeled in part on Sophia, is "so child-like, so wayward, in her singular character, so apart from ordinary rules" (9:264), yet this young woman, by her restoration of the mysterious portrait of Edward Randolph, the most tyrannical ruler in American colonial history, warns her uncle, Lieutenant–Governor Hutchinson, that an oppressed people will resort to violence and bloodshed if pushed beyond their limit.

In a letter of 1838, Sophia informed her mother that Mr. Hawthorne "said he had imagined a story of which the principal incident is my cleaning that picture of Fernandez. To be the means, in any way, of calling forth one of his divine creations is no small happiness."[68] Yet whereas the picture Sophia restored became lustrous and gorgeous, the one in Hawthorne's "divine creation" starts and ends as horrific.[69] In its blackened state, the portrait is the subject of rumors: "One of the wildest, and at the same time the best accredited, accounts, stated it to be an original and authentic portrait of the Evil One, taken at a witch meeting near Salem" (9:260). Through the restoration efforts of Alice, it becomes, instead, a portrait of Edward Randolph, suffering like a victim in hell: "The expression of the face . . . was that of a wretch detected in some hideous guilt, and exposed to the bitter hatred, and laughter, and withering scorn, of a vast surrounding multitude. There was the struggle of defiance, beaten down and overwhelmed by the crushing weight of ignominy. The torture of the soul had come forth upon the countenance" (9:267). Given the origins of Hawthorne's story in the *Cuba Journal*, Robert Cantwell has speculated that Hawthorne "imagined on the basis of Sophia's unguarded words, the political situation in the island and the predicament of the de Zayas."[70] Transposing Cuba to New England, Hawthorne, Cantwell writes, conceived of "the young Cuban aristocrats as colonists at a moment of fateful decision in their country's history."[71] If this interpretation is valid, as I believe it is, then Hawthorne understood, as Sophia apparently did not, that tyranny and insurrection make a hellish couple in any time or place, including Santo Domingo, Cuba, or Boston.

Eric Sundquist has criticized Hawthorne for being "strangely blind" to the paradox of American liberty rising simultaneously with the rise of slavery, yet Hawthorne's "blindness" can best be understood as a belief that slavery was but one of many evils afflicting humanity and provoking reform or rebellion. In "The Procession of Life," he praises "the genuine benefactors of the race" who have worked to end all forms of human misery: "The prison, the insane asylum, the squalid chambers of the alms-house, the manufactory where the demon of machinery annihilates the human soul, and the cotton-field where God's image becomes a beast of burthen; to these, and every other scene where man wrongs or neglects his brother, the apostles of humanity have penetrated" (10:216). As for the metaphor of blindness, in Hawthorne's view, it suited those idealists and reformers who devoted themselves to only one species of reform and failed to see beyond their own narrow focus, including the consequences of their own actions. In "Septimius Norton" (a later version of "Septimius Felton"), he responds to the American Revolution and the Civil War simultaneously by observing, "Not only soldiers (who have a dispensation for drinking blood) but statesmen, quiet, elderly people, who have never hurt a fly, bring about the deaths of myriads, by blunders, mistakes, or even of fell purpose, and never dream of immorality" (13:432). The humility couched in such a political vision becomes less and less tolerable as the need for decisive action becomes more and more apparent to partisan observers.

Abolitionism and Violence

The persistent resistance to the abolitionist movement that Hawthorne showed throughout his career arose not from any sympathy toward slave owners but, rather, from aversion to radicalism in whatever form it took. (Emerson shared this aversion, at least until the 1850s, and thus his 1844 antislavery address praises the docility with which the slaves in the British West Indies greeted news of their emancipation in 1833 and 1838.) Although there were those within the early antislavery movement who sought to end slavery by gradual means (e.g., the apprenticeships used by the British to stage emancipation in the West Indies), it was Garrison's radical rhetoric calling for immediate and unqualified emancipation that sparked the most controversy and concern.[72] Inspired by the activities of black abolitionists in Boston, Garrison founded his abolitionist newspaper, *The Liberator,* in 1831, and within months, Nat Turner's notorious Southampton slave rebellion occurred, during which Turner and his band of some sixty to eighty slaves killed over sixty white men, women, and children. The revolt generated suspicion and panic throughout the South, and countless blacks were tortured and killed in retaliation. Even the editor of the Richmond *Whig* lamented this "feature of the Southampton Rebellion . . . We allude to the slaughter of many blacks without trial and under circumstances of great barbarity."[73] Although Turner's only reading material had been the Bible, Garrison and the *Liberator* were widely perceived as instigators of the rebellion. Garrison received assassination threats from the South and New England both.[74] Undeterred, a year later, he warned his readers that if "the glorious day of universal emancipation" did not arrive, "woe to the safety of this people! . . . A cry of horror, a cry of revenge, will go up to heaven in the darkness of midnight, and re-echo from every cloud. Blood will flow like water—the blood of guilty men, and of innocent women and children. Then will be heard lamentations and weeping, such as will blot out the remembrance of the horrors of St. Domingo."[75]

Not surprisingly, Garrison became a polarizing public figure, and in 1835, an antiabolitionist mob pulled him from a meeting of the Boston Female Anti-Slavery Society and dragged him through the streets with a rope around his neck, before he was rescued and put in jail for protection. Public opinion weighed heavily against Garrison, who was blamed for the riot. The *Salem Gazette* claimed, "the tendency of the labors of such men, is to convert this 'happy land' into scenes of blood and carnage, and to induce the blacks to cut the throats of the whites."[76] Similarly, the *Boston Post* responded by asserting, "we deplore the madness of the abolitionists and condemn their measures."[77] Hawthorne apparently agreed that at least some abolitionists were indeed "mad," and in the fall of 1835, soon after the mob riot in Boston, he made the following entry in his notebook:

> A sketch to be given of a modern reformer,—a type of the extreme doctrines on the subject of slaves, cold water, and other such topics. He goes about the streets haranguing most eloquently, and is on the point of mak-

ing many converts, when his labors are suddenly interrupted by the appearance of the keeper of a mad-house, whence he has escaped. Much may be made of this idea. (8:10)

Hawthorne never wrote a tale or romance with this plot as he advised himself to do, but Hollingsworth, of *The Blithedale Romance,* displays some of the traits of this "modern reformer." One reader, Theodore Parker, reportedly believed that Garrison was the model for Hollingsworth.[78]

Today, we regard the early abolitionists as heroic moral leaders of their age, but in the 1830s, they were seen by most Americans, in the North and South, as fanatics threatening the stability of society, the virtue of white citizens, and the lives of all. Most Northerners regretted the existence of slavery, but they saw the abolitionists as misguided fanatics. They distinguished, in other words, between support of abolition and support of abolitionists. In an August 1833 editorial in the *New York Evening Post,* editor William Cullen Bryant expressed his and his readers' opposition to slavery but declared, "There is not the slightest disposition to interfere in any improper and offensive manner, except among certain fanatical persons, and those few in number, we regard it to be as well settled as any fact in relation to public opinion ever discussed in the public journals."[79] Many otherwise progressive supporters of the antislavery movement feared the consequences of immediate emancipation, especially the prospect of large numbers of ex-slaves joining Northern society and its labor force.[80]

It was not the abolitionists, however, but their opponents who instigated the most political violence in the 1830s, forming mobs that attacked Negroes and abolitionists. This hostility grew out of the belief that Negroes were unfit to live in a white society; that slavery was a local, not a national, matter; that foreigners (namely, British abolitionists) were interfering in American affairs; and that immediate emancipation would lead to violence and race war.[81] They claimed that an interracial society was "unnatural" and would lead to various forms of depravity and social ills, especially if emancipation were not followed by deportation. James Fenimore Cooper warned in *The American Democrat* (1838) that if and when American slavery ceased, "two races will exist in the same region, whose feelings will be embittered by inextinguishable hatred, and who carry on their faces, the respective stamps of their factions. The struggle that will follow, will necessarily be a war of extermination. The evil day may be delayed, but can scarcely be averted."[82] Such a perspective led to support for the colonization movement, even by ardent abolitionists. At the end of *Uncle Tom's Cabin* (1852), Stowe calls Americans to first educate the emancipated slaves "until they have attained to somewhat of a moral and intellectual maturity, and then assist them in their passage to those shores [of Africa], where they may put in practice the lessons they have learned in America."[83]

Less explicitly, but with some conviction, Hawthorne supported the activities of the American Colonization Society with his editing of *Journal of an African Cruiser* (1845), written by his friend Bridge, telling about a recent cruise on the West Coast of Africa to protect American trade and stop slavers.[84] Throughout that work, as will be discussed in chapter 4, Hawthorne inserts a pacifism suggesting that violence is an ineffective means of achieving political ends. For Hawthorne, the passion and excitement generated by the abolitionists brought out the worst, not the best, in human behavior. Thus the young boy who counseled, "By reason my life let me square," became a man who felt the same way.

CHAPTER 2

Witchcraft and Abolitionism

It is not enough that you agree with them [the Massachusetts Republicans].
You must say your creed in their words with their intonation and just when
they bid you or they hang or burn you as a heretic.

—Letter of Emory Washburne to Robert C. Winthrop, June 7, 1856

During his apprentice years as a writer, Hawthorne studied the history of
witchcraft even more intently than he did the American Revolution, spurred
by the central role played by his great-grandfather Judge John Hathorne
(known as the witch judge) and by public interest in witchcraft as a social
and political phenomenon. Before the witchcraft hysteria ended in 1693,
Judge Hathorne's "examinations" of accused witches and wizards led to the
imprisonment of more than 150 persons, the hanging of nineteen innocent
persons, and the death by torture of another. In the preface to *The Scarlet
Letter*, Hawthorne declares that this ancestor "inherited the persecuting
spirit, and made himself so conspicuous in the martyrdom of the witches,
that their blood may fairly be said to have left a stain upon him." Referring
to him and another ancestor—John's father William, who had persecuted the
Quakers—Hawthorne writes, "I, the present writer, as their representative,
hereby take shame upon myself for their sakes, and pray that any curse in-
curred by them—as I have heard, and as the dreary and unprosperous condition of the race, for many a long year back, would argue to exist—may be

now and henceforth removed" (1:10). Though this confession and professed atonement are light and humorous or at least intentionally melodramatic, it appears that Hawthorne indeed felt guilty about the role his ancestors played in Puritan history.[1] Consequently, he regarded with suspicion the role of judge as well as appeals to his passions seeking condemnation of others.

The Study of Witchcraft

Hawthorne's readings in the history of Salem witchcraft included such works as Cotton Mather's *The Wonders of the Invisible World* (1693), Robert Calef's *More Wonders of the Invisible World* (1700), Thomas Hutchinson's *The History of the Colony of Massachusetts* (1765), and Charles Upham's *Lectures on Witchcraft* (1831), all of which reveal that the specter evidence used to convict the accused witches was obviously fabricated and that anyone guided by reason, rather than superstition, would have dismissed it. Yet it prevailed. From this result, Hawthorne focused on three causes of the witchcraft delusion relevant to his political vision: (1) the false accusations made by supposedly "afflicted" persons, including some of the accused; (2) the fanaticism and cruelty of the ministers, judges, and magistrates, who evoked and perpetuated the hysteria; and (3) the gullibility of the populace, who believed the lies of the accusers and trusted the judgment of the leaders of the community. For him, superstition and fear went hand in hand, evoking sensational tales of specters, ghosts, and devils, which led to the torture and death of the innocent. Salem witchcraft, in other words, taught him to be deeply skeptical of fearmongering and demonizing, especially when practiced by self-righteous leaders and accepted without question by their gullible followers.

Recently, historians and sociologists have traced the Salem witchcraft hysteria to a number of economic, political, and social causes, including factional conflicts between Salem Town and Salem Village; long-term personal grudges between the Putnam and Porter clans; strife in the Salem Village church and a falling away of attendance; growing antagonism toward independent and combative women; anxiety about the Massachusetts government, which existed in a state of uncertainty after the colonists imprisoned the royal governor Edmund Andros and awaited his replacement; and perhaps most significant, horror-filled Indian attacks on the Massachusetts frontier, which drove many traumatized and fearful colonists back to communities such as Salem.[2] These recent explanations run counter to the blame placed on the Puritan leaders by Hawthorne and his contemporaries.[3] It seems that Hawthorne displaced onto Cotton Mather the guilt generated by Hawthorne's knowledge of his great-grandfather's role in the witchcraft delusion. In their histories, Upham and George Bancroft similarly vilified Mather, along with the Reverend Samuel Parris, thus giving Judge Hathorne a free pass, perhaps out of consideration for Hawthorne, who was their well-regarded acquaintance.

While the causes of events in Salem in 1692 remain open to scholarly investigation and interpretation, Hawthorne, in all of his sources, encountered a group of facts that have long been known and agreed upon, which indicated how lies, self-righteousness, and gullibility can degrade a society. The first fact is that in January 1692, Betty Parris, the nine-year-old daughter of the minister in Salem Village, Samuel Parris, fell ill and suffered violent fits, throwing herself about, striking out, and shrieking. Soon, her eleven-year-old cousin, Abigail Williams, also living in the Parris home, experienced the same symptoms. Parris consulted the local physician, William Griggs, who warned that the "Evil Hand" could be the cause of the girls' malady, but when Parris met with nearby ministers, they cautioned patience and joined him in prayer. At the suggestion of a near neighbor, Mary Sibley, Parris's slaves, Tituba and John Indian, baked a "witch cake" with the girls' urine to feed to the Parrises' dog, presumably the devil's familiar. Learning of this attempt to cure the girls, Parris denounced Sibley from his pulpit, on March 27, 1692.

> [W]hen these calamities first began, which was in my own family, the affliction was several weeks before such hellish operations, as witchcraft, was suspected. Nay, it never brake forth to any considerable light, until diabolical means were used, by the making of a cake by my Indian man, who had his direction from this our sister, Mary Sibley; since which apparitions have been plenty, and exceeding much mischief hath followed. But by this means (it seems) the devil hath been raised amongst us, and his rage is vehement and terrible, and when he shall be silenced, the Lord only knows.[4]

By the time Parris delivered this sermon, seven or eight other girls had joined Betty Parris and Abigail Williams in having fits. Under questioning by adults, they had accused Tituba, Sarah Good, Sarah Osborne, Rebecca Nurse, and Martha Corey of bewitching them.

John Hathorne and Jonathan Corwin examined the first three women to be accused, Tituba, Good, and Osborne, on March 1, 1692. Their examinations were recorded in transcripts that served as the primary evidence used later at the women's trials, which began on June 2, with Lieutenant–Governor William Stoughton presiding. (Hathorne served as one of the seven members of the court who heard evidence against the accused, none of whom had legal counsel.) Most of these transcripts still exist, and they clearly reveal the polemical fierceness with which Hathorne dealt with the accused. Good and Osburn denied the charges against them, as did Tituba at first. But under stern questioning by Hathorne, Tituba confessed, telling a fabulous tale about doing the devil's bidding. Tituba declared that the devil appeared sometimes as a hog, sometimes as a great black dog, and sometimes as a man with black clothes and white hair. In all forms, she said, he told her time and again to serve him and to hurt the children.

When Hathorne asked Tituba what form the devil assumed at first, her answer suggests he appeared in a dream. She replied, "one like a man Just as I was goeing to sleep Came to me this was when the Children was first hurt he sayd he would kill the Children & she would never be well, and he Sayd if I would nott Serve him he would do soe to mee." She said this man had a yellow bird "and more pretty things" he promised to give her if she would serve him. She admitted that he had appeared to her the previous night, along with four women, including Goody Osburn, Goody Good, and two women from Boston she did not recognize. They all rode on sticks to Thomas Putnam's home and there hurt his child. When asked by Hathorne, "doe you goe through the trees or over them?" Tituba replied, "we see no thing but are there presently." When asked, "why did you not tell your master?" she replied, "I was afraid they said they would cut off my head if I told." Under further questioning, she claimed to have seen Goody Osborn with "a thing with a head like a woman with two leggs and wings" and "a thing all over hairy, all the face hayry & a long nose." She added, "I don't know how to tell how the face looks w'th two Leggs, itt goeth upright & is about two or three foot high & goeth upright like a man & last night itt stood before the fire In mr parris's hall." She also testified that she saw Sarah Good set a wolf upon Elizabeth Hubbard. (Elizabeth had reported being attacked by the specter of a wolf.)[5]

In her second examination, the next day, Tituba elaborated on her sensational story, saying that the man who appeared to her told her that he was God and that she must believe him and serve him for six years. If she did so, she said, "he would give me many fine things." She added that he said he would "Come the Next time & show me a book." This detail, known as crucial evidence proving one a witch, provoked leading questions from Hathorne, who asked, "did nott he make you write yo'r Name?"—a question that led to the following exchange:

A. noe nott yett for mistris Called me into the other roome.
Q. whatt did he say you must doe in that book?
A. he Sayd write & sett my name to itt.
Q. did you write?
A. yes once I made a marke in the Booke & made itt with red Bloud.

When asked how many other marks there were in the book, she says nine, which Hathorne finds of great interest, of course.

Q. you Say that there was Nine did he tell you whoe they were?
A. noe he noe lett me See but he tell me I should See them the next tyme
Q. what sights did you see
A. I see a man, a dogge, a hogge, & two Catts a black and Red & the strange monster was Osburne that I mentioned before this was was the hayry Imp. the man would give itt to mee, but I would nott have itt.
Q. did he show you in the Book w'ch was Osburne & w'ch was Goods mark?
A. yes I see . . .
Q. did he tell you where the Nine Lived?
A. yes, Some in Boston & Some herein this Towne, but he would nott tell mee wher thay were.[6]

Obviously, the slave Tituba provided the sensational testimony she believed Hathorne and others wanted to hear, and it is not difficult to see that she was forced "to serve" (the refrain of her answers), whether the demand comes from Hathorne, her slave master Parris, or the spectral devil.

Tituba was unique in the witchcraft trials by occupying two subject positions at the same time, witch and slave (ironic, since to be a witch required the exercise of free will). This fact complicated the reading of marks on her body. Thomas Hutchinson, in his *History*, identifies her as an Indian woman from New Spain, who, "upon search," was "found to have scars upon her back which were called the devil's mark, but might as well have been supposed those of her Spanish master."[7] A common test for witchcraft was finding a scar or mole on the body of the accused, the devil's mark, not to be confused with the witch's mark, an unusual protuberance or teat from which demons might suck in the form of familiars. Tituba's judges chose to read her scars as the mark of the devil, but after the trials ended, she admitted that she had lied, "that her Master did beat her and otherways abuse her, to make her confess and accuse (such as he call'd) her Sister-Witches, and that whatsoever she said by way of confessing or accusing others, was the effect of such usage."[8] We may assume, then, that her scars were also effects of such usage. Master and devil and minister were one.

Tituba's false and sensational testimony gave credence to the girls' accusations and led to the hunt for other witches in the community's midst. (As a key witness against others, Tituba was not hanged; Sarah Osborne, however, died in jail on May 10, and Sarah Good was hanged on July 19.) As John Hale later put it, "the success of Tituba's confession encouraged those in Authority to examine others that were suspected, and the event was, that more confessed themselves guilty of the Crimes they were suspected for. And thus was this matter driven on."[9] Ten days after Tituba's first examination, Ann Putnam Jr. accused Martha Corey of witchcraft, and seven days later, Abigail Williams accused Rebecca Nurse.

The false accusations of Tituba and the children acquired political power through a judicial process marked by credulity, bias, and cruelty. Judge Hathorne's examination of Corey on March 21, in the packed Salem Village meetinghouse, was especially coercive, probably because he knew she had expressed disdain for the proceedings. Because his questioning reveals the "persecuting spirit" his great-grandson found repellent (and because the specifics of his persecution are relatively unknown), I here provide an extended quotation from the *Salem Witchcraft Papers*.

MR HATHORNE: "You are now in the hands of Authority tell me now why you hurt these persons
MARTHA KORY: I do not.
Q. who doth?
A. Pray give me leave to goe to prayer [This request was made sundry times]

Q. We do not send for you to go to prayer But tell me why you hurt these?

A. I am an innocent person: I never had to do with Witchcraft since I was born. I am a Gospel Woman . . .

Q. If you expect mercy of God, you must look for it in Gods way by confession Do you think to find mercy by aggravating your sins

A. A true thing

Q. Look for it then in Gods way

A. So I do

Q. Give glory to God & confess then

A. But I cannot confess

Q. Do not you see how these afflicted do charge you

A. We must not beleive distracted persons

Q. Who do you improve to hurt them

A. I improved none

Q. Did not you say our eyes were blinded you would open them

A. Yes to accuse the innocent . . .

Q. Tell us who hurts these: We came to be a Terror to evil doers You say you would open our eyes we are blind

A. If you say I am a Witch

Q. You said you would show us [She denied it.]

Q. Why do you not now show us

A. I cannot tell: I do not know . . .

Q. Do you beleive these children are bewitcht

A. They may for ought I know I have no hand in it

Q. You say you are no Witch, may be you mean you never Covenanted with the Devil. Did you never deal w'th any familiar

A. No never . . .

Q. Do you beleive you shall go unpunished

A. I have nothing to do w'th witchcraft

Q. Did you not say you would open our eyes why do you not

A. I never thought of a Witch

Q. Is it a laughing matter to see these afflicted persons [She denied it]

Q. Severall prove it

A. Ye are all against me & I cannot help it[10]

Judge Hathorne's questioning continued in the same vein until Ann Putnam cried out that there was a black man whispering in Corey's ear, which Mary Walcott confirmed. (This spectral sighting by the girls may have been informed by their knowledge that Corey, before her marriage to Giles Corey, had borne a mulatto son.)[11] Hathorne's treatment of Corey shows grave prejudice (she was hanged on September 22), and with other defendants, his prejudice and cruelty did not abate.[12]

In their examinations, Hathorne and Corwin rushed to judgment and accepted the lies of the accusers at face value, even their claims that specters of the accused had tormented them. Because Hathorne and Corwin proceeded on the assumption that the devil could not assume the shape of an innocent person, they treated specter evidence as undeniably incriminating. At least a few colonists privately questioned this evidence, especially in the case of the elderly Rebecca Nurse (hanged on July 19), who had lived a saintly life. But Judge Hathorne showed no doubts. On May 10, as he was examining George Jacobs Sr., the following exchange took place.

JACOBS: You tax me for a wizard, you may as well tax me for a buzard I have done no harm.
HATHORNE: Is it no harm to afflict these?
JACOBS: I never did it.
HATHORNE: But how comes it to be in your appearance?
JACOBS: The Devil can taken any likeness.
HATHORNE: Not without their consent.[13]

Jacobs was hanged on August 9 because, as Nathaniel Hawthorne sarcastically explained in "Main-street" (1849), "the miserable sinner was prevailed with to mount into the air, and career among the clouds; and he is proved to have been present at a witch-meeting as far off as Falmouth, on the very same night that his next neighbors saw him, with his rheumatic stoop, going in at his own door" (11:74).

Thus delusions and/or lies proved deadly for those persons charged with witchcraft, and even the hearsay testimony of ghosts, heard by a child, was permitted to weigh against the accused. In the trial of a former Salem Village minister who had moved to Maine, John Burroughs (hanged on August 9), little Ann Putnam, aged eleven, claimed that one evening she saw the apparition of Burroughs, who tortured her and urged her to write in his book. He told her, she said, that his first two wives would appear to her and tell her many lies, and the women then appeared in their winding sheets. They spoke angrily to Burroughs and told him that their blood cried out for vengeance against him and that he should be cast into hell. At this, his apparition vanished, and the two ghostly women told Ann that Burroughs had murdered them. The ghost of the first wife showed Ann where Burroughs had stabbed her under the left arm and said that it happened when she and Burroughs lived in the house the Parris family now inhabited.[14] A host of other Salem and Andover residents made similar, though less spectacular, accusations against Burroughs. His conduct at the gallows raised doubts about his guilt, however, when he spoke to the crowd and said the Lord's Prayer perfectly, which a witch or wizard supposedly could not do; but Cotton Mather interceded, addressing the people from horseback and reminding them that the devil could appear as an angel of light.[15] In "Main-street," Hawthorne recreated the scene using heavy irony: "wise Cotton Mather," he writes, "as he sits there on his horse, speaks comfortably to the perplexed multitude, and tells them that all has been religiously and justly done, and that Satan's power shall this day receive its death-blow in New England" (11:77).

Despite Judge Hathorne's firm belief in specter evidence, the growing number of accusations in the summer of 1692 led Increase Mather to write a treatise warning against the exclusive use of specter evidence, asserting that Satan may "appear in the Shape of an Innocent and Pious, as well as of a Nocent and Wicked Person, to Afflict such as suffer by Diabolical Molestations."[16] Fourteen ministers formally concurred with him. Also, in the fall of 1692, Samuel Willard, writing under a pseudonym, condemned the trials, and Thomas Brattle, a Boston merchant, wrote a now-famous letter criticizing the Salem examinations and trials, especially the testimony of the "afflicted persons," whose behavior made him "strongly suspect that the Devill imposes upon their brains, and deludes their fancye and imagination; and that the Devill's book (which they say has been offered them) is a mere fancye of theirs, and no reality: That the witches' meeting, the Devill's Baptism, and mock sacraments, which they oft speak of, are nothing else but the effect of their fancye, depraved and deluded by the Devill, and not a Reality to be regarded or minded by any wise man."[17] As a result of such growing skepticism, especially Increase Mather's treatise, Governor William Phips dissolved the Court of Oyer and Terminer and later pardoned all those still in custody, awaiting trial or execution.

Puritan Decline

For Nathaniel Hawthorne, the zeal, self-righteousness, and delusion of the Puritan witch-hunters at the end of the seventeenth century signified a decline in the piety and wisdom of the early Puritans as a group and served as a warning to future generations. In the procession scene at the end of *The Scarlet Letter,* which takes place in 1649, he dramatizes the sobriety, fortitude, and self-reliance of the early Puritans and compares these traits to the "preternatural activity" of the younger generation, represented by the effete and deceitful Arthur Dimmesdale. The first governors of the Massachusetts Bay Colony—Simon Bradstreet, John Endicott, Thomas Dudley, and Richard Bellingham—resemble Fanshawe standing triumphant on his cliff or the Gray Champion planted before the king's oncoming troops: "They had fortitude and self-reliance, and, in time of difficulty or peril, stood up for the welfare of the state like a line of cliffs against a tempestuous tide" (1:238). The shift from strength and stability to weakness and instability constitutes Hawthorne's primary narrative of historical change, and he attributes national significance to it: "the generation next to the early emigrants," he writes near the end of *The Scarlet Letter,* "wore the blackest shade of Puritanism, and so darkened the national visage with it, that all the subsequent years have not sufficed to clear it up" (1:246).

Obviously, Hawthorne, unlike so many New Englanders, did not admire the residual Puritanism of his region. In "Main-street," he becomes explicit about the nature of the transformation he observed: "The sons and grandchildren of the first settlers were a race of lower and narrower souls than their progenitors had been. The latter were stern, severe, intolerant, but not superstitious, not even fanatical; and endowed, if any men of that age were, with a far-seeing worldly sagacity" (11:68). Although Hawthorne never asserts that his contemporaries represent a further decline in the New England character, his social satires, such as "The Celestial Railroad" (discussed in chapter 4), indicate he suspects as much.

Within Hawthorne's myth of Puritan decline into the fanaticism represented by the Salem witchcraft trials, John Endicott assumes a transitional role (as Michael Davitt Bell has shown), and his alteration indicates those Puritan traits found most objectionable when embodied in a political leader or the people he leads. Hawthorne portrays Endicott as courageous and manly in his early activities, as in the 1634 incident portrayed in "Endicott and the Red Cross" (1837), where Endicott speaks "under strong excitement, yet powerfully restraining it," as he defies the king of England. As persecutor of the Quakers in 1659, however, Endicott, as portrayed in Hawthorne's "The Gentle Boy" (1831), becomes "a man of narrow mind and imperfect education, and his uncompromising bigotry was made hot and mischievous by violent and hasty passions; he exerted his influence indecorously and unjustifiably to compass the death of the enthusiasts; and his whole conduct, in respect to them, was marked by brutal cruelty" (9:69). In the first, 1832 version of "The Gentle Boy," Hawthorne offers extenuations for Endicott's treatment of the Quakers and even places some blame on these "enthusiasts" themselves, citing their opposition to "all established governments" (9:614). More specifically, he writes that "after all allowances, it is to be feared that the death of the Quakers was principally owing to the polemic fierceness, that distinct passion of human nature, which has so often produced frightful guilt in the most sincere and zealous advocates of virtue and religion" (9:615). Thus, despite Hawthorne's admiration for the Quakers' devotion to peace, their "polemic fierceness" stands out as behavior one must fear. When he collected "The Gentle Boy" for the 1837 *Twice-Told Tales,* Hawthorne deleted this passage, apparently realizing by then how unjust it was to the Quakers, with whom he came to identify, especially near the end of his life. By then, of course, the Quakers were known for their commitment to peace, not their zealous opposition to government.

Hawthorne's sense of the links among witchcraft, rebellion, and violence, which I see as central to his major works, remains for the most part implied. Yet the three become explicitly entwined at times, as in the late unfinished romance "Grimshawe." There, the "hereditary growth of the frame of public mind which produced the witch-craft delusion" (12:382) generates an attack on the English-born Grimshawe by a mob, "off-scourings of the recently finished war, old soldiers, rusty, wooden-legged; [and] sailors, ripe for any kind of mischief," who shout, "Hang him. Tar and feather the infernal Tory. The wizard! . . . Kill him! Kill him!" Meanwhile, the "respectable" men of the town merely look on (12:384). Hawthorne thus connects the witchcraft hysteria of 1692 with the violence against Tories some one hundred years later and attributes both to an inflamed public mind.

Witchcraft and Blame

In the historical accounts of the Salem witchcraft delusion, Hawthorne discovered ample evidence that impassioned attempts to rid the world of evil could produce results just the opposite of those desired. Cotton Mather's behavior provided him with a telling example. In *Grandfather's Chair,* Hawthorne has Grandfather relate that Mather "believed that there were evil spirits all about the world. . . . He supposed that these unlovely demons were everywhere, in the sunshine as well as in the darkness, and that they were hidden in men's hearts, and stole into their most secret thoughts" (6:94). Such an obsession, Hawthorne believed, evoked the demonic, and Mather's writings suggested as much. In his 1689 volume *Memorable Providences, Relating to Witchcrafts and Possessions,* Mather practically wrote the script for events in Salem by warning of the devils and witches abroad in the land and describing the afflictions of the Goodwin children at Boston who suffered fits and "other bewitchments." After the executions were well underway, Mather, in the fall of 1692, sought to defend the examinations, trials, and hangings in his *The Wonders of the Invisible World* (1693), in the process showing some self-doubt: "I have indeed set myself to countermine the whole PLOT of the Devil, against *New-England,* in every branch of it, as far as one of my *darkness* can comprehend such a *Work of Darkness.*"[18] Mather's ardent foe, Boston merchant Robert Calef, in his *More Wonders of the Invisible World* (1700), was one of the first to indict Mather by tracing events in Salem not to a "plot of the Devil" but to "a Biggotted Zeal, stirring up a Blind and most Bloody rage, not against Enemies, or Irreligious Proffligate Persons, But (in Judgment of Charity, and to view) against as Vertuous and Religious as any they have left behind them in this Country, which have suffered as Evil doers with the utmost extent of rigour."[19] In other words, Calef argued that Mather created the evil he sought to destroy.

Calef's indictment of Mather served as the basis for later historical accounts that Hawthorne also knew well. The second volume of Thomas Hutchinson's *The History of the Province Massachusetts-Bay* (1767) begins by observing that Mather's *Memorable Providences* "obtained credit sufficient, together with other preparations, to dispose the whole country to be easily imposed upon by the more extensive and more tragical scene, which was presently after acted at Salem and other parts of the county of Essex."[20]

Similarly, in his 1831 *Lectures on Witchcraft,* Charles Upham, a friend of Hawthorne's at the time, presents an overwrought indictment of Mather and Parris, both of whom he claims sought to increase their own influence "over an infatuated people." Perhaps revealing more about himself than about Mather, Upham confesses concerning Mather, "I cannot, indeed, resist the conviction, that, not withstanding all his attempts to appear dissatisfied, after they had become unpopular, with the occurrences in the Salem trials, he looked upon them with secret pleasure, and would have been glad to have had them repeated again in Boston."[21] George Bancroft's third volume of his monumental *History of the United States from the Discovery of the American Continent* (1840) draws on Upham in his condemnation of Mather but exonerates the people of Salem for their contributions to the delusions and deaths. He traces the beginning of the troubles to Parris and his congregation, pointing out that there was "a strife so bitter" between the two that "it attracted the attention of the general court."[22] Parris, Bancroft claims, was "moved by personal malice, as well as by blind zeal,"[23] while Cotton Mather acted out of vanity and self-righteousness: "As the affair proceeded, and the accounts of the witnesses appeared as if taken from his own writings, his boundless vanity gloried in 'the assault of the evil angels upon the country, as a particular defiance of—himself.' Yet the delusion, but for Parris, would have languished."[24] As for Tituba, Bancroft, following Calef, points out, "Tituba, an Indian female servant, who had practiced some wild incantations, being betrayed by her husband, was scourged by Parris, her master, into confessing herself a witch."[25]

Like Hawthorne, Bancroft perceived the relation between revolutionary violence and witchcraft: "Rebellion, it was said, is as the sin of witchcraft; and Cotton Mather, in his Discourse, did but repeat the old tale: 'Rebellion is the Achan, the trouble of us all.'" The rebellion, though, was ideological, rather than physical; that is, religious authority, rather than political power, was under attack. As Bancroft points out, the cry of witchcraft was never raised "except when free inquiry was advancing."[26] Because Bancroft's overriding thesis in his *History* is the value and progress of democracy, he claims that the "common mind of Massachusetts was more wise" than Mather and that "to the west of Massachusetts, and to Connecticut, to which the influence of Cotton Mather and its consequences did not extend, we must look for the unmixed development of the essential character of New England." As for the responsibility of the people of Massachusetts, Bancroft asserts, "Of the magistrates at that time, not one held office by the suffrage of the people: the tribunal, essentially despotic in its origin, as in its character, had no sanction but an extraordinary and an illegal commission. . . . The responsibility of the tragedy, far from attaching to the people of the colony, rests with the very few, hardly five or six, in whose hands the transition state of the government left, for a season, unlimited influence."[27]

Hawthorne disagreed with Bancroft's judgments. In *Grandfather's Chair,* he praises the "brilliancy" (6:138) of Bancroft's *History,* but in private, he considered Bancroft himself, who was his political patron, a liar.[28] He could not agree with Bancroft that the blame for the witchcraft delusion rested solely on five or six community leaders. For him, almost everyone in the colony was complicit. In *Grandfather's Chair,* when Grandfather comments on the Salem witchcraft trials, his auditors "shuddered to hear that a frenzy, which led to the death of many innocent persons, had originated in the wicked arts of a few children" (6:77). Grandfather explains that "the children would pretend to be seized with strange convulsions, and would cry out that the witches were afflicting them." As for the Puritan leaders, Grandfather says that "unfortunately, the ministers and wise men were more deluded than the illiterate people." The result was that lies and falsehoods proliferated: "The number of those, who pretended to be afflicted by witchcraft, grew daily more numerous; and they bore testimony against many of the best and worthiest people" (6:78). When the children listening to his tale question whether there are truly such things as witches, Grandfather emphatically declares, "there are none; and our forefathers soon became convinced, that they had been led into a terrible delusion" (6:79). In *The House of the Seven Gables,* Hawthorne similarly refers to "that terrible delusion which should teach us, among its other morals, that the influential classes, and those who take upon themselves to be leaders of the people, are fully liable to all the passionate error that has ever characterized the maddest mob. Clergymen, judges, statesmen—the wisest, calmest, holiest persons of their day—stood in the inner circle roundabout the gallows, loudest to applaud the work of blood, latest to confess themselves miserably deceived" (2:7–8). For Hawthorne, then, "passionate error" had afflicted leaders and followers alike, especially because they failed to remain calm and reasonable.

Witchcraft Tales

A number of Hawthorne's early tales that he burned apparently dealt with Salem witchcraft in rather sensational ways, if the narrator of "The Devil in Manuscript" (1835) is to be believed. He has Oberon say to his friend,

> You have read them, and know what I mean,—that conception in which I endeavored to embody the character of a fiend, as represented in our traditions and the written records of witchcraft. Oh, I have a horror of what was created in my own brain, and shudder at the manuscripts in which I gave that dark idea a sort of material existence! (11:171)

A few of these creations, it seems, survived, including his very first published tale, "The Hollow of the Three Hills" (1830), which attempts to treat "that dark idea" of witchcraft. The tale is so steeped in gothic conventions, however, that it lacks force and becomes a sad account of sin and guilt. Set amid "strange old times, when fantastic reveries were realized among the actual circumstances of life," it features an "evil" old crone who conjures up visions to torment a beautiful guilt-ridden lady who has apparently deserted her parents, husband, and child. At the end, when the lady has been rendered lifeless, the crone, who has acted as a cruel ethical agent, cackles, "Here has been a sweet hour's sport!" (9:204).

The tale gives little indication of Hawthorne's later intense scrutiny of the import of what happened in Salem in 1692. In an 1845 letter to Evert Duyckinck, he indicated his awareness of the complexity of the history of Salem witchcraft, which Duyckinck asked him to write. "A mere narrative," Hawthorne replied, "to be sure, might be prepared easily enough; but such a work, if worthily written, would demand research and study, and as deep thought as any man could bring to it. The more I look at it, the more difficulties do I see—yet difficulties such as I should like to overcome. Perhaps it may be the work of an after time" (16:126–27). Although Hawthorne never wrote the history, two of his early tales written after "The Hollow of the Three Hills" show his growing appreciation of the complexity of witchcraft and his desire to critique the sensationalism that impelled it. "Alice Doane's Appeal" (1835) and "Young Goodman Brown" (1835) both explore psychological states grounded firmly in the actual historical context of Salem and the dangers of specter evidence and mass delusion. They thus anticipate Hawthorne's two most accomplished romances, *The Scarlet Letter* and *The House of the Seven Gables,* and provide insight into the development of his political vision.

In "Alice Doane's Appeal," Hawthorne pairs one of his earlier sensational gothic tales with an imaginative re-creation of a scene on Gallows Hill in 1692, as the accused witches are led to their execution. He frames the composite work with a visit to Gallows Hill in the present by the narrator and two pretty female companions, whom he tries to impress. The first inner narrative is a gothic tale the narrator reads from a manuscript he has written. It features a young man named Leonard Doane, in love with his sister Alice, who is seduced by an unknown youth named Walter Brome, whom Leonard murders. These events, it turns out, result from the machinations of a wizard "who had cunningly devised that Walter Brome should tempt his unknown sister to guilt and shame, and himself perish by the hand of his twin-brother." The story climaxes in a crowded graveyard, where a "company of devils and condemned souls come on a holiday, to revel in the discovery of a complicated crime; as foul a one as ever was imagined in their dreadful abode" (11:277). Not surprisingly, the young ladies laugh at this story, for it is "too grotesque and extravagant, for timid maids to tremble at." In his own defense, the narrator points out that "in old witch times," such a narrative would "have brought even a church deacon to Gallows Hill"—that is, to be hanged. He then detains the ladies "a while longer on the hill" and makes "a trial whether truth were more powerful than fiction" (11:278).

In Hawthorne's tale, truth does prove more powerful than fiction, as the second story draws on his historical knowledge of what happened in Salem and on Upham's *Lectures on Witchcraft* (which Hawthorne praises in passing), to evoke sympathy for the accused witches and loathing for Cotton Mather, "the representative of all the hateful features of his time." As the imagined procession of "the virtuous" walk up Gallows Hill, one by one, the narrator describes them sympathetically.

> Here tottered a woman in her dotage, knowing neither the crime imputed her, nor its punishment; there another, distracted by the universal madness, till feverish dreams were remembered as realities, and she almost be-

lieved her guilt. One, a proud man once, was so broken down by the intolerable hatred heaped upon him, that he seemed to hasten his steps, eager to hide himself in the grave hastily dug, at the foot of the gallows. (11:278–79)

Following these comes an "ordained pastor" (obviously Burroughs), "who walked onward to the same death; his lips moved in prayer, no narrow petition for himself alone, but embracing all, his fellow sufferers and the frenzied multitude; he looked to heaven and trod lightly up the hill." The "afflicted" accusers follow, "a guilty and miserable band," made up of "villains," "wretches," "lunatics," and "children, who had played a game that the imps of darkness might have envied them, since it disgraced an age, and dipped a people's hands in blood." In the rear of the procession rides Cotton Mather, "the one blood-thirsty man, in whom were concentrated those vices of spirit and errors of opinion, that sufficed to madden the whole surrounding multitude" (11:279). By thus describing the scene, the narrator achieves his goal of making his companions tremble and cry. He also substantiates what he declared at the outset, that Gallows Hill was "the spot, where guilt and phrenzy consummated the most execrable scene, that our history blushes to record. For this was the field where superstition won her darkest triumph; the high place where our fathers set up their shame, to the mournful gaze of generations far remote" (11:267). Hawthorne's own mournful gaze—focused on his "fathers," I wish to emphasize—contributed to his skepticism about the "phrenzy" and "madness" that caused "feverish dreams" to be "remembered as realities" leading to the death of the innocent.[29]

In many ways, "Alice Doane's Appeal" marks Hawthorne's rejection of his own gothic sensationalism and of narratives growing out of "passionate impulses," such as those surrounding the witchcraft delusion. Nina Baym has argued that the tale suggests "the danger of the diseased imagination," and she speculates that Hawthorne may have been influenced by Upham's "seminal lectures on Salem witchcraft, delivered in Salem at just the time Hawthorne was working on this fiction."[30] "The confluence of imagination and passion, so heartily deplored by Upham," Baym writes, "is of course the ground of this early writing by Hawthorne. Upham's commonsense point is that imagination, like a wild beast, is inherently dangerous."[31] While Baym's speculation certainly seems plausible, I would qualify it somewhat by pointing out that Hawthorne, as an artist, appreciated the imagination in ways Upham apparently did not. In his *English Notebooks,* for example, Hawthorne comments on the new spiritualism fad by declaring that "these enthusiasts, who adopt such extravagant ideas, appear to me to lack imagination, instead of being misled by it, as they are generally supposed to be" (21:230). In other words, they fail to imagine other, more logical, explanations for the phenomena they witness. Hawthorne always noticed how stories were told, especially the ways the imaginary could combine with the actual. His theory of romance famously centers on just this combination. When the imaginary becomes pure fantasy, however, and is confused with reality, then, Hawthorne believed, it could indeed delude and harm. In a letter of October 18, 1841, to his fiancée, Sophia, warning her away from mesmerism, he advises her, "Keep thy imagination sane—that is one of the truest conditions of communion with Heaven" (15:590). Such a warning reveals his knowledge that imagination could be dangerous, and as Baym points out, "his work after 1830 shows one attempt after another to write more rational and conservative fiction."[32]

In Hawthorne's masterpiece of short fiction, "Young Goodman Brown," he draws on Salem witchcraft to construct an elaborate tale showing the irreversible harm caused by the inability to distinguish between that which is imaginary and that which is real. David Levin and Michael Colacurcio have persuasively argued that the subject of the tale is not the depravity of humankind but, rather, the power of specter evidence.[33] All that Goodman Brown sees as real is but a delusion, a projection of his own mind, as Hawthorne's many references to shapes and figures suggest. After Brown enters the forest, for example, he exclaims, "What if the Devil himself should be at my very elbow!" and immediately beholds "the figure of a man" who tells him he has made the trip from Boston to Salem Village in fifteen minutes. This figure holds a staff in the likeness of a great black snake that appears "to twist and wriggle itself, like a living serpent" (10:76), and as they walk, the "figure" of Goody Cloyse appears at his bidding, then disappears when he throws his staff down at her feet. The devil's arguments are so apt that they seem "rather to spring up in the bosom of his auditor than to be suggested by himself" (10:80), and after he vanishes, Brown hears "a confused and doubtful sound of voices" (10:82) and thinks he hears the deacon and the minister and his wife, Faith, among them. Rushing through the forest, he finally comes upon the fantastic witches' meeting, where the "Shape of Evil" attempts to baptize Brown and his wife, Faith. As Brown resists, the scene disappears, and in answer to the question of whether Brown had "only dreamed a wild dream of a witch-meeting," Hawthorne writes, "Be it so, if you will. But, alas! It was a dream of evil omen for young Goodman Brown" (10:89). Brown is changed into a desperate man by the experience, and what he has taken for reality has affected him profoundly. In fact, as Hawthorne well knows, just such visions had deadly consequences in Salem in 1692. As Cotton Mather asserted, when Burroughs, accused of witchcraft, distrusted his wife and told her he could read her thoughts, he thus divulged that "by the assistance of the *Black Man,* he might put on his *Invisibility,* and in that *Fascinating Mist,* gratifie his own Jealous Humour, to hear what they said of him."[34] For Mather and others, such evidence, along with sightings of Burroughs's specter and the ghosts of his wives, was sufficient to justify his hanging.

For Hawthorne, to dream was a misleading human activity that deserved skeptical consideration. Thus he shows that Young Goodman Brown's belief in his dream brings him endless gloom. (Tituba, one should recall, said she encountered the devil as she was falling asleep, leading to a dreamlike vision that, when recounted, precipitated her imprisonment and the death of others.) The creation of realities, in Hawthorne's belief system, was God's work. In *The Scarlet Letter,* he critiques Dimmesdale's character by insisting that realities "were meant by Heaven to be the spirit's joy and nutriment. To the untrue man the whole universe is false,—it is impalpable,—it shrinks to nothing within his grasp" (1:145). In *The House of the Seven Gables,* Hawthorne presents a character who, in contrast to Goodman Brown and Dimmesdale, understands this point. Hawthorne writes that even if Holgrave's "early faith should be modified by inevitable experience," he would not lose his faith; rather, it "would be well bartered for a far humbler one, at [life's] close, in discerning that man's best-directed effort accomplishes a kind of dream, while God is the sole worker of realities" (2:180). To cite just one more example, when Hawthorne informed Sophia of his worries about her seeing a mesmerist for her headaches, he tells her that what she has experienced

are dreams, my love—and such dreams as thy sweetest fancy, either waking or sleeping, could vastly improve upon. And what delusion can be more lamentable and mischievous, than to mistake the physical and material for the spiritual? What so miserable as to lose the soul's true, though hidden, knowledge and consciousness of heaven, in the mist of an earth-born vision? Thou shalt not do this. (15:589)

One could argue that Hawthorne felt no one should manipulate his fiancée but himself, yet while this may be true, he also sought to protect her from purveyors of fantasies.

Delusions and Mists

To observe the dichotomy between humans' dreams and God's realities in Hawthorne's thinking clarifies much about his politics, as well as his art. In fact, I would like to suggest that the dreams of Goodman Brown and Holgrave anticipate the infamous passage about slavery in Hawthorne's *The Life of Franklin Pierce,* where he asserts that from one point of view, slavery appears to be "one of those evils, which Divine Providence . . . by some means impossible to be anticipated . . . it causes to vanish like a dream" (23:352). If I am right that Brown's vision of the witches' Sabbath, which vanishes like a dream when he shouts, "Faith, Faith," is somehow linked to Hawthorne's assertion that the evil of slavery may somehow vanish like a dream if we trust in divine providence, then what, one may ask, is the connection between the two? Blind faith in the power of God? Perhaps. But Brown's predicament encourages us to consider another possibility: that in the crucible of Hawthorne's mind, the horrors of witchcraft and of slavery become falsehoods and delusions, mere specter evidence not to be trusted.

It is important to notice the priority Hawthorne gives to faulty perception in his treatment of witch-hunters, abolitionists, and self-righteous reformers, for in his view, the violence they cause represents not malice but a failure of vision. In his discussion of John Brown's hanging for trying to stage a slave insurrection, Hawthorne writes, "He himself, I am persuaded, (such was his natural integrity) would have acknowledged that Virginia had a right to take the life which he had staked and lost; although it would have been better for her, in the hour that is fast coming, if she could generously have forgotten the criminality of his attempt in its enormous folly" (23:428). Folly, delusion, madness—these were the visual and mental defects Hawthorne saw animating those intent on ridding the land of evil, whether that evil was witchcraft, Indians, or slavery. In his biography of Pierce, in the passage that has become notorious, Hawthorne calls abolitionism "the mistiness of a philanthropic theory," and it is important to recognize the delusion inscribed in this characterization. The relevant passage reads:

> [Pierce] fully recognized, by his votes and by his voice, the rights pledged to the South by the Constitution. This, at the period when he so declared himself, was comparatively an easy thing to do. But when it became more difficult, when the first imperceptible movement of agitation had grown to be almost a convulsion, his course was still the same. Nor did he ever shun the obloquy that sometimes threatened to pursue the northern man who dared to love that great and sacred reality—his whole, united, native country—better than the mistiness of a philanthropic theory. (23:292)

Hawthorne did not share Pierce's love of the Union, yet what is more striking about the dichotomy he deploys here, between the "reality" of the United States and the "mistiness" of abolitionism, is that he impugns an effect, not a cause.

Beyond its reference to climatic conditions, the term *mistiness* can also refer (as the *Oxford English Dictionary* points out) to the obscuring of mental vision or outlook, when the real character of a thing is veiled from one's eyes and mind. For Hawthorne, mist also suggested ocular and mental deception, such as that surrounding visions of specters and ghosts. Hawthorne's contemporaries shared his familiarity with this usage, as their writings show. Margaret Fuller, in a well-known dispatch she wrote from Scotland in September 1846, tells about a mist that arose on Ben Lomond before she could descend and about the night she spent on the mountain, during which she saw "visionary shapes, floating slowly and gracefully, their white robes would unfurl from the great body of mist in which they had been engaged, and come upon me with a kiss pervasively cold as that of Death."[35] In *Walden,* Thoreau also suggests the supernatural and bewitching effects of the mist, as he describes how the rising sun revealed the "soft ripples" and "smooth reflecting surface" of the pond, "while the mists, like ghosts, were stealthily withdrawing in every direction into the woods, as at the breaking up of some nocturnal conventicler."[36] In Hawthorne's writings, mists and mistiness are used to suggest not only ghosts and witchcraft but also mental failure. Clifford goes into a mist in *The House of the Seven Gables* when his mental torpor settles upon him; Priscilla appears as behind a mist in *The Blithedale Romance* after she enters her trance as the veiled lady.

When individuals in Hawthorne's works suffer from the inability to see beyond their narrow obsessions, it is often an *ism*—such as Puritanism, transcendentalism, or abolitionism—that has blinded them. (For Sophia, the danger was mesmerism.) These are the "theories" or enthusiasms that Hawthorne thought preyed on the weak-minded and harmed actual persons. When he comments in his notebook, "I find myself rather more of an abolitionist in feeling than in principle" (8:112), he is showing his privileging of persons over abstractions. At this moment, he admits to being moved by the plight of the slaves yet resists generalizing his experience. The way Sophia put it in their journal was to say that her husband was "without theories of any kind,"[37] which distinguished him from their Concord neighbors. In "The Christmas Banquet" (1844), written in Concord, Hawthorne pairs a miserable theorist "smitten with grief" by "the incredulity of mankind" with a distraught clergyman who had "wandered into a cloud region, where everything was misty and deceptive, ever mocking him with a semblance of reality, but still dissolving when he flung himself upon it for support and rest" (10:302). Thus theorist and clergyman inhabit the same unreal estate, and their isms are interchangeable.

In "The Celestial Railroad" (1843), Hawthorne emphasizes these points using a cave by the wayside, occupied by the "Giant Transcendentalist" who has displaced those "vile old troglodytes" Pope and Pagan. In other words, Catholicism, paganism, and transcendentalism at one time or another prey on the gullible. The giant looks "like a heap of fog and duskiness" and fattens unsuspecting travelers for his table by feeding them "plentiful meals of smoke, mist, moonshine, raw potatoes, and saw-dust" (10:197). Less comically, Hawthorne places his protagonist in "Septimius" within the heart of transcendentalism, the town of Concord, and shows him struggling unsuccessfully to make his way out of this bewitched land: "with every step that he took, it seemed as if he were coming out of a mist, out of an enchanted land, where things had seemed to him not as they really were." Linking the mist to witchcraft, Hawthorne claims that Septimius had wandered unawares into a mental landscape inconsistent "with all that really is, with men's purposes, fates, business; into such a misty region had he been, and strayed many days, deeming himself at home; but now the mists were thinning away, he was passing the witch-like boundaries, and might never find his way over them again" (13:129).

For Hawthorne, a persistent danger of New England righteousness was its tendency to lead followers into confusing darkness rather than clear light (as happens quite literally to Edward Digby in "The Man of Adamant"). In Cotton Mather's *Memorable Providences, Relating to Witchcrafts and Possessions* (1689), which Hawthorne knew well, Mather sought to stir his readers by telling them that "there are Devils & Witches" and that "tho those night-birds least appear where the Day-light of the Gospel comes, yet New-Engl. has had Exemples of their Existence & Operation."[38] The result, as we have seen, was witchcraft hysteria and the execution of innocent people. Three years later, after the witch scare had taken twenty lives, Increase Mather sought to bring clarity to the issue of specter evidence and the assumption that the devil could not take the appearance of the innocent, by warning his readers, "He that can in the Likeness of Saints encourage Witches to Familiarity with Hell, may possibly in the likeness of a Saint afflict a Bewitched Person. But this we see from Scripture, Satan may be permitted to do."[39] In other words, when it comes to the devil at work in the world, argues Mather, beware of appearances, and do not rely on them as evidence of guilt or innocence. Hawthorne's familiarity with the writings of both Mathers appears to have informed his writing of "The Old Manse," where he satirizes the preeminent transcendentalist, Emerson, by observing that in his home at the opposite end of town, he shines like an "intellectual fire," attracting "bats and owls, and the whole host of night-birds," who are victims and agents of confusion. These "uncertain, troubled, earnest wanderers," Hawthorne writes, "flapped their dusky wings against the gazer's eyes, and sometimes were mistaken for fowls of angelic feather." To Hawthorne, these "hobgoblins of flesh and blood," as he calls them, become "delusions" that mislead (10:30). As for Emerson, when he figures in Hawthorne's works (e.g., as Mr. Smooth-it-away in "The Celestial Railroad"), he is not to be trusted.

In Hawthorne's works, magistrates, judges, and ministers betray the public's trust by failing to provide clear-sighted leadership. In his study of the Salem witchcraft delusion, Hawthorne would have become familiar with Reverend John Hale's moving 1702 *A Modest Enquiry,* which admits that, "by their inchantments," the witch accusers "have raised mists, strange sights, and the like, to beget admiration, and please Spectators" and that those, including Hale himself, "who were most concerned to act and judge in those matters, did not willingly depart from the rules of righteousness." Hale argues that "such was the darkness of that day, the tortures and lamentations of the afflicted, and the power of former presidents [*sic*], that we walked in the clouds and could not see our way."[40] Hale's use of mists and clouds to explain what happened in Salem is of course his way of absolving himself from guilt. And even if Hawthorne recognized only subconsciously the psychohistorical parallels between the Salem witchcraft delusion that he, too, felt guilty about and the Concord isms that came to possess and mystify his friends and family, his resistance to and comments on the latter become more understandable, if not less morally questionable.

One indication of his awareness of these parallels appears in *The Blithedale Romance,* where Coverdale identifies the closest friend of Hollingsworth as "the cold, spectral monster which he had himself conjured up, . . . and of which, at last—as these men of a mighty purpose so invariably do—he had grown to be the bond-slave. It was his philanthropic theory!" (3:55). Late in the romance, as Hollingsworth's coldness and cruelty emerge, especially in his treatment of Zenobia, Coverdale declares, "I saw in Hollingsworth all that an artist could desire for the grim portrait of a Puritan magistrate, holding inquest of life and death in a case of witchcraft." Hollingsworth condemns Zenobia, who loves him, and her "trial" foreshadows her fate. Coverdale observes, "Had a pile of faggots been heaped against the rock, this hint of impending doom would have completed the suggestive picture" (3:214). Within hours of Hollingsworth's condemnation, Zenobia drowns herself, inspiring lifelong guilt in the puritanical reformer, who abandons his spectral "theory," which he at last admits transformed him into a murderer.

When George William Curtis, in his condemnation of Hawthorne in 1864, claimed that Hawthorne failed to appreciate "the fine moral heroism" and "the spiritual grandeur" of the Puritans, he anticipated the link I have been trying to forge between seventeenth-century witch-hunting and nineteenth-century abolitionism. In the process, Curtis also unwittingly supported Hawthorne's case against the abolitionists. Referring to "Young Goodman Brown" in his argument, Curtis assailed Hawthorne's pacifism about slavery by asserting, "that the Devil, in the form of an elderly man clad in grave and decent attire, should lead astray the saints of Salem village, two centuries ago, and confuse right and wrong in the mind of Goodman Brown, was something that excited [Hawthorne's] imagination, and produced one of his weirdest stories. But that the same Devil, clad in a somber sophism, was confusing the sentiment of right and wrong in the mind of his own countrymen he did not even guess."[41] Curtis would have it that Hawthorne himself was in league with the devil, saying, "the mind of Justice Hathorn's descendant was bewitched by the fascination of a certain devilish subtlety working under the comeliest aspects in human affairs. It overcame him with strange sympathy. It colored and controlled his intellectual life."[42] Curtis not only misread Hawthorne's short story and its critique of specter evidence but also unwittingly put himself in the false position of the Puritan witch-hunter. He indicts Hawthorne for failing to see the devil at work in the slavocracy, thus making himself an advocate for those willing to kill the innocent in order to drive the devil from the land.[43]

Witch-Hunting and Abolitionism

Hawthorne perceived the Puritan backgrounds of contemporary abolitionists and the ways their behavior mirrored that of the Puritan witch-hunters of colonial Salem and Boston. As he critiqued one explicitly, he was able to critique the other implicitly. They formed a particularly strong bond in his mind, based on parallels in addition to a failure of vision caused by fanaticism and madness. These included a Puritan religiosity intent on ridding the devil from the land, the sensationalistic demonization of others (accused witches and slave masters, respectively), and obsession with forbidden sexual relations (e.g., concubinage and amalgamation). These associations shaped his political and moral vision, especially during the 1840s and 1850s, for he sensed, as did many of his contemporaries, that Puritanism and the warrior spirit of Cromwell was alive and well in New England, despite the efforts of the Unitarians and transcendentalists to proffer a new view of humankind. Moral purity remained the national goal.

By the beginning of the Civil War, as Joanne Pope Melish has observed, "the New England nationalist trope of virtuous, historical whiteness, clothed as it was in a distinctive set of cultural, moral, and political values associated with New England's Puritan mission and Revolutionary struggle, had come to define the Unionist North as a whole."[44] Although Hawthorne himself at times seems a proponent of Puritanism, especially due to his skeptical view of human nature, he is also its harshest critic, dramatizing its narrowness and blindness—most famously in *The Scarlet Letter*. While intellectual historians have credited the "erosion of Calvinist orthodoxy and the emergence of a powerful alternative often labeled liberal Protestantism" with becoming the "primary source for abolitionist arguments about the inherent brutality of slavery,"[45] a Puritan sensibility nevertheless inspired much of the righteous indignation of antislavery thought. The Virginian Moncure Conway, who became an abolitionist and friend of Emerson, astutely observed John Brown's Puritan appeal: "it appears to me now that there had remained in nearly every Northern breast, however liberal, some unconscious chord which Brown had touched, inherited from the old Puritan spirit and faith in the God of War. I had been brought up in no such faith, but in the belief that evil could be conquered only by regeneration of the evil-doer."[46]

Hawthorne shared the Puritans' grim assessment of human nature, but he rejected the intolerance, cruelty, and self-righteousness they exhibited. As a consequence, his critique of his reform-minded contemporaries, including the bloodthirsty Whigs (as he called them), coincided with his critique of his ancestors. At their worst, all could become iron men whose repressed fears and desires became externalized in demonic shadow figures resembling themselves. In "Alice Doane's Appeal," Cotton Mather appears riding at the rear of a procession of witches and is described as "a figure on horseback, so darkly conspicuous, so sternly triumphant that my hearers mistook him for the visible presence of the fiend himself" (11:279). In "Main-street," Hawthorne likewise depicts Mather on horseback overseeing a pitiful group of witches being taken to the gallows. There, Hawthorne asks, "May not the Arch Fiend have been too subtle for the court and jury, and betrayed them— laughing in his sleeve the while—into the awful errors of pouring out sanctified blood as an acceptable sacrifice upon God's altar? Ah! No; for listen to wise Cotton Mather, who . . . tells them that all has been religiously and justly done, and that Satan's power shall this day receive its death-blow in New England" (11:77). Hawthorne's heavy irony here suggests that Mather has unwittingly placed himself in league with the devil, under the delusion that he has successfully resisted him.

In a similar psychological process, the devil in "Young Goodman Brown" bears "a considerable resemblance to [Brown], though perhaps more in expression than features. Still, they might have been taken for father and son" (10:76). As Brown rushes deeper into the forest, "brandishing his staff with frenzied gestures, now giving vent to an inspiration of horrid blasphemy, and now shouting forth such laughter, as set all the echoes of the forest laughing like demons around him," he has become a demon himself and generated a nightmare world of his own creation. In "The Hall of Fantasy" (1843), delusion and doubling receive additional, yet less serious, treatment, as Hawthorne satirizes a "herd of real or self-styled reformers," many of whom "had got possession of some crystal fragrance of truth, the brightness of which so dazzled them that they could see nothing else in the wide universe." Among them stands the abolitionist, "brandishing his one idea like an iron flail" (10:180), and the resemblance of this figure to a demonic slave master, whip in hand, is surely intentional.

As he read accounts of the Salem witchcraft delusion, Hawthorne also encountered imagery linking witch-hunters, devils, and slave masters, as well as witches and slaves. He would also have noticed the ways in which the evil perceived by the most prominent witch-hunters revealed more about themselves than about the devil. The most striking example appears in the case of the Reverend Samuel Parris, whose slave Tituba, as we have seen, told her wild tale of how the devil became her master—"he Tell me he god, & I must believe him and Serve him."[47] After the executions stopped, she declared "that her Master [Parris] did beat her and otherways abuse her, to make her confess and accuse (such as he call'd) her Sister-Witches."[48] (For a nineteenth-century depiction of the devil abusing witches, see figure 2.) Thus Parris, leading witch-hunter and enemy of Satan, becomes, as Bancroft puts it, "the beginner and procurer of the sore afflictions to Salem village and the country."[49] In 1862, Hawthorne reminded himself, as he planned "Septimius Felton," "The clergyman is the more terribly earnest in his religion, because he is conscious of the devil in his blood" (13:515).

Other ministers in Salem Village during the witchcraft trials used imagery linking the devil to slave masters and, indirectly, to themselves. Reverend Deodat Lawson, Samuel Parris's predecessor, declared in a sermon delivered in Salem during the trials, "It is a matter of terror, amazement, and astonishment, to all such wretched souls . . . as have given up their names and souls

George Cruikshank, *Black John Chastising the Witches* (detail), from *Twelve Sketches Illustrative of Sir Walter Scott's "Demonology and Witchcraft"* (London: Robins, 1830). (Author's collection.)

to the Devil; who by covenant, explicit or implicit, have bound themselves to be his slaves and drudges, consenting to be instruments in whose shapes he may torment and afflict their fellow-creatures (even of their own kind) to the amazing and astonishing of the standers-by."[50] Mercy Short, an unstable young woman in Cotton Mather's congregation, whom Mather claimed to save through his fasts and counsel in the fall of 1693, apparently fought off the devil's attempt to make her his slave. According to Mather, his efforts prevented Short's evil angels from tormenting her, and she "could see their 'Black Master' strike and kick them, 'like an Overseer of so many Negro's' until tiring of their useless attempts they said furiously, 'Well you shant be the last,' and flew from the room."[51] As Mercy's minister, Mather was her overseer—from his pulpit, he literally oversaw all in his congregation. If religious oppression was a cause of the demonic possession performed by Mercy and the hysterical girls of Salem Village, then what spills forth from their frenzy are forms of religious rebellion. (Mercy's invisible tormentors, Mather reported, frequently indulged in "Railing and Slander against a certain Person in the Town"—Mather himself.)[52] In "The Old Manse" preface Hawthorne alludes to the doubling he sees afflicting Puritans like Mather, when he observes that his own dark study was "made still blacker by the grim prints of Puritan ministers that hung around. These worthies looked strangely like bad angels, or, at least, like men who had wrestled so continually and so sternly with the devil, that somewhat of his sooty fierceness had been imparted to their own visages" (10:5).

The demonization of one's enemy is clearly a transhistorical, cross-cultural phenomenon, yet in American history, an unusually full and various set of persons have been demonized. As Michael Rogin points out, "the Indian cannibal, the black rapist, the papal whore of Babylon, the monster-hydra United States Bank, the demon rum, the bomb-throwing anarchist, the many-tentacled Communist conspiracy, the agents of international terrorism"[53] are a consistent, repressed feature of American sociopolitical history. Rogin does not mention the Salem witches, but they, too, form part of this series, as does the Southern slave owner in abolitionist literature, speeches, and iconography. I would assume that the latter fact has not been a topic of interest in recent American studies because it serves no obvious purpose in advancing a politics of liberation or "transformative social action";[54] however, it would not have escaped Hawthorne's notice, not only because of its link to the Puritan past, but also because of its application to his friend Pierce.

During the campaign of 1852, the figure of Pierce appeared in a broadside showing him bowing down across the Mason-Dixon Line to the devil while a Southern slaveholder declares, "Save the Union / And with the meanest Yankee grease / Smear the hinges of your knees / And in silence pray for peace." Pierce is identified in the cartoon as "one of the Southern dirt eaters saving the Union" (see figure 3). After Pierce's election, passage of the Kansas-Nebraska Act and the rendition of Anthony Burns raised the level of abolitionist vituperation directed at Pierce and the South. Moncure Conway, the Virginian turned New England abolitionist, after participating in the famous protest meeting in Framingham Grove, Massachusetts, on July 4, 1854, which featured speeches by Thoreau, Sojourner Truth, and Garrison, de-

Position of the Democratic Party in 1852, 1852. Lithograph on wove paper. (Courtesy of the Library of Congress.)

cided, "I could not join the Antislavery Society. There was a Calvinistic accent in that creed about the 'covenant with death and agreement with hell' [Garrison's description of the Constitution]. Slavery was not death, nor the South hell. . . . my peace principles inclined me to a separation between sections that hated each other. Yet I knew good people on both sides."[55] Thoreau, in a journal entry he used in his speech, identified Pierce as "the Devil" and sarcastically observed, "Men are surprised because the devil does not behave like an angel of light."[56]

Just as John Hathorne and Cotton Mather sought to drive Satan from New England, the abolitionists and Conscience Whigs sought to drive him from the Union. In Mather's eyes, the devil had "decoy'd a fearful knot of proud, froward, ignorant, envious and malicious creatures, to lift themselves in his horrid Service. . . . each of them have their *Spectres,* or Devils, commission'd by them, & representing of them, to be the Engines of their Malice. By these wicked *Spectres,* they seize poor people about the Country, with

CRUELTIES OF SLAVERY.

Cover, *Anti-Slavery Record*, May 1835. (Courtesy of the Boston Public Library.)

various & bloody *Torments*."[57] For Garrison, whose rhetoric, like Mather's, drew upon the Bible, Southern slave owners were the devil's agents, "an adulterous and perverse generation, a brood of vipers, hypocrites, children of the Devil, who could not escape the damnation of hell."[58] Such demonization appeared in iconography as well as rhetoric, outraging those accused of depravity. In the summer of 1835, Senator John Tyler of Virginia, future president of the United States, held up a copy of the *Anti-Slavery Record* and showed his fellow Southerners "a picture upon the external covering, designed to represent each of you gentlemen. A scourge is in your hand, and three victims bound and kneeling at your feet. You are represented as demons in the shape of men" (see figure 4).[59] As Bertram Wyatt-Brown has pointed out, "the abolitionists looked to the past for their imagery, and primitive woodcuts of lustful masters and abject slaves became the gargoyles and relics of a gothic revival."[60]

The provocative iconography of the abolitionists often satisfied Northern fascination with the sexual relations between Southern masters and their female slaves (coded as "concubinage," not rape, by male abolitionists) and mirrored seventeenth-century Puritan fascination with the sexual relations between the devil and his concubines. Licentiousness took on political significance, and the black female body, like the bodies of accused witches, could be identified as a threatening site of sin and vice.[61] Few noticed the injustice of blaming the victim such identification involved. Drawing on first-hand knowledge, one assumes, Thomas Jefferson addressed this aspect of the relationship between slave and master in his *Notes on the State of Virginia,* warning that slavery allowed "a perpetual exercise of the most boisterous passions, the most unremitting despotism on the one part, and degrading submissions on the other."[62] Just as the religious persecution of witches, especially in Europe, involved avid exploration of the "filthy rites" practiced by the devil and his female worshipers, so, too, the abolitionists focused on the appetites and lusts of the slave masters, indulged through the bodies of their female slaves.[63] Donald M. Scott has pointed out, "The most vivid result of slavery (to which abolitionists turned again and again) was a system of lust, of unleashed, illicit sexuality. Slavery made the female slave the helpless victim of the master's insatiable sexual desires, since under slavery, one early abolitionist wrote, 'the marriage relation, the source of all others, is out of the question. And in its stead is introduced a system of Universal Concubinage.'"[64] The eminent abolitionist Wendell Phillips indulged in blaming the victim by calling the South "one great Brothel, where half a million of women are flogged to prostitution, or worse still, are degraded to believe it honorable."[65] Similarly, Hawthorne's brother-in-law Horace Mann, in his "Speech on the Institution of Slavery" (1852), identified slave owners as those wanting to "introduce a foul concubinage in place of the institution of marriage, and who would remorselessly trample upon all the tenderest and holiest affections which the human soul is capable of feeling."[66]

Abolitionist attacks on the "luxurious" South and its "sinful" liaisons revealed a level of sexual anxiety and prurience reminiscent of earlier Puritan culture. In "Young Goodman Brown," Hawthorne explores such anxiety by dramatizing the competing desires of the "holiest affections" of marriage and the unholy sexual attractions offered by the devil and his sex slaves. Brown's departure from his wife, Faith, to pursue forbidden sexual knowledge deep in the forest demonstrates his moral weakness, as does his susceptibility to spectral evidence, which he accepts as real. The explicit focus of the tale is witchcraft in Salem, not slavery, yet the racial fantasies of New Englanders linking blackness and sexuality surely inform the work.[67] Thus, when the "dark figure" of the devil in "Young Goodman Brown" reappears as the "Black Man" in *The Scarlet Letter,* the issues of witchcraft, sexuality, and slavery merge, as do the imageries of witchcraft, slavery, and revolutionary violence. *The Scarlet Letter* warns against those persons suffering the delusion that the devil, rather than their own guilt-ridden fantasies, haunts the borders of civilized life. Although the book has been interpreted in countless ways over the years, on the political level, as I discuss in chapter 5, it offers a cautionary tale directed at Puritans, abolitionists, and politicians alike who take an obsessive interest in ridding the world of evil. Just as the devil emerged as the shadow self of Puritan divines, such as Parris and Mather, the "Black Man" becomes Arthur Dimmesdale's own negative identity, emerging most clearly after he reexperiences illicit desire in the forest and returns to town having acquired "sympathy and fellowship with wicked mortals and the world of perverted spirits" (1:222).[68] Hawthorne's romance is thus of a piece with "Young Goodman Brown," which shows more harm being done to Brown by his attraction to the thought of evil than by evil itself.

Witchcraft, Voodoo, and Tituba

For Hawthorne, mental weakness, self-delusion, and outright lies go hand in hand, and the "uninstructed multitude," when aroused by false stimuli, especially if sensational, can be positively fatal. In antebellum America, witchcraft and slave insurrection contributed imagery to a national imaginary dominated by fears of dark racial Others. The strong emotional and intellectual link between the two sources arose in part from voodoo, as practiced in Haiti and introduced into the United States.[69] The voodoo religion was one of the most spectacular features associated with the Santo Domingo slave revolt. According to various reports, the nocturnal meetings of slave leaders in the summer of 1791 involved various voodoo rites, including blood oaths and animal sacrifice. Alfred Hunt points out, "Voodoo played a shadowy role in the initial stages of the slave revolt in St. Domingue if only because it gave slaves a common bond and perhaps some sense of power in the belief that spirits were on their side. Whites looked upon black rituals as both primitive and potentially savage."[70] Because planters, slaves, and free people of color emigrated from Haiti into Louisiana territory during and after the Haitian Revolution, a dread of voodoo and slave insurrection became widespread among slave owners of the region. In New Orleans, the police arrested groups of blacks they caught meeting unlawfully to engage in voodoo cere- monies.[71] In the summer of 1851, for example, New Orleans newspapers re- ported the arrest of "no less than fifteen or twenty colored women engaged in the mysterious rites of Voudou. . . . Most of them were dancing at the time around a fowl, a toads head and other articles which are considered indis- pensable to the proper observance of the ceremonies. . . . The police suc- ceeded in capturing a round dozen of the Voudoux, and marched them off to jail."[72] Another "voudou assemblage," reported by the *New Orleans Bee,* in- volved five free women of color and a slave girl, whom police discovered in a house on Gravier Street at midnight "lying in a state of nudity within a chalked circle on the floor, mumbling some nonsensical incantations. A caul- dron of water, containing a large snake, was boiling in the fireplace, and a table was spread with roasted oysters, hard boiled eggs, and liquor, of which free indulgence had been made." When the police broke in, the women "were awaiting the arrival of an old negro hag, who possesses reputed powers of witchcraft, to complete and effect the charm."[73] The parallels between such forbidden assemblies in the antebellum South and tales of witchcraft in New England in the late seventeenth century may explain why Tituba, the Indian slave from Barbados accused of witchcraft in Salem in 1692, metamorphosed into a Negro slave practicing voodoo in the literary and historical accounts of Salem witchcraft.

As Chadwick Hansen has shown, in the colonial court documents and narratives, Tituba is clearly a Carib Indian experienced in fortune-telling, but during the nineteenth century, her race and magic become more black and African.[74] Charles Upham's *Salem Witchcraft* (1867) not only focuses on Tituba's race but magnifies the significance of her religion, suggesting that she and her husband, John, "may have originated the 'Salem witchcraft.'" Up- ham observes, "They are spoken of as having come from New Spain, as it was then called,—that is, the Spanish West Indies, and the adjacent main- lands of Central and South America,—and, in all probability, contributed, from the wild and strange superstitions prevalent among their native tribes, materials which, added to the commonly received notions on such subjects, heightened the infatuation of the times, and inflamed still more the imaginations of the credulous."[75] A year after Upham's history appeared, Longfellow, in his verse drama *Gils Corey of the Salem Farms,* gave Tituba an Indian mother and a "black and fierce" African father, who taught her African magic. In George Bancroft's revised *History of the United States* (1876), she becomes "half-Indian, half-negro," although in the earlier editions of his history, she was an Indian. Over the years, Tituba's metamorphosis continued, and as Hansen has pointed out, the last vestige of her actual race disappeared in Arthur Miller's play *The Crucible* (1953), where she is a dramatic black voodoo priestess, chanting over a boiling kettle in a dark forest while the girls of Salem engage in naked dancing. It thus seems that the "horrors of Santo Domingo" provided a colored lens through which witchcraft in Salem was viewed, making Tituba seem more African and dangerous than she was.[76]

Hawthorne's "Septimius Norton" (ca. 1861–62) alludes to the racial transformation of Tituba, using her as a figure to evoke memories of Salem witchcraft and also to racialize those memories and problematize them—perhaps in response to the issue of miscegenation that dominated the recent presidential campaign, which resulted in Lincoln's election. In one of the later drafts of the romance, Tituba is identified as the great-aunt of the protagonist's mixed-race aunt. Aunt Keziah, or Nashoba, as she is called in "Septimius Norton," is said "to have had a very dark skin, the straight black hair, and that Indian form of the face, and Indian eye, lineaments which are said to be harder to eradicate . . . than those of the negro race" (13:266). More sinned against than sinning, her appearance and mysterious knowledge of poisonous plants and her racial hybridity combine to marginalize her. As she says, "it is a dismal world enough for those that are out of place in it, and who can never find their like, such as we of the Indian blood, or of a strange new blood made out of two races, and so that we are a kind of monster in the world" (13:425). Despite her "strange new blood," Aunt Nashoba, as she dies, proclaims her innocence in relation to the Black Man: "Now I'm a Christian woman, and believe my Bible, and I've always defied Satan (or the Black Man, as they used to call him,) though, if he'd happened to tempt me at the right time, I can't say but I might have yielded, as well as my great-aunt Tituba" (13:426). Despite Nashoba's confession, the irony Hawthorne weaves into his narrative is that she, like Tituba, is an innocent victim of the man of the house and misunderstood by the public: "She was not so malign an old woman as people supposed her; sometimes, if they had listened with charitable ears, they might hear her muttering a prayer; but such was their notion of the acridity, bitterness, pepperiness, of the old thing's disposition, and so little of the angel was there in her looks, that they probably mistook these utterances under her breath for curses on them and herself" (13:402). Clearly, Nashoba's independence and perversity, like Goody Corey's, marginalized her as much as did her race.

Witchcraft, the Black Man, and revolutionary violence figure prominently in a number of Hawthorne's other works, most notably *The Scarlet Letter*. As Jean Fagan Yellin has pointed out, Hawthorne draws on abolitionist iconography and rhetoric throughout that novel. He uses the image of a forcibly exposed and enchained woman to describe Hester's condition in Boston.[77] He links Arthur to a Southern slave master by means of his whip, his lust, his hypocrisy, his dominance over young women, and his refusal to acknowledge his child. Hawthorne hints at "the sinfulness of black sexuality," perhaps drawing on "travelers' reports of black Africans, of wild dancing in the woods." In Yellin's view, the Black Man desires the bodies and souls of the white women of Boston, and they, in turn, constitute "an alternative society" bound by witchcraft. She observes that "although this diabolical *society* is never taken seriously, when 'black' is read as a racial, and not a moral, descriptive, the text of *The Scarlet Letter* reveals an obsessive concern with blacks and blackness, with the presence of a dangerous dark group within society's midst—a concern that is characteristic of much American writing in the last decades before emancipation."[78] While Yellin's argument certainly has merit, especially given the nightmare generated in white psyches by the Haitian Revolution and Nat Turner's bloody slave revolt, Hawthorne, as I will show in chapter 5, sought to critique this fearful dream work as he exploited it for literary purposes. Fearmongering was second only to warmongering in his hierarchy of political sins.

CHAPTER 3

Racism, Slave Narratives, and the Body as Evidence

Our cautious and truth-loving people in New-England would never have believed this testimony, in proof of my identity, had it been borne by an abolitionist. Not that they really think an abolitionist capable of bearing false witness intentionally; but such persons are thought fanatical, and to look at every thing through a distorted medium.

—Frederick Douglass, reply to A. C. C. Thompson, slaveholder

I could ruin myself, any week, if I had not laid down a rule to consider every applicant for assistance an imposter, until he proves himself a true and responsible man—which it is very difficult to do.

—Hawthorne, *English Notebooks*

If Hawthorne indeed conflated witch-hunting Puritans with his abolitionist contemporaries, using specter evidence as one point of comparison, then one may ask if this means he disbelieved stories he heard and read about the demonic behavior of slave masters. The answer is apparently yes, and the primary reason seems to be that he doubted their veracity.[1] He knew Tituba as accused witch, slave, and fabricator, whose testimony propelled the hysteria in Salem in 1692, and this knowledge may have informed his skepticism about the narratives of contemporary fugitive slaves. He also saw that abolitionist literature was imbued with a crude gothicism that made it seem less than credible as nonfiction. As Wyatt-Brown has pointed out, the abolitionists' vision "included a gothic terror that granted masters and slaves less than their due as human beings. An anti-slavery tract was like a Brontë novel: a mixture of revealing insights into evil and thrusts into popular bathos."[2] Hawthorne's racism surely hardened his skepticism, leading him to doubt that the suffering of slaves exceeded—in severity or importance—that of other victims of oppression and cruelty. Perhaps the only positive thing that can be said about his racism is that it was less virulent and more benign than that of many other New England intellectuals, including the transcendentalists. In fact, as this chapter will show, Hawthorne possessed the heart of a reformer (though he tried to hide this fact, which embarrassed him). Yet he responded to the problem of human brutality—of bodies beaten, tortured, and marked—not emotionally but rationally, taking a careful and systematic approach to the problem, devoid of the zeal that animated abolitionism and other reform movements.

Transcendental Racialism

I have mentioned that the general antagonism toward the abolitionists grew out of fear and hatred of Negroes. Miscegenation, known at the time as amalgamation, was a potent related issue. It informed not only the abolitionists' verbal assaults on slave owners in the South but also mob violence against abolitionists and Negroes in the North. As Leon Litwack has pointed out, "discrimination against the Negro and a firmly held belief in the superiority of the white race were not restricted to one section but were shared by an overwhelming majority of white Americans in both the North and the South. Abraham Lincoln, in his vigorous support of both white supremacy and denial of equal rights for Negroes, simply gave expression to almost universal American convictions."[3] Negrophobia permeated white society, high and low, and racialist "science" endowed it with respectability.

In the 1820s and 1830s, the threat of amalgamation inspired mob action against people of color in a number of Northern cities, and much of the violence was caused by race hatred, unrelated to the issue of slavery. In *Reaping the Bloody Harvest*, John M. Werner records forty-one riots involving "race" in the United States between 1824 and 1849, while Leonard L. Richards, in his study of antiabolition mobs in Jacksonian America, notes sixty-one "anti-abolition and anti-Negro mobs" in New England between 1833 and 1837.[4] In a more recent study, Joanne Pope Melish points out that hostility toward free blacks in the North predated the antiabolitionist riots and that "the characterizations of actual people of color as disorderly and dependent, and the literary and graphic invention of imaginary people of color who were upstart, savagely ridiculous, and demonic fueled this out-pouring of frenzied anger and resentment."[5] In other words, hostility directed at abolitionists began with fear and hatred of people of color. Surprisingly, mob action against abolitionists was organized and led by "gentlemen of standing and property," that is, "prominent and articulate men—doctors and lawyers, merchants and bankers, judges and Congressmen,"[6] who feared the disruption of established economic, social, religious, and racial boundaries that they saw the abolitionists threatening with their rhetoric and activities.

To argue against slavery and on behalf of the Negro were two separate and distinct activities in antebellum America, although antiabolitionist mobs merged the two in their propaganda. Even the most ardent abolitionists—with a few exceptions, such as John Brown and his family—could not accept Negroes as their social equals. Abraham Lincoln expressed a nationwide sentiment among whites when he declared that "there is a physical difference between the white and black races which I believe will forever forbid the two races living together on terms of social and political equality."[7] William and Jane Pease point out that much of what the abolitionists said "betrayed an implicit and at times explicit belief in racial inferiority. . . . Occasionally crude, more often hidden in underlying assumptions or in appeals to science, prejudice played a more pervasive role than the logic of consistency would admit."[8] Such prejudice can be seen in Lydia Maria Child's 1836 claim that "by universal emancipation we want to *stop* amalgamation"; in Angelina Grimké's condescending 1837 letter to Sarah Douglass praying, "May the Lord lift you from the dung hill and set you among princes"; and in Theodore Parker's 1860 letter from Rome declaring, "the Anglo-Saxon with common sense does not like this Africanization of America; he wishes the superior race to multiply rather than the inferior."[9] In 1858, Walt Whitman, as editor of the *Brooklyn Daily Times,* argued on behalf of ridding the country of Negroes, writing, "Who believes that the Whites and Blacks can ever amalgamate in America? Or who wishes it to happen? Nature has set an impassable seal against it. Besides, is not America for the Whites? And is it not better so? As long as the Blacks remain here, how can they become anything like an independent and heroic race? There is no chance for it."[10]

Some members of the American Anti-Slavery Society were willing to allow Negroes into white churches, but leaders of the movement, including William Green, John Rankin, and William Jay (members of the society's executive committee) hesitated when it came to giving blacks any prominence in the society. According to Wyatt-Brown, when Lewis Tappan, cofounder of the society, "suggested Theodore S. Wright, a Negro Presbyterian minister, as a speaker at the anniversary meeting, Jay threatened to resign. He argued that neither the public nor abolitionists themselves were ready for so revolutionary a step."[11] As Wyatt-Brown points out, when Tappan "rode from Philadelphia to Harrisburg for a state convention meeting in 1837, he reported in the *Emancipator* that his white companions defied the other white railroad passengers by sitting with the Negro delegates. When it came to dining in public, however, some of the whites proved more squeamish and moved to separate tables."[12] In defense of the abolitionists, Leon Litwack has argued that the extent of their racism is difficult to determine and that "[m]ore significant, perhaps, is the fact that abolitionists could hold differing views on the propriety of social relations with Negroes and still combine to assist northern Negroes to secure equal political rights and economic improvement."[13] Their accomplishments included repeal of the ban on interracial marriages, on Jim Crow seating in railroad cars, and on segregation in Boston public schools.

As is generally known, racial prejudice in antebellum America was supported and advanced by so-called scientific studies that placed the Negro at the bottom of a hierarchy of races. Major intellectuals of the period, including Hawthorne, did not question the validity of these studies, which seemed authoritative and informed. The most prominent race scientist of the 1830s was Samuel Morton of Philadelphia, whose *Crania Americana* (1839), based on his collection of thousands of skulls, ranked the races in descending order from Caucasian to American Negroes, Hottentots, and aboriginal Australians. In *Crania Aegyptiaca* (1844), Morton and his collaborator, English Egyptologist George R. Gliddon, extended Morton's findings to northern Africa, "proving" the Egyptians could not have been Negroes. As Louis Menand has pointed out, Morton "made elementary statistical errors. But his studies, published in oversized volumes with elegantly designed plates and charts, were widely circulated, and his results were cited as authoritative by scientists in the United States and Europe."[14]

The Southern race scientist Josiah Nott joined Morton and Gliddon in arguing that the Negro represented a degraded stage of human being, and he used his work as an argument against amalgamation and as an apology for slavery. Nott's first published article, "The Mulatto a Hybrid—Probable Extermination of the Two Races if the Whites and Blacks are Allowed to Intermarry," argued that mulattos were less fertile than whites or blacks and that any line they established would die out in three or four generations. Writing a Southern friend, he described his field of study as "the nigger business" or "niggerology."[15] Despite its proslavery bias, his *Types of Mankind* (1855), published in Philadelphia and London, was a massive and best-selling study that established a hierarchy of races and argued that the "inferior races," after serving their purposes, would become extinct. He summarizes his thesis as follows:

> Lofty civilization, in all cases, has been achieved solely by the "Caucasian" group. Mongolian races, save in the Chinese family, in no instance have reached beyond the degree of semi-civilization; while the Black races of Africa and Oceanica, no less than the *Barbarous* tribes of America, have remained in utter darkness for thousands of years. Negro races, when *domesticated,* are susceptible of a limited degree of improvement; but when released from restraint, as in Hayti, they sooner or later relapse into barbarism.[16]

The work of Morton, Gliddon, and Nott was accepted as scientifically credible by the New England intelligentsia, including members of Hawthorne's Saturday Club, a group of authors and academics who represented, according to him, "the most enlightened public opinion of New England" (18:544). Oliver Wendell Holmes and Louis Agassiz, who had sterling scientific credentials, spoke out forcefully on the "natural" superiority of the white race. Holmes, poet, doctor, and dean of the Harvard Medical School, asserted, "The Creator has hung out the colors that form the two rallying points, so that they shall be unmistakable, eternal. . . . The white man must be the master in effect, whatever he is in name."[17] Agassiz, famed professor of natural history at Harvard, who emigrated to America from Switzerland in 1846, joined with Morton, Gliddon, and Nott in proving "scientifically" that the Negro was the lowest form of human being, "incapable of living on a footing of social equality with the whites, in one and the same community, without becoming an element of social disorder." In 1847, Agassiz drew on "authoritative" data to inform a Charleston audience, "The brain of the Negro is that of the imperfect brain of a 7 month's infant in the womb of a White."[18]

As for Emerson, another Saturday Club member, he lacked the insight or intent to consider the Negro race equal to the white. At his intellectual best, as Lawrence Buell has persuasively argued, Emerson "opened up the prospect of a much more profound sense of the nature, challenge, and promise of mental emancipation, whatever one's race, sex, or nation might be," yet he also failed at times "to free his mind from parochial entanglements."[19] One of these entanglements was Negrophobia, which in his case could be rather virulent. (In 1849, James Russell Lowell thought, perhaps incorrectly, that Emerson was prepared to blackball Frederick Douglass from the Boston Town and Country Club if the matter was put to a vote.)[20] While Hawthorne's racism has become a major issue in discussions of his politics, Emerson's racism has been discounted because of his antislavery activities. Nevertheless, when examined, it can shock. At age eighteen, he wrote in his journal, "I saw, ten, twenty, a hundred large lipped, lowbrowed black men who, except in the mere matter of languages, did not exceed the sagacity of the elephant."[21] Accepting prevailing notions of the hierarchy of the races, he believed that the destiny of blacks was to "serve & be sold & terminated."[22] As for the role of whites in their "termination," an 1848 journal entry by Emerson declares, "It is better to hold the negro race an inch under water than an inch over." On the same page, he wrote, "You cannot preserve races beyond their term."[23]

Like the witch-hunters of Salem that Hawthorne so detested, Emerson conflated victims and victimizers, asserting that a "secret" the abolitionists did not know was that the Negro and the slaveholder were of one party; they stand "in nature below the series of thought, & in the plane of vegetable & animal existence, whose law is to prey on one another, and the strongest has it."[24] In an 1853 meditation on the abolitionists, Emerson observed that even when the slaveholders "are extinguished, & law, intellectual law prevails, it will then appear quickly enough that the brute instinct rallies & centres in the black man. He is created on a lower plane than the white, & eats men & kidnaps & tortures, if he can. The Negro is imitative, secondary, in short, reactionary merely in his successes, & there is no origination with him in mental & moral sphere."[25] As late as 1854, Emerson was writing in his journal, "The dark man, the black man declines. . . . It will happen by & by, that the black man will only be destined for museums like the Dodo. Alcott compassionately thought that if necessary to bring them sooner to an end, polygamy might be introduced & these made the eunuchs, polygamy, I suppose, to increase the white births."[26]

This compassionate conservatism on the part of Amos Bronson Alcott, ordinarily the most liberal and idealistic of the transcendentalists, startles like a distant cry and makes one wonder about its source. The South in general and the Old Dominion in particular emerge as possibilities. Although Alcott grew up in Connecticut, his personality and social outlook were shaped by the five years he spent traveling throughout the South as a Yankee peddler in the early 1820s. His visits to the plantation homes of the Virginia aristocracy especially impressed him, and he later recalled, "I owe more to those as regards culture than to any school of instruction."[27] As Madelon Bedell has pointed out, "This life of the southern aristocracy which he so much admired was built on slavery. Although Alcott was to become one of the foremost antislavery advocates of his time, he never seems to have quite made this connection, but persisted in his admiration of the wealthy southern style of life to the end of his days."[28] In the Southern colonies during the eighteenth century, castration of black males, both free and slave, existed as lawful punishment, and although the laws had been repealed by the beginning of the nineteenth century for humanitarian reasons, the motives behind them persisted, namely, the desire to protect the white race from contamination, especially white women by black men, and the "generalized need in white men to persuade themselves that they were really masters and in all ways masterful."[29] Alcott was, of course, familiar with racialist thought, and he prided himself on his Anglo-Saxon heritage, which endowed him, he believed, with his blond hair and blue eyes, as contrasted with the dark skin and dark eyes of his wife, Abba May, and his daughter Louisa May, who may have had Portuguese and Jewish ancestors.[30] As Sarah Elbert has pointed out, in 1846, Bronson "referred to Louisa and her mother at one difficult moment in Louisa's childhood as 'two devils, as yet, I am not quite divine enough to vanquish the mother fiend and her daughter.' He joked that Louisa was a 'true-blue May, or rather, a brown.'"[31]

Other transcendentalists held similar racialist views. Thoreau, whose mother and sisters were more active in the antislavery movement than he was, helped runaway slaves make their way to Canada but regarded them with racial prejudice. In his journal, he compared the African with the Indian and declared that the former "will survive, for he is docile, and is patiently learning his trace and dancing at his labor; but the Indian does not often dance, unless it be the war dance."[32] As for the suffering of black slaves, Thoreau could take a rather callous view of it. He wrote in an 1845 journal entry, "the degradation & suffering of the black man—will not have been in vain if they contribute thus indirectly to give a loftier tone to the religion and politics of this country."[33] One assumes he means the religion and politics practiced by whites. As Michael Meyer has shown, there is evidence indicating that in the 1850s, Thoreau found racial mixing a threat to whites and felt that colonization for blacks was a solution to the problem of "intermingling."[34] Thoreau's lecture and essay "Slavery in Massachusetts" argues not against the suffering or oppression of actual slaves but, rather, against what he perceived as his enslavement in Massachusetts caused by the state's compliance with the Fugitive Slave Act.

Margaret Fuller, while more positive about racial mixing, accepted the findings of the racial theorists, as evident in her observations on Native Americans in *Summer on the Lakes, in 1843*. There she laments the "degradation" of the Indian and declares, "Amalgamation would afford the only true and profound means of civilization. But nature seems, like all else, to declare, that this race is fated to perish. Those of mixed blood fade early, and are not generally a fine race."[35] Fuller's sometime friend Elizabeth Peabody, in an 1851 essay on slavery in the *North American Review*, similarly echoed the race scientists and argued that "if the two races, after the slaves are set free, remain together at the South, we can foresee nothing but evil. If amalgamation should take place, it would create a third race, certainly inferior to the white, and probably inferior to the negro." "Of specific remedies," she concludes, "we know only one, and that is colonization."[36] She and Hawthorne, her brother-in-law, thus held similar views of emancipation, amalgamation, and the benefits of colonization, which is a little-known fact that even Elizabeth seems to have ignored. Because of Hawthorne's friendship with Franklin Pierce (and Pierce's close ties to Southern slaveholders), both of Sophia's sisters, Mary and Elizabeth (ignoring the complexity of their own racial attitudes), accused the Hawthornes of proslavery sentiments, which Sophia denied, to no avail.

Hawthorne's Racial Prejudices

Long after Hawthorne's death, Elizabeth Peabody asserted, with only slight exaggeration, that Hawthorne "knew *nothing* about Slavery. He had never been in the South. He never saw a slave or a fugitive slave. He looked at all antislavery literature as beneath the consideration of a reasonable man."[37] Her charges are valid for the most part, yet while Hawthorne had no truck with abolitionists, his racism was actually milder than that of Peabody and other transcendentalists. In fact, his boyhood acquaintance, William Symmes, a dark mulatto one year older than Hawthorne, credited him with a rare lack of prejudice. Late in life, Symmes, who seems a reliable source, told others that Hawthorne and another childhood friend, William Pitt Fessenden, "were the only two white boys and men who never by word or look offended him in the matter of his color."[38]

Symmes, born in Portland, Maine, recalled of the beginning of their relationship,

> I lived with one of the few men who visited Richard Manning, and used to go there often with my foster father. Nat Hawthorne and I were nearly of the same age and often played together. Thomas Pond, a beautiful sheet of water, lay about a half a mile to the eastward of his mother's house, the outlet of which is the creek running between Manning's house and that of his sister. We used to go to the pond, and on a large flat rock, partly covered with water, fish for perch and minnows, and try our skill at throwing stones as far as we could into the pond.[39]

Symmes went to sea as a sailor at age twenty but later occasionally saw Hawthorne by chance: "He never forgot me, and once, after he graduated, came on board a vessel in Salem harbor and stayed with me two hours. I was then before the mast. I have heard people say Hawthorne was cold and distant; if he was so, there was one of his youthful associates who, as the world goes, was not his equal socially, certainly not intellectually, who was never forgotten. The last time I saw him we were in Liverpool; he recognized me across the street, and 'hove me to.' We had a long talk, and he conversed in that easy, bewitching style, of which he was perfect master when he pleased."[40]

While he was in college, Hawthorne socialized with another mulatto, John Russwurm, a fellow member of the Athenean Club, and on his travels, he occasionally encountered free blacks, which evoked his admission that he found himself "more of an abolitionist in feeling than in principle" (8:112). His notebook entries, while racist, tend to be more condescending than hostile. In August 1838, he recorded his response to a group of Negroes congregated near the meetinghouse at Williamstown, Massachusetts, including one "old fellow" who talked "with a strange kind of pathos, about the whippings he used to get, while he was a slave—a queer thing of mere feeling, with some glimmerings of sense. Then there was another gray old negro, but of a different stamp, politic, sage, cautious, yet with boldness enough, talking about the rights of his race, yet so as not to provoke his audience, discoursing of the advantages of living under laws—and the murders that might ensue, in that very assemblage, if there were no laws. In the midst of this deep wisdom, turning off the anger of a half drunken fellow, by a merry retort, a leap in the air, and a negro's laugh" (8:112). As a fellow storyteller, Hawthorne appreciated not only the "deep wisdom" of this former slave but also his narrative skill, his ability to control the reactions of his auditors. In a less admiring and less admirable observation, Hawthorne reports amusement at seeing "the look of scorn, and shame, and sorrow, and painful sympathy" that one of a group of "well dressed and decent negro wenches" bestowed on a drunken Negro ascending the meetinghouse steps.

In another entry made near this time, Hawthorne describes "a negro respectably dressed, and well-mounted on horseback, travelling on his own hook, calling for oats and drinking a glass of brandy and water at the bar—like any other Christian. A young man from Ouisconsin said, 'I wish I had a thousand such fellows in Alabama.' It made a queer impression on me—the negro was really so human—and to talk of owning a thousand like him" (8:151). What is "queer" about the feeling Hawthorne has is not only the shock of a reality so at odds with prevailing stereotypes of the Negro as not fully human (which Hawthorne apparently held as one of his unexamined theoretical assumptions) but also the irony of a prospective Southerner demonstrating his lack of humanity by talking "of owning a thousand like him." Hawthorne does not complete the thought in the entry, because it goes beyond the bounds of logic and Northern ideology. The young man jars him toward the recognition that the South and the North "were two distinct nations in opinion and habits, and had better not try to live under the same institution,"[41] a view he maintained during the Civil War. "What ever happens next," he wrote to Bridge in May 1861, "I must say that I rejoice that the old Union is smashed. We never were one people, and never really had a country since the Constitution was formed" (18:381).

A year later, when he traveled with Dicey near Manassas, they aided a group of runaway slaves, giving "them food and wine, some small sums of money, and got them a lift upon a train going Northwards,"[42]—all facts that Dicey reported and Hawthorne suppressed in his own account of this encounter. Near the end of Hawthorne's life, while visiting the home of James T. Fields, he asked Moncure Conway to tell him about any Negro ghost stories he had heard, and Conway later recalled, "One of these was of a negro who saw an enormous conflagration near by, but on reaching the spot found only one firecoal and heard a dog bark. Hawthorne was interested in this, and spoke in a sympathetic way about the negroes that I did not expect."[43] Conway, like Elizabeth Peabody, assumed that Hawthorne's politics included Negrophobia, yet his racism never equaled that of Emerson, who became an ardent abolitionist. Hawthorne's ironic perspective on human pride kept him from subscribing to Emerson's sense of Anglo-Saxon racial superiority (or white supremacy, if you wish) that distinguishes so much of Emerson's writings, especially *English Traits* (1856).[44]

Hawthorne, unlike most of his white contemporaries, seems to have been aware of the prevalence and injustice of racism, if only at second hand. When he edited *Journal of an African Cruiser,* from materials provided by his friend Bridge, he added both his characteristic irony and a number of moral observations focused on the issue of race. Near the conclusion of Bridge's account of his voyage along the coast of Africa in 1843, either he or Hawthorne explicitly addresses the matter of racial prejudice and its cultural relativity.

When the white man sets his foot on the shore of Africa, he finds it necessary to throw off his former prejudices. For my own part, I have dined at the tables of many colored men in Liberia, have entertained them on shipboard, worshipped with them at church; walked, rode, and associated with them, as equal with equal, if not as friend with friend. Were I to meet those men in my own town, and among my own relatives, I would treat them kindly and hospitably, as they have treated me. My position would give me confidence to do so. But, in another city, where I might be known to few, should I follow the dictates of my head and heart, and there treat these colored men as brethren and equals, it would imply the exercise of greater moral courage than I have ever been conscious of possessing. This is sad; but it shows forcibly what the colored race have to struggle against in America, and how vast an advantage is gained by removing them to another soil.[45]

Despite the understanding in evidence here, Hawthorne, in a jocular letter to Bridge in April 1844, revealed both the depth and limits of his own racism as he responded to Bridge's account of a skirmish between American sailors and their officers (including Bridge) and five tribes of African natives, some of whom had plundered and burned an American vessel and murdered its captain and crew. Hawthorne tells Bridge to stay aboard ship the next time: "In the sight of God, one life may be as valuable as another; but in our view, the stakes are very unequal. Besides, I really do consider the shooting of these niggers a matter of very questionable propriety; and am glad, upon the whole, that you bagged no game on either of these days. It is a far better deed to beget a white fellow-creature [Hawthorne's daughter Una had just been born], than to shoot even a black one" (16:26). This statement, true to Hawthorne's pacifism, is the racist version of his opposition to warfare and violence.

Antislavery Horror Stories

Hawthorne's racial prejudices no doubt influenced his disdain for antislavery literature—Peabody's most accurate charge against him. This literature's sensationalism and its mediation by polemical abolitionists also undermined its credibility. Hawthorne's study of Salem witchcraft, as I have mentioned, taught him to be suspicious of sensational testimony about torment and bodily pain, and antislavery tracts made liberal use of descriptions of imprisonment and entrapment, scenes of violence, rapes, whippings, dismemberments, lustful masters, terrified slaves, and assorted instruments of torture. Authors of slave narratives, as Teresa Goddu has pointed out, faced "the difficulty of representing a gothic history through gothic conventions without collapsing the distinctions between fact and fiction, event and effect."[46] Most slave narratives, however, were unable to overcome this difficulty.

In the writings of the abolitionists, the sensational predominated, and horror stories, as Elizabeth Clark has pointed out, "proved to be among the most effective and dramatic weapons in the reform arsenal: speakers often righteously denied any intention to 'harrow up' an audience's feelings before going on to dwell enthusiastically on atrocities."[47] One particularly harrowing example appeared in multiple publications, including David L. Child's *The Despotism of Freedom; or, The Tyranny and Cruelty of American Republican Slave-Masters, Shown to Be the Worst in the World* (1833), John Rankin's *Letters on American Slavery* (1833), and Lydia Maria Child's *An Appeal in Favor of that Class of Americans Called Africans* (1833). It gained additional impact because it featured a nephew of Thomas Jefferson, who killed a young slave. Rankin's version, told in a letter from the Reverend William Dickey, reads,

In the county of Livingston, Ky. near the mouth of Cumberland, lived Lilburn Lewis, a sister's son of the venerable Jefferson. He "who suckled at fair Freedom's breast" was the wealthy owner of a considerable number of slaves, whom he drove constantly, fed sparingly, and lashed severely. The consequence was, they would run away. This must have given, to a man of spirit and a man of business great anxieties until he found them, or until they had starved out, and returned. Among the rest was an ill grown boy about seventeen, who having just returned from a skulking spell, was sent to the spring for water, and in returning let fall an elegant pitcher. It was dashed to shivers upon the rocks. . . . It was night, and the slaves all at home. The master had them collected into the most roomy negrohouse, and a rousing fire made. When the door was secured, that none might escape, either through fear of him or sympathy with George, he opened the design of the interview, namely, that they might be effectually taught to stay at home and obey his orders. All things being now in train, he called up George, who approached his master with the most unreserved submission. He bound him with cords, and by the assistance of his younger brother, laid him on the broad bench or meat block. He now proceeded to WHANG off George by the ancles!!! It was with the broad axe!—In vain did the unhappy victim SCREAM AND ROAR! He was completely in his master's power. Not a hand amongst so many durst interfere. Casting the feet into the fire, he lectured them at some length. He WHACKED HIM OFF below the knees! George roaring out, and praying his master to BEGIN AT THE OTHER END! He admonished them again, throwing the legs into the fire! Then above the knees, tossing the joints into the fire! He again lectured them at leisure. The next stroke severed the thighs from the body. These were also committed to the flames. And so off the arms, head and trunk, until all was in the fire! Still protracting the intervals with lectures, and threatenings of like punishment, in case of disobedience, and running away, or disclosure of this tragedy. Nothing, now remained, but to consume the flesh and bones; and for this purpose the fire was briskly stirred, until two hours after midnight. When, as though the earth would cover out of sight, the nefarious scene, and as though the great master in Heaven would put a mark of his displeasure upon such monstrous cruelty, a sudden and surprising shock of Earthquake overturned the coarse and heavy backwall, composed of rock and clay, which completely covered the fire, and the remains of George. This put an end to the amusements of the evening. The negroes were permitted to disperse, with charges to keep this matter among themselves, and never to whisper it in the neighborhood, under the penalty of a like punishment. When he retired, the lady exclaimed, "O! Mr. Lewis, where have you been and what have you done!" She had heard a strange pounding, and dreadful screams, and had smelled something like fresh meat burning! He said that he had never enjoyed himself at a ball so well as he had enjoyed himself that evening.

The letter goes on to say that the Negroes "whispered the horrid deed" and that Lewis was arrested and committed suicide awaiting trial. Dickey's letter is followed by the date "October 8, 1824," and the note "N. B. This happened in 1811, if I be correct, the 16th of December. It was the Sabbath!"[48] (Dickey's account is factually accurate, although his heavy-handed dramatization makes it seem fictional.)[49]

From about 1831 to the Civil War, narratives featuring the horrors of slavery gained increasing popularity, and as Frances Smith Foster has pointed out, "under the label of education, scenes of violence and cruelty were presented which not only could awaken moral outrage against slavery but at the same time satisfy the public's appetite for sensationalism."[50] In the middle of the nineteenth century, as Clark has pointed out, "slave narrators competed with each other to produce ever more sensational effects, using such titles as *Life and Narrative of William J. Anderson, Twenty-Four Years a Slave; Sold Eight Times! In Jail Sixty Times! Whipped Three Hundred Times!!!*"[51] Between 1831 and 1861, more than eighty slave narratives were published, most under the auspices of white abolitionists. Several were exposed as hoaxes, including the *Narrative of James Williams, an American Slave, Who Was for Several Years a Driver on a Cotton Plantation in Alabama* (1838), edited by John Greenleaf Whittier;[52] however, the exposure did not affect the popularity of the genre. Among the best sellers were *Narrative of the Life of Frederick Douglass, an American Slave, Written by Himself* (1845), which sold some thirty thousand copies within five years; *Narrative of William Wells Brown, a Fugitive Slave, Written by Himself* (1847), which sold eight thousand copies in less than eighteen months; and *Truth Stranger than Fiction: Father Henson's Story of His Own Life* (1858), which sold six thousand copies in three years and eventually over one hundred thousand copies, after it was learned that Henson served as the model for Stowe's Uncle Tom. By comparison, *The Scarlet Letter* had sold only seventy-eight hundred copies by the end of Hawthorne's life, an average of six hundred copies a year.

In the works they brought before the public, abolitionist editors encouraged not only certain obligatory scenes (whippings, the coffle or chain gang, the auction block, the separation from other family members) but also obligatory emotions, especially grief and anger. In his preface to Douglass's *Narrative*, Garrison practically blackmails the reader in order to evoke the emotions sought.

> He who can peruse it without a tearful eye, a heaving breast, an afflicted spirit,—without being filled with an unutterable abhorrence of slavery and all its abettors, and animated with a determination to seek the immediate overthrow of that execrable system,—without trembling for the fate of this country in the hands of a righteous God, who is ever on the side of the oppressed, and whose arm is not shortened that it cannot save—must have a flinty heart, and be qualified to act the part of a trafficker in slaves and the souls of men.[53]

Garrison's heavy-handed mediation exemplifies abolitionist control of the fugitive slaves' experience, which even Frederick Douglass eventually found oppressive.

Ironically, as abolitionists collected, edited, framed, and published slave narratives, they undermined the credibility of the slaves' testimony. John W. Blassingame, responding to the need to collect as much evidence as possible, concedes that since the antebellum narratives were frequently dictated to and written by whites, it is difficult to arrive at an understanding of the slave's unmediated interpretation of his or her experience. (Later transcribed or recorded interviews present a similar problem, of course.) Although Blassinggame argues for the integrity of the abolitionist editors, based on their professional standing, he concedes that

> many of the more reliable accounts contain elements that cannot be attributed to the blacks. Certain literary devices which appear in the stories were clearly beyond the ken of unlettered slaves. First, many of the narratives contain long dialogues that can only represent approximations of the truth. Sometimes it is obvious that the editors fleshed out the sparse details supplied by the fugitives to heighten the dramatic effect.[54]

This dramatic effect, often gothic in nature, can subordinate the slave's pain to the white reader's response. "Paradoxically," as Goddu has shown, "the gothic effect subsumes the gothic even as it testifies to its horrors." She cites as an example Sarah Grimké's account of her departure from the South and slavery.

> As I left my native state on account of slavery, and deserted the home of my fathers to escape the sound of the lash and the shrieks of tortured victims, I would gladly bury in oblivion the recollection of those scenes with which I have been familiar; but this may not, cannot be; they come over my memory like gory specters, and implore me with resistless power, in the name of a God of mercy, in the name of a crucified Savior, in the name of humanity; for the sake of the slaveholder, as well as the slave, to bear witness to the horrors of the southern prison house."[55]

From a skeptical perspective, such as Hawthorne's, Grimké's account of her own feelings (which displace the slave's pain) would appear more gothic fantasy than historical fact, and her gory specters not as realities but, rather, as psychological projections, telling us more about the perceiver than the perceived.[56]

The male and female abolitionists engaged in bringing the slave's experience before the public showed little self-consciousness about the problem of appropriation, yet they were highly sensitive to the problem of credibility and used various means to treat it. Garrison, in his preface to Douglass's *Narrative,* addresses the problem head-on, as was his wont.

> So profoundly ignorant of the nature of slavery are many persons, that they are stubbornly incredulous whenever they read or listen to any recital of the cruelties which are daily inflicted on its victims. They do not deny that the slaves are held as property, but that terrible fact seems to convey to their minds no idea of injustice, exposure to outrage, or savage barbarity. Tell them of cruel scourings, of mutilations and brandings, of scenes of pollution and blood, . . . and they affect to be greatly indignant at such enormous exaggerations, such wholesale misstatements, such abominable libels on the character of the southern planters! . . . Skeptics of this character abound in society.[57]

Because of this skepticism, Douglass himself was delighted when a Southerner challenged what he said about his former masters in his *Narrative.* After sarcastically thanking his detractor for inadvertently acknowledging that Douglass had indeed been a slave, he declared, "Our cautious and truth-loving people in New-England would never have believed this testimony, in proof of my identity, had it been borne by an abolitionist. Not that they really think an abolitionist capable of bearing false witness intentionally; but such persons are thought fanatical, and to look at every thing through a distorted medium."[58] Douglass fully understood the demands placed on him for authenticity and credibility, but he also felt the need to construct his narrative so as to advance the cause of abolition. In an 1848 letter to his former master, Thomas Auld, Douglass warns him, "I intend to make use of you as a weapon with which to assail the system of slavery—as a means of concentrating public attention on the system, and deepening their horror of trafficking in the souls and bodies of men."[59] A year later, however, in a "friendly epistle" to Auld, Douglass admits that some of his charges were undeserved, especially his having accused Auld of brutality toward Douglass's grandmother.[60]

Douglass, Henry "Box" Brown, and other fugitive slaves took their anti-slavery message to England while Hawthorne was there during 1853–57, and Hawthorne surely noticed their activities, which were greeted by large crowds and extensive newspaper coverage. The sensational dominated these appearances, which often featured large panoramas showing scenes of American slavery, displays of instruments of torture used in slavery, and revelations of personal scars.[61] The events also took political stands. At a huge meeting in Manchester on August 1, 1854, Brown and leading American abolitionist Parker Pillsbury dramatized the brutality of slavery and also indicted President Pierce, whom Pillsbury called in his speech "a Northern democrat, but a Northern man with Southern principles, in so far as he has any principles at all," a description met with laughter.[62]

In both the United States and England, imposters posed a problem for abolitionists and their supporters, further damaging the credibility of actual fugitives. The Boston Vigilance Committee, which provided fugitives with cash, clothes, shelter, and jobs, checked out each fugitive's story but could not eliminate deception.[63] In England, as Audrey Fisch has shown, the most notorious impostor was Rueben Nixon, a petty thief, gambler, and con artist, who traveled throughout England collecting money from sympathizers. On February 6, 1857, the *Montrose, Arbroath and Brechin Review* praised his lecture given under the name William Love. A week later, the paper reported the news that from evidence obtained, it is clear that Love/Nixon "has never been a slave, except to his inveterate habit of lying and deception; and, though often a fugitive, his flying has only been from those whom he has duped and fleeced. He has a new story for almost every place in which he appears, and a different name for each character he assumes."[64] Other imposters had different methods, and Fisch notes that an untitled article in the *Liverpool Mercury* reported the arrest, conviction, and eighteen-month sentence of a Negro called the Reverend Alfred Thomas Wood, DD, who had "been going about in this country and in Ireland during the greater part of last year, collecting subscriptions professedly for completing a new church in Monrovia, in the republic of Liberia. . . . He had represented himself in different places as an Episcopalian, an independent, and a Baptist, according to circumstances."[65] Such prevarication, coupled with the sensationalism of antislavery tracts, suggests that there were more reasons for Hawthorne's disdain of the abolitionists than just the sins of racism, coldheartedness, and membership in the Democratic Party. As someone who was "cautious and truth-loving," especially when it came to tales of torment and abuse, such as those told by the young girls in Salem in 1692, he examined such violent matters carefully and dispassionately. His consular letters from England, discussed in the next section, show this most clearly.

Hawthorne as Reformer

As U.S. consul to Liverpool, Hawthorne became increasingly involved in dealing with the brutalization of sailors, black and white, on American ships, and he sought ways to help the victims both through modest immediate assistance and by seeking government action that would address the systemic causes of the cruelty he witnessed. In July 1854, he informed Secretary of State William Marcy that the current mode of impressing United States seamen

> operates not only to the immediate injury and demoralization of the sailor, but produces the further bad effect, that, for greater and easier gain, an inferior class of men are engaged by unprincipled and irresponsible Shipping Masters. As an almost inevitable consequence, the officers are irritated into the maltreatment of these men, who have been imposed upon them as seamen, often without any claim to that character. . . . I feel it a duty to express my opinion, that, if competent persons were appointed by our government to investigate this matter, great evils would certainly be exposed, and a wholesome and effective remedy might be suggested. (19:190–91)

Getting no response to this suggestion, Hawthorne wrote Marcy again nine months later, providing evidence of the cruelty that needed to be addressed. He submitted papers relating to his own investigation of the case of Daniel Smith, a small farmer kidnapped at Charleston and forced to work as a sailor on the American ship *George A. Hopley* bound for Liverpool. During the voyage, Davis had been beaten senseless, and once in port, he had been abandoned, dying and starving. When Hawthorne first interviewed him, Smith told what had happened. "They had beaten him shamefully," Hawthorne recorded in his notebook, "of which he bore grievous marks about his face and eyes, and bruises on his head and other parts of his person; and finally the ship had sailed, leaving him behind. I never in my life saw so forlorn a fellow, so ragged, so wretched; and he seemed as if his wits had been beaten out of him" (21:165). Hawthorne visited Smith in the hospital several weeks later, just hours before he died, and as the victim lay writhing on his bed, unable to speak, Hawthorne noticed tattoos of nautical emblems on his arms. He later wrote in his notebook, "This might be of some importance, because the dying man had told me, when I first saw him, that he was no sailor, but a farmer, and that this being his first voyage, he had been beaten by the captain for not doing a sailor's duty, which he had no opportunity of learning. These sea-emblems indicated that he was probably a seaman of some years' service" (21:166–67).

Frustrated in his attempt to read Smith's body as a reliable text. Hawthorne read letters that Smith had on his person when he died and concluded from these that the man had indeed told the truth about his vocation and fate. In his notebook, Hawthorne then recorded his deep dismay that a free citizen of the United States "should be absolutely kid-napped, carried to a foreign country, treated with savage cruelty . . . and left to die on his arrival" (21:169). Three days later, he sent Secretary of State Marcy papers related to Smith's death, including a coroner's report he had requested. He added in a cover letter, "The circumstances are narrated in my Certificate and shew [sic] the case to be one of great cruelty, and I submit whether it is not one in which an example ought to be made of the offender. . . . I on a former occasion suggested a commission to ascertain the merits or rather demerits of the system & the best mode of reform, & I still think that would be the best course to adopt" (19:294–95). (More than a year later, Marcy replied that "the pressure of public business" prevented anyone in the State Department from acting on Hawthorne's suggestion.)[66]

In a related effort to initiate U.S. government action, Hawthorne wrote to his friend Charles Sumner, leading abolitionist in the Senate, asking for his help "in bringing the condition of our mercantile marine before Congress." He tells Sumner, "Every day, some miserable cruelty and carnage is brought under my notice." He gives as examples the abuse and death of Smith and the fatal shooting of three other sailors by their officers, adding, "the most perplexing part of the matter is, that all this bloodshed and cruelty seems to be strangely justifiable, and almost inevitable under the circumstances" (17:344). Hawthorne lays the blame not on officers or the sailors but on the practice of using shipping masters to supply seamen for vessels in return for a percentage of wages, with the result that inexperienced men are tricked or kidnapped and find themselves being abused at sea before they know what has happened to them. (Of course, drunkenness plays its part in this deception.) Hawthorne tells Sumner, "You would have to make inquiries into their system, on your side of the water; and I could help you to many atrocities which come to my knowledge through the statements of seamen. These shipping-masters should be annihilated at once;—no slave-drivers are so wicked as they, and there is nothing in slavery so bad as the system with which they are connected" (17: 345). Sumner, perhaps piqued, never answered. He forwarded the dispatch to Attorney General Caleb Cushing, who ignored it. Nevertheless, Hawthorne continued to work on behalf of reform, and his consular letters are filled with official accounts of abuse at sea, showing an author resisting the impulse to jump to conclusions and trying to adjudicate complex issues fairly.[67]

In *Our Old Home*, Hawthorne sets out the problems he faced as consul and the difficulty he had in getting at the truth to his satisfaction.

> Scarcely a morning passed, but that some sailor came to show the marks of his ill-usage on shipboard. Often, it was a whole crew of them, each with his broken head or livid bruise, and all testifying with one voice to a constant series of savage outrages during the voyage; or, it might be, they laid an accusation of actual murder, perpetrated by the first or second officers with many blows of steel knuckles, a rope's end, or a marline-spike, or by the Captain, in the twinkling of an eye, with a shot of his pistol. Taking the seamen's view of the case, you would suppose that the gibbet was hungry for the murderers. Listening to the Captain's defence, you would seem to discover that he and his officers were the humanest of mortals, but were driven to a wholesome severity by the mutinous conduct of the crew, who, moreover, had themselves slain their comrade in the drunken riot and confusion of the first day or two after they were shipped. Looked at judicially, there appeared to be no right side to the matter, nor any right side possible in so thoroughly vicious a system as that of the American mercantile marine. (5:31–32)

Yet Hawthorne did arrive at judicial decisions regarding cases he investigated, and he often used physical evidence to do so. In a letter of August 14,

1857, to Lewis Cass, he explains his decision to refuse the certificate of registry of the ship *AZ* of New York because the captain had beaten and tortured the steward and cook under his command and refused to pay them what he owed them.

> In all cases of this kind, depending entirely on the evidence of Seamen (who seem to have their own peculiar notions on the subject) it is extremely difficult to arrive at the truth, but looking at the evidence before me in this case, the admission of the Captain [that he did beat the men some], and the condition of the men described in the accompanying copy of surgeon's certificate (enclosure No3) [indicating multiple contusions, abrasions, and fractures], I was forced to the conclusion that Wheeler and McDonald had been very cruelly used by the Captain, and were entitled to their discharge. (20:171–72)

As Bill Ellis, editor of Hawthorne's consular letters, points out, by the end of his term, Hawthorne was taking decisive actions as consul, "siding, for instance, with the black seaman William Valentine of the *Vanguard*, who, threatened and goaded by his white superiors, finally turned on one of his oppressors with a knife and was in return beaten senseless" (19:28). Hawthorne defended Valentine and sought prosecution of the officers, who had been "very tyrannical," he told the U.S. secretary of state, and "had grossly ill-treated the men" (20:154).

The reading of the body as text that Hawthorne was forced to do in his investigations figured prominently in the antislavery movement, of course, where scars served as irrefutable evidence of abuse. Frederick Douglass reputedly discovered this when he overcame the incredulity of a London audience who could not believe that the person before them, speaking so eloquently, had ever been a slave. Douglass stripped off his shirt and displayed his scarred back to the audience, overcoming their disbelief.[68] For Hawthorne, though, reading the body as text required caution, for he knew that the Salem girls showed various marks on their bodies to substantiate their false accusations. When Goodwife Corey bit her lip during her examination, for example, the "bewitched" children "were bitten on their arms and wrists and produced the Marks before the Magistrates, Ministers and others. And . . . if she did but Pinch her Fingers, or Graspe one hand hard in another, they were Pinched and produced the Marks before the Magistrates, and Spectators."[69] (When Arthur Dimmesdale rips open his shirt at the end of *The Scarlet Letter*, Hawthorne provides multiple readings of the mark on his chest—including denial of any mark at all—to emphasize, contra the Salem Puritans, the difficulty of reading such texts.) In the case of Wheeler and McDonald, Hawthorne, after determining the captain's guilt and ordering him to pay three months advance wages, added, in the interests of truthfulness, "I feel it proper to say that Captain Simpsons general treatment of his crew appears to have been unexceptionable and that he seemed to me on the whole a kind hearted man, but to be afflicted with a temper easily kindled to violence and not easily pacified" (20:177). After Hawthorne moved to Rome, he heard from his efficient head clerk, Henry Wilding, who re-presented the difficulties Hawthorne had dealt with: "I am still at the Consulate, battling with hard captains and sailors,—struggling to do right amid threats and discouragements, when the truth is hard to find."[70]

While the charge of callousness leveled at Hawthorne may be justified in terms of what we now know about the realities of slavery, one needs to hesitate when it comes to assuming he took no interest in ridding the world of horrific behavior. Reluctant to judge precipitously or to accept the charges of accusers at face value, as his great-grandfather had done, Hawthorne approached conflicting testimony circumspectly, seeking truth in the midst of falsehoods and deceptions. One small indication of his success is that in 1859, Richard Monckton Milnes, later Lord Crewe, brought the issue of cruelty on board English and American merchant ships before the House of Commons, using a letter Hawthorne provided for the purpose.[71] Citing Hawthorne by name, Milnes moved that Queen Victoria enter into negotiations with the government of the United States "for the purpose of preventing the assaults and cruelties committed on merchant seamen engaged in traffic between this country and the United States, and of bringing to justice the perpetrators of such offences, many of whom at present escaped with impunity in consequence of the defects in the system of international jurisdiction."[72] The motion passed. Despite his failure to enlist legislative support for reform from the United States, Hawthorne, as Ellis writes, "did more than any other consul in the British Isles to bring abuses of seamen to the State Department's attention, and his direct legal efforts to find unorthodox ways to bring brutal ships' officers to justice seem without precedent."[73] In a letter of October 8, 1857, to his outspoken sister-in-law Elizabeth Peabody, Hawthorne misleadingly told her, "I do not know what Sophia may have said about my conduct in the Consulate. I only know that I have done no good; none whatever" (23:465). He had no desire to be thought a member of the group of reformers Peabody so visibly represented.

CHAPTER 4

Accord in Concord

How gently, too, did the sight of the old Manse—best seen from the river, overshadowed with its willow, and all environed about with the foliage of its orchard and avenue—how gently did its gray, homely aspect rebuke the speculative extravagances of the day!

—Hawthorne, "The Old Manse"

The three preceding chapters of this study have focused on the backgrounds and expression of Hawthorne's political values as they relate to his study of revolution and witchcraft, which informed his attitude toward the abolitionists, their literature, and their activities. I have also tried to show that Hawthorne's racism should not be singled out as an attitude that somehow differentiates him from other New England intellectuals, especially the transcendentalists. This chapter will advance the argument that during his stay in Concord in the early 1840s, Hawthorne was actually in agreement with his transcendentalist neighbors with regard to such issues as reformers, reform, and the role of the scholar-artist in American society. In other words, the transcendentalists were no more "abolitionist" than Hawthorne at this period, though recent scholarship and criticism have tended to make it seem that they were.

Hawthorne's rivalry with Emerson and his satires of reform and reformers have received much attention over the years, but the degree to which his sociopolitical outlook coincided with those of the transcendentalists has gone relatively unexamined. I do not wish to suggest that Hawthorne did not find himself at odds with this group, for he did. Their optimism and his pessimism obviously took them down different paths of thought. Moreover, as the lone fiction writer among them, his human interests were somewhat broader, as a comparison of their respective notebooks can show, and he was drawn toward individuals marginalized by class and race, at least as an observer. As his sister Elizabeth put it, he possessed "a power of adapting himself to the minds of others whose culture and pursuits were unlike his own."[1] Still, the congruence of his sociopolitical outlook with those of Emerson, Thoreau, Fuller, and Alcott was remarkable, and the clear division between them occurred years later, caused not by contrasting views of slavery or the slave, as so many commentators have asserted, but by Hawthorne's inveterate pacifism and their willingness to condone violence to effect political change. Thus Hawthorne's "fall," as it was called, marked a movement on their part, not his.

The "Newness" and Concord

On July 9, 1842, when Hawthorne arrived with his new bride, Sophia, to take up residence in the Old Manse, he had completed his stints as measurer in the Boston Custom House (1839–40) and resident at Brook Farm (1841). The customhouse appointment came through the assistance of Elizabeth Peabody and the political clout of George Bancroft, who was emerging as leader of the Massachusetts Democrats at the same time he was making his mark as major historian of the United States. Hawthorne, during his tenure, came to hate political office and politicians. He wrote to his fiancée, Sophia, on May 15, 1840, "I do detest all offices—all, at least, that are held on a political tenure. And I want nothing to do with politicians—they are not men; they cease to be men, in becoming politicians. Their hearts wither away, and die out of their bodies. Their consciences are turned to India-rubber—or to some substance as black as that, and which will stretch as much" (15:422). He later excepted only his friend Pierce from this characterization, though he even doubted Pierce's humanity at times.

The reason for Hawthorne's hostile attitude toward politicians in 1840 lies perhaps in his sense of Bancroft's deviousness or in the fate of his college friend Jonathan Cilley, an aggressive and effective Democratic congressman from Maine who, because of his politics, was killed in a duel with William J. Graves, a Whig congressman from Kentucky, on February 24, 1838. In a memorial essay written for O'Sullivan's *Democratic Review* after Cilley's death, Hawthorne praised Cilley's character and political success and condemned those who had silenced him. O'Sullivan had asserted that the Whigs, with their "bitter and ferocious spirit of party,"[2] had plotted Cilley's murder, but Hawthorne does not go this far, though he recognized the political context of the challenge (later revealed to have been written by the leading Whig senator Henry Clay).[3] Hawthorne declares, "A challenge was never given on a more shadowy pretext; a duel was never pressed to a fatal close, in the face of such open kindness as was expressed by Mr. Cilley; and the conclusion is inevitable, that Mr. Graves, and his principal second, Mr. Wise, have gone farther than their own dreadful Code will warrant them, and overstepped the imaginary distinction which, on their own principles, separates Manslaughter from Murder" (23:119).[4]

Hawthorne later expressed pride in the restraint he managed in his essay on Cilley. "Written," he told his friend Hillard, "in the very midst of my grief, and when every other man in the nation, on both sides, was at fever-heat, it is, though very sad, as calm as if it had been written a hundred years after the event; and, so far as I recollect it, it might as well have been written by a Whig as by a Democrat" (16:277). The piece itself, though perhaps nonpartisan, helped gain Hawthorne his appointment to the Boston Custom House (Bancroft mentioned it in his appointment letter). At times, Hawthorne's principled efforts to rise above party politics advanced his career, as he perhaps knew they would.

With the election of Whig president Harrison in 1840, Hawthorne lost almost all immediate prospects for a new political appointment (though the Tyler presidency renewed his hopes somewhat), and he had become disenchanted with Brook Farm after spending seven months there in 1841. By moving to Concord after his marriage in 1842, he entered a small world dominated by what was called the "Newness." Although Emerson was viewed as the inspirational leader of those who sought ways to bring idealism to bear upon life in America, he was politically more conservative than Hawthorne, having been raised in the Federalist environment of Boston and become a supporter of the Whig Party. Emerson viewed Jackson and his followers with a certain elitist disdain, though he professed to admire the principles of the Democratic Party. His biographer Ralph Rusk explains, "He undoubtedly had the feeling that property was safer with the Whigs than with the Democrats, yet his own modest possessions did not blind him to the rights of the unpropertied."[5] The "modest possessions" Rusk mentions included Emerson's first wife's share of the Tucker estate, some twelve thousand dollars in stocks and cash, which he had secured from members of her family through a lawsuit (she had died at age nineteen, before coming into her inheritance). He would add to this inheritance through wise investments in stocks and real estate, reaching an estimated net worth of $50,000 by 1851 (the equivalent to more than a million today), and dying a wealthy man.[6] As James Russell Lowell so aptly put it, he possessed "A Greek head on right Yankee shoulders, whose range / Has Olympus for one pole, for t' other the Exchange."[7]

The most significant differences between Hawthorne and the Concord transcendentalists had more to do with money than politics, though the two are of course inseparable. During their first stay in Concord, from July 1842 to October 1845, the Hawthornes suffered from severe poverty, which embarrassed them and generated various forms of tension. Thoreau, for example, had unconventional notions about how to economize, as the first chapter of *Walden* makes clear, and although Hawthorne had the highest regard for him as a scholar and a person, he later told Monckton Milnes, "in his presence one feels ashamed of having any money, or a house to live in, or so much as two coats to wear" (17:279). Hoping to establish a conventional middle-class family, Hawthorne was frustrated during his years at the Manse because others failed to pay him what he was due. Charles A. Dana and George Ripley, directors of Brook Farm, would not send him the outstanding $524 they owed him, and editors O'Sullivan and Lowell did not send him payment for his contributions to their periodicals. The result was that after his "fellowship of toil and impracticable schemes, with the dreamy brethren of Brook Farm" (1:25), he found himself unable to pay the rent on the Manse or at times even to buy food.

Emerson's condescending attitude did little to help. On August 2, 1845, Emerson, unasked, tried to persuade Caroline Sturgis to live with the Hawthornes as a boarder, telling her, "They are, as I understand it, still without any resource, & contented enough with Concord. It is still doubtful whether Mr Ripley get here this winter, and if not, your living with them would enable H. to pay his rent, which, Mr R told me yesterday, had not been paid since the first year."[8] Sturgis declined. One month later, Sophia wrote to her mother about "the perplexities that have vexed my husband the last year, and made the place painful to him . . . It is wholly new to him to be in debt, and he cannot 'whistle for it,' as Mr. Emerson advised him to do, telling him that everybody was in debt, and that they were all worse than he was."[9] Emerson, I think, got a secret delight out of Hawthorne's embarrassments.[10]

Despite his dire poverty (countered in "The Old Manse" by an emphasis on fecundity), Hawthorne wrote some twenty-one tales and sketches at the Manse. One, "The New Adam and Eve," condemns the results of the new capitalism and "the great and miserable fact" that one portion of the earth's inhabitants are "rolling in luxury" while the multitude is "toiling for scanty food" (10:262–63). In other tales from *Mosses from an Old Manse*, Hawthorne turns his attention to contemporary American culture more directly than ever before, and throughout these pieces, he expresses his political beliefs by lauding what he calls "the institutions that had grown out of the heart of mankind" (10:26), while critiquing "the speculative extravagances of the day" (10:25).

His new literary interests seem clearly the result of the intense intellectual stimulation of Concord, generated by Emerson, who had settled in the town in 1835. The Transcendental Club, the *Dial,* and Brook Farm were three early manifestations of the innovative ideas circulating within the Concord community, but probably even more influential in evoking Hawthorne's satire were the more unusual visitors who came to Concord to seek Emerson's advice and support. Such men as Ellery Channing, Jones Very, and Bronson Alcott fell into this category, and in "The Old Manse," Hawthorne describes them as "a variety of queer, strangely dressed, oddly behaved mortals, most of whom took upon themselves to be important agents of the world's destiny, yet were simply bores of a very intense water" (10:31–32). Of the leading transcendentalists—Emerson, Thoreau, Fuller, and Alcott—only Alcott seemed "ultra" in his views, for his idealism left his family dependent on the charity of his wife's relatives and of Emerson as well. Yet even Alcott, ironically enough, shared Hawthorne's disdain for ardent abolitionists in the 1840s, because of their fierce polemics. Although the transcendentalists, because of their well-known idealism, are often seen as central to the New England reform movement of the 1840s, they neither identified with reformers nor particularly cared for them. Their emphases were on personal and individual reform rather than on collective action, and in this regard, their attitudes accorded with Hawthorne's.

In November 1840, Emerson satirized those attending the Convention of Friends of Universal Reform in Boston, observing,

> A great variety of dialect and of costume was noticed; a great deal of confusion, eccentricity, and freak appeared, as well as of zeal and enthusiasm. If the assembly was disorderly, it was picturesque. Madmen, madwomen, men with beards, Dunkers, Muggletonians, Come-outers, Groaners, Agrarians, seventh-day-Baptists, Quakers, Abolitionists, Unitarians and Philosophers,—all came successively to the top, and seized their moment, if not their hour, wherein to chide, or pray, or preach, or protest. The faces were a study.

Emerson identifies as participants Alcott, Garrison, Parker, Very, "and many other persons of a mystical or sectarian or philanthropic renown." He adds, "there was no want of female speakers."[11] Hawthorne shared Emerson's bemused attitude toward these advocates of the "Newness," and although he had been willing to participate in the social experiment at Brook Farm, he refused to attach any absolute value to such efforts. In "Earth's Holocaust," he calls the "Titan of innovation" "angel or fiend, double in his nature, and capable of deeds befitting both characters." This Titan, the narrator records, at first shook "down only the old and rotten shapes of things" but "had now, as it appeared laid his terrible hand upon the main pillars, which supported the whole edifice of our moral and spiritual state"(10:400). Marriage and the family were probably the main two pillars Hawthorne had in mind at the time, for a number of the emerging experiments, such as Fourierism and the women's rights movement, saw both as oppressive and outdated.[12]

Three of the pieces Hawthorne wrote at the Manse, "The Hall of Fantasy," "The Celestial Railroad," and "Earth's Holocaust," directly satirize the host of new social, religious, and political experiments that gained traction following the financial panic and depression beginning in 1837. Hawthorne wrote "The Hall of Fantasy" (1843) during the winter of 1842, at about the same time that Bronson Alcott and his English friends Charles Lane, Lane's son William, and Henry Gardiner Wright arrived in Concord and began planning their ill-fated utopian community called Fruitlands. (Hawthorne and Sophia were expecting at the time.) Although Emerson took great interest in these folks and hosted meetings in his home where they could discuss their plans with others, including Hawthorne and George Ripley, he never considered joining their enterprise, which he regarded as foolish, as did Hawthorne. In "The Hall of Fantasy," Hawthorne describes visitors to an imaginary place where dreams abound. He includes among them a number of American authors, businessmen with wild commercial schemes, inventors of fantastic machines, noted reformers of the day, and religious fanatics. "Here, also," he writes, "was Mr. Alcott, with two or three friends, whom his spirit has assimilated to itself and drawn to his New England home, though an ocean rolled between." The narrator's guide lauds Alcott as "a bodiless idea," a prophet, whose "influence will have impregnated the atmosphere, and be imbibed by generations that know not the original apostle of the ideas, which they shall shape into earthly business." (Buford Jones has argued persuasively that the guide is based on Thoreau, who admired Alcott inordinately.)[13] The narrator is not so admiring: " 'At all events, he may count you as a disciple,' said I, smiling; 'and doubtless there is the spirit of a system in him, but not the body of it' " (10:638).

Alcott's partnership with Lane in founding Fruitlands made him seem radical in numerous ways, even though his political outlook matched Hawthorne's in its appreciation of civility and disdain for fanaticism. The Fruitlanders' plan was to replace the family by establishing a consociate community, in which members would live an ideal spiritual life. Wishing not to subjugate men or animals, they proposed not to wear leather, wool, or cotton; to avoid the use of oxen or horses for farming; to eat only native grains, fruits, and vegetables, preferably those that grew upward; and to drink only water. Lane also argued for celibacy, which Mrs. Alcott resisted. Eventually they purchased a farm some twenty miles west of Concord, at Harvard, Massachusetts, near the Shaker community there. But before they did, they considered purchasing the Manse and its grounds as their site. On May 21, 1843, Ellery Channing wrote to Margaret Fuller about the "Vegetable Eaters," who were seeking a location for their utopian experiment. He informed her that they had considered a number of places. "Now," writes Channing, "some notion of buying the Manse capers in their airy sconces, to be met by some other light dancing fancy, & the two locking arms presented disappear into gaseous fixtures."[14] One can imagine how annoying this must have been to the Hawthornes, who, though renters at the Manse, nevertheless considered it their sacred home. Their writing on a window of the house, on April 3, 1843, indicated a desire to declare the place theirs. "Man's accidents are God's purposes" is the initial inscription, inspired perhaps by Sophia's recent miscarriage, yet also expressing Hawthorne's deepest religious and political conviction.

In "The Hall of Fantasy," Hawthorne sketches Emerson's figure as well as Alcott's and accords the former slightly more respect: "Mr. Emerson was likewise there, leaning against one of the pillars, and surrounded by an admiring crowd of writers and readers of the Dial, and all manner of Transcendentalists and disciples of the Newness, most of whom betrayed the power of his intellect by its modifying influence upon their own" (10:637). Hawthorne's skepticism about Emerson becomes more pronounced in the second satire he wrote in the spring of 1843, "The Celestial Railroad." In this work, the skepticism appears not only in the commentary on the Giant Transcendentalist, who feeds visitors on "moonshine and mist," but also in his characterization of the spiritual guide for the modern pilgrims, Mr. Smooth-it-away, who blithely remarks that "Tophet has not even a metaphorical existence" (10:194) and that the Slough of Despond could "easily be converted into firm ground" (10:187). Although, according to almost everyone who met or knew him, Emerson exuded geniality and benevolence throughout his life, Hawthorne apparently saw him as an urbane devil of sorts. In "The Celestial Railroad," Mr. Smooth-it-away undergoes a transformation at the end of the tale as he waves to the narrator and other passengers who have boarded a steam ferryboat supposedly taking them to heaven: "And then did my excellent friend, Mr. Smooth-it-away, laugh outright; in the midst of which cachinnation, a smoke-wreath issued from his mouth and nostrils; while a twinkle of lurid flame darted out of either eye, proving indubitably that his heart was all of a red blaze" (10:206). As the pilgrims sail on to their destination (presumably hell), the narrator awakens from the dream in which this vision appeared.[15] Whenever Hawthorne contemplated the person of Emerson, he similarly tended to focus on his not being what he seemed. In a conversation Hawthorne had with Margaret Fuller in the summer of 1844 concerning the Emersons' marriage, he reportedly told her that the difficulty of her single state was "nothing compared with that of those who have entered into those relations but not made them real: who only *seem* husbands, wives, & friends."[16]

In his third satire of reform, "Earth's Holocaust" (1844), Hawthorne focuses on misguided attempts to purify the world by burning all sources of moral corruption, including titles, family crests, pedigrees, priestly robes, crosses, alcohol, tobacco, weapons, gunpowder, the guillotine, the gallows, money, laws, pamphlets, and books—even the Bible. But after these are thrown into a gigantic bonfire, the focus turns to what has been forgotten: "The Heart—the Heart—there was the little, yet boundless sphere, wherein existed the original wrong, of which the crime and misery of this outward world were merely types. Purify that inner sphere; and the many shapes of evil that haunt the outward, and which now seem almost our only realities, will turn to shadowy phantoms, and vanish of their own accord" (10:403–4). This assertion anticipates the notorious comment Hawthorne made later, in *The Life of Franklin Pierce*, about slavery vanishing; and it harks back to the moral of "Young Goodman Brown": the evils one sees are projections from within, or, as Emerson puts it in *Nature*, "What we are, that only can we see."[17]

Given Hawthorne's satirical treatments of Emerson and his followers, one would expect some resentment on Emerson's part, yet there was apparently none.[18] In fact, after reading "The Celestial Railroad," Emerson recommended it to Thoreau, telling him that it "has a serene strength which one cannot afford not to praise,—in this low life."[19] What was the reason behind this accord? Emerson as well as Thoreau shared Hawthorne's belief that self-reform should take precedence over any schemes to perfect society through external means, whether a utopian commune, a celestial railroad, or the immediate abolition of slavery.

Hawthorne and Amalgamation

Hawthorne shared his contemporaries' racialist belief that amalgamation between whites and people of color would degrade American civilization and lead to various social ills, such as "strange pursuits, ill-temper, passionateness, secret grudges" (13:266). Nevertheless, he evidenced a more nuanced attitude toward those of mixed blood than did the transcendentalists, with their celebration of muscular Anglo-Saxonism. Hawthorne's interest in the mysteries and dangers of amalgamation (later termed miscegenation) has been discerned in "Rappaccini's Daughter" (1844), *The Scarlet Letter* (1850), *The House of the Seven Gables* (1851), and *The Marble Faun* (1860).[20] What I would like to point out here is that despite his racism, Hawthorne consistently showed sensitivity to the injustice suffered by those who inherited Indian or African blood, and he may even have identified with those estranged by their racial genealogy. In his introduction to *The Scarlet Letter,* for example, when Hawthorne refers to the crimes of his Puritan ancestors and asserts that the "strong traits of their nature have intertwined themselves with mine," his use of the term "intertwined" resonates with racial meaning, for he conceived of miscegenation in botanical terms, as did many of his contemporaries. In "The Old Manse," he describes how grapevines can "unite two trees of alien race in an inextricable twine, marrying the hemlock and the maple against their will, and enriching them with a purple offspring, of which neither is the parent" (10:23). At the time he wrote this, he had recently completed "Rappaccini's Daughter," featuring the poisonous purple flower in the midst of Dr. Rappaccini's experimental garden.

As Anna Brickhouse has shown, the issue of miscegenation lies at the heart of "Rappaccini's Daughter," for Beatrice "is characterized as the product of a kind of botanical miscegenation. She is a 'sister' to those cross-bred flowers in her father's garden that 'would have shocked a delicate instinct by an appearance of artificiality indicating that there had been such commixture, and, as it were adultery, of various vegetable species, that the production was no longer of God's making, but the monstrous offspring of man's depraved fancy, glowing with only an evil mockery of beauty'" (10:110).[21] Although the "commixture" of plants in the garden is unnatural and monstrous, Beatrice's "unnatural" qualities—her "hybridity," if you will—are not essential but man-made. In her discussion of Hawthorne's "covert aversion to racial mixture" in the tale, Brickhouse has identified Beatrice as one of the "monsters" in it, yet I would point out that Beatrice figures more prominently as the innocent victim of the three men who control her fate: her father, Rappaccini, who tries to play God; his rival Baglioni, who engineers Beatrice's death; and Baglioni's protégé, Giovanni, the young man whose passion or lust overcomes his reason, precipitating Beatrice's suicide. Although Beatrice asks Giovanni to "forget that there ever crawled on earth such a monster as poor Beatrice" (10:125), the narrator identifies her as "the poor victim of man's ingenuity and of thwarted nature" (10:128). In other words, she may be poisonous, but it is clearly because she has been poisoned. By structuring his tale to focus on misogyny, Hawthorne thus avoids the tradition of blaming the female victim in matters of sexual abuse and racial degradation.[22]

Even Emerson, perhaps because of his Negrophobia, was guilty of following this tradition at times, as in his essay "American Civilization" (1862), in which he describes the South as a country "where the position of the white woman is injuriously affected by the outlawry of the black woman"[23]—as if the female slave were to blame for the adultery of the white master. In contrast, Hawthorne, writing at almost the same moment as Emerson, defends the black female's honor. In *Our Old Home* (1863), after criticizing the attitude of "Englishmen of station" who take advantage of "the lower orders of their countrywomen," he adds,

> The distinction of ranks is so marked, that the English cottage-damsel holds a position somewhat analogous to that of the negro girl in our Southern states. Hence comes inevitable detriment to the moral condition of those men themselves, who forget that the humblest woman has a right and a duty to hold herself in the same sanctity as the highest. The subject cannot well be discussed in these pages. (5:241)

In other words, any woman, whether white and poor or black and enslaved, deserves power over her own sexuality, and if a man ignores that right, he is degraded, not she.

That the mulatto population of the South was growing as a result of rape was the scandal of the antebellum South, as abolitionists repeatedly pointed out, and all antislavery fiction dealt with the sin of miscegenation. Nancy Bentley has explained, "Biracial characters were made the symbols of an inescapable history of Southern guilt. And the miscegenation crimes of the slavocracy were not sins of sexual violation only; the scandal of race 'confusion' was an odious crime in itself, and white writers often had their characters express this confusion as a painful lived experience."[24] In Hawthorne's last romances, racial mixing is treated as a blessing as well as a curse, granting his protagonists superior abilities. In *The Marble Faun*, we learn that "[T]here was something in Miriam's blood, in her mixed race, . . . which had given her freedom of thought and force of will" (4:403). In the unfinished "Septimius

Felton," the mixed blood of Septimius and his Aunt Keziah accounts for their violent tendencies and their marginal status in their community, which is clearly Concord, Massachusetts, yet it also elevates them. Before a long account of the mixed blood his protagonist has inherited, Hawthorne reminds himself, "The mixture of race a crime against nature, therefore pernicious" (13:256), which applies not only to Septimius personally but also to racial relations in New England and the country over the course of several centuries. Yet apparently for Hawthorne, as for Melville (both of whom were familiar with the tradition of the cursed gothic hero), pain and grief could lead to depth of thought and feeling. Thus, Septimius's mixed blood (like Beatrice's and Miriam's) accounts not only for his latent deadliness but also for his intellectual and emotional superiority. Hawthorne writes, "This mixture of bloods had given him a strange and exceptional nature; and he had brooded upon the legends that clung around his race, following his ancestry, not only to the English universities, but into the wild forest, and hell itself" (13:512). Hawthorne thus Americanizes and racializes his Byronic protagonist, and in a scene symbolizing the superiority Hawthorne attributes to him (and to himself?), Septimius stands high on the hillside behind his house and observes the homes of Rose Garfield, his beloved, and Robert Hagburn, his friend. (The site, of course, is based on the hill behind Hawthorne's Wayside house.) As Septimius looks literally and figuratively down on Rose and Hagburn from his elevated position, he wonders "if it would not have been better for Rose's happiness if her thoughts and virgin fancies had settled on that frank, cheerful, able, wholesome young man, instead of on himself, who met her on so few points; and, in relation to whom, there was perhaps a plant that had its root in the grave, that would entwine around his whole life, overshadowing it with dark, rich foliage, and fruit that he could only feast upon alone" (13:43–44). Obviously, both admiration and identification adhere in Hawthorne's characterization of his protagonist, who, though lacking the mundane traits of cheerfulness and wholesomeness, has access to knowledge that enriches and deepens his life. In the "Septimius Norton" version of the manuscript, Hawthorne reminds himself in a note, "Make his nobility of character grow upon the reader, in spite of all his defects" (13:528).

Like Septimius, the character of Aunt Keziah (later Nashoba) shows a mixture of defects and virtues. "Scalp him," she urges in one version of Hawthorne's plot, "whatever of witch and Indian squaw there was in her

. . . triumphing over what civilization & Christianity had been trying for a century and a half to do towards taming her" (13:241–42). This fierce aunt acts as Septimius's housekeeper, and they trace their mutual ancestry to a Puritan who married the daughter of an Indian Sagamore. Among later descendants are a half-breed woman executed "during the prevalence of the witchcraft delusion." The injustice of her fate and its link to false witnessing is explained by Hawthorne yet also attributed to this person herself: "the wild traits of her heathen ancestry overpowered those of the civilized race with which her blood was mingled; she was said, too, to have had a very dark skin, the straight black hair, and that Indian form of the face, and Indian eye, lineaments which are said to be harder to eradicate . . . than those of the negro race. Something, also, perhaps of the fierce and cruel Indian temper, and generally, a cast of character that made her disliked by her neighbors" (13:266). Hawthorne here anticipates the causal connection between difference and martyrdom, which modern scholars have found informing the witchcraft phenomenon.

Keziah is a combination of Hawthorne's own Aunt Hannah (a family servant during his youth) and Mrs. Peters, a free black servant of the Hawthornes when they lived in the Berkshires. Hawthorne's daughter Rose, who declared that Mrs. Peters "no doubt stood for a suggestion of Aunt Keziah," recalled her as "an invaluable tyrant, an unloaded weapon, a creature who seemed to say, 'Forget my qualities if you dare—there is one of them which is fatal!' As my parents possessed the capacity to pay respect where it could be earned, the qualities of Mrs. Peters were respected, and she found herself in a sort of heaven of courteous tolerance."[25] Hawthorne's pairing of Septimius and Keziah in a house based on his own may represent his attempt to come to terms with his own racial heritage. He may even have imagined some familial tie with blacks, such as Mrs. Peters, if only because, like Poe, his troubled lineage made him both identify with and feel disdain toward blacks, as cursed outsiders.

In "Septimius," he combines Puritan witch-hunter and Indian witch within the same house or family line, yet "[s]omething in the mixture of bloods, first of Indian and civilized blood, then of this with the hostile blood of the Puritans, had not amalgamated well" (13:266). Secluded in his study, Septimius, student of theology, after killing a British officer, contends not only with the enemy of all mankind, Death (seeking the elixir of life by deciphering a torn manuscript the dying soldier gave him), but also with his own racial heritage and, by extension, the dark and bloody presence within the emergent nation itself. When a red flower grows from the grave of the British redcoat, Septimius plucks it to make a trial effort at creating the elixir of immortality, but when he gives the elixir to Aunt Keziah, who has become critically ill, the drink kills, rather than saves, her. In this sense, her fate is like Beatrice's at the hands of Giovanni and company. Hawthorne thus thematizes the poisonous effects of good intentions, especially the harm inflicted on racial Others by those (e.g., Puritan divines, British redcoats, and New England scholars) deluded into thinking they are the Others' more civilized saviors. In one of his plans for the romance, Hawthorne tells himself, "Perhaps the moral will turn out to be, the folly of man in thinking that he can ever be of any importance to the welfare of the world; or that any settled plan of his, to be carried on through a length of time, could be successful" (13:529). As this study has pointed out previously, such a humbling thought lies at the heart of Hawthorne's politics.

In the summer of 1863, as the Civil War raged and "Septimius Felton" lay unfinished, Hawthorne accused his sister-in-law Elizabeth Peabody of being "disturbed by the potent elixir of political opinion" that emanated from "the abolition papers." Thus, in Hawthorne's imagination, the abolitionists, like other self-righteous reformers, offered cures more deadly than the ills they sought to overcome, with amalgamation perhaps being one of these. He also blamed the abolitionists, as some later historians would, for precipitating the Civil War, which, he told Peabody, "will only effect by a horrible convulsion the self-same end that might and would have been brought about by a gradual and peaceful change" (18:590). Whether the moral absolutism of the abolitionists made the war inevitable remains a matter of long-standing debate; but it is certain that for many Northerners, the abolitionists' activities eventually brought slavery to the center of national attention.

Concord and Antislavery

In the 1830s, as Sandra Harbert Petrulionis has shown, Concord "was essentially a provincial town with large anti-abolitionist, if not pro-slavery, views, and Garrison and his band of rabble-rousers enjoyed little support."[26] The local antislavery movement, inspired by a visit of the Grimké sisters, involved the activities of a small group of women, including Cynthia, Sophia, and Helen Thoreau (Henry's mother and sisters) and Lidian Emerson. Abba Alcott, when her family lived in Concord during 1840–48 and from 1857 to her death in 1877, was also very active in the female antislavery society.[27] As for Emerson's participation, Phyllis Cole has shown that two women—his wife, Lidian, and his aunt Mary Moody Emerson—exerted pressure on him to commit to the antislavery cause, but he resisted.[28] His racism made him discount the pain and suffering of the slave, which the abolitionists emphasized. A journal entry of 1837 makes this clear: "Lidian grieves aloud about the wretched negro in the horrors of the middle passage; and they are bad enough. But to such as she, these crucifixions do not come. They come to the obtuse & barbarous to whom they are not horrid but only a little worse than the old sufferings. They exchange a cannibal war for a stinking hold. They have gratifications which would be none to Lidian."[29] In other words, Emerson argued that relatively speaking, the slaves did not suffer as Lidian would but, rather, only a little more than they did in Africa, even being somehow grateful for the change. (After Emerson, preparing for his 1844 antislavery address, read Thomas Clarkson's well-informed and horrific *History of the Abolition of the African Slave-Trade* [1808], he could no longer maintain this absurd opinion.)[30]

In the early 1840s, however, Emerson, like Thoreau, worried most about individual spiritual emancipation and thought slaves, not others, were responsible for their plight.

> Nobody can oppress me but myself. Once more, the degradation of that black race, though now lost in the starless spaces of the past, did not come without sin. The condition is inevitable to the men they are, & nobody can redeem them but themselves. An infusion from God of new thought & grace can retrieve their loss, but nothing less. The exertions of the abolitionist are nugatory except for themselves.[31]

When Emerson first participated in antislavery activities, he did so to please the women in his family; moreover, he apparently felt degraded by the effort. After giving the 1844 "Address on the Emancipation of the Negroes in the British West Indies" at the request of the Concord Female Antislavery Society, he wrote to Thomas Carlyle, "though I sometimes accept a popular call, & preach on Temperance or the Abolition of slavery, as lately on the First of

August, I am sure to feel before I have done with it, what an intrusion it is into another sphere & so much loss of virtue in my own." As for the abolitionists, in his journal, he calls them "an altogether odious set of people, whom one would be sure to shun as the worst of bores & canters."[32]

Emerson's new friend Margaret Fuller likewise shunned the abolitionists and their cause. She refused to allow the topic of slavery to be introduced into her "conversations" during 1839–44, and she freely admitted that she found the abolitionists too fanatical in their activities. In a letter to Maria Weston Chapman, declining a request to support the annual Anti-Slavery Fair and to devote a conversation to abolition, Fuller bluntly declared, "The Abolition cause commands my respect, as do all efforts to relieve and raise suffering human nature. The faults of the party are such as, it seems to me, must always be incident to the partizan spirit." Referring to the rights of women that the abolitionists had begun to discuss, Fuller added, "The late movements in your party have interested me more than those which had for their object the enfranchisement of the African only. Yet I presume I should still feel sympathy with your aims only not with your measures."[33] It was not until Fuller went to work on the *Tribune* in 1845 that she started to align herself with the antislavery cause. From Italy in 1847, she wrote in one dispatch, "How it pleases me here to think of the Abolitionists! I could never endure to be with them at home, they were so tedious, often so narrow, always so rabid and exaggerated in their tone."[34]

During March 1844, as Hawthorne sought ways to make ends meet, Emerson and Thoreau addressed an audience made up of members of various reform societies at Amory Hall in Boston, where they positioned themselves as skeptical observers of the beliefs and practices of their audience and other speakers in the series, including Garrison, Charles Lane, and Wendell Phillips. As Linck Johnson has pointed out, Emerson remained "a distant observer rather than an active sympathizer in the reforms he surveyed at Amory Hall," while Thoreau, "with an impressive lack of tact, . . . challenged the motivation and efficacy of the Amory Hall lectures themselves."[35] Like Hawthorne in "Earth's Holocaust," Emerson satirized the various theories for saving the world as proposed by proponents of health and moral reform, especially the associationists in general and Alcott and Lane in particular (whose Fruitlands experiment failed after six months). "The criticism and attack on institutions which we have witnessed," he declared, "has made one thing plain, that society gains nothing whilst a man, not himself renovated, attempts to renovate things around him: he has become tediously good in some particular, but negligent or narrow in the rest; and hypocrisy and vanity are often the disgusting result."[36] He claimed that he and his audience (composed of reformers) wished "to be shamed out of our nonsense of all kinds, and made men of, instead of ghosts and phantoms. We are weary of gliding ghostlike through the world, which is itself so slight and unreal. We crave a sense of reality, though it comes in strokes of pain."[37] As an alternative means of achieving this sense of reality, Emerson advocated self-reliance and inward change: "Each man, if he attempts to join himself to others, is on all sides cramped and diminished of his proportion; and the stricter the union, the smaller and the more pitiful he is. . . . The union must be ideal in actual individualism."[38] In other words, Emerson argued that power and freedom are achieved from within. He concluded with questions suggesting how self-reform should occur: "Shall not the heart which has received so much, trust the Power by which it lives? May it not quit other leadings, and listen to the Soul that has guided it so gently, and taught it so much, secure that the future will be worthy of the past?"[39] For Emerson, self-reliance and God-reliance were one.

Like Emerson, Thoreau, in his Amory Hall lecture, titled "Conservatives and Reformers," rejected the various schemes of reformers and argued that true reform begins with the individual, who then serves as an example to others. In an especially insulting part of the lecture, he implied that the social ills the reformer sees are projections from within, an idea Thoreau returned to in the opening chapter of *Walden:* "I believe that what so saddens the reformer is not his sympathy with his fellows in distress, but, though he be the holiest son of God, is his private ail. Let this be righted, let the spring come to him, the morning rise over his couch, and he will forsake his generous companions without apology."[40] Apparently, his discussions with William Henry Channing had led him to this conclusion. Thoreau, like Emerson, sought by such rhetoric to justify his detachment from reformers, whom he viewed with disdain.

Even Bronson Alcott, despite his rarified idealism, joined with Emerson and Thoreau in viewing Garrison's radicalism as unseemly. In a journal entry of February 14, 1850, Alcott recorded a visit from Emerson: "E. said that he could never speak handsomely in presence of persons of G's class. And I, too, plead to the like infirmity . . . . The spirit and grain of this class is essentially discourteous, and there is fight and desperation in the blood, manners, and speech of the creature."[41] Alcott would harbor fugitive slaves in his home, serve on the Boston Vigilance Committee, participate in the attempt to prevent the rendition of the fugitive slave Anthony Burns, and befriend John Brown and his family; nevertheless, he could never go along with the political passion of Garrison or Parker. When his fellow abolitionists attacked Webster for his infamous speech of March 7, 1850, in favor of the Compromise, Alcott described himself in terms that could easily apply to Hawthorne: "I am incapable of becoming a partisan; and while I accept and am proud of the declarations of my friend who pleads the cause of civility and justice with an eloquence so fervent and convincing, I yet must cry for the awards of justice and civility to Webster, Clay, Calhoun, and the conservatives of slavery even."[42] Alcott's wife, Abba, and his daughter Louisa were the bolder abolitionists in the family. Louisa's short stories of the 1860s even dealt sympathetically with interracial romance and armed slave rebellion.[43] Her father, however, remained genteel in his thought and action.

Detachment and serenity seemed necessary for the kind of intellectual and spiritual growth that the men at both ends of Concord valued during the early 1840s. Emerson posed this rhetorical question in his journal for 1840: "Does he not do more to abolish Slavery who works all day steadily in his garden, than he who goes to the abolition meeting & makes a speech? . . . He who does his own work frees a slave. He who does not his own work, is a slave-holder."[44] In *Walden*, Thoreau made this case even more defiantly: "I sometimes wonder that we can be so frivolous, I may almost say, as to attend to the gross but somewhat foreign form of servitude called Negro Slavery, there are so many keen and subtle masters that enslave both north and south. . . . What a man thinks of himself, that is it which determines, or rather indicates, his fate. Self-emancipation even in the West Indian provinces of the fancy and imagination,—what Wilberforce is there to bring that about?"[45] In the 1845 journal passage from which the preceding quote was taken, Thoreau added, "One emancipated heart and intellect—It would knock off the fetters from a million slaves."[46]

Writing for the *Tribune* in the summer of 1845, Fuller expressed almost the same thought. After lamenting the existence of slavery in the United States, she asserted that "in private lives, more than in public measures must the salvation of the country lie." At present, she claimed, the country lacked "men ripened and confirmed for better things. They leaned too carelessly on one another; they had not deepened and purified the private lives from which the public must spring."[47] Obviously, all of these friends were in agreement with Hawthorne's assertion at the end of "Earth's Holocaust" that one's focus should be on "The Heart. The Heart." The argument was that if one purified the heart, the shapes of evil that seemed realities would vanish.[48]

Hawthorne's Ideal Artist

Hawthorne's fabled shyness and reserve informed his aversion to group endeavors, but he also remained enough of an idealist after his Brook Farm experience to believe he could benefit his fellow man through his detached thought and creative work.[49] In "The Procession of Life" (1843), Hawthorne, though defiantly unsentimental, expresses respect for all of those people whose "pervading principle is Love" (10:215). He includes in this category philanthropists, reformers (including abolitionists), educators, missionaries, and nurses, all "whose impulses have guided them to benevolent actions," and he adds to his list others

> to whom Providence has assigned a different tendency and different powers. Men who have spent their lives in generous and holy contemplation for the human race; those who, by a certain heavenliness of spirit, have purified the atmosphere around them, and thus supplied a medium in which good and high things may be projected and performed,—give to these a lofty place among the benefactors of mankind, although no deed, such as the world calls deeds, may be recorded of them. (10:216–17)

For Hawthorne, someone like John Eliot would be such a visionary benefactor, as would the artist of Kouroo whom Thoreau describes in *Walden*. They resolutely pursued perfection, despite worldly distractions, and by doing so, they altered the world. Even though Hawthorne chose to become a husband and a father, this solitary role long appealed to him. The sanctity he attached to the towered studies in which he wrote attests to this. If Hawthorne had remained single and solvent, it was a role he would probably have sought for himself.

In "Old News," Hawthorne summarizes his sense of the individual's relation to time and eternity: "In this world, we are the things of a moment, and are made to pursue momentary things, with here and there a thought that stretches mistily toward eternity, and perhaps may endure as long." He cautions against disregard of the world, however, by adding, "All philosophy, that would abstract mankind from the present, is no more than words" (11:133). For Hawthorne, someone like Alcott, whom he called "this airy Sage of Apple Slump!" (23:453), embodied such unworldliness. Hawthorne's ideal intellectual, by contrast, engages the world as an observer and then transforms reality into art that enhances the world. His story "The Artist of the Beautiful" presents Owen Warland struggling with such a task. This young man withdraws from others in order to study nature and then, drawing on his study, creates an exquisite work of art—in this case, a mechanical butterfly, destroyed by the Danforths' child. More important than the artifact, the narrator claims, is the idea that impelled it: "When the artist rose high enough to achieve the Beautiful, the symbol by which he made it perceptible to mortal senses became of little value in his eyes, while his spirit possessed itself in the enjoyment of the Reality" (10:475). Owen has several flaws, of course, not least of which is his physical separation from his fellow man, which is often the burden borne by the "scholar-idealist," whom Randall Stewart has called "the most important single type of character in Hawthorne's works."[50]

Perhaps the one scholar-idealist in Hawthorne's writings least burdened by apparent flaws and internal conflicts appears in his nonfictional account of Emanuel Leutze, whom he visited in 1862, when Leutze was in the initial stages of painting his now-famous gigantic mural *Westward the Course of Empire Takes Its Way* (see figure 5). Hawthorne came upon the artist hidden behind a wooden enclosure in the Capitol Building in Washington, D.C., where he was creating his visual paean to American expansionism as the Civil War raged outside. Hawthorne reports,

> It was an absolute comfort, indeed, to find Leutze so quietly busy at this great national work, which is destined to glow for centuries on the walls of the Capitol, if that edifice shall stand, or must share its fate, if treason shall succeed in subverting it with the Union which it represents. It was delightful to see him so calmly elaborating his design; while other men doubted and feared, or hoped treacherously, and whispered to one another that the nation will exist only a little longer. . . . But the artist keeps

right on, firm of heart and hand, drawing his outlines with an unwaver-
ing pencil, beautifying and idealizing our rude, material life, and thus
manifesting that we have an indefeasible claim to a more enduring national existence. (23:409–10)

Such a passage allows a glimpse of Hawthorne's sense of himself as an artist
and patriot—someone physically detached from his country, like Leutze behind his scaffolding, but intellectually and emotionally engaged in modeling
its future, knowing full well its precious fragility and his own limitations.[51]

Although it is possible to identify Thoreau and Emerson as committed
abolitionists due to their activities during Hawthorne's years at the Manse,
such linkage, which has become prevalent in recent scholarship, misrepre-
sents their perspective on current events.[52] They were certainly not irresponsible dreamers, as Arthur Schlesinger Jr. and other historians have portrayed
them, but they were also not yet political activists. Organized reform still repelled them. As Thoreau humorously put it in *Walden*, "If I knew for a cer-
tainty that a man was coming to my house with the conscious design of doing me good, I should run for my life."[53] His *Dial* essay "Herald of Freedom"
(1844) has been cited as evidence of his sympathy toward antislavery activism, but though it extends praise to Nathaniel Rogers, editor of an antislavery newspaper, this praise is for his unique prose style, which, Thoreau
writes, advertises "that, unlike most reformers, his feet are still where they
should be, on the turf, and that he looks out from a serener natural life into
the turbid arena of politics."[54] Similarly, Thoreau's praise of the abolitionist
leader Wendell Phillips in a letter to the editor of the *Liberator* on March 12,
1845, focuses not on Phillips's reform activities but, rather, on his "freedom
and steady wisdom, so rare in the reformer, with which he declared that he
was not born to abolish slavery, but to do right."[55] In other words, Thoreau
identified Rogers and Phillips with himself and his own individualism and extended little sympathy to "most reformers."

Thoreau and other transcendentalists began to alter their political behavior near the end of Hawthorne's early association with them, but not a great
deal. In the summer of 1845, Thoreau went to jail in protest over the annexation of Texas and extension of slavery, and Fuller used the columns of the
Tribune to protest the same issues, yet both stayed true to their commitment
to individualism, as opposed to collective action. "In private lives, more than
in public measures must the salvation of the country lie," Fuller declared in

Emanuel Gottlieb Leutze, *Westward the Course of Empire Takes Its Way* (mural study, U.S. Capitol), 1861. (Smithsonian American Art Museum, bequest of Sara Carr Upton.)

her "Fourth of July" column for 1845.[56] Similarly, Emerson, even though he delivered his famous 1844 antislavery address, did not join the abolitionist movement at that time. As Albert von Frank has accurately observed, the address, "while it clearly embraced abolitionist aims, need not (indeed should not) be read as an endorsement of collective strategies or tactics."[57] Ironically, as far as collective action with regard to slavery is concerned, Hawthorne's editorial work on Horatio Bridge's *Journal of an African Cruiser* (1845) put forth some of the most informed and progressive thoughts to be found in the writings of the Concord authors.

Emerson, Hawthorne, and British Philanthropy

When Emerson agreed to give his antislavery address, along with Samuel Joseph May, Frederick Douglass, and others, before a meeting arranged by the Women's Anti-Slavery Society, all the local churches refused to host the event, so Hawthorne offered the avenue of the Manse. Because it rained on the morning of the event, it was held in the hall of the courthouse instead, and one suspects that Hawthorne attended, if only as a courtesy.[58] If he was there, he probably agreed with the substance, if not the tone, of what he heard, especially from Emerson. The two authors shared a political fatalism; yet Emerson's was always optimistic, Hawthorne's skeptical. Emerson's address pays notice to the suffering of slaves, but it shies away from the moral outrage and calls to action of the abolitionists. It celebrates the abolitionist cause, especially in England, but uses Emerson's own ideals of individualism, self-reliance, and racial determinism to do so. At the beginning of the anti-slavery address, he introduces a folktale that seems to blame the victim for his plight.

> Very sad was the negro tradition, that the Great Spirit, in the beginning, offered the black man, whom he loved better than the buckra or white, his choice of two boxes, a big and a little one. The black man was greedy, and chose the largest. "The buckra box was full up with pen, paper, and whip, and the negro box with hoe and bill; and hoe and bill for negro to this day."[59]

The hope for change Emerson holds out to the Negro relies not on the aid of others. "I say to you," he declares in a key sentence, "you must save yourself, black or white, man or woman; other help is none."[60] (Although this may sound like a call to revolution, it refers to self-reform and moral development.) He laments the "want of men" among American congressmen and asserts that "it now appears, that the negro race is, more than any other, susceptible of rapid civilization."[61]

Emerson's argument contains a sizable stipulation, often overlooked, that runs counter to abolitionist discourse. His method is to meld this discourse with his own theory of racial evolution based on the power of individualism and to go no farther than noticing signs and omens of the black man's moral progress. Notice, for example, how heavily qualified his central point is: "If the black man is feeble, and not important to the existing races not on a parity with the best race, the black man must serve, and be exterminated. But if the black man carries in his bosom an indispensable element of a new and coming civilization, for the sake of that element, no wrong, nor strength, nor circumstance, can hurt him: he will survive and play his part."[62] Although Emerson praises Toussaint for showing the courage and character a black man can display, he obviously viewed Toussaint as exceptional.[63] Emerson's point here, as elsewhere, is that individuals, not groups, alter history. He would repeat this argument in England in 1848 as he tried to come to terms with the apparent success of the socialist movement.[64]

Thus Emerson's stipulation was a crucial qualification of his with regard to the future of the Negro race. In his "Ode, to William H. Channing" (1846), Emerson reveals that his political fatalism even exceeded Hawthorne's at times, for he includes the following lines in the poem: "The over-god / Who marries Right to Might, / Who peoples, unpeoples,—/ He who exterminates / Races by stronger races, / Black by white faces,—/ Knows to bring honey / Out of the lion."[65] The end of his antislavery address likewise depends on the combination of racial destiny and free will, and it features the bright future of the white race: "There is a blessed necessity by which the interest of men is always driving them to the right; and, again, making all crime mean and ugly. The genius of the Saxon race, friendly to liberty; the enterprise, the very muscular vigor of this nation, are inconsistent with slavery."[66]

Len Gougeon has persistently argued, most notably in *Virtue's Hero* (1990), that the 1844 address marked Emerson's commitment to abolitionism, yet Gougeon relies for evidence on the response the address received among abolitionists, who assumed Emerson had joined their ranks. In the 1850s, he would; but the 1844 address trumps their methods as much as it supports their goals. So why did the abolitionists interpret it so favorably? One reason is that Emerson's rhetoric often rises to a level of generality that allows his audience to arrive at conclusions that Emerson himself refrained from making. Auditors of Emerson's lectures tended to hear what they wanted and expected to hear.[67] As von Frank points out, the abolitionists were eager to have Emerson for an ally, yet there is a question of whether they "felt any pressing need to understand his views precisely."[68] Also, Emerson early acquired the habit of refusing to explain himself or correct a false impression.[69] When he provoked outrage at Harvard with his address to the Divinity School, for example, he refused to respond publicly to the charges of irreligion made against him. He let such friends as George Ripley, James Freeman Clarke, and Theodore Parker debate for him, asserting that he was unable to do well in such a contest. In many ways, Emerson imagined himself not unlike the

L. Grozelier, *Heralds of Freedom. Truth, Love, Justice*, 1857. Lithograph. *Clockwise from top:* Emerson, Wendell Phillips, J. R. Giddings, Theodore Parker, Gerrit Smith, Samuel J. May, and Garrison. (Courtesy of the Massachusetts Historical Society.)

angel Uriel in his poem of that title, who boldly disturbs the "stern old war-gods" of heaven but then modestly withdraws "into his cloud," leaving his "fire-seed" behind to triumph over the mistaken "celestial kind."[70] As Leonard Neufeldt has pointed out, "Pulling back is personally and strategically imperative for heaven's most beautiful angel."[71] Fittingly, Emerson's angelic image would be featured in an abolitionist poster of 1857 (see figure 6), where he appears as the topmost "herald of freedom."

Hawthorne, I believe, was seldom deceived by Emerson and, in fact, identified with him at times, even as he opposed him. *Journal of an African Cruiser* (1845), the editing project Hawthorne turned to five months after Emerson delivered his antislavery address, reveals their shared interest in the fate of free blacks, disdain for politicians, and belief in divine providence. Hawthorne, I think, responded to the heightened praise for British reformers that Emerson doled out, by adding ironic commentary to the factual information in Bridge's manuscript journal. In his address, Emerson reviews the efforts of the British abolitionists who effected the 1834 emancipation in the West Indies and concludes, "I think the whole transaction reflects infinite honor on the people and parliament of England."[72] *Journal of an African Cruiser,* in contrast, asserts that "however benevolent may be the motives that influence the action of Great Britain, in reference to the slave-trade, there is the grossest cruelty and injustice in carrying out her views" (*JAC,* 51). Bridge reports that the British cruisers, after intercepting slave ships and "rescuing" captive natives, take them not back to Africa and their homes but, rather, to the West Indies, where they work for British planters as free labor or perish by starvation. Although the British cruisers could anchor at the mouths of the rivers and prevent the slavers from putting to sea, they instead wait to capture the vessels away from the coast, for then "the captors receive £5 per head for the slaves on board, and the government has more 'emigrants' for its West Indian possessions" (*JAC,* 52). As for the fate of these "emigrants," the *Journal* declares that their conditions in Trinidad or Jamaica are more wretched than those of the slaves in Cuba. The account concludes with the observation, "English philanthropy cuts a very suspicious figure, when, not content with neglecting the welfare of those whom she undertakes to protect, she thus attempts to ma[k]e them subservient to national aggrandizement" (*JAC,* 51).[73] The facts are Bridge's, but the irony is surely Hawthorne's.

The Bridge-Hawthorne *Journal* shares with Emerson's 1844 antislavery address not only an interest in British philanthropy but also observations on the Negro race and the complicity of New England in the perpetuation of slavery. Because Hawthorne identifies himself as merely the "editor" of Bridge's *Journal,* the book is not included in *The Centenary Edition of the Works of Nathaniel Hawthorne,* and it has received little notice from Hawthorne critics and biographers, who have tended to dismiss it as a journalistic task, undertaken to help a friend and make some money. Hawthorne's contributions to the book, however, are not unsubstantial, and as a comparison of the published text with a portion of Bridge's manuscript can show, the editing displays key features of Hawthorne's political vision, including his circumspection and pacifism, as well as his skepticism.

In the spring of 1843, Hawthorne learned that Bridge had been selected as purser on the USS *Saratoga,* the flagship of Commodore Matthew C. Perry's African Squadron charged with patrolling the west coast of Africa to suppress the slave trade. He urged Bridge to write letters for magazine publication that could later be collected in a book. He also offered to help him with the writing, telling him in a letter of May 3, 1843, "After you have had due time for observation, you may then give grave reflections on national character, custom, morals, religion, the influence of peculiar modes of government, &c; and I will take care to put these in their proper places, and make them come in with due effect" (15:687). Knowing that interest in the slave trade was high, Hawthorne advised Bridge, "You must have as much as possible to say about the African trade, its nature, the mode of carrying it on, the character of the persons carrying it on &c.—in order to fit the book for practical men" (16:26). Bridge followed this advice, and Hawthorne's "editing" added his own political slant to the material. On April 7, 1845, Hawthorne wrote to Evert Duyckinck, "My own share of it is so amalgamated with the substance of the work, that I cannot very well define what it is; but all the solid and material merit is due to my naval friend" (16:86).

In one of the few substantive studies of the *Journal,* Patrick Brancaccio has speculated that Hawthorne used his editorial influence to give qualified support to colonization in order to advance his political career. "This position [colonization]," Brancaccio writes, "helped to reassure influential Democrats about the former Brook Farmer and may have helped clear the way to his appointment as Surveyor of the Custom House at Salem in

1846."[74] Wineapple has similarly regarded the work as a form of political opportunism, declaring that "Bridge's memoir could bolster Hawthorne's credentials, particularly since Bridge had much to say on the slavery problem. In fact, his support of colonization as the solution to the slavery question might actually placate antislavery Democrats and pacify southern ones at the same time."[75] Actually, however, the colonization movement had become discredited in the North and South by the 1840s, and while Hawthorne was certainly not above political scheming and maneuvering in order to secure a government office, the only political benefit he could expect to derive from the project was to solidify his friendship with Bridge, who had influential political connections. Moreover, the positive treatment of the colonization effort within the *Journal* pointedly critiques the use made of the movement by Southerners, to remove troublesome free slaves.

The American Colonization Society (ACS) had been established in late 1816 by Robert Finley, a Presbyterian minister, with the goal of deporting free blacks to Africa, based on the belief that American racial prejudices were natural and unalterable.[76] The first and largest colony that the ACS founded was Liberia, where Bridge went ashore numerous times on his eighteen-month voyage. Liberia was comprised of a strip of land 130 miles long and 40 miles wide, bounded on the east by the Atlantic. It was acquired on December 15, 1821, from the reluctant King Peter of Africa, by agents for the ACS who pointed a loaded pistol at his head and threatened to kill him.[77]

Early settlers in Liberia had to cope with disease, hunger, starvation, and attacks by the African natives, problems that persisted even as the colony grew. In 1832, the ACS board of managers reported that since 1820, twenty-two expeditions had gone to Liberia; in the first eighteen, just under 1,500 persons had been transported, and 230 of these died, mostly from malaria.[78] *The African Repository,* the official organ of the ACS, persistently used racist arguments to encourage deportation of free blacks, even as it admitted that the colony aided the slave trade: "Rum, gunpowder, and spear-pointed knives, have been among the regular exports from this country to the colony of Liberia. These are sold to the natives, and especially to the slave traders, being the indispensable articles of their traffic, and the causes of the wars that furnish captives to be sold to them as slaves. The slave trade, instead of being repressed (as had been pretended) had been stimulated and encouraged."[79] Bridge, however, defended the colony from this charge, calling it "not true," and pointed the finger at the British colonies: "The only places where the traffic is carried on, north of the line, are in the neighborhood of the most powerful English settlements on the whole coast; while even British authority does not pretend that the vicinity of the American colonies is polluted by it" (*JAC*, 52).

The colonization movement gained popularity during the turbulent 1820s and early 1830s and had two kinds of supporters: first were the racists who wanted to rid the United States of its so-called degraded and dangerous Negro population; second were the humanitarians who wanted to provide blacks with the opportunity to achieve political and social equality. By the mid-1830s, however, colonization was "reduced to irrelevance even among leading proponents of philanthropy and reform," as George M. Frederickson has pointed out.[80] Northern abolitionists, influenced by the hostile reaction to colonization by free blacks in Boston and Baltimore, attacked the movement as racist and impractical, while Southern slave owners attacked it as a long-term threat to slavery. Garrison and Douglass were especially strident in their accusations that the ACS was trying to banish blacks from white society. During the 1850s, colonization enjoyed a brief resurgence, gaining the support of the Republican Party and its presidential candidate, Abraham Lincoln.[81] But when Bridge's *Journal* appeared in 1845, the ACS was struggling to maintain its minimal viability.

Bridge and Hawthorne had to be acutely aware of the tensions between the colonizationists and abolitionists, and the *Journal* strives to be balanced in its observations and conclusions. The preface identifies Bridge as "a northern man, but not unacquainted with the slave institutions of our own and other countries—neither an Abolitionist nor a Colonizationist—without prejudice, as without prepossession" (*JAC*, v–vi). The preface also claims that the value of Bridge's observations on the condition and prospects of Liberia derives from "his freedom from partisan bias, and his consequent ability to perceive a certain degree of truth, and inclination to express it frankly" (*JAC*, ix). The *Journal* has been characterized as racist by several scholars,[82] yet its estimation of the abilities of free blacks is actually higher than that found in Emerson's antislavery address and may be one of the least racist of any work approved by the ACS. Whereas the primary trait Emerson praises among liberated slaves is docility, the narrator of the *Journal* details the intelligence, sagacity, and diplomacy of African American colonial leaders.

In Bridge's account of his visit with Governor Roberts, Hawthorne, as editor, adds a compliment to the ACS for rescuing Roberts from slavery: "the friends of Colonization can hardly adduce a stronger argument in favor of their enterprise, than that it has redeemed such a man as Governor Roberts from servitude, and afforded him the opportunity (which was all he needed) of displaying his high natural gifts, and applying them to the benefit of his race" (JAC, 49).[83] For the most part, however, the Journal does not have much positive to say about the freed slaves in the colony. For example, Bridge writes, "Accustomed to be ruled and taken care of by others, they are no better than mere children, as respects the conduct and economy of life" (JAC, 34). Brancaccio sees in such a statement a "racist belief in infantilism of slaves," and Wineapple has said that Bridge's Journal thus reflects the sentiment that "Africans, and especially African-Americans, are childlike creatures." Yet the point Bridge was making, it seems to me, was that while some Negroes, those who had been slaves, were like children, those Negro colonists never enslaved were not. In other words, Bridge indicated that the character flaws of the former resulted from nurture, not nature—an observation that strikes at the heart of all the racialist science then shaping American racism. Here's what the Journal says, which includes criticism of the ACS:

I perceive, in Colonization reports, that the owners of slaves frequently offer to liberate them, on condition of their being sent to Liberia; and that the Society has contracted debts, and embarrassed itself in various ways, rather than let such offers pass. In my opinion, many of the slaves, thus offered, are of little value to the donors, and of even less to the cause of Colonization. Better to discriminate carefully in the selection of emigrants, than to send out such numbers of the least eligible class, to become burdens upon the industrious and intelligent, who might otherwise enjoy comfort and independence. Many a colonist, at this moment, sacrifices his interest to his humanity, and feels himself kept back in life by the urgent claims of compassion. . . . Fifty young or middle-aged men, who had been accustomed to self-guidance in America, would do more to promote the prosperity of the colony, than five hundred such emigrants as are usually sent out. (JAC, 34)

The praise accorded John Roberts and John Russwurm in the Journal are of a piece with this discriminating evaluation. After watching Governor

Roberts skillfully acquire territory for the colonists by means of a "palaver," or meeting, with hostile native neighbors, Bridge praises his "sagacity and diplomatic shrewdness" (*JAC*, 63). Elsewhere, Bridge declares, "The Governor is certainly no ordinary person. . . . His deportment is dignified, quiet, and sensible. He has been tried in war as well as in peace, has seen a good share of fighting, and has invariably been cool, brave, and successful" (*JAC*, 5). Similarly, he calls the mulatto colonial agent John Russwurm "a man of distinguished ability and of collegiate education" (*JAC*, 37).

Bridge's personal relation with Russwurm surely affected his positive estimate of the American colonies in Africa. Russwurm was one of the first blacks to graduate from college in the United States, and Bridge, in his *Personal Recollections of Nathaniel Hawthorne* (1893), recalls that Russwurm "lived at a carpenter's house, just beyond the village limits," at Bowdoin, "where Hawthorne and the writer called upon him several times, but his sensitiveness on account of his color prevented him from returning the calls."[84] After graduating from college, Russwurm, the son of a prosperous merchant and his Jamaican "housekeeper," coedited the *Freeman's Journal,* in which he protested against the ACS and extolled the virtues of Haiti. In 1829, however, frustrated at various forms of racial injustice, he had a change of heart and decided to emigrate to Liberia under the auspices of the ACS, after announcing to his readers, "We consider it a mere waste of words to talk of ever enjoying citizenship in this country: it is utterly impossible in the nature of things."[85] In 1830, Russwurm founded the first newspaper in Liberia, the *Liberia Herald,* which Hawthorne drew on as he edited Bridge's *Journal.* Russwurm also became the first governor of the Maryland colony in Africa, in 1836. As a political leader, he advocated that the various settlements confederate to enhance their means of self-protection. In 1839, this plan became a reality.[86]

As Hawthorne read Bridge's manuscript materials telling of what he had seen and done during his time in the African Squadron, he added his own touches. As Brancaccio has observed, "the thematic organization and ironic and morally ambiguous point of view clearly betray Hawthorne's hand."[87] In a letter of March 2, 1845, to Evert Duyckinck, Hawthorne explained, "As he gave me pretty large license, I have re-modeled the style, where it seemed necessary, and have developed his ideas, where he failed to do it himself, and have put on occasional patches of sentimental embroidery—at the same time avoiding to tamper with his facts, or to change the tenor of his observations upon them; so that the work has not become otherwise than authentic, in my hands" (16:82). A portion of Bridge's original materials exists in manuscript at the New York Public Library and allows insight into the nature of Hawthorne's "remodeling" and "developing."

In the original journal, Bridge's entries show him to be rather blunt, crude, and callous. Even in the edited *Journal,* not all of these traits disappear. For example, in discussing arranged marriages, Bridge blithely mentions that when a husband is displeased with his new bride, "she is tied, starved, and severely beaten; a mode of conjugal discipline which generally produces the desired effect" (*JAC,* 18). In anticipation of the execution of a slave who tried to run away from his native captors, Bridge writes: "the poor wretch will stand little chance for mercy at the hands of these barbarians, frenzied with rum, and naturally blood-thirsty. We are all anxious to go on shore, to see the ceremonies, and try to save the destined victim; or, if better may not be, to witness the thrilling spectacle of a human sacrifice, which, being partly a religious rite, is an affair of a higher order than one of our civilized executions" (*JAC,* 127–28). Bridge's ship departs before this "higher order" spectacle transpires.

While unable to tone down all of Bridge's callousness, Hawthorne, as a comparison of the unedited and edited versions of Bridge's journal shows, endows Bridge with a thoughtful sensibility. On a simple level, there's the matter of animal cruelty. In his original manuscript, Bridge tells of seeing a crocodile laying on a log with his mouth wide open, catching flies. A member of their party goes over and fires a full charge of shot into the animal's mouth, causing it to swim away wounded. Hawthorne, as he edits this, removes the detail of the wanton shooting. He similarly alters a scene in which Bridge beats a Negro who helps him ashore at Porto Praya in the Cape Verde Islands. Here's the account from Bridge's handwritten manuscript:

Beached the boat. Large negro with a ragged red shirt, waded out and took me on his shoulders, sword & all. As we left the boat a heavy "roller" came in. The negro lost his foot-hold, I my balance, and down we plunged into the surf. The negro held on by my legs stoutly, the tendency of which was to keep my head under water. Not being ready to be drowned by a Sansculotte negro, I gave him a vigorous kick, sprang to my feet, and seizing him by his ambrosial curls pushed his head under water in his turn.[88]

In Hawthorne's reworking, the Negro becomes "my sable friend." Instead of the declaration "Not being ready to be drowned by a Sansculotte negro," Hawthorne writes, "Having no taste for a watery death," thus eliminating the class-conscious racism. Following the account, Hawthorne has Bridge declare, "An abolitionist, perhaps, might draw a moral from the story, and say that all, who ride on the shoulders of the African race, deserve nothing better than a similar overthrow" (*JAC*, 11). Hawthorne thus allows Bridge to be more circumspect than he actually was. (Bridge, by the way, must have been a heavy burden to carry, for he was a gigantic man.)[89]

Hawthorne's pacifism also enters into the *Journal* with regard to larger acts of violence. Whereas Bridge takes certain pleasure in both witnessing and participating in violent acts, Hawthorne registers a disapproval of them. Following Bridge's account of two tribes near Grand Drewin that have been at war for more than a year, Hawthorne adds a comment on "the absurdity of war, as the ultimate appeal of nations" (*JAC*, 120). When Bridge records his part in the raids undertaken on native towns along the coast below Berebee to punish the people for their attack on the American ship *Mary Carver* the year before, Hawthorne likewise interjects his pacifism. In a dramatic scene, Bridge and a midshipman by themselves come upon a hamlet of three native houses set apart from the towns the Americans have already burned. Bridge's manuscript reads:

> It was a pretty spot, about 50 yards in diameter with a tree of very dark foliage in the centre, and three neat houses around it. An impervious hedge surrounded the whole except two similar entrances one of which we first described. The slight doors of the houses were fastened but we beat them all in with our muskets, one keeping guard while the other sacked the hamlet. It was not much of a sacking, for every article of furniture had been carried off. I tried to set it on fire by flashing my pistol among the thatch and then by firing my musket into it, but unsuccessfully. Another party soon came in and burnt it down. This was doubtless the settlement of one family, who had been living in comfort till we came. Apart from the rest of the tribe they were all in all to each other.[90]

Hawthorne's edited published version reads:

> Forcing our way through one of these narrow portals, we beheld a grassy
> area of about fifty yards across, overshadowed by a tree of very dense fo-
> liage, which had its massive roots in the centre, and spread its great pro-
> tecting branches over the whole enclosure. . . . This small, secluded ham-
> let had probably been the residence of one family, a patriarch, perhaps,
> with his descendants to the third or fourth generation—who, beneath
> that shadowy tree, must have enjoyed all the happiness of which unculti-
> vated man is susceptible. Nor would it be too great a stretch of liberality,
> to suppose that the green hedge of impervious thorns had kept out the
> vices of their race, and that the little area within was a sphere where all
> the virtues of the native African had been put in daily practice. These
> three dwellings, and the verdant wall around them, and the great tree that
> brooded over the whole, might unquestionably have been spared, with
> safety to our consciences. But when man takes upon himself the office of
> an avenger by the sword, he is not to be perplexed with such little scrupu-
> losities, as whether one individual or family be less guilty than the rest.
> Providence, it is to be presumed, will find some method of setting such
> matters right. (*JAC*, 83)

Hawthorne's "editing" of this entry allows Bridge to see more deeply into the
immorality of his conduct and of warfare itself. In a paragraph concluding
the full account of the events that day, Hawthorne adds his observations on
the transformative doubling that occurs when a person engages in violence
and warfare: "though the burning of villages be a very pretty pastime, yet it
leaves us in a moralizing mood, as most pleasures are apt to do; and one
would fain hope that civilized man, in his controversies with the barbarian,
will at length cease to descend to the barbarian level, and may adopt some
other method of proving his superiority, than by his greater power to inflict
suffering" (*JAC*, 85).

During the whole period of their cruise off the coast of West Africa, the
African Squadron captured no slave ships flying the American flag or run by
American citizens. Because the coast was so long and because the means of
subterfuge was so simple (e.g., flying the flag of another nation), Bridge is not
surprised at this result or at the willingness of merchants to deal with slave
traders. He points out that the United States conducts a vigorous trade with

native Africans, with more vessels coming from Salem than any other port. All of them, the *Journal* reports, "bring New England rum, leaf-tobacco, powder, guns, large brass pans, and cotton cloth" (*JAC*, 110). A large number of ships, the *Journal* continues, "whether English or American, do a considerable part of their business either with the slavers, or with natives settled at the slave-marts, and who, from their connection with the trade have plenty of money. . . . The merchant at home, possibly, is supposed to know nothing of all this. It is quite an interesting moral question, however, how far either Old or New England can be pronounced free from the guilt and odium of the slave-trade, while, with so little indirectness, they both share its profits and contribute essential aid to its prosecution" (*JAC*, 112). Such a concern with guilt distinguishes Hawthorne from his transcendentalist friends, who preferred to celebrate the antislavery movement rather than question its claims to success. This distinction is minor, however, when compared to Hawthorne's and the transcendentalists' shared opposition to the twin aristocracies of Northern capitalists and Southern planters.[91] Although Hawthorne, by the end of his life, would be regarded as a rogue of sorts by his Concord friends, he and they lived in relative harmony during the 1840s, sharing a sense of moral and intellectual superiority to both ardent reformers and conventional money-driven souls in the rest of the nation.

CHAPTER 5

Lies, Specters, and the "Black Man"

Ghostland lies beyond the jurisdiction of veracity.
—Hawthorne, *English Notebooks*

I must confess, it stirs up a little of the devil within me, to find myself hunted by these political bloodhounds. If they succeed in getting me out of office, I will surely immolate one or two of them.
—Hawthorne, letter to Longfellow, June 5, 1849

After Hawthorne left Concord, he spent about four and a half years living in Salem, where his political thought acquired a cutting edge that made his literary irony more serious and, to some readers, more offensive. His struggle to secure a political appointment, his subsequent firing from the customhouse, and his defeat at the hands of the Salem Whigs strengthened his hostility toward self-righteous reformers and their followers. His political foes were probably not as vicious as he suspected, nor the people of Salem as gullible; nevertheless, he imagined himself the victim of both and drew on the imagery of revolution and witchcraft while doing so. As this chapter will show, these images also informed his major two romances, *The Scarlet Letter* and *The House of the Seven Gables,* both of which mount memorable critiques of the moral absolutism, faulty vision, and political violence of seventeenth-century Puritans and those he saw as their nineteenth-century counterparts.

Seeking Office

Hawthorne, like his friend O'Sullivan and his former patron Bancroft, had long identified with the Van Buren wing of the Democratic Party and had hoped the former president would gain his party's nomination. However, the election in 1844 centered on the annexation of Texas, thanks to the efforts of outgoing President Tyler, who thought he could gain reelection by outmaneuvering Van Buren and the leading Whig candidate, Henry Clay, both of whom wished to keep annexation and slavery out of the campaign. Tyler, a former Democrat turned Whig, had become president upon the death of President Harrison in April 1841, and he brought annexation to the floor of Congress, signing a compromise measure hours before his term expired in January 1845. Annexation was popular among voters in the West and the South, so when Clay and Van Buren went public with their joint opposition to it, they undermined their chances at the presidency. In fact, Van Buren lost the nomination of his party, which turned to the dark horse James K. Polk, a slave owner from Tennessee, supported, albeit reluctantly, by Andrew Jackson. (Tyler, an outsider to both major parties, was forced to drop out of the race.)

Whereas Bancroft and O'Sullivan rather opportunistically shifted their allegiance to Polk when it appeared he would emerge as the party's nominee, Hawthorne continued to disapprove of him and his expansionist platform even after the election. He apparently agreed with Van Buren and Clay that annexation would provoke sectional passions that could destroy the nation. According to James Mellow, Hawthorne, in an unrecovered letter to Park Benjamin, dated December 17, 1844, and sold at auction in 1921, "vigorously attacks the election of Polk to the Presidency. [The] whole administration is violently attacked. He says that if Texas is annexed, the Union will be broken by a separation between free and slave states; this he regards as inevitable and imminent."[1] Hawthorne was right that the acquisition of new territories would lead to secession, but he was wrong that this was "imminent." Fifteen years would transpire before the nation split apart.

Bancroft convinced himself that annexation could be accomplished peacefully, and although he was a friend and supporter of Van Buren, he helped swing the presidential nomination to Polk during the voting at the 1844 Democratic National Convention. When Polk's nomination was assured, Bancroft immediately sent him a letter informing him of this fact and detailing his role in bringing it about. After the election, as Lilian Handlin reports, Bancroft also "penned a masterful letter [to Polk] with just the right combination of shrewdness, flattery, and fortitude"; the letter stressed his role in Polk's success but said nothing about Van Buren and mentioned no reward.[2] The result for Bancroft was an appointment as secretary of the navy, in charge of patronage in New England. Although Hawthorne disapproved of Polk's agenda and had contempt for Bancroft as a politician, he nevertheless hoped that they would offer him a political office that would solve his financial problems.

In his quest for a government office, Hawthorne depended on his influential friends to assist him, but he also did what he could to help himself, specifically by courting those who had political influence and trying to remove those who stood in his way. Although his efforts proved successful, his primary political antagonist in Salem, the Reverend Charles Upham, eventually proved more skillful at manipulating the political system. Hawthorne's first inkling that perhaps Upham was not as good a friend as he thought appears in a letter to Sophia in December 1844, where Hawthorne relates that the good reverend, with whom he had dined at the Emersons, returned to Salem and "told the most pitiable stories about our poverty and misery; so as almost to make it appear that we were suffering for food. Everybody that speaks to me seems tacitly to take it for granted that we are in a very desperate condition, and that a government office is the only alternative of the almshouse" (16:70–71). (Emerson seems the most likely source of this gossip.) Despite Hawthorne's indignation, his financial situation was indeed desperate, and he borrowed money from Bridge and engaged in various forms of political intrigue because of it.

Eyeing the plum federal office of postmaster in Salem, Hawthorne asked Bridge to use his influence to prevent the confirmation by the Senate of Benjamin F. Browne, who had been nominated for the office by President Tyler before the 1844 election. "If I am not misinformed, Tyler had actually appointed me," Hawthorne writes, "but was afterwards induced to change it. He will probably leave it to the next administration to make a new appointment" (16:65). Hawthorne had known Browne, an apothecary and leader in Salem Democratic politics, for a number of years. In a letter of March 1845, O'Sullivan told Hawthorne that he had "written to Bancroft again about the

Salem P.O., though I do not believe Brown [sic] will be removed. Bancroft spoke of him as an excellent and unexceptionable man. I did not speak of the other places you named at Salem, because you say the emoluments are small."[3] Unsuccessful in his efforts to sabotage Browne's appointment and reappointment (which ran from 1845 to 1849), Hawthorne ingratiated himself with the postmaster at the end of 1845, by editing his memoir "Papers of an Old Dartmoor Prisoner," which appeared in the *Democratic Review* from January through September 1846. On October 28, 1845, Browne, now a Hawthorne supporter, wrote a letter to President Polk recommending Hawthorne for surveyor of the Salem customhouse.[4]

Through the support of friends, both Democrats and Whigs, Hawthorne became one of the few Van Buren supporters to gain patronage under Polk, who excluded Northern Democrats from his administration, thus splitting the party and allowing the Whigs to elect Zachary Taylor in 1848. As soon as Polk's victory was assured, O'Sullivan, Bridge, and Pierce went to work to persuade Bancroft to appoint Hawthorne to a lucrative post. O'Sullivan had worked tirelessly on Polk's behalf during the campaign and even persuaded Van Buren to write an election-eve endorsement of the candidate. He thus gained some influence over patronage, but not as much as he thought he deserved. O'Sullivan and Van Buren had been allies since the founding of the *Democratic Review* in 1837, yet in his editorials, O'Sullivan argued persistently for party unity and did his best to promote goodwill between the Northern and Southern wings of the party. After the election of 1844, O'Sullivan sought appointments for a number of Van Buren Democrats, provoking Polk in the process, but he reserved his most strenuous efforts for his friend Hawthorne. In a letter of March 21, 1845, to Hawthorne, he asked,

> What would you say to go out as a consul to China with A.H. Everett?
> . . . At any rate, something satisfactory *shall be done* for you. For the purpose of presenting you more advantageously, I have got Duyckinck to write an article about you in the April Democratic; and what is more, I want you to consent to sit for a daguerreotype, that I may take your head off in it. . . . By manufacturing you thus into a Personage, I want to raise your mark higher in Polk's appreciation.[5]

Obviously, O'Sullivan, like Hawthorne's other good friends, was willing to go to great lengths to obtain a government position for him.

Hawthorne appreciated O'Sullivan's efforts, but if he had known the argument O'Sullivan was making on his behalf (citing his poverty), he might not have been so pleased. "Hawthorne is dying of starvation," O'Sullivan wrote Bancroft, "and I of anxious suspense on his behalf—meanwhile not even a word to know what to expect or hope for him" (16:93 n. 2). Hawthorne's friend Charles Sumner, then a Whig, similarly stressed Hawthorne's poverty in a letter he sent to Bancroft's wife, telling her, "I have heard to-day of the poverty of Hawthorne. He is very poor indeed. He has already broken up the humble and inexpensive house which he had established in Concord, because it was too expensive. You know how simply he lived. He lived almost on nothing; but even that nothing has gone. . . . I plead for him earnestly, and count upon your friendly interference to keep his name present to the mind of your husband."[6] In his reply to Sumner, Bancroft sarcastically commented, "I am glad you go for the good rule of dismissing wicked Whigs and putting in Democrats"; then he promised to find Hawthorne an office.[7]

Bridge's efforts on Hawthorne's behalf involved putting him in contact with influential political figures, which the reserved author at first found objectionable. In a letter of June 10, 1845, to Bridge, Hawthorne declared, "So far from imagining that my visit to you could be productive of any influence towards receiving an office, I had no intention of making the said visit, unless I should have first have obtained the office. I have said nothing about your plan to Sophia, knowing that she would not be aiding and abetting towards it" (16:102). Hawthorne apparently swallowed his pride, for he and Sophia did join Bridge at his quarters at the navy yard near Portsmouth, New Hampshire, for a two-week visit during July and August of 1845, along with other invited guests—Senator and Mrs. Charles Atherton of New Hampshire, Senator John Fairfield of Maine, and former senator Franklin Pierce and Mrs. Pierce. All three senators subsequently wrote recommendations for Hawthorne. Of the three, Pierce surely had the most influence. He and Polk had been friends when they served together in Congress, and as fellow conservative "Hunkers," they shared a dislike for Van Buren, belief in an aggressive foreign policy, and desire for new territory. On May 12, 1846, Pierce wrote to Bancroft on Hawthorne's behalf, declaring, "if he is not provided for in some way it will fill me with regret and I shall never cease to feel that a thing has been omitted that was due from *this* Administration."[8] Hawthorne's appointment to the Salem customhouse thus resulted not from any political "services" to the party but, rather, from his financial need, his literary stature, and his influential friends. His claim in "The Custom-House" and elsewhere that he "neither received nor held his office with any reference to political services" (1:13) has some basis in truth, though once in office, he did engage in party "services," including a kickback scheme involving threats to fire two subordinates who balked at donating part of their extra pay to the Democratic Party.

Hawthorne, Manifest Destiny, and the Mexican War

Hawthorne took his oath of office on April 9, 1846. Two weeks later, the Mexican War began, with the April 25 killing of General Taylor's quartermaster by Mexican guerrillas near the Rio Grande. President Polk, despite his public commitment to a diplomatic solution to the problem of relations with Mexico, had secretly desired and provoked war by sending troops into the contested area occupied by Mexicans south of the Nueces River. His long-range goal was to acquire California and other Mexican territory, even if it meant the unconstitutional invasion and occupation of a sovereign nation and the loss of moral stature in the eyes of the world. Van Buren explained in a public letter before the election, "It has hitherto been our pride and our boast that whilst the lust of power, with fraud and violence in its train, has led other and differently constituted governments to aggression and conquest, our movements in these respects have always been regulated by reason and justice."[9] Bancroft, Van Buren's former supporter and an antislavery advocate, argued that annexation was in the best interests of the United States and would actually prevent the spread of slavery. He reasoned that if Texas remained independent, it could engage in the slave trade and import more slaves, whereas if it became part of the Union, it could not. He also argued that if California was purchased from Mexico, the balance of power in Congress between free states and slave states could be preserved.[10]

During the summer of 1845, O'Sullivan also insisted, in the *Democratic Review,* that annexation would prove beneficial to the country and that it would not mean war or the extension of slavery. Using a phrase that would make him famous, he asserted "our manifest destiny to overspread the continent allotted by Providence for the free development of our yearly multiplying millions."[11] As O'Sullivan's recent biographer Robert D. Sampson has said, "it is a terrible irony" that a phrase associated with violence and conquest was coined by a pacifist who sought to end war and capital punishment.[12] Sampson points out that for O'Sullivan, "'manifest destiny' was essentially a peaceful and gradual process as befits someone who, at about the time he wrote this essay for the June 1845 *Democratic Review,* was warning the Polk administration of the danger of war with Mexico."[13]

Given his pacifism, Hawthorne would have found the arguments of Bancroft and O'Sullivan appealing, though his skepticism surely made him doubt their validity. According to a March 1845 letter that Sophia sent to her mother, Hawthorne was neither as pessimistic as Conscience Whigs about the extension of slavery nor as optimistic as Northern Democrats about preserving the Union. "My husband," she asserted, "says he has not wholly thought out the subject of the annexation of Texas; but he does not think it such a calamity as many do. He says he should be glad of the separation of the South from the North, for then he should feel as if he had a country, which he can never do while that weight of slavery hangs on our skirts. He does not believe it will make any difference about perpetuating Slavery—& he thinks it better to be at peace with the nations."[14] While either Hawthorne or Sophia probably tailored the sanguine attitude here to suit Mrs. Peabody's antislavery politics, the disunionism the letter expresses is identifiably Hawthorne's, as is the stated desire for peace.[15]

Throughout his career, Hawthorne maintained that if the South persisted in maintaining its "peculiar institution," the Union was not an imagined community worth waging war to preserve. Only the elimination of slavery eventually made war seem justifiable to him. Before the Civil War, support for disunion was maintained by only a small group of Garrison's followers, many of whom, including Frederick Douglass, eventually abandoned it. The overwhelming number of Whigs and Democrats alike preferred to see the nation expand, and while they disagreed in the 1840s and 1850s about war and slavery, they agreed on expansion. For Whigs, the growth of a market-based economy seemed particularly desirable. For Democrats, especially the Young Americans, led by O'Sullivan, expansion into the western territories meant cheap land for the working class and the spread of democratic principles. Once the war with Mexico broke out, in the spring of 1846, most Americans, including Hawthorne, felt compelled to support it. At Polk's urging, Congress quickly granted the resolution of war he asked for, with the House voting 174–14 in favor and the Senate 40–2. Only antislavery Whigs opposed. They and their New England constituents—mainly abolitionists and transcendentalists—saw the war as an immoral attempt to extend slavery. Thoreau, as is well known, protested the war by refusing to pay his poll tax and spent a night in jail, which resulted in his lecture and essay known as "Civil Disobedience." Fuller, in a *Tribune* dispatch from Europe, denounced "this horrible cancer of Slavery, and this wicked War, that has grown out of it."[16] Theodore Parker, combining pacifism with racism, charged that Polk had misled the public into supporting an unchristian war of aggression against a degraded and half-civilized people. The United States would one day dominate the continent, he asserted, because "the Mexicans cannot stand before this terrible Anglo-Saxon race, the most formidable and powerful the world ever saw. . . . They must melt away as the Indians before the white man"; yet this must happen, he insisted, not by warfare but by "the steady advance of a superior race, with superior ideas and a better civilization."[17] Though one of the boldest antislavery advocates in the country, Parker nevertheless held strong views in line with white supremacy.

Emerson, like Parker, opposed the war, yet he also believed that in the long run, it would not matter how Anglo-Saxon racial superiority triumphed. In a journal entry of 1844 (the same year as his fatalistic antislavery address), he observed, "It is very certain that the strong British race which have now overrun so much of this continent, must also overrun that tract [Texas], & Mexico & Oregon also, and it will in the course of ages be of small import by what particular occasions & methods it was done. It is a secular question."[18] Later, in *The Conduct of Life* (1860), he again rationalized the war and expansionism by asserting, "out of Sabine rapes, and out of robbers' forays, real Romes and their heroisms come in fulness of time. . . . The agencies by which events so grand as the opening of California, of Texas, of Oregon, and the junction of the two oceans, are effected, are paltry . . . ; most of the great results of history are brought about by discreditable means."[19]

Hawthorne, of course, lacked Emerson's ability to accept "discreditable means" in light of "great results," as shown by his many studies of how "the wrong-doing of one generation lives into the successive ones" (2:2); moreover, the theft of land and property by a supposedly superior race became a chief sin he explored, most notably in *The House of the Seven Gables* (1851). It is difficult not to see in that romance a veiled critique of the Mexican War and the ill-gotten gain of massive new territory, including California, where the discovery of gold set off the mad gold rush of 1849. In his preface to *The House of the Seven Gables*, Hawthorne claims as his "moral" or "truth" "the folly of tumbling down an avalanche of ill-gotten gold, or real estate, on the heads of an unfortunate posterity" (2:2). Although his immediate reference is to the Pyncheons of Salem, he surely has the American people in mind as well.

In a sketch Hawthorne wrote a year earlier, in the wake of the Mexican War, he directed sly satire at the discourse used to justify aggression and conquest as inevitable results of manifest destiny and Anglo-Saxon racial superiority. "Main-street" (1849) features a narrator-showman who uses puppets and a malfunctioning mechanical panorama to tell a dubious providential history of Salem, beginning in precolonial times and intended to end in the present. The displacement of the original inhabitants of the Salem site, the Indians, initiates the "progress" the showman illustrates, yet a rather grouchy spectator sitting in the front row questions the props at the outset. Not unlike Mark Twain enumerating Cooper's literary offenses, this "acidulous-looking gentleman" refuses to succumb to the showman's visual and historical artifice. "The whole affair is a manifest catch-penny," he observes at the beginning. "The trees look more like weeds in a garden, than a primitive forest; the Squaw Sachem and Wappacowet are stiff in their pasteboard joints; and the squirrels, the deer, and the wolf, move with all the grace of a child's wooden monkey, sliding up and down a stick" (11:52). As the showman tries to represent the Indians' early encounter with the settlers, he similarly fails to satisfy his critic's demand "to see things just as they are." The showman asserts, "the Indians, coming from their distant wigwams to view the white man's settlement, marvel at the deep track which he makes, and perhaps are saddened by a flitting presentiment, that this heavy tread will find its way over all the land; and that the wild woods, the wild wolf, and the wild Indian, will alike be trampled beneath it. Even so shall it be. The pavements of the Main-street must be laid over the red man's grave" (11:55). The most meaningful words here are "trampled" and "must," the first suggesting willful aggression, the other suggesting an inevitable progression. By putting them side by side and letting free will dominate fate, Hawthorne discredits the showman's providential narrative. In *The House of the Seven Gables*, he would develop this theme more fully, as Colonel Pyncheon builds his mansion "over an unquiet grave," the site of Matthew Maule's hut (2:9), and seeks to claim a vast "unexplored and unmeasured tract of eastern lands" (2:18), supposedly deeded by the Indians.

In several later scenes of "Main-street," Hawthorne explicitly critiques the racial thinking used to justify white theft of Indian land. After describing the arrival of Governor Endicott and other colonists, the showman declares, "you perceive that the Anglo-Saxon energy—as the phrase now goes—has been at work in the spectacle before us. So many chimneys now send up their smoke, that it begins to have the aspect of a village street" (11:57). As the settlers construct their house of worship, which in time confines more than it liberates, the showman commands, "Look again at the picture, and observe how the aforesaid Anglo-Saxon energy is now trampling along the street, and raising a positive cloud of dust beneath its sturdy footsteps" (11:58). The repetition of the word "trampling," as Colacurcio has pointed out, assures "us that the great theme of Manifest Destiny is indeed the subtext of this otherwise unassuming little pageant."[20] The showman's Indians become aware "that the street is no longer free to them, save by the sufferance and permission of the settlers," and the show of English power effects their awe. A "mail clad band" advances up the street: "There they come, fifty of them, or more; all with their iron breastplates and steel-caps well burnished, and glimmering bravely against the sun; their ponderous muskets on their shoulders, their bandaliers about their waists, their lighted matches in their hands, and the drum and fife playing cheerily before them. See! Do they not step like martial men?" (11:59–60). This show of military might, like others in Hawthorne's works, is an exciting spectacle that deflects attention from the moral stakes involved in its use.

Published in the midst of the excitement surrounding the return of soldiers from the Mexican War and of the exaggerated heroism accorded them in story, poetry, and song,[21] "Main-street" ends by satirizing Salem's celebration of the election of General Zachary Taylor. (In Whig-dominated Salem, Taylor received 64 percent of the vote.) The showman had planned, he says, to bring his show down to the present and illuminate current events, but a wire breaks, halting the machinery, and keeping the miniature street buried beneath the great snow of 1717, a "catastrophe," he earnestly declares, parallel to "the fate of Herculaneum and Pompeii" (11:81). With such humor, Hawthorne reveals his growing hostility toward his native town, which would reach its peak of ironic intensity in "The Custom-House." His wicked wit here surely informs his choice of a literal deus ex machina to bury the miniature Salemites, who had built their town over the graves of Indians. Hawthorne concludes the sketch with tongue in cheek by having the showman lament the permanent "burial" of the town, saying, "I had expended a vast deal of light and brilliancy on a representation of the street in its whole length, from Buffum's Corner downward, on the night of the grand illumination for General Taylor's triumph" (11:81).

Like the American public and even antislavery reformers, Hawthorne distinguished between those political figures who initiated wars and the soldiers who fought in them, often unaware of the issues at stake. In *The Life of Franklin Pierce* (1852), written four years after the end of the Mexican War, Hawthorne praises the citizen soldiers and credits them with a "spirit of romantic adventure which more than supplies the place of disciplined courage" (23:318). Superimposing medieval romantic conventions on his material, he claims of the soldiers, "All of them, from the rank of general downward, appear to have been animated by the spirit of young knights, in times of chivalry, when fighting for their spurs" (23:346). Did Hawthorne know better?[22] He should have, for the newspapers had described the atrocities committed by American troops, and Pierce's diary itself provided a window upon the degradation a war could provoke. In one entry, Pierce meditates on what it means for a civilized nation to wage war.

> *War* has been *declared,* but with all our battles, all our brilliant victories, and the loss of all the valuable lives *war* has not yet been *prosecuted* I could desire that it may not be, but from the little I have observed I believe, that it *must* be before a peace can be *"conquered."* I mean war as it has been recognized for the last 200 years in the most civilized Nations. No, not as it has been recognized, but *war* as it has actually been carried on, with its fruits & its results. *War,* that actually carries, wide spread woe & dessolation to the *conquered* and tacitly at least, allows pillage & plunder with accompanyments not to be named during a campaign like this Even in a private journal. . . . If my boy should ever read this daily journal I desire that he may not misunderstand his father—I hate war in all its aspects, I deem it unworthy of the age in which I live & of the Govt in which I have borne some part. All I mean to say is, that there can be no such thing as a profound sense of justice, the sacredness of individual

rights and the values of human life connected with human butchery, and all men, who think & feel as I think & feel and yet are found on fields of slaughter are in a false position from education and the force of circumstances. (23:492–93)

The next day, Pierce regretted writing this "digression" (as he called it), and Hawthorne omitted it from his published transcription of the diary, yet it contains one of the most profound insights Pierce ever expressed.

Americans in Mexico eventually "prosecuted" the war, to the everlasting shame of the United States. General Winfield Scott admitted that the army of volunteers under his command "committed atrocities to make Heaven weep and every American of Christian morals blush for his country. Murder, robbery and rape of mothers and daughters in the presence of tied-up males of the families have been common all along the Rio Grande."[23] Lieutenant George C. Meade reported that the volunteers were "driving husbands out of houses and raping their wives. . . . They will fight as gallantly as any men, but they are a set of Goths and Vandals without discipline, making us a terror to innocent people."[24] According to a number of other eyewitnesses, both Mexican and Anglo, the Texas Rangers were especially brutal and cruel in their treatment of Mexican civilians, and although Anglo-American historians have claimed that the Rangers' actions cannot be judged by standards imposed from outside the context of border warfare, Larry McMurtry has fashioned a damning response: "Why they can't is a question apologists for the Rangers have yet to answer. Torture is torture, whether inflicted in Germany, Algiers, or along the Nueces Strip. The Rangers, of course, claimed that their end justified their means, but people who practice torture always claim that."[25]

Hawthorne's admiration for James Russell Lowell's *Biglow Papers,* serialized in 1846 and published as a book in 1848, also suggests that he knew more about the dark side of the Mexican War effort than *The Life of Franklin Pierce* reveals. Lowell's fictional letters from young Birdofredom Sawin, "Private in the Massachusetts Regiment," direct devastating satire at the Polk administration's war propaganda using realities of the war itself: "nimepunce a day fer killin' folks comes kind o' low fer murder." Although Lowell supported abolitionism and Hawthorne did not, they agreed, as Birdofredom puts it,

Ez fer war, I call it murder,—
There you hev it plain an' flat;
I don't want to go no furder
Than my Testyment fer that.[26]

Hawthorne, when asked by Monckton Milnes in 1854 for "half a dozen good American books," included in his choices Lowell's *Biglow Papers,* calling it "the best thing he has written" (17:261).

Decapitated Surveyor

Despite his aversion to war, Hawthorne at times expressed admiration for those who approached battle reluctantly, dispassionately, and with kindness in their hearts, as if that were possible. In "The Custom-House," he describes the old general James Miller in such terms. In the War of 1812, among other feats, Miller led a charge on the hill at Lundy's Lane and, in intense and deadly fighting, captured the British battery there. Hawthorne writes,

> What I saw in him—as evidently as the indestructible ramparts of Old Ticonderoga, already cited as the most appropriate simile—were the features of stubborn and ponderous endurance, . . . and of benevolence, which, fiercely as he had led the bayonets on at Chippewa or Fort Erie, I take to be of quite as genuine a stamp as what actuates any or all the polemical philanthropists of the age. He had slain men with his own hand, for aught I know;—certainly they had fallen, like blades of grass at the sweep of a scythe, before the charge to which his spirit imparted its triumphant energy;—but, be that as it might, there was never in his heart so much cruelty as would have brushed the down off a butterfly's wing. (1:22)

Ironically, the political manipulation of this old warrior by Hawthorne's allies became the primary reason Hawthorne lost his own job as surveyor.

According to the Salem Whigs, the old general faced "privation and suffering"[27] because of the machinations of Hawthorne and his fellow Salem Democrats, who apparently persuaded the general to step down from his job as collector before Taylor took office. With the post vacated, Polk replaced the general with his son Colonel Ephraim Miller (a friend of Hawthorne and other Democrats), who, as a nominal Whig, did not face removal by Taylor.

In exchange for his appointment, the younger Miller secretly agreed not to replace the Democrats in the customhouse with Whigs.[28] Hawthorne participated in this intrigue in December 1848 by sending to his new acquaintance Senator Atherton the petition calling for Ephraim Miller's appointment, asking him to take "the trouble of laying it before the President." Hawthorne attached a note declaring, "I certify that the gentlemen, whose signatures are contained in the within list, are persons known to me, & that they comprise to the best of my recollection all the leading merchants & importers of this district" (16:253 n. 1). According to Sophia Hawthorne, Charles Upham, leader of the Salem Whigs, having read the petition in Washington in the summer of the following year, copied it incorrectly to use against Hawthorne.

> He left out "to the best of his recollection," and made it read that these were *all* the merchants of Salem. Stephen C. Phillips's name was not signed. And so Mr. U. brings this to prove that Mr. Hawthorne is impeachable for want of veracity! He tried hard to find that my husband acted politically with regard to Colonel Miller's appointment; and as this was impossible, he thought he would try to prove him a false witness. . . . He is, my husband says, the most satisfactory villain that ever was, for at every point he is consummate.[29]

Upham's "villainy," if that is what it was, arose out of frustration with the Democrats' success at maintaining control of the customhouse, even after they lost the 1848 election. Colonel Ephraim Miller stalled the Whigs by claiming that before he replaced any of the inspectors under his authority, he wished to follow the lead of the Taylor administration, which controlled the federal appointments, including the surveyorship. This tactic outraged the Salem Whigs, and they decided to call for Ephraim's ouster and Hawthorne's. Referring to Ephraim, Upham declared,

> It was evident that the Collector relied upon our not being able or willing to touch that office [the surveyorship], on account of Mr. Hawthorne's literary character. That gentleman was placed as a barrier in our way. The Collector and his official associates planted themselves, as they thought, securely behind him, and actually made his removal necessary before we could advance a step in obtaining our rightful authority over the Custom House. . . . Mr. Hawthorne owes the application for his removal entirely

to the folly of his friend, the Collector and his other advisors, who placed him between themselves and the power of the administration.[30]

In March 1849, when Hawthorne got wind of the Whigs' move to replace him, he asked his friend Hillard to line up influential Boston Whigs to support him, claiming, "I was not appointed to office as a reward for political services, nor have I acted as a politician since," which was half true, half false. Hillard obliged and secured letters from Rufus Choate, Horace Mann, Charles Sumner, and Daniel Webster, among others, all of whom argued on behalf of Hawthorne's retention. Meanwhile, the Salem Whigs sent to Washington a "petition" signed by thirty "gentlemen" of Salem, calling for Hawthorne's ouster. In late June 1849, when it looked as if Hawthorne might succeed in regaining his office, the Salem Whigs became more aggressive, exposing more of what they knew about Hawthorne's customhouse politics. Upham made two trips to Washington in June to lobby for Hawthorne's removal, and after the Whigs met and agreed on a course of action, Upham prepared a "Memorial" charging Hawthorne with "official extortion and corruption."[31]

The "Memorial" is a curious document, combining high praise of Hawthorne ("one of the most amiable and elegant writers of America, which his fellow-citizens, of all parties, cherish and appreciate, and none more than the Whigs of his native city") with exaggerated accounts of his complicity in corrupt political practices ("the Whig Inspectors were robbed of their just dues, they were systematically oppressed, and their feelings constantly outraged").[32] The kickback scheme, enforced with the threat of dismissals, signed by Hawthorne, was pretty irrefutable, which even Hawthorne had to admit in a private letter to Horace Mann on August 8, 1849.

[M]y idea is (I may be mistaken, but it is founded on some observation of the manoeuvres of small politicians, and knowing the rigid discipline of Custom houses as to party-subscriptions) that there really was an operation to squeeze an assessment out of the recusant Inspectors, under the terror of an impending removal or suspension;—that one of the Inspectors turned traitor, and was impelled, by the threats and promises of Mr Upham and his coadjutors, to bring his evidence to a pretty direct point on me;—and that Mr Upham, in his memorial to the Treasury Department, defined and completed the lie. (16:292)

By the time Hawthorne wrote this letter, he had accepted his fate. In private letters and "The Custom-House," he revealed his sense of persecution and martyrdom. Even though he had brought on his own public ouster by signing off on the corrupt practices within the customhouse, by participating in the failed scheme of the Democrats to keep control of the customhouse, and by resisting his removal on the false grounds of nonpartisanship, he nevertheless chose to blame Upham and the Salem Whigs for hounding him unfairly from office.

The Scarlet Letter and Specter Evidence

During Hawthorne's struggles in Salem, the satirical attitude toward reformers that infused his *Mosses from an Old Manse* transformed into a rather bitter hostility toward the "besom of reform," as he calls the Whig's campaign to "decapitate" him. The imagined connection between Whigs and self-righteous Puritans that Hawthorne acquired living and struggling in Salem inform both *The Scarlet Letter* and *The House of the Seven Gables*. The connection he imagined had some basis in fact, because the Whigs, especially the Conscience Whigs outside of Boston, traced their ancestry to rugged Puritan stock and saw themselves as moral stewards, which is why they became prominent in the antislavery movement.[33]

Early antislavery efforts in America began with the Puritans' hated rivals, the Society of Friends, or Quakers, who by 1670 sought to prevent the holding of slaves by any of its members. For the Quakers, opposition to slavery became part of their overall opposition to war in all its forms and of the cultivation of peace and goodwill among all humankind. Organized antebellum abolitionism, which, starting in the 1830s, became aggressive in its attack on slavery in the South, has been traced to the influence of the British antislavery movement and to American evangelical Christianity, but its warlike rhetoric owes much to a residual Puritanism still vital in parts of New England, especially among the Whigs of Massachusetts.[34] As David Donald long ago pointed out, almost all of the leading abolitionists were Whigs, not Democrats: "William Lloyd Garrison made his first public appearance in Boston to endorse the arch-Whig Harrison Gray Otis: James G. Birney campaigned throughout Alabama to defeat Jackson; Henry B. Stanton wrote editorials for anti-Jackson newspapers. Not merely the leaders but their followers as well seem to have been hostile to Jacksonian democracy, for it is estimated that fifty-nine out of sixty Massachusetts abolitionists belonged to the Whig party."[35]

Webster's Cotton Whigs (proslavery because of economic ties to Southern cotton) controlled Boston politics, but Conscience Whigs (decidedly antislavery) were in the majority in Massachusetts outside of Boston, including Concord and Salem.[36] According to Michael Holt, Webster lamented that the Massachusetts Whig party was "sorely afflicted" with abolitionists, including the Reverend Charles Upham in Salem, for whom Websterites in Salem refused to vote in the Essex County elections of August and November 1850.[37] The Free-Soil candidate for Congress defeated Upham, in part because the Webster Whigs abstained. Holt writes that in a letter of November 20 to Henry L. Dawes, Upham in turn "castigated Webster for exercising 'a fatal influence' in New England because he whored after southern support for the presidency."[38] In many ways Upham's ambition and his politico-religious zeal made him a perfect representative of the type of self-righteous Puritan Salem had long harbored, at least in Hawthorne's imagination.

Even if he had not been a leading minister and politician known as an expert in witchcraft, Upham would have seemed to Hawthorne like a modern-day Cotton Mather who had fixed on Hawthorne as his victim. After *The Scarlet Letter* appeared, Hawthorne informed Bridge that "The Custom-House" "has caused the greatest uproar that ever happened here since witch-times. If I escape from town without being tarred and feathered, I shall consider it good-luck" (16:329). This imagery, drawn from witchcraft and insurrection, portrays Hawthorne's sense of martyrdom, but other imagery reveals his thirst for revenge. "I must confess, it stirs up a little of the devil within me," he wrote to Longfellow in the summer of 1849, "to find myself hunted by these political bloodhounds. If they succeed in getting me out of office, I will surely immolate one or two of them" (16:269). Hawthorne thus imagines himself as a persecuted witch and runaway slave but also a participant in the burning or lynching of his antagonists. As writer and politico, Hawthorne had a flair for the dramatic, and to imagine himself both victim and victimizer came naturally to him, enabling him to be in and out of the political game at the same time, standing both here and there at once, as witch, slave, or their devilish counterpart.

What seems to have bothered Hawthorne most about his imagined victimization in Salem is the false testimony brought against him, which also harkened back to the witchcraft trials. In a letter of April 13, 1850, he informed Bridge that the Salem people "certainly do not deserve good usage at my hands . . . after permitting me to be deliberately lied down—not merely once, but at two several attacks—on two false indictments—without hardly a voice being raised on my behalf" (16:329). The lies and delusion of Salem in 1692 thus reappear in Hawthorne's Salem of 1849 and make their way into his novel about Boston in 1642–49. The way in which he introduces the story of Hester Prynne to the reader shows his self-conscious use of unreliable narration, for he not only disavows it as his own story (the manuscript is prepared by Surveyor Pue) but also locates its origins in "oral testimony," told not by eyewitnesses but, rather, by "aged persons, alive in the time of Mr. Surveyor Pue" (1:32). This dubious line of transmission alerts the reader to the unreliability of all that follows. The explicit moral of the book, "Be true! Be true! Be true!" (1:260), often ridiculed, has political resonance for an author victimized by enemies who have turned the public against him.

"The Custom-House" is a transparent hoax, of course, and Hawthorne challenges the reader to see through it and through the lies and superstitions controlling those in his fictional world as well. He claims that his dead predecessor Surveyor Pue haunts the customhouse and "with his own ghostly hand . . . imparted to me the scarlet symbol, and the little roll of explanatory manuscript" (1:33). Surveyor Hawthorne, who "dresses up" the tale, is also a ghost, who has suffered a political beheading at the hands of "blood-thirsty" Whigs. "The moment when a man's head drops off is seldom or never, I am inclined to think, precisely the most agreeable of his life," he declares, adding that he at least takes satisfaction in thus showing his loyalty to "his brother Democrats," who had doubts about him before "he had won the crown of martyrdom, (though with no longer a head to wear it on)" (1:41–42). He extends his joke by claiming that after his firing, the newspapers "kept me, for a week or two, careering through the public prints, in my decapitated state, like Irving's Headless Horseman" (1:42–43).

Although intended for humorous effect, Hawthorne's joke about the ghosts of the customhouse serves as a link between his politics and his art. First, his representation of himself as a martyred political figure is a fiction intended to veil his involvement in party politics and to counter the charges made against him by the Salem Whigs. He once told a friend seeking political office, "A subtile boldness with a veil of modesty over it, is what is needed" (16:649). Second, as the allusion to Irving's "The Legend of Sleepy Hollow" suggests, Hawthorne knows himself to be not dead at all but a rough-and-tumble trickster intent on mischief, not unlike Irving's Brom Bones, whose masquerade scares his rival, the gullible Yankee schoolmaster Ichabod Crane, out of the territory. Ichabod's fatal weakness, we know, is his belief in ghosts (his favorite author is the "invaluable" Cotton Mather, Puritan expert on witchcraft and specters). Upham, Hawthorne's chief antagonist among the Salem Whigs and also an expert on witchcraft, specters, and politics, suffers from Hawthorne's sly revenge in *The House of the Seven Gables,* where he appears as the villainous Judge Pyncheon. Hawthorne's professed detachment and serenity in "The Custom-House" masks his thirst for revenge, and thus Surveyor Hawthorne "in so far as he shows himself in a false light," becomes, like Hawthorne's other characters, "a shadow, or, indeed, ceases to exist." Thus, as we are told, the romance may "be considered as the 'Posthumous Papers of a Decapitated Surveyor'" (1:43).

At both the personal and political levels, the novel focuses on the spectral, and it explores its origins and the effects it produces. While Chillingworth is clearly duplicitous, all the main characters of *The Scarlet Letter* are liars and deceivers. They lie primarily through silences, by what they choose not to say. Whereas Arthur hides his paternity, Hester hides her continuing love for Arthur. They both thus have one face in public and another in private, which creates a wide path to dissolution. "No man, for any considerable period, can wear one face to himself, and another to the multitude, without finally getting bewildered as to which may be the true," Hawthorne declares in chapter 20, "The Minister in a Maze" (1:216). Such deceit not only reduces one to confusion but also dissolves the world and the self. "To the untrue man, the whole universe is false,—it is impalpable,—it shrinks to nothing within his grasp. And he himself, in so far as he shows himself in a false light, becomes a shadow, or, indeed, ceases to exist" (1:145–46). Both Arthur and Hester undergo such dissolution during the course of the novel, as they deceive others and even themselves about their true identities. They become shadows, ghosts, specters; and the romance becomes a ghost story, warning not only against false witnessing but also against becoming a ghost oneself, like the decapitated surveyor.

A primary specter in *The Scarlet Letter* is the "Black Man," but there is no actual Black Man, of course, just as there was no Black Man in Salem Village in 1692. Hawthorne's allusions make it clear that he is a creation of the colony's religion and a projection of each sinful person's guilt-ridden mind. Melville, in his review of *Mosses,* referred to Hawthorne's "appeals to that Calvinistic sense of Innate Depravity and Original Sin, from whose visitations . . . no deeply thinking mind is always and wholly free,"[39] but Hawthorne was more interested in experiential sins than religious dogma. For him, danger lay in those irrational passions—lust, anger, egotism, revenge—that some persons and nations do not repress. In a tale flanked at the beginning by the Whigs, with their "fierce and bitter spirit of malice and revenge" (1:41), and at the end by the Spanish sailors, with their gleaming eyes and "animal ferocity" (1: 232), the main characters of *The Scarlet Letter* become victims of irrational passions they cannot control. Chillingworth, like many of Hawthorne's villains, suffers from coldheartedness, as his name implies, yet at the other emotional extreme are Arthur and Hester, who in their moments of weakness display an excess of emotion, which peaks in the ironically titled chapter 17, "The Pastor and His Parishioner." Their inability to stay within the confines of these roles leads to a dissolution of character that makes them appear as ghosts.

As chapter 17 opens, they discover their transformation: "So strangely did they meet, in the dim wood, that it was like the first encounter, in the world beyond the grave, of two spirits who had been intimately connected in their former life. . . . Each a ghost, and awe-stricken at the other ghost!" (1:190). Arthur, who puts forth his hand, which is cold as death, and touches the chill hand of Hester, has become a ghost not because of some supernatural force, the "dark necessity" Chillingworth conjures up to justify his conduct, but because of his own weak humanity. As Hawthorne explains, "It is the unspeakable misery of a life so false as his, that it steals the pith and substance out of whatever realities there are around us, and which were meant by Heaven to be the spirit's joy and nutriment" (1:145). Hester, too, because she is an unrepentant penitent, becomes a specter as she remains in Boston and "haunts the spot where a marked event has given color to her lifetime." Near the end of the novel, as she awaits Arthur in the marketplace, her face "was like a mask; or rather, like the frozen calmness of a dead woman's features; owing this dreary resemblance to the fact that Hester was actually dead, in respect to any claim of sympathy, and had departed out of the world with which she still seemed to mingle" (1:226). Thus *The Scarlet Letter* becomes a ghost story, told by a ghost, and as fabulous as the testimonies given in the Salem witchcraft trials.

In his preface (written after completing the novel), Hawthorne claims that as long as he remained in the customhouse, his characters "retained all the rigidity of dead corpses, and stared me in the face with a fixed and ghastly grin of contemptuous defiance. 'What have you to do with us?' that expression seemed to say" (1:34). Their lack of reality and vitality prepares us for the effects of their actions. Although Chillingworth is the conventional villain of the romance, becoming darker and more deformed as he exacts his revenge, Arthur, because of his guilt, imagines the devil at his own elbow. Hester, too, when she peers in Pearl's face, sees something "fiend-like" and "full of malice," as if an "evil spirit" is there. What they see is an amalgamation of superstition and guilt. Despite rumors of Pearl being a demon offspring, the actual "Black Man" who has fathered her is of course Arthur. Hester tells Pearl she met the Black Man only once, and we know she met not the devil but the Reverend Arthur Dimmesdale and that forbidden desire impelled their union. When Arthur appears emerging from the mist in the forest, Pearl asks, "is it the Black Man?" and Hester replies, "silly child. . . . It is the minister" (1:187).

In the climactic scene that follows, Hester reveals the nature of her previous relationship with Arthur, as she gives in to a passion she has hidden for years, taking off her letter, taking off her cap, letting her "dark and rich" hair down, and displaying "a crimson flush" that glows with sexual arousal on her cheek. Whether we wish to conclude that, eight years in the past, the minister seduced his beautiful, married parishioner, she seduced him, or they both succumbed to their mutual attraction for one another, the fact remains that their union is illicit, despite Hester's assertion that it has "a consecration of its own." Hester is free to divorce, albeit with difficulty, and Arthur is free to marry, albeit with loss of admiration, yet they disregard these challenging public proceedings and act on their secret desires. When they do this a second time, as an act of free will, Arthur appears to become the "Black Man" of Hester's imagination. Plunging through the forest, not unlike Goodman Brown, he makes his way through a dreamscape, and "at every step he was incited to do some strange, wild, wicked thing or other, with a sense that it would be at once involuntary and intentional" (1:217). Hawthorne thus dramatizes the pernicious and insubstantial effects of being caught up in the "contagion of the hour," which soon wears off after Arthur's election-day sermon.

Before his triumph on that day, the people of Boston are said to see their ailing young minister as a victim of the devil, struggling against the devil's power unsuccessfully. The sexton, too, assumes that the devil dropped Arthur's glove on the scaffold to falsely incriminate him. Yet both the people and Arthur suffer from delusions. Chillingworth, the man of science, pointedly tells Hester, "With the superstition common to his brotherhood, he fancied himself given over to a fiend, to be tortured with frightful dreams, and desperate thoughts, the sting of remorse, and despair of pardon; as a foretaste of what awaits him beyond the grave. But it was the constant shadow of my presence!—the closest propinquity of the man whom he had most vilely wronged!—and who had grown to exist only by this perpetual poison of the direst revenge!" (1:171–72). In other words, Arthur sees the spectral fiend that is not there and overlooks the mortal villain that is. As a scholar and scientist, Chillingworth does not share Arthur's superstition and even admits the fiendishness of his own behavior. The brilliance of Hawthorne's psychological and political insight here is that specters, ghosts, and fiends are projections of an individual's or a society's own repressed fears and desires.

Hester, as a martyr to a harsh Puritan community sustained by sermons of the ministers and spread by the gossip of the people, stands forth as an admirable and almost heroic victim on the scaffold. The narrator identifies with her in this role. However, when, in the forest scene, she tempts Arthur a second time, her role becomes that of a rebel, and the narrator's sympathies seem to disappear. Drawing on revolutionary imagery, Hawthorne presents her as a goddess of liberty leading a wild assault on a citadel, yet, as I have noted elsewhere, "her victory, like that of the first Bastille day, sets loose forces of anarchy and wickedness."[40] Arthur experiences "the exhilarating effect—upon a prisoner just escaped from the dungeon of his own heart—of breathing the wild, free atmosphere of an unredeemed, unchristianized, lawless region" (1:201). In chapter 13, "Another View of Hester," we learn that Hester lives in a time when "[m]en of the sword had overthrown nobles and kings. Men bolder than these had overthrown and rearranged . . . the whole system of ancient prejudice, wherewith was linked much of ancient principle." As a result of imbibing the spirit of the age, Hester entertains thoughts, "shadowy guests, that would have been as perilous as demons to their entertainer, could they have been seen so much as knocking at her door" (1:164). These dangerous specters, whether generated by revolution, regicide, or the Reformation, enhance the appeal of the devil or of unsanctioned action. Hester confides to Mistress Hibbins, "if they had taken Pearl I would have signed my name in the Black Man's book and that with mine own blood" (1:117). To what end would she have done so? To seek revenge? No. To show her loss of faith in a benevolent God? Perhaps. As an act of rebellion? Definitely. Hawthorne's insight here is that what it took to make a "witch" was the misuse of power—oppression. Witchcraft indeed equaled rebellion, as Cotton Mather claimed.

The "Black Man" thus takes on a political manifestation as the fabulous ally of those, such as Hester, who cannot find justice among God's so-called saints. Hester thinks of turning to him in order to obtain justice if her child is taken from her by those in power. In desperation, she will align herself with the "Black Man" at war with the established authorities of the land. Ultimately, Hawthorne wishes us to discover that the most dangerous persons in the novel are not those characters who conjure up the specter of the devil by following their unruly passions—that is, Chillingworth, Arthur, Hester, Pearl, and Mistress Hibbins—but those who perpetuate a society masking cruelty as righteousness, despotism as justice. While ministers and magistrates focus on the power of the devil, so as to maintain their authority, the people, in their ignorance, respond with fear and anger. Thus the "gossips" who surround the scaffold reveal a frightening bloodlust, wanting Hester to be branded or executed. As one puts it, "This woman has brought shame upon us all, and ought to die" (1:51). (The actual Mistress Hibbins, whom Hawthorne includes as a character in his novel, calling her "insane," died at the hands of God-fearing Puritans in 1646. She was executed as a witch.) Before Hester is allowed to return to her prison cell, "the eldest clergyman of Boston," the Reverend John Wilson, subjects the crowd to a "discourse on sin," referring continually to Hester's scarlet letter: "So forcibly did he dwell upon this symbol, for the hour or more during which his periods were rolling over the people's heads, that it assumed new terrors in their imagination, and seemed to derive its scarlet hue from the flames of the infernal pit" (1:68–69).[41] He thus demonizes Hester and makes his listeners believe she is in league with the devil. Consequently, when she is led back to prison, "it was whispered, by those who peered after her, that the scarlet letter threw a lurid gleam along the dark passage-way of the interior" (1:69). His fearmongering has done its work.[42]

Whether Arthur should be viewed as escaping from his own delusions at the end of *The Scarlet Letter* and thereby allowing his parishioners a glimpse of his true character remains an open question. Given Hawthorne's emphasis on deceptions of all kinds, one suspects the pietà tableau at the end of the novel should be read as ironic. Time and again in his works, Hawthorne shows that only self-delusion allows one to claim the ability to triumph over evil and do good in the world; however, Hawthorne's emotional reaction as he read the ending of the novel to Sophia suggests that perhaps it lost its irony as he confronted what he had wrought; that is, the trickster may have tricked himself. In his *English Notebooks,* he recalls "my emotions when I read the last scene of the Scarlet Letter to my wife, just after writing it—tried to read it, rather, for my voice swelled and heaved, as if I were tossed up and down on an ocean, as it subsided after a storm" (21:339–40). He thus joined those many readers who find Arthur's mock confession persuasive and the resolution moving, even given how staged it seems. As Hawthorne would later admit in his comments on John Brown, "What right have I to complain of any other man's fool impulses, when I cannot possibly control my own!" (23:428).

The House of the Seven Gables and the Means of Political Power

As he prepared *The Scarlet Letter* for publication, Hawthorne discussed the title of the book with his publisher James T. Fields. Hawthorne suggested that they print the title in red ink, because it would prove "attractive to the great gull whom we are endeavoring to circumvent" (16:308), that is, the reading public. He wrote his next romance, *The House of the Seven Gables,* in the Berkshires in the fall and winter of 1850, filling it with images of sunshine yet writing in the light of a smoldering resentment toward self-serving political figures and a gullible public that could be manipulated by lies and appeals to their passions. In the book, he continued to explore the themes of false witnessing, unreliable evidence, and the doubling of victim and victimizer, all linked to Salem witchcraft and its legacy.

Before leaving Salem, Hawthorne let several correspondents know how he felt about Upham and his constituents. In a letter of June 5, 1849, Hawthorne wrote to Longfellow, "I may perhaps select a victim, and let fall one little drop of venom on his heart, that shall make him writhe before the grin of the multitude for a considerable time to come" (16:270). Readers of *The House of the Seven Gables* soon recognized Upham as the model for the despicable Judge Pyncheon. Hawthorne's hostility was more sweeping, though, for he also felt "infinite contempt" for the people of Salem, who listened to the "false indictments" against him with "hardly a voice being raised in my behalf; and then sending one of the false witnesses to Congress, others to the State legislature, and choosing another as their Mayor" (16:329). As part of his revenge, he set his romance in Salem and began by recalling the most shameful event in Salem's past, the witchcraft delusion. He used it as an analogue for current events, and by insisting that "the wrongdoing of one generation lives into the successive ones" (2:2), he made sure Salem and its inhabitants could not escape guilt for their past, especially the fictional Judge Pyncheon, who enjoys "eminent respectability" (2:228) while deceiving almost everyone in town with his "unctuous benignity" (2:117).

The judge is paired with his Puritan ancestor Colonel Pyncheon, and they prey on the poor and the weak—Clifford Pyncheon and Matthew Maule, respectively—to satisfy their lust for wealth and power. Just as the colonel, described as "the iron-hearted Puritan—the relentless persecutor—the grasping and strong-willed man" (2:15), demonstrates the evil he accuses Matthew Maule of practicing as a wizard, the judge, too, indulges in the "unscrupulous pursuit of selfish ends through evil means" and, like his ancestor, acts "under a delusion"—not belief in the devil but belief in "the secret which he supposed Clifford to possess." Hawthorne generalizes about the doggedness behind such delusion: "Men of his strength of purpose, and customary sagacity, if they chance to adopt a mistaken opinion in practical matters, so wedge it and fasten it among things known to be true, that to wrench it out of their minds is hardly less difficult than pulling up an oak" (2:242). The only defense available against such persecution is the curse, the desperate turn to witchcraft or wizardry, as an act of rebellion against one's oppressor. Yet Hawthorne dramatizes the doubling that occurs as a result, causing victims to become victimizers as the generations unfold. Few of the characters in the novel—Maules and Pyncheons alike—stand forth as totally admirable, yet

Hawthorne declares disingenuously that their defects do not "redound, in the remotest degree, to the discredit of the venerable town, of which they profess to be inhabitants" (2:3). His thick irony, which may have gone unnoticed by some readers, would not have been lost on his friends. They knew the contempt that he confessed he felt toward the people of Salem and their "venerable town."

The one person in Salem he most detested ran for national office in 1850, as Hawthorne was writing his romance. Hawthorne followed the good reverend's political fortunes with much interest. Upham had served as state representative from 1840 to 1849, and in 1850, he ran for a seat in the U.S. House of Representatives, which had become a highly charged political arena due to the debate about the expansion of slavery. Spurred by David Wilmot's unsuccessful proviso (which called for the prohibition of slavery in the territory acquired from Mexico), a North-South division opened up in both major parties at this time and led to the rise of the Free-Soilers, a coalition of Conscience Whigs and antislavery Democrats who could not stomach the Compromise of 1850, with its hated Fugitive Slave Act. In Massachusetts, the alliance was led by ex-Democrats, such as Amasa Walker, and ex-Whigs, such as Charles Sumner, who positioned themselves as opponents of what Jonathan Earle has called "the twin aristocracies personified by the northern Money power and the southern slave power."[43] Hawthorne supported this Free-Soil alliance, although his political friends in Salem remained loyal to the Democratic Party there. In the congressional election held in Salem in the fall of 1850, Upham, the Whig candidate, failed to get the majority vote needed to win, in part because four candidates were running, in part because, as I mentioned earlier, the Whigs loyal to Webster did not vote for him.

Hawthorne was delighted. He wrote to Zachariah Burchmore, "I must confess I have enjoyed our reverend friend's defeat, and hope he will have a worse whipping at his next trial" (16:365). To help bring this about, he asked Burchmore, "In the canvass against Upham, did you remind the public of the fact of his refusing to read the Declaration of Independence one Fourth of July, some years ago, on the pleas that he did not assent to its principles? Pike told it for a fact" (16:366). Before learning of Upham's political fate (he was defeated by the Free-Soil candidate in April 1851 by 953 votes), Hawthorne killed off his fictional counterpart with rather sadistic glee in his ironically titled chapter "Governor Pyncheon." Clearly, Judge Pyncheon dies a natural death, choking on his own blood, but in a figurative sense, he is murdered by the author, who seems to delight in the judge's abrupt cessation of life. He carefully describes a fly, "which has smelt out" the body, crawling across the judge's face toward his wide-open eyes to inflict ultimate humiliation upon him. Such a torture fantasy one would think beneath Hawthorne's sensibility, but apparently it was not.

As part of his rather unseemly treatment of Judge Pyncheon (or, rather, his corpse), Hawthorne blackens the body as he sends the judge's soul to hell (the devil apparently awaits, in the form of the cat Grimalkin, to receive it). If Upham's abolitionist leanings were known to Hawthorne—as they apparently were, for he asked Burchmore about the possibility "of a compromise between the Whigs and Freesoilers in favor of Upham" (16:364)—there is an added irony in the following description, which undermines the dead judge's racial purity.

> The gloom has not entered from without. . . . The judge's face, indeed, rigid, and singularly white, refuses to melt into this universal solvent. . . . Has it yet vanished? No!—yes!—not quite! And there is still the swarthy whiteness—we shall venture to marry these ill-agreeing words—the swarthy whiteness of the Judge's face. The features are all gone. There is only the paleness of them left. And how looks it now? There is no window! There is no face! An infinite, inscrutable blackness has annihilated sight! Where is our universe? All crumbled away from us. (2:276)

As David Anthony points out, Judge Pyncheon's face seems here to be the face of elitist American culture itself: "Increasingly diluted by differences of class and race, that face appears here to reflect a failed last moment in the maintenance of upper-class whiteness."[44] I would add that if Judge Pyncheon is indeed based on Charles Upham, Hawthorne would have enjoyed imposing a form of amalgamation on a Conscience Whig suspected of abolitionism. When the judge does not show up at the dinner in Boston, attended by a group of political insiders who plan to run him for governor, they conclude "that the Free Soilers have him," and they "fix upon another candidate" (2:275). While imagining his absence in Boston, the author racializes the judge even more, becoming a bit demonic himself. He taunts the "great, black bulk" that the judge's corpse has become, "Rise up, thou subtile, worldly, selfish, iron-hearted hypocrite, and make thy choice, whether still to be subtile, worldly, selfish, iron-hearted, and hypocritical, or to tear these sins out of thy nature, though they bring the life-blood with them! The Avenger is upon thee! Rise up, before it be too late!" (2:283). Of course, it is already too late, as narrator and reader well know.

On its surface, *The House of the Seven Gables* delineates and celebrates the social changes wrought by a new market economy and the displacement of old gentility, represented by Hepzibah and Clifford, by an emergent plebianism, represented by Holgrave and Phoebe. The hateful Judge Pyncheon, however, represents a degraded form of his cousins' gentility, for, as Walter Benn Michaels has observed, he "is certainly more capitalist than nobleman."[45] Indeed, the unseen power of money to corrupt and deceive poses the greatest threat to the town and nation, though few of the characters seem to understand this fact. Holgrave, who professes radical political notions, holds forth about the burden of the past and the oppression of "Dead Men's books," "Dead Men's forms and creeds," "Dead Men's diseases," and "Dead Men's houses" (2:183). Yet after Judge Pyncheon's death, he becomes willing to accept the country estate that he and his bride Phoebe will call home, thus making his reformist principles seem susceptible to corruption by money as well.

The happy ending of the novel, which resolves the tension in the romance between old gentility and new plebianism (neither of which are portrayed very favorably), obscures the underlying point of the romance, which is the baseness at the heart of the current political system. Although the judge dies, this baseness lives on. As Hawthorne puts it in "Governor Pyncheon," "ambition is a talisman more powerful than witchcraft" (2:274), and "the tall and stately edifice" built by men like the judge and filled with the external phenomena of life, "such as gold, landed estate, offices of trust and emolument, public honors," contains a "decaying corpse within," which is "that secret abomination," the builder's "miserable soul!" (2:229–30). The men in Boston waiting for the judge, whom they plan to make governor, "steal from the people . . . the power of choosing its own rulers," and "the popular voice, at the next gubernatorial election, though loud as thunder, will be really but an echo of what these gentlemen shall speak, under their breath, at your friend's festive board" (2:274). This is Hawthorne's contemporary version of what happened in Salem in 1692, when "clergymen, judges, statesmen" (2:8) exerted undue influence on the people and contributed to their fears and hatreds. The main difference between 1692 and 1850 is that the religious justification for political demagoguery has become less apparent.

Although Judge Pyncheon is the obvious villain of the novel, his villainy is veiled from the people of Salem. Even the charming plebian Phoebe Pyncheon, whose cheerfulness and efficiency shine forth for all to see, becomes complicit in the judge's villainy, by her failure to see that his political and economic success is fraudulent, built on a foundation of lies and intimidation. In this sense, Hawthorne makes her a representative of those townspeople who once succumbed to the witchcraft delusion and continue to be duped by their political leaders. Some passages in the novel grant Phoebe insight and the ability to make real that which is only fanciful. As part of his courtship, Holgrave flatters her in his description of life as a complex riddle: "It requires intuitive sympathy, like a young girl's, to solve it. A mere observer, like myself (who never have any intuitions, and am, at best only subtile and acute) is pretty certain to go astray" (2:179). Hawthorne, as narrator, also flatters Phoebe (and Sophia, her model?) by observing, "these transparent natures are often deceptive in their depth; those pebbles at the bottom of a fountain are farther from us than we think" (2:182). Yet during the course of the novel, he provides Phoebe little intellectual depth and limits her skills to good housekeeping and adept salesmanship. In Hepzibah's cent shop. Phoebe proves popular with the people of Salem, for like them, she is willing to ignore all that might disturb her equanimity and geniality. She does not "exactly comprehend" Holgrave (2:93); she ignores "whatever was morbid" in Clifford's "mind and experience" (2:143); and she is taken in by the judge's expressed desire to make Clifford happy: "Is he so very wicked?" she asks. "Yet his offers were surely kind!" (2:131). Hawthorne describes her mind as of "the trim, orderly, and limit-loving class" (2:131). She is willing to grant the smiling judge the status he assumes as a political figure who says and does all the right things, making him seem admirable.

Phoebe shows an instinctual reaction to the judge, drawing away when he tries to kiss her, but she quickly overcomes it. When he speaks benevolently to Clifford, she feels "very much in the mood of running up to Judge Pyncheon and giving him, of her own accord, the kiss from which she had so recently shrunk away" (2:128). Happily, she fails to act on this impulse, yet she stays confused about why Hepzibah and Clifford feel threatened by him, and she attributes their hostility to an ancient family feud. When told by

Hebzibah that the judge "has a heart of iron," she finds herself perplexed about

> whether judges, clergymen, and other characters of that eminent stamp and respectability, could really, in any single instance, be otherwise than just and upright men. A doubt of this nature has a most disturbing influence, and, if shown to be a fact, comes with fearful and startling effect, on minds of the trim, orderly, and limit-loving class, in which we find our little country-girl. Dispositions more boldly speculative may derive a stern enjoyment from the discovery, since there must be evil in the world, that a high man is as likely to grasp his share of it, as a low one. A wider scope of view, and a deeper insight, may see rank, dignity, and station, all proved illusory, so far as regards their claim to human reverence, and yet not feel as if the universe were thereby tumbled headlong into chaos. But Phoebe, in order to keep the universe in its old place, was fain to smother, in some degree, her own intuitions as to Judge Pyncheon's character. (2:131–32)

Thus Hawthorne sets out the terms for his critique of political power and its abuse: there are indeed cruel and evil men who attain high office and control over affairs of state, yet those who fail to perceive their true nature and trust them are almost as culpable for the harm they cause. Phoebe thus represents the electorate—or, more accurately, that "great gull," the public—which fails to show the "wider scope of view," the "deeper insight," needed to penetrate the illusions of "rank, dignity, and station" these iron men create.

As Phoebe becomes entranced as Holgrave reads to her, the moon, Hawthorne writes, climbs overhead, "unobtrusively melting its disk into the azure—like an ambitious demagogue, who hides his aspiring purpose by assuming the prevalent hue of popular sentiment" (2:213), and it only becomes discernible as darkness falls. Hawthorne describes Phoebe "as unconscious of the crisis through which she had passed, as an infant of the precipice to the verge of which it has rolled" (2:212). Thus her manipulation by Holgrave's voice parallels the public's manipulation by demagoguery, both processes resulting from an infantile level of consciousness that fails to perceive the dangers at hand. The male "younger crowd" of Salem shows less obliviousness but greater prejudice. The cruel young boys, whom Hepzibah imagines directing taunts, cries, and laughter at Clifford if he walked the streets, are but smaller versions of their benighted parents: they "have no more reverence for what is beautiful and holy, nor pity for what is sad—no more sense of sacred misery, sanctifying the human shape in which it embodies itself—than if Satan were the father of them all!" (2:247). Even the comical little Ned Higgins starts "sputtering with wrath" (2:290) when frustrated in his search for treats within the house. He is about to throw a stone through the front window when a stranger stops him and sends him off to school, where he may or may not learn to behave.

Within *The House of the Seven Gables,* only the independent Maules display the ability to discern realities amid appearances. The first Matthew Maule, victim that he is, nevertheless perceives "the bitterness of personal enmity" (2:8) behind the colonel's persecution of him, as well as the medical condition that could prove fatal to the colonel some day. When he fashions his curse, "God will give him blood to drink!" it is, we later learn, "probably founded on a knowledge of the physical predisposition in the Pyncheon race" (2:304). His son, the architect Thomas Maule, perceives that the Indian deed is the most valuable document the colonel has in his possession, so he hides it behind the portrait, escaping the charge of robbery, yet frustrating the Pyncheons by making the figure of the colonel stand between them and their dreams of great wealth. As for the second Matthew Maule, he, too, must be credited with more intelligence and insight than Gervayse Pyncheon and his daughter Alice, the Europeanized Pyncheons, who view him with condescension. Hawthorne, because he did not believe in the reality of witchcraft, uses mesmerism to approximate its putative effects, and when Alice Pyncheon falls victim to the second Matthew Maule's mesmeric powers and behaves like the so-called bewitched girls of Salem, it is not because she is in fact bewitched but because she has succumbed to Maule's superior mental strength. The function of mesmerism within the romance is thus to reveal the susceptibility of certain people, those without power of insight, to become entranced by a reining ism. Although Maule's hypnotizing of Alice has obvious malevolent features, including his enslavement of her, his behavior is redeemed somewhat by the knowledge that his ongoing torment of the young woman has its limits. She catches cold by coming through the rain at his command to attend the bride in the bridal chamber at his wedding, and she subsequently sickens and dies, an event he did not desire, for "[h]e meant to humble Alice, not to kill her" (2:210). Like all of Hawthorne's would-be re-formers, he ends up doing more harm than good.

Holgrave, the character with the most admirable qualities in the romance (though Hepzibah certainly has her heroic moments), observes and under-stands the nature and behavior of all the other characters and, by refusing to use his power over Phoebe to do her any harm, resists the temptation his grandfather succumbed to. Holgrave allows Phoebe to come out of the trance his story of Alice has placed her in and to regain her self-assurance. His love expresses itself through respect, not possession, and Phoebe's natural joy in turn warms his personality. Hawthorne obviously admires Holgrave and makes the reader do so as well, granting him "the rare and high quality of reverence for another's individuality" (2:212). His art, like that Hawthorne aspired to, allows him not only to distinguish illusory appearance from spir-itual reality but also to take the measure of public men and women. As Baym has pointed out, "His daguerreotypes, taken with the help of the sunlight that is his friend and ally, show Pyncheon's true nature, illuminating his vil-lainy and identifying him with his persecuting ancestor."[46] The only insight denied to Holgrave is recognition of his own folly in accepting the judge's es-tate. Perhaps only those who have experienced dire poverty, as Hawthorne surely had, can overlook the sacrifice of principle that such an acceptance in-volves.

CHAPTER 6

Transformative Violence at Home and Abroad

> He never yet was guilty of an effort to cajole his fellow citizens, to operate
> upon their credulity, or to trick them ever into what was right; and therefore
> all the victories which he has ever won in popular assemblies, have been tri-
> umphs doubly honored, being as credible to his audience as to himself.
>
> —Hawthorne, *The Life of Franklin Pierce*

Hawthorne's knowledge of the witchcraft delusion, of the ways in which political and religious leaders could lead the public astray through demagoguery and sensationalism, made him resist appeals to his emotions during
the "impending crisis" that dominated the news in the United States throughout the 1850s.[1] The antislavery movement's turn toward violence as a means
to effect political change, coupled with Southerners' increasing intransigence
and offense at perceived insults to their honor and way of life, generated a
heightened political environment that swept up in its passion even the likes of
Fuller, Thoreau, and Emerson. As I will argue in this chapter, the monomania
critiqued in *The Blithedale Romance* (1852) and the transformative murder
of *The Marble Faun* (1860) have as their backdrop this rising tide of violence.[2] The European revolutions of 1848–49, especially Margaret Fuller's
radical activities in Italy, prefigured a major change in antislavery thinking in
the United States, influenced the prowar attitudes of some of its most important Northern intellectual advocates, and reaffirmed Hawthorne's commitment to political pacifism.[3]

Fuller and the Turn to Violence

In her *New York Tribune* dispatches from Italy during 1848–50, Fuller argued on behalf of revolutionary violence in order to overthrow absolutist rule and establish a republican government. She had met the Italian revolutionary Joseph Mazzini in England before taking up residence in Rome in the fall of 1847, and her willingness to accept violence partly flowed from her support of his radical position within the Italian Risorgimento. Mazzini (whose motto was "God and the People") had plotted a number of insurrections against Italian rulers throughout the 1820s and 1830s. He lived in exile under sentence of death until he returned to Rome after the flight of the pope in the fall of 1848. Fuller's most dramatic and central example of defending Mazzini's revolutionary politics was her approval of the assassination of Count Pellegrino Rossi. On November 16, 1848, Rossi, the new prime minister of the Papal States, was stabbed in the throat as he entered the Chamber of Deputies. In the *Tribune,* Fuller reported that afterward, soldiers and citizens joined in singing "Blessed the hand that rids the earth of a tyrant," and she added, "Certainly, the manner was grandiose."[4] This was her private sentiment as well, and she told her mother, "For me, I never thought to have heard of a violent death with satisfaction, but this act affected me as one of terrible justice."[5] Mazzini's violent methods had lasting influence: ten years later, while Hawthorne was in Rome, a former Mazzini follower, Felice Orsini, tried unsuccessfully to assassinate Napoleon III in Paris by throwing bombs at his carriage, killing 8 people and wounding 142.

Hawthorne's reaction to Fuller's radical political activities can be discerned in his portrayal of Hester, especially as a figure of Liberty, intent on the overthrow of an oppressive patriarchal order.[6] Hester, we are told, looked from her "estranged point of view at human institutions, and whatever priests or legislators had established; criticizing all with hardly more reverence than the Indian would feel for the clerical band, the judicial robe, the pillory, the gallows, the fireside, or the church" (1:199). Without the influence of Pearl, she "might, and not improbably would, have suffered death from the stern tribunals of the period, for attempting to undermine the foundations of the Puritan establishment" (1:165).

In *The Blithedale Romance,* written the year after Fuller, her husband, and her child all drowned in the shipwreck of the *Elizabeth* off the coast of

Fire Island, New York, Hawthorne again drew on his reaction to Fuller and revolutionary violence in his portrayal of Zenobia, who at one point has the look of a woman about to plunge a dagger into her rival, an act of passion more likely "in Italy, instead of New England" (3:78). As Thomas R. Mitchell has shown, Hawthorne's characterization of Zenobia "conflates Fuller's earlier ideological fight for women's rights and for a reformation of the institution of marriage with her fight, the military fight, to overthrow the worldly power of one of the oldest institutions of arbitrary lordship, the Papacy."[7] Despite Zenobia's passion and aggressiveness, or perhaps because of them, she clearly fascinates author and narrator. However, she falls victim to Hollingsworth's self-righteous machinations, as he courts her for her money and then rejects her when he apparently learns she has none, blaming her for unspecified sins. When Coverdale comes upon them as they confront one another, he declares, "I saw in Hollingsworth all that an artist could desire for the grim portrait of a Puritan magistrate, holding inquest of life and death in a case of witchcraft;—in Zenobia, the sorceress herself, not aged, wrinkled, and decrepit, but fair enough to tempt Satan with a force reciprocal to his own" (3:214). As Hollingsworth, the modern-day Puritan, enforces his will, the imagery shifts from male witch-hunting to female rebellion: "In Zenobia's whole person, beholding her more closely, I saw a riotous agitation; the almost delirious disquietude of a great struggle, at the close of which, the vanquished one felt her strength and courage still mighty within her, and longed to renew the contest. My sensations were as if I had come upon a battle-field, before the smoke was as yet cleared away" (3:215). When the smoke does clear, Zenobia's stiff and pierced corpse, dragged from the river, reveals her hands "clenched in immitigable defiance" (3:235). Though she kills herself, her last words curse Hollingsworth as her murderer.[8]

Fuller's defiant example needs to be viewed as part of the international political unrest that followed the revolutions of 1848–49 and that captured Hawthorne's attention as it caused increasingly violent political rhetoric and action throughout the 1850s. The transcendentalists and abolitionists Hawthorne knew personally were often at the center of this development, which focused on the slavery issue. Thoreau's essay "Resistance to Civil Government," for example, which appeared alongside Hawthorne's "Main-street" in Elizabeth Peabody's *Aesthetic Papers* (1849), hints at what lies ahead. In it, Thoreau asks, "But even suppose blood should flow. Is there not a sort of blood shed when the conscience is wounded? Through this wound a man's real manhood and immortality flow out, and he bleeds to an everlasting death."[9] Thoreau's later defense of John Brown in "A Plea for John Brown" proceeds logically from such thinking and allows him to repress his knowledge of the Pottawatomie Massacre, when Brown and seven other men dragged five Southern settlers from their homes on the night of May 24–25, 1856, and split open their skulls with broadswords.[10]

Among some radical abolitionists, signs of a turn from moral suasion to violence had begun in the 1840s, led by outspoken leaders of Northern blacks. David Walker's *Appeal* (1829) advocated violence against slaveholders and struck a responsive chord among many slaves, including perhaps Nat Turner.[11] In 1843, at the National Colored Convention in Buffalo, Henry Highland Garnet echoed Walker by voicing the following message for American slaves: "You cannot be more oppressed than you have been—you cannot suffer greater cruelties than you have already. *Rather die freemen than live to be slaves.* Remember that you are FOUR MILLIONS! . . . Let your motto be resistance! resistance! RESISTANCE!"[12] In 1849, Walker's *Appeal* and Garnet's address were published together in a pamphlet reportedly paid for by an impoverished New York farmer, John Brown.[13] That same year, Frederick Douglass, in a speech at Boston's Faneuil Hall, announced his new commitment to violent means by alluding to the revolutions of 1848. As reported in the *Liberator* on June 8, 1849, he declared,

> I should welcome the intelligence to-morrow, should it come, that the slaves had risen in the South, and that the sable arms which had been engaged in beautifying and adorning the South, were engaged in spreading death and devastation there. (Marked sensation.) . . . Why, you welcomed the intelligence from France, that Louis Phillipe had been barricaded in Paris—you threw up your caps in honor of the victory achieved by Republicanism over Royalty . . . and joined heartily in the watchword of "Liberty, Equality, Fraternity"—and should you not hail, with equal pleasure, the tidings from the South, that the slaves had risen, and achieved for himself, against the iron-hearted slave-holder, what the republicans of France achieved against the royalists of France? (Great applause and some hissing.)[14]

In the 1850s, while William Lloyd Garrison and his followers continued to argue for nonresistance, others in addition to Douglass—such as Angelina Grimké Weld, Samuel May, Wendell Phillips, Henry Wright, and Parker Pilsbury—abandoned their "peace principles" and argued for armed resistance.[15] Pilsbury even told the Massachusetts Anti-Slavery Society that "he longed to see the time come when Boston should run with blood from Beacon Hill to the foot of Broad Street."[16] Passage of the Compromise of 1850, with its divisive Fugitive Slave Act, contributed substantially to this change in attitude within the abolitionist movement. The act empowered federal marshals to require all citizens to aid in the capture and return of fugitive slaves to their owners. This provoked the outrage and defiance of many white Northerners who saw the act as making them personally complicit with slavery. In his journal, Emerson called it "the most detestable law that was ever enacted by a civilized state" and swore, "I will not obey it, by God."[17] Parker's 1850 sermon *The Function and Place of Conscience in Relation to the Laws of Men* declared to the congregation that "it is the natural duty of citizens to rescue every fugitive slave from the hands of the marshal who essays to return him to bondage; to do it peaceably if they can; forcibly if they must, but by all means to do it. . . . if I were a fugitive, and could escape in no other way, I would kill him [the slave-catcher] with as little compunction as I would drive a mosquito from my face. It is high time this was said."[18] (Though a minister, Parker kept a loaded pistol in his desk and a drawn sword within reach of his right hand.)[19]

Acting upon his sense of outrage, Parker formed the Boston Vigilance Committee, with the intent of resisting the new law, by force if necessary. In October 1850, members of this committee thwarted the seizure of runaway slaves William and Ellen Craft. Elsewhere, other abolitionists did the same. In February 1851, a group of black abolitionists rushed into a Boston courtroom and rescued the fugitive slave Shadrach, helping him escape to Canada; and in October 1851, a mob of more than two thousand people stormed a courthouse at Syracuse, New York, and rescued Jerry McHenry, a fugitive in custody.[20]

The Free-Soil Party benefited from Northern reaction to the Fugitive Slave Act. In Massachusetts, long a Whig stronghold, a coalition of Democrats and Free-Soilers won a majority of seats in the state legislature in the elections of 1850 and sent the former Whig Charles Sumner to the U.S. Senate as a Free-Soiler.[21] "Among the conservative and propertied class, in New York, Boston, and elsewhere," David Potter has observed, "a vigorous sentiment of support for the law itself and for Daniel Webster as its sponsor was strongly in evidence."[22] Hawthorne, however, stood not among these conservatives but with the coalition of Democrats and Free-Soilers. In May 1851, he wrote to Longfellow lauding the election of their mutual friend Sumner to the Senate, adding that he felt no "pre-eminent ardor" for the abolitionist cause and identifying the Fugitive Slave Law as "the only thing that could have blown me into any respectable degree of warmth on this great subject of the day—if it really be the great subject—a point which another age can determine better than ours" (16:431). Several months later, he elaborated upon his political shift, telling his friend Burchmore in Salem that he was glad that Burchmore had "stood out so stiffly against all compromise with the Free-Soilers," but explaining,

> As for myself, being entirely out of political life, I act upon other considerations. I have not, as you suggest, the slightest sympathy for the slaves; or, at least, not half so much as for the laboring whites, who, I believe, as a general thing, are ten times worse off than the Southern negros. Still, whenever I am absolutely cornered, I shall go for New England rather than the South;—and this Fugitive Law cornered me. Of course, I knew what I was doing when I signed that Free-Soil document, and bade farewell to all ideas of foreign consulships, or other official stations. (16:456)

Like many other Northern Democrats who aligned themselves with the Free-Soilers due to the Fugitive Slave Law, Hawthorne returned to his old party in 1852, earning a foreign consulship by doing so. His rationale most likely matched that of William Cullen Bryant and many other Barnburners turned Free-Soilers who thought that the Southern hold on the party had been broken in 1850 and that, as Jonathan Earle puts it, "the Democratic Party, at least in the North, had been redeemed."[23] Even Van Buren (who ran for president on the Free-Soil ticket in 1848) decided to return to the Democratic Party. Although Hawthorne remained someone who would always "go for New England rather than the South," he nevertheless appreciated those Democrats, such as Franklin Pierce and John O'Sullivan, who tried to unify the party and the country. A number of other Democrats felt the same. Earle notes that "for fourteen months after the 1852 election, Free Soil—as a movement, an ideology and a party—was practically moribund."[24]

The Blithedale Romance and *The Life of Franklin Pierce:* A Political Diptych

Hawthorne began writing *The Blithedale Romance* (1852) in the fall of 1851, and he used the novel to set out his opposition not to the utopian experiment at Brook Farm (though he found Fourierism repugnant) but to reformers like Hollingsworth, whose philanthropy masked destructive and deadly egotism. As with his creation of Surveyor Hawthorne in *The Scarlet Letter,* Hawthorne uses an unreliable first-person narrator, Coverdale, to essay his political views and critique them at the same time. (He would do the same in "Chiefly about War-Matters," using editorial footnotes to question his own statements in the text.) As a minor poet, Coverdale indulges in obsessive voyeurism and speculation, especially about Zenobia and Hollingsworth, both of whom he finds physically attractive. But as he criticizes their activism and deceit, he indicts his own detachment and timidity. As in *The Scarlet Letter,* all of the characters become spectral and ghostlike at times, especially when they masquerade as something they are not. But Hollingsworth's iron will controls the action and leads to tragedy.

Hawthorne assigns Hollingsworth the central role of the deluded adversary of the devil, who discovers that his own deity "is but a spectrum of the very priest himself, projected upon the surrounding darkness." Coverdale claims to love Hollingsworth, yet he uses metaphors of violence that provide a powerful explanation of why such men need to be resisted: "They will keep no friend, unless he make himself the mirror of their purpose; they will smite and slay you, and trample your dead corpse under foot, all the more readily, if you take the first step with them, and cannot take the second, and the third, and every other step of their terribly straight path" (3:70). Zenobia becomes the main victim of Hollingsworth's monomania, and her "dead corpse" brings Coverdale's metaphors to life in the novel's catastrophe.

Thomas R. Mitchell has provided a useful summary of what Fuller contributed to Hawthorne's creation of the character of Zenobia, including her intellectual attractiveness and vitality, her fight for women's rights, her pride and apparent arrogance, and her death by drowning.[25] Hollingsworth, by comparison, seems to have no one model but to be a composite of several reformers Hawthorne knew well. Like Emerson, he attracts others through his eloquence and idealism yet treats them with coldness when they approach too close. Like such strong-willed reformers as Parker, Garrison, and even Orestes Brownson, he exudes power through his rhetoric and demeanor. (Sophia Hawthorne described Parker as "bold and unscrupulous" and observed that "the moment any person thinks he is particularly original, and the private possessor of truth, he becomes one-sided and a monomaniac.")[26] Ironically, Parker thought Hollingsworth a portrait of Garrison. "He thinks Garrison will flinch at Hawthorne's picture of the philanthropist," Mary Mann wrote to her husband, Horace.[27]

As for Coverdale, many readers have identified him with Hawthorne, emphasizing their shared propensity for voyeurism, irony, and political detachment. At one point in the narrative, Coverdale declares, "Were there any cause, in this whole chaos of human struggle, worth a sane man's dying for, and which my death would benefit, then—provided, however, the effort did not involve an unreasonable amount of trouble—methinks I might be bold to offer up my life. If Kossuth, for example, would pitch the battle-field of Hungarian rights within an easy ride of my abode, and choose a mild, sunny morning, after breakfast, for the conflict, Miles Coverdale would gladly be his man, for one brave rush upon the leveled bayonets. Farther than that, I should be loth to pledge myself" (3:246–47). Kossuth, of course, was the famous Hungarian freedom fighter who briefly headed the Hungarian Republic of 1849 before the combined forces of Austria and Russia overpowered his army and drove him from the country. Imprisoned for a time in Turkey, he made his way to the United States in December 1851, seeking money and arms to continue his revolutionary efforts. Richard Brodhead, in his influential essay "Hawthorne and the Fate of Politics," has used Coverdale's humorous comments on Kossuth as support for his argument that "typically, the quickening of Hawthorne's sense of involvement in the larger struggles of a society in conflict ends up producing not deepened commitment but deepened irony toward such commitment. The main source of this irony is Hawthorne's unregenerate fantasy."[28] This is both a reasonable and now prevalent view of Hawthorne's politics, but Brodhead's argument overlooks as much as it reveals. Unlike Coverdale, Hawthorne had steel in his character, and as a writer and public intellectual, he boldly adhered to his political pacifism, drawing on a courage (or stubbornness, if you will) that his self-ef-facing humor veiled from his readers. What has been called Hawthorne's "re-treat" or "escape" into fantasy, then, can also be seen as his means of secur-ing and maintaining an independent and complex understanding of current events.

His satirical treatment of Coverdale and Kossuth, I would argue, is a covert expression of Hawthorne's pacifism, spurred most likely by the irra-tional Kossuth "fever" sweeping the country at the time. Banquets, parades, and speeches honored the Hungarian revolutionary wherever he went, in-cluding Concord, where Emerson gave a speech on his behalf in May 1852 and hosted a reception in his honor. Hawthorne declared himself "as enthu-siastic a lump of frozen mud" (16:537) about Kossuth before seeing him at West Newton, and the Hungarian's commitment to violence and warfare could not have impressed him. Responding to his welcome in Concord, Kos-suth declared, "I have never yet heard of a despot who had yielded to the moral influence of liberty. The ground of Concord itself is an evidence of it. The doors and shutters of oppression must be opened by bayonets, that the blessed rays of your institutions may penetrate into the dark dwelling-house of oppressed humanity."[29] (The image of a military assault on the dwelling of oppressed persons perhaps says more about the noble Magyar's disdain for the Slavs of Hungary than he wished.) During his tour of the United States, Kossuth refused to talk about Negro slavery, despite his emphasis on Hun-garian "liberty," and the abolitionists faulted him for his diplomatic silence. Surprisingly, Hawthorne, too, found this objectionable. In a letter of June 14, 1854, to George Sanders, Hawthorne reacted to a public letter of Kossuth's and asked, "Does he not trim and truckle a little? Doubtless, he says nothing but what is perfectly true; but yet it has not the effect of frank and outspoken truth. I wish he had commenced his reply with a sturdier condemnation of slavery" (17:230).

In the first half of *The Blithedale Romance,* the reader often finds Hollingsworth, because of his strength of character, more appealing than the timid Coverdale, making it easy to understand why the two main women prefer him to the effete poet. Moreover, even at the end, Hawthorne grants the debilitated Hollingsworth some compassion when he appears as an en-lightened, yet ruined, man—one haunted by the dead Zenobia, who charged him with her murder. The moral Coverdale then offers—though perhaps not to be trusted, given its deliverer—accords with Hawthorne's own belief system as expressed elsewhere. Coverdale argues,

> Admitting what is called Philanthropy, when adopted as a profession, to be often useful by its energetic impulse to society at large, it is perilous to the individual, whose ruling passion, in one exclusive channel, it thus becomes. It ruins, or is fearfully apt to ruin, the heart; the rich juices of which God never meant should be pressed violently out, and distilled into alcoholic liquor, by an unnatural process; but should render life sweet, bland, and gently beneficent, and insensibly influence other hearts and other lives to the same blessed end. (3:243)

The rejection of a singular "ruling passion" and of feelings "pressed violently out," coincides with Hawthorne's increasing dismay at the political activism he saw growing around him, especially in Concord, where he had just bought his new home, the Wayside, purchased from the Alcotts, next door to Ephraim Bull, producer of the Concord grape.[30]

Hawthorne's *The Life of Franklin Pierce,* written several months later, during July and August 1852, stands as a companion piece to *The Blithedale Romance.* In it, Hawthorne paints a portrait of his ideal political activist, who rises above any singular ism to work for the good of humanity as a whole. Whereas the reformer of *The Blithedale Romance* is willing to sacrifice others and their peaceful community to his own narrow cause, the Pierce of Hawthorne's later book devotes himself to others and approaches political issues in the broadest terms for the good of the nation. Hawthorne includes an account of Pierce's service in the Mexican War ("a gallant soldier in the hour of your country's need") but works to present him essentially "as a man of peaceful pursuits. 'Cedant arma togae.' ['Let wars yield to peace']" (16:561–62.). All evidence indicates that General Pierce, as he was called, indeed shared Hawthorne's commitment to peace.

In 1852, the campaign strategy of both the Democrats and the Whigs was to focus on personalities and avoid raising the emotional issue of slavery, for they knew whatever was said on the issue could alienate one section of the country or another. The party platforms of both major parties thus stressed unity and endorsed the Compromise of 1850 and the Fugitive Slave Act. Only the Free-Soil Party, with Senator John P. Hale of New Hampshire as its candidate, took a sectional stand: its platform declared "that slavery is a sin

against God and a crime against man" and demanded the immediate and total repeal of the Fugitive Slave Act.[31] (Hale garnered 5 percent of the popular
vote.) Placing himself at odds with the Democratic Party's campaign strategy,
Hawthorne chose to address the slavery issue in *The Life of Franklin Pierce*,
perhaps because he understood how important the issue was among his own
family and friends in Massachusetts (his brother-in-law Horace Mann was
running for governor on the Free-Soil ticket),[32] perhaps because he found it
cowardly to "trim and truckle," as he would accuse Kossuth of doing. In a
letter of July 5, 1852, he wrote to Pierce,

> I am sensible of a very difficult and delicate part of my task, in your con-
> nection with the great subject of variance between the North and South.
> There is no way, however, open to my perception—no course either of
> true policy, or worthy either of you or your biographer—save to meet the
> question with perfect candor and frankness, and to state what has been
> your action, and what your position; not pugnaciously, and, by no man-
> ner of means, defensively, but so as to put you on the broadest ground
> possible, as a man for the whole country. I suppose I shall see my way
> clearer, when I actually approach these knotty points; but at all events,
> they are not to be shirked nor blinked. (16:561)

Because of this resolve, Hawthorne organized his biography around
Pierce's support of the Compromise of 1850, but by doing so, he allowed his
future biographers and critics to misinterpret his own political views by
conflating them with Pierce's. The most well-known example of this occurs in
Sacvan Bercovitch's highly acclaimed *The Office of "The Scarlet Letter"*
(1991), which bases its interpretation of Hawthorne's masterpiece on the assumption that Hawthorne supported the Compromise of 1850, an assumption gained primarily from *The Life of Franklin Pierce*.[33] While Hawthorne
indeed tried to make the best case he could for Pierce's politics, they were not
his own, and he identified with the Pierce he created no more than he did
with the admirable characters in his fiction, whose motives and perspectives
he illuminated for his readers.

To justify Pierce's most objectionable political stance (in the eyes of
Northern voters), Hawthorne structured the biography in such a way as to
make Pierce's support of the Compromise of 1850 seem a natural and admirable effect of his lifelong patriotism. His book thus begins by focusing not

on Pierce himself or his ancestry but on his father, General Benjamin Pierce, who fought in the American Revolution and helped found the nation. In his second chapter, Hawthorne stages a reunion between the old general and his surviving "comrades at arms," who reminisce about "the era of seventy-six" as young Franklin looks on. "A scene like this," Hawthorne writes, "must have been profitable for a young man to witness, as being likely to give him a stronger sense, *than most of us can attain,* of the value of that Union which these old heroes had risked so much to consolidate—of that common country which they had sacrificed every thing to create" (23:284–85, emphasis added). Later, when he summarizes Pierce's service in the House of Representatives, Hawthorne again credits him with a national perspective (which Hawthorne himself did not share).

> Without loving New England less, he loved the broad area of the country more. He thus retained that equal sentiment of patriotism for the whole land, with which his father had imbued him. . . . His sense of the value of the Union, which had been taught him at the fireside, from earliest infancy, by the stories of patriotic valor that he there heard, was now strengthened by friendly association with its representatives from every quarter. (23:293–94)

When Hawthorne finally arrives at the recent and volatile topic of the Compromise, he attributes Pierce's vote and voice to "the principles which he had long ago avowed" (23:350), thus distinguishing him from Clay and Webster, both regarded as political opportunists, seeking the presidency. "We have sketched some of the influences amid which he grew up," Hawthorne writes, "inheriting his father's love of country, mindful of the old patriot's valor in so many conflicts of the Revolution, and having close before his eyes the example of brothers and relatives, more than one of whom have bled for America, both at the extremist North and farthest South; . . . Such a man, with such hereditary recollections, and such a personal experience, must not narrow himself to adopt the cause of one section of his native country against another" (23:351–52). Using such qualifications, Hawthorne avoids casting disapproval upon those New Englanders, including himself, who opposed the Compromise, while he also presents Pierce not as proslavery but as patriotically pro-Union.

Hawthorne's own political views emerge most noticeably when he briefly turns his attention from Pierce to political figures in general. In a little-known passage, he describes three kinds of men found in the political arena: (1) opportunists, or "mere politicians of the moment"; (2) theorists; and (3) historically informed statesmen endowed with practical sagacity. He obviously admires the latter most, and as he explains how they are formed, he seems to be referencing himself.

[W]hen the actual observation of public measures goes hand in hand with study, when the mind is capable of comparing the present with its analogies in the past, and of grasping the principle that belongs to both, this is to have history for a living tutor. If the student be fit for such instruction, he will be seen to act afterwards with the elevation of a high ideal, and with the expediency, the sagacity, the instinct of what is fit and practicable, which make the advantage of the man of actual affairs over the mere theorist. (23:293)

Thus, whereas Hollingsworth, the slave of his theory, can only see things from his own narrow point of view, the true statesman draws from the past and present, the ideal and the actual, to attain the wider scope of view and deeper insight needed to understand the world.

Despite the political differences separating Hawthorne and Pierce, they agreed on the benefits of restraint and the destructiveness of "agitation" (23:351)—that is, the rhetoric and actions of "the fiercest, the least scrupulous, and the most consistent of those, who battle against slavery" (23:350). While offering no apology for slavery in the biography, Hawthorne argues for making its abolition part of a broader conception of philanthropy, restating in new terms the central idea that underlies his politics: "There is no instance, in all history, of the human will and intellect having perfected any great moral reform by the methods which it adapted to that end; but the progress of the world, at every step, leaves some evil or wrong on the path behind it. . . . Whatever contributes to the great cause of good, contributes to all its subdivisions and varieties" (23:352). Thus Hawthorne argued that the election of Pierce, a good man motivated by "liberal, generous, catholic sympathy" (23:282), should have the support of "the lover of his race, the enthusiast, the philanthropist of whatever theory" (23:352).

Through his writing of Pierce's biography, Hawthorne came to admire the man's administrative skills. Until recently, he has been one of the few commentators on Pierce who has expressed such admiration. In a private letter, Hawthorne told Bridge,

> I have come seriously to the conclusion that he has in him many of the chief elements of a great ruler. . . . His talents are administrative; he has a subtle faculty of making affairs roll onward according to his will, and of influencing their course without showing any trace of his action. There are scores of men in the country that seem brighter than he is; but Frank has the directing mind, and will move them about like pawns on a chessboard, and turn all their abilities to better purpose than they themselves could. Such is my idea of him, after many an hour of reflection on his character, while making the best of his poor little biography. He is deep, deep, deep. (16:605–6)

Pierce's most recent biographer, Peter A. Wallner, arrives at the same conclusion, at least with regard to Pierce's winning the presidential nomination as a dark horse. Wallner credits Pierce with "a masterful job of political manipulation" and points out, "He had cleverly allowed his name to surface while professing reluctance for the nomination. By working behind the scenes with his loyal New Hampshire supporters, Washington friends, and Mexican War colleagues, Pierce set himself up as the perfect compromise choice. . . . So subtle was his touch that even the members of the Concord clique may not have realized how completely Pierce had controlled the entire operation."[34]

Thanks to the return of many Northern Democrats, such as Hawthorne, to the party and thanks also to the support of Cotton Whigs (whom Webster, distraught at his failure to win his party's nomination, encouraged to vote for Pierce), the 1852 presidential election proved one-sided with regard to electoral votes (254 to 42). Yet neither Winfield Scott, known for his pomposity, nor Pierce, a political unknown, generated much excitement, and as election day approached, Hawthorne wrote to Bridge, "I do not feel very sanguine about the result of this election. There is hardly a spark of enthusiasm in either party; but what there is, so far as I can judge, is on the side of Scott. The prospect is none of the brightest, either in New York, Ohio, or Pennsylvania; and unless [Frank] gets one of them he goes to the wall" (16:606). Pierce won all three of the states Hawthorne mentioned and twenty-seven of the thirty-one states in all. He failed to win the popular vote in the Northern states, however, and he favored Southerners in his political appointments, including Jefferson Davis as his secretary of war, which evoked strong objections from voters in New England.

Pierce rewarded one New Englander, however, with the Liverpool consulate, the most lucrative post at his disposal. Hawthorne was confirmed without objection in the Senate, and the new Free-Soil senator from Massachusetts, Charles Sumner, quickly congratulated him.

> My dear Hawthorne,
>
> "Good!" "good,"—I exclaimed aloud on the floor of the Senate, as your nomination was announced.
>
> "Good!" "good,"—I now write to you on its confirmation.
>
> Nothing could be more grateful to me. Before you go I hope to see you.
>
> > Ever Yours
> > Charles Sumner
> > "Senate Chamber, March 26th '53[35]

Ironically, Sumner would become Pierce's most bitter political foe, but Hawthorne maintained his friendship with Sumner, while reserving his greatest sympathy for Pierce, whose administration proved a disaster. Hawthorne professed disinterest in the effect his connection to Pierce had on his own reputation (though his sisters-in-law Mary Mann and Elizabeth Peabody expressed repeated concern), and while he continued to differ with Pierce on a number of political issues, such as the importance of keeping the South in the Union, he remained loyal to Pierce personally. What did distress Hawthorne during his seven years abroad was the increasing violence in the United States caused by the slavery issue. As the decade of the 1850s progressed, the "agitation" grew in intensity, leading to "Bleeding Kansas" and the Civil War.

The Events of 1854 and Their Aftermath

When the Pierce administration began, it seemed that the slavery controversy was quieting down and that national attention was turning to other domestic and foreign issues. However, the popular success of Stowe's *Uncle Tom's Cabin* (1852) and the introduction of the infamous Nebraska Bill by Senator

Stephen A. Douglas of Illinois changed all that. For a mixture of motives, Douglas proposed to divide the Nebraska territory into two regions, Nebraska and Kansas, and to allow the "citizens" of each territory to decide whether or not to allow slavery within their borders. The bill explicitly (in an amendment added to gather Southern support) repealed the Missouri Compromise of 1820, which had designated lands of the Louisiana Purchase north of 3630' latitude as permanently free of slavery. In the North, the Nebraska Bill provoked immediate and furious outrage, and Pierce, who had reluctantly agreed to support it, was vilified as "the tool of the slave-holding power."[36] A group of Free-Soil congressmen, led by Senators Salmon P. Chase of Ohio and Sumner, launched an immediate attack; their widely circulated "Address of the Independent Democrats, to the People of the United States" denounced the bill "as a gross violation of a sacred pledge, as a criminal betrayal of precious rights, as part and parcel of an atrocious plot to exclude from a vast unoccupied region, immigrants from the Old World and free laborers from our own States, and convert it into a dreary region of despotism, inhabited by masters and slaves."[37] Both Whigs and Democrats lost supporters by passing the bill, 37–14 in the Senate, 113–100 in the House. Horace Greeley later recalled, "The passage of the Nebraska Bill was a death-blow to Northern quietism and complacency, mistakenly deeming themselves conservatism. To all who fondly dreamed or blindly hoped that the Slavery question would somehow settle itself, it cried, 'Sleep no more!' in thunder-tones that would not die unheeded. . . . Systematic, determined resistance was now recognized as imperative duty."[38] Thus was born the Republican Party. Thus, also, began a renaissance of Puritan rhetoric. As Potter points out, the opponents of slavery in Congress "had a strength which derived not only from the righteousness of their cause but also from the technical skill of a distinctive style of publicity, which discredited their opponents as not only wrong on principle but also morally depraved and personally odious."[39]

In England, Hawthorne, reading the vicious partisan charges and countercharges, felt more and more alienated from his country and his own party. On March 30, 1854, he wrote to Bridge, "It sickens me to look back to America. I am sick to death of the continual fuss, and tumult and excitement, and bad blood, which we keep up about political topics." He was particularly concerned about how Pierce was holding up, especially given his struggles with alcohol in the past: "I wish you would send me the most minute particulars about Pierce—how he looks and behaves when you meet him—how his health and spirits are—whether he has any secret bad habits—and, above all, what the public really thinks of him; a point which I am utterly unable to get at, through the newspapers" (17:188). Several months later, on July 3, 1854, Sophia Hawthorne wrote to her sister Mary Mann,

> at this quiet distance from the scene & the turmoil, you cannot think how insane all America seems to us about the Nebraska bill, & now I find you share the frenzy too. We recieve hundreds of newspapers—whig, democrat, free soil & all kinds, from Washington, New York, Boston & Salem—giving us every one of the speeches in Congress—& all the comments, criticisms, abuse, vituperation, indignation & every thing else going in those great United States.[40]

The effect of reading numerous American newspapers (almost all of which had party alliances), as opposed to reading say just one, was to be struck by the differences caused by partisan thought and feeling, that is, by the lack of truthfulness each party engaged in to gain political advantage. In the wake of the Kansas-Nebraska Act, a profusion of political parties and alignments emerged, most notably the nativist Know-Nothings, and the Pierce administration was subjected to heavy partisan abuse. Thus Hawthorne would write to Pierce in the summer of 1855, "What a storm you have had to face! And how like a man you have faced it" (17:351). To his publisher Ticknor, he wrote, "I find it impossible to read American papers (of whatever political party) without being ashamed of my country" (17:237). To be an American in England, especially in an official capacity, was to represent America, to be called on to defend the policies and practices of the administration that appointed him, yet Hawthorne found this increasingly difficult to do, especially given England's commitment to antislavery.

As the debate over the Nebraska Bill raged in the spring of 1854, the case of the fugitive slave Anthony Burns added to the political passion that the Hawthornes found appalling. Burns, who had been working in a Boston clothing store, was arrested on May 24 by Southern slave hunters and, after being identified by his owner, was locked up in the courthouse to await a judicial decision on his fate. Headlines from the antislavery *Commonwealth* proclaimed, "ANOTHER MAN SEIZED IN BOSTON BY THE MAN

HUNTERS!! THE DEVIL-BILL RENEWING ITS VIGOR AND GETTING UP A JUBILEE AMONG US ON THE PASSAGE OF THE NEBRASKA BILL!!!"[41] The Boston Vigilance Committee held an excited and confused protest meeting in Faneuil Hall, at which Wendell Phillips and Theodore Parker spoke passionately about the need for action;[42] meanwhile, their friend, transcendentalist minister Thomas Higginson, and a mob of followers battered down the courthouse door in an attempt to rescue Burns, killing a volunteer guard, an Irishman named James Batchelder, in the process. (Bronson Alcott provided belated support on the scene.) The newspapers aligned with the Pierce administration characterized the attack on the courthouse as treason. The *Boston Post,* for example, declared, "The abolitionists and their confederates did all they could to subserve the cause of mob law! Their treasonable meeting at Faneuil Hall was not enough. It was not enough that Parker, and Phillips, and their associates excited the passions of their deluded dupes up to the pitch of destruction and murder, nor that seditious handbills startled the passers-by at the corners of the streets."[43] John Mitchel's *Citizen* declared that of all the "coteries" of Boston, "the most pestiferous and despicable is the Parker-Phillips assembly of fanatics and fools, with their double-distilled moonshine of universal brotherhood, while they excite a mob to murder; and their maudlin transcendentalism which staggers through our libraries in such a pitiable state, that one would like to send it to the watch-house, where Don Quixote's vagrant volumes were detained."[44] Even the usually sedate *Dodge's Literary Museum* berated the abolitionists "demoniac zeal" and claimed that "the Passionate demagogues" had "inflamed the passions of the ignorant and reckless, incited them to tumult and violence and murder, and left no stone unturned by which to stain our streets with the blood of anarchy."[45]

After a futile defense mounted by Richard Henry Dana Jr., Judge Edward Greely Loring ordered Burns returned to his master, Charles Suttle. Wendell Phillips delivered the bad news to Burns in his cell and later recalled, "There I vowed anew before the ever-living God I would consecrate all the powers He had given me to hasten the time when an innocent man should be safe on the sacred soil of the Puritans."[46] To ensure no additional rescue would succeed, President Pierce, declaring that "the law must be executed," sent federal troops to escort Burns to the harbor, as thousands of Bostonians, offended at this insult to their independence, looked on with anger and dismay.

Buildings were draped in black, and black-edged American flags flew above the street. The *National Era* asked, "Is this offensive interposition of the Federal Power, within a sovereign State, a safe precedent? Is this constant resort to a Standing Army, to enforce an odious Federal enactment, favorable to the stability of Republican institutions?"[47] The Hawthornes' friend James Freeman Clarke, the minister who married them, delivered a sermon titled "A Discourse on the Rendition of A Burns," which denounced the "SLAVE POWER, which has triumphed in Congress over the Rights of the North" and blamed the "false policy of those who have sought to conciliate the South by concession." Clarke vowed, "Henceforth I shall reckon it no small part of my professional work to speak, to act, and to pray for the American Slave."[48]

On July 4, 1854, Sophia Hawthorne wrote to her father,

We have seen in the papers accounts on all sides of the great slave case in Boston. The abolitionists certainly seem raving distracted, but not in the least brave. . . . Oh how much harm to the wretched slave these crazy men do! Mr Parker was far more the murderer of that officer than the man who shot him. How bloodthirsty he is. How like madmen they behave— & all to no purpose. The poor slave will doubtless suffer more for the trouble his capture has cost his master than if he had taken him quietly.[49]

Although one has to question Sophia's misplaced anger here (directed not at the slaveholder but at those who would thwart him), she correctly assumed that an example would be made of Burns upon his return to Richmond, where he was kept four months tightly shackled in a slave pen, becoming seriously ill. The poor health he developed from this torture led to his death at the age of twenty-eight.

As Hawthorne became increasingly distressed about the rising tide of violence in his own country, his Concord neighbors were contributing to this change through their new political commitments. When the huge antislavery rally to protest the Nebraska Bill and the Burns "kidnapping" was held at Framingham Grove on July 4, 1854, Thoreau joined the speakers, who included Frederick Douglass, Sojourner Truth, and Garrison. The latter brought cheers from the crowd of three thousand with an onstage burning of copies of the Fugitive Slave Act, the court's decision in the Anthony Burns case, and the U.S. Constitution. The speech Thoreau wrote for the occasion,

"Slavery in Massachusetts," also attracted favorable attention, at least among abolitionists. It was published in the *Liberator* on July 21 and reprinted in the *New York Tribune* on August 2 and in the *National Anti-Slavery Standard* on November 12—in the latter, under the title "Words That Burn." The speech drew upon a series of Thoreau's journal entries, which reveal his immediate outrage at Burns's remission. In one, he declared, "Rather than thus consent to establish Hell upon earth—to be a party to this establishment—I would touch a match to blow up earth & hell together. I will not accept life in America or on this planet on such terms."[50] In his essay, he broadened this declaration to read: "I need not say what match I would touch, what system endeavor to blow up—but as I love my life, I would side with the light, and let the dark earth roll from under me, calling my mother and brother to follow."[51]

Thoreau engaged in no suicide bombing, of course, but he heaped contempt on the government and its representatives, especially the marines and militia who carried out orders from above. Thoreau called the attack on the Boston courthouse "bloody & disinterestedly heroic."[52] Parker had condemned the slain Batchelder, writing, "a man has been killed. He was a volunteer in this service. He liked the business of enslaving a man, and has gone to render an account to God for his gratuitous wickedness."[53] Thoreau expressed a similar estimate of the police and marines, for they, he claimed, "were not men of sense nor of principle—in a high moral sense they were not *men* at all." "What is wanted," he declared, "is men, not of policy, but of probity—who recognize a higher law than the Constitution."[54] In his most threatening entry, he asserted, "I am calculating how many miscreants each honest man can dispose of. I trust that all just men will conspire."[55] In "Slavery in Massachusetts," he rephrased this to read: "My thoughts are murder to the State, and involuntarily go plotting against her."[56] Though he did not join a plot against the state, his friends Parker, Higginson, and Franklin Sanborn did, joining with three others as John Brown's "Secret Six," who provided Brown with weapons and money for his activities in "Bleeding Kansas" and his raid on Harpers Ferry.[57]

Higginson, the most devoted member of the group, had been inspired by Fuller's revolutionary example. As a boy, he knew Fuller as a fascinating friend of his older sister, and he identified with her willingness to convert ideas into political action. She "had upon me, through her writings, a more immediate intellectual influence than any one except Emerson, and possibly Parker," he declared in the biography of her he later wrote.[58] After leading the abortive attack on the Boston courthouse to free Burns, Higginson defended himself in a sermon by saying he had discovered that he was living under a despotism and that he must become a rebel: "I see now, that while Slavery is national, law and order must constantly be on the wrong side. I see that the case stands for me precisely as it stands for Kossuth and Mazzini, and I must take the consequences."[59] In 1856, he followed in Fuller's footsteps by becoming a correspondent for Greeley's *Tribune,* traveling to "Bleeding Kansas," where he wrote dispatches comparing antislavery setters to European revolutionaries and comparing the United States to Austria and Russia, known for their despotism.[60]

His reports contributed to the sensationalism and propaganda that surrounded the violence in Kansas. Potter points out that "by far the most active newspaper in reporting affairs in Kansas was the New York *Tribune* edited by Horace Greeley, who proved a true field marshal in the propaganda war."[61] As an example, Potter cites the sacking of Lawrence, Kansas, by Sheriff Jones and his large "posse" of Missouri "ruffians." The *Tribune* reported the event under the headlines "STARTLING NEWS FROM KANSAS—THE WAR ACTUALLY BEGUN—TRIUMPH OF THE BORDER RUFFIANS— LAWRENCE IN RUINS—SEVERAL PERSONS SLAUGHTERED—FREEDOM BLOODILY SUBDUED." Several days later, in less sensational style, the paper acknowledged that scarcely anyone in Lawrence had gotten hurt.[62]

Both antislavery settlers and proslavery settlers in Kansas were being killed, however, and in May 1856, a dispatch that appeared in the *New York Daily Tribune* accurately observed, "No man's life is safe; no kind of property secure. A Guerrilla war exists in Kansas, and unless the people in the States come to our rescue and relief speedily, we shall all likewise perish."[63] In a resolution that same month, the American Anti-Slavery Society blamed the president for the violence.

We are living under the sway of "Border-Ruffianism," incarnated in the person of Franklin Pierce—no longer the legitimate President of the United states, but one deserving of immediate impeachment and removal for his perfidy and treason as the unscrupulous tool of the Slave Power; and, therefore, that we are in the midst of a revolution to throw off the chains of a slave holding oligarchy a thousand times more intolerable to be borne than any ever imposed upon our Revolutionary fathers by the mother country.[64]

As part of this so-called revolution, John Brown and his sons took it upon themselves to revenge the sacking of Lawrence and the previous murder of two young antislavery men, John Jones and John Stewart, by riding to Pottawatomie Creek on the night of May 24 and murdering five proslavery settlers living there. As reported in the *New York Herald,* "[t]hese devils in human form dragged their captives just outside" their cabins and left them "cold and dead upon the ground, gashed, torn, hacked and disfigured to a degree at which even Indian barbarity would shudder. The windpipe of the old man, for instance, was entirely cut out, his throat cut from ear to ear. The body of one young man has the face and head sacrificed, and the hands are cut and chopped up with a bowie knife."[65] Brown proclaimed he was acting for God and the Army of the North.

The United States seemed especially violent and bloody in the spring of 1856. On May 22, the day after the sack of Lawrence and two days before the Pottawatomie Massacre, South Carolina congressman Preston Brooks assaulted Charles Sumner without warning in the Senate chamber, beating him with a heavy cane until he was lying bloody and unconscious on the floor. Sumner's injuries, both physical and psychological, were severe, and he did not return to the Senate for three and a half years. Northerners were outraged by the barbaric assault. (See figure 7, which obscures the face of Brooks and conveys the idea that his violence represents "Southern chivalry." The pen in Sumner's hand and the cudgel in Brooks's are meant to characterize the different modes of behavior in the two sections of the country.) At a protest meeting in Concord on May 26, 1856, Emerson asserted that the assault "taught us the lesson of centuries. I do not see how a barbarous community and a civilized community can constitute one state."[66]

For Southerners, Brooks's "chastising" of Sumner represented an honorable defense of Southern honor, provoked by the abuse heaped by Sumner upon the South in general and particularly upon Brooks's uncle, Senator Andrew Pickens Butler of South Carolina. In his two-day speech titled "The Crime against Kansas," Sumner had combined invective against Pierce's Kansas policy with ridicule of Butler and damnation of the South. Butler,

J. L. Magee, *Southern Chivalry: Argument Versus Club's*, 1856. Lithograph.
(Print Collection, Miriam and Ira D. Wallach, Division of Art, Prints, and Pho-
tographs, New York Public Library, Astor, Lenox and Tilden Foundations.)

who had challenged Sumner's commitment to the Constitution, suffered
from a speech impediment, and Sumner had alluded to this by recalling that
Butler had "overflowed with rage at the simple suggestion that Kansas had
applied for admission as a State, and, with incoherent phrases discharged the
loose expectoration of his speech, now upon her representative, and then
upon her people. . . . He cannot open his mouth, but out there flies a blun-
der."[67] More provocatively, Sumner had pressed two hot buttons of Southern
pride and shame, the rape of a white woman by a black man and the lust of
a white man for his black mistress. He had identified the "crime" against
Kansas as "the rape of a virgin territory, compelling it to the hateful embrace
of slavery," and he had accused Butler of having chosen as a mistress "polluted in the sight of the world . . . the harlot, slavery."[68] When Senator Douglass, author of the Nebraska Bill, had objected to Sumner's speech, Sumner
had called Douglass a "noisome, squat, and nameless animal" who switched
"out from his tongue the perpetual stench of offensive personality."[69]

In the months following the assault on Sumner, Southerners sent Brooks new canes—to replace the one he broke caning Sumner—and staged rallies in his honor, including a huge barbecue and ball attended by some five to eight thousand people.[70] Sumner's Republican Party, on the other hand, gained many new members due to his martyrdom. Those who opposed the party in Massachusetts, the wounded Sumner claimed, were "in sympathy, open or disguised, with the vulgar enemy, quickening everywhere the lash of the taskmaster, and helping forward the Satanic carnival of slavery."[71] The rhetoric was effective, but some of those who refused to condemn the assault and endorse Sumner's "defence of human rights and free territory" faced abolitionist wrath. Emory Washburne, Whig ex-governor of Massachusetts, put it in terms of the witchcraft hysteria: "It is not enough that you agree with them. You must say your creed in their words with their intonation and just when they bid you or they hang or burn you as a heretic."[72]

Even before Sumner's beating, Emerson, like Thoreau, had succumbed to the polarizing rhetoric of the day, becoming more committed to political violence each year. Emerson's "Lecture on Slavery," given on January 25, 1855, shows a marked change in attitude toward group effort. "Whilst I insist on the doctrine of the independence and the inspiration of the individual, I do not cripple but exalt the social action," he said, adding, "It is so delicious to act with great masses to great aims."[73] In his speech at a Kansas relief meeting in Cambridge on September 10, 1856, he advocated sending arms to the Kansas settlers and adopted the rhetoric and perspective of Greeley's *Tribune,* claiming, "There is this peculiarity about the case of Kansas, that all the right is on one side. We hear the screams of hunted wives and children answered by the howl of the butchers."[74] When John Brown came east some three months later, seeking money and guns to continue his fight in Kansas, he received a warm welcome from Emerson and others. He visited Sumner in Boston in early 1857 and asked to see the bloody coat he was wearing when he was assaulted. According to David Donald, "Painfully Sumner had hobbled to his closet and handed the garment, still stiff with blood to Brown, who closely examined it and 'said nothing . . . but . . . his lips compressed and his eyes shown like polished steel.'"[75]

Brown also paid a visit to Concord, where he met with Thoreau and Emerson, the latter inviting him to spend the night in a guest room he reserved in a nearby farmhouse.[76] According to David Reynolds, the transcendentalists knew about Brown's role in the Pottawatomie murders "yet em-

braced him anyway. . . . They were thoroughly familiar with—and support-
ive of—his overall violent strategy."[77] Petrulionis has offered a more
qualified description of their support, pointing out that "those abolitionists
who did read sketchy reports about Brown's role in the Pottawatomie murders could easily dismiss such stories as half-truths, as proslavery cant, especially when Brown categorically denied involvement."[78] Brown's self-presen-
tation, perhaps more than his actions, impressed the transcendentalists, and
as Robert Richardson has concluded, "Emerson recognized and approved of
John Brown's apocalyptic finality and his intransigent moral absolutism."[79]
For Hawthorne, such recognition and approval were misplaced.

Brown's sensational speech in the Concord town hall in early March 1857
struck a responsive chord in his auditors, for it overflowed with selective gory
details, which Brown dramatized by holding up a trace chain he said had
bound one of his sons dragged to prison by a Missouri ruffian. He also said
he had lost two sons in Kansas, one murdered and one driven insane by torture at the hands of proslavery invaders.[80] In his journal, Emerson recorded,
"Captain John Brown of Kansas gave a good account of himself in the Town
Hall, last night, to a meeting of Citizens. One of his good points was, the
folly of the peace party in Kansas, who believed, that their strength lay in the
greatness of their wrongs, & so discountenanced resistance. He wished to
know if their wrong was greater than the negro's, & what kind of strength
they gave to the negro?"[81] According to Emerson's son Edward, his father
gave generously to Brown's efforts in Kansas, knowing full well that weapons
would be purchased.[82] When Brown returned to Concord in the spring of
1859, he led his audience to believe he was still struggling to make Kansas a
free state, but he was actually planning his raid on Harpers Ferry, which took
place on October 16, 1859.

The Marble Faun: Forgiveness versus Vengeance

The literary consequences of Hawthorne's reading about the growing crisis in
the United States during his years abroad can be found in his next romance,
The Marble Faun, which combines descriptions of Italian art, architecture,
and scenery with an exploration of the psychological effects of killing on behalf of the oppressed. Like many of Hawthorne's earlier works, the romance
draws on images of witchcraft and revolution as it examines the attempt to

destroy evil, personified by Miriam's model and linked through superstition to the so-called "Spectre of the Catacombs," the "Man-Demon" who haunts that underground region seeking "to beguile new victims into his own misery" (4:33). The character Hawthorne creates to rid the world of this devil—and thus to become demonic himself—is not an older villain on the order of Chillingworth or Judge Pyncheon but an innocent young Italian, Donatello, a sylvan figure resembling the "faun" of the title. Donatello rehearses the familiar political transformation in Hawthorne's imagined world, turning from an innocent youth to a savage adult under the influence of momentary passion—in this case, rage inspired by Miriam's distress.

Miriam's rebellious character seems based in part on Fuller's revolutionary activities in Rome during 1848–49, especially her public approval of Rossi's assassination,[83] while Donatello shares many of the traits Hawthorne associated with Thoreau. In *The Marble Faun,* as Thomas R. Mitchell points out, Hawthorne creates "a parallel to Fuller's efforts to articulate an ideological justification for the republican insurrection in Rome by linking it to democratic revolutions of the past." Mitchell points to one passage in particular: "Miriam directs Donatello to Pompey's forum immediately after the murder and 'treading loftily past,' proclaims: 'For there was a great deed done here! . . . a deed of blood, like ours! Who knows, but we may meet the high and ever-sad fraternity of Caesar's murderers, and exchange a salutation?'"[84] Obviously, Hawthorne understood Fuller's perspective on the assassination of the pope's minister in 1848, but he revealed his skepticism about it by having Miriam refer to Brutus and his coconspirators as "murderers." Behind all the art and aestheticism of *The Marble Faun* stands Hawthorne's political purpose: to critique the notion of righteous violence.

Hawthorne's pacifism faced a powerful challenge from Fuller's dispatches from Rome, Thoreau's "Slavery in Massachusetts," Emerson's addresses, and the sermons of Parker, Higginson, and Clarke, all of which condemned slavery and condoned violence—even killing—on behalf of liberty. *The Marble Faun* responds to this challenge by alluding to parallel examples of such violence in classical mythology, the Bible, and world history, all of which are subtly criticized by means of an alternative value system based on Christian love, peace, and forgiveness. The fact that Miriam is rumored to have Negro blood in her veins (just one of many speculations about her past) introduces the issue of slavery and miscegenation into the romance. (According to one rumor, she is the "offspring of a Southern American planter, who had given her an elaborate education and endowed her with his wealth" [4:23].) Donatello's killing of her oppressor, with her approval, gains additional political significance from Donatello's own racial traits, which, as Nancy Bentley first pointed out, link him to racialist discourse emphasizing the primitive and brutelike character of Negroes.[85]

Hawthorne's preface to *The Marble Faun*, often cited to show his blindness to the evil of slavery, needs to be interpreted as somewhat ironic, given his concern that America itself was bitterly divided over slavery and was on the precipice of civil war.

> No author, without a trial, can conceive of the difficulty of writing a Romance about a country where there is no shadow, no antiquity, no mystery, no picturesque and gloomy wrong, nor anything but a commonplace prosperity, in broad and simple daylight, as is happily the case with my dear native land. (4:3)

Such a statement can be paired with Hawthorne's insistence, in his preface to *The House of the Seven Gables*, that he cherishes "a proper respect" for the people of Salem, as well as with his claim, in the preface to *The Blithedale Romance*, that his characters "are entirely fictitious" and have no reference to those he knew at Brook Farm. To "gull" his obtuse readers seems to have been one of Hawthorne's small pleasures in life.

Hawthorne was keenly aware that his "dear native land" was suffering from "gloomy wrong" that threatened to tear it apart. In a letter to Bridge of December 14, 1854, Hawthorne told his friend that the United States had become "so convulsed with party-spirit as it is, so crochetty, so restless, so ill-tempered. From this distance, it looks to me as if there were an actual fissure between the North and the South, which may widen and deepen into a gulf, anon" (17:294).[86] Two years later, he lamented the news from his own country and declared to William Ticknor, "I find myself less and less inclined to come back. . . . I sympathize with no party, but hate them all—free-soilers, pro-slavery men, and whatever else—all alike In fact, I have no country, or only just enough of one to be ashamed of; and I can tell you, an American finds it difficult to hold up his head, on this side of the water, in these days" (17:559).

After moving to Italy in 1858, Hawthorne was visited from March 10 to April 19 by an old friend, ex-president Franklin Pierce, who brought an insider's perspective (albeit darkly colored) on recent political developments. A month later, as Hawthorne was collecting material with the intent "of writing a little romance" about the faun, he discussed "Bleeding Kansas" with the poet and newspaper editor William Cullen Bryant, who had been instrumental in establishing the Free-Soil Party and, in 1856, the national Republican Party.[87] In a notebook entry of May 22, 1858, Hawthorne wrote,

> I introduced the subject of Kansas, and methought his face forthwith assumed the bitter keenness of the Editor of a political newspaper, while speaking of the triumph of the administration [Buchanan's] over free soil opposition. I inquired whether he had seen Sumner recently; and he gave a very sad account of him as he appeared at their last meeting, which was in Paris. (14:222–23)

Kansas, as Hawthorne well knew, had become increasingly violent, and Sumner was still recovering from having been beaten senseless on the floor of the Senate. Sumner recovered from his physical wounds, but as Bryant told Hawthorne, it seemed "that the shock upon his nerves had extended to his intellect, and was irremediable." Hawthorne found this information "about as sad as anything can be," adding, "He was merely (though with excellent abilities) one of the best fellows in the world, and ought to have lived and died in good-fellowship with all the world" (14:223).[88]

In *The Marble Faun*, Hawthorne's interest in the American political scene combines with his heightened awareness of European art. He uses the relations among his four main characters—two American artists, one Anglo-Italian-Jewish artist, and one Italian nobleman—to explore multiple perspectives on a mysterious crime, the assassination of a shadowy figure who once posed as a model. From the outset, Miriam's art and her identification with Beatrice Cenci suggest her willingness to use violent means against an oppressor, and Donatello's devotion to her, along with his own latent savagery, foreshadow the murder of the model, who becomes representative of a corrupt and despotic government. (Near the end, we learn that the model has entered the priesthood.) As several commentators have pointed out, the setting of the romance, present-day Rome, retains the tense political atmosphere it had ten years before, during the days of the Roman Republic, and Fuller's presence hovers over the work, along with those of revolutionaries (e.g., Mazzini) who fought against the pope, the French, and the Austrians. Robert Levine has pointed out, "Hawthorne continually reminds the reader of the coercive presence throughout Rome of the French military."[89] This is particularly apparent during the Roman Carnival, where, Hawthorne writes,

> Detachments of French infantry stood by their stacked muskets in the Piazza del Popolo, at one extremity of the course, and before the palace of the Austrian embassy, at the other, and by the column of Antoninus, midway between. Had that chained tiger-cat, the Roman populace, shown only so much as the tips of his claws, the sabers would have been flashing and the bullets whistling, in right earnest, among the combatants who now pelted one another with mock sugar-plums and wilted flowers. (4:441)

The Marble Faun examines the complexities of sin and guilt, as Hawthorne does in almost all of his works, but here, stirred by past and present political tensions, Hawthorne expands his canvas to examine dramatically not merely the moral dilemmas of individuals but the morality of a political principle as well. In his attempt to instruct his readers, he uses an approach he praised in *The Life of Franklin Pierce*: "comparing the present with its analogies in the past, and of grasping the principle that belongs to both" (23:293). Thus Donatello, though apolitical and naive, becomes, through his association with Miriam, a representative political agent, a rebel, acting on behalf of an obscure cause that neither he nor the reader can discern.

Levine has made a persuasive case for reading Miriam "as an anti-Catholic revolutionary, perhaps even an assassin, of 1848," and he argues that the murder "can be viewed as a republican revolutionary assassination of a tyrannizing Catholic who sought to keep her in thrall."[90] This certainly seems reasonable, especially given the Cenci material, as does Levine's argument that the Carnival becomes "a ritual of revolution that restages the Protestant-republican revolution of 1848" (28), with Kenyon role-playing as the pope's prime minister, Rossi.[91] At the Carnival, Kenyon is surrounded by a mob of fantastic figures, including a gigantic woman who draws "a huge pistol," takes "aim right at the obdurate sculptor's breast," and pulls "the trigger"(4:446). Yet though events of 1848 informed Hawthorne's romance, his intent went beyond them. He uses Miriam's paintings to remind us that political violence is ongoing and that myth, legend, and history are filled with analogous violent events, many perpetrated by women. Miriam's identification with Beatrice Cenci, for example, as John Carlos Rowe has pointed out, "not only enhances the aura of Italian 'ruin' but warns . . . readers of the dangers of this historical repetition-compulsion, whereby both women's rights and republican revolution will follow a venerable will-to-power and cycle of revenge."[92] The painting of the archangel Michael slaying the monster Satan, however, also reminds us that killing, as opposed to victimization, is weighted toward males.

As a childlike sylvan figure and savage political agent, Donatello shares many of the traits attributed to Fuller's Italian lover, Count Ossoli, yet he also seems modeled on Thoreau, whose recent published thoughts were "murder to the state."[93] In Concord, Thoreau was known as a modern-day Pan, a joyful flute player, at home among nature, animals, and children. In the early 1840s, he and Hawthorne boated on the Concord River together; talked "about pine-trees and Indian relics, in his hermitage at Walden" (1:25); and went ice-skating together with Emerson on the river behind the Manse, where Thoreau performed his "dithyrambic dances and Bacchic leaps."[94] This side of Thoreau was no doubt evoked by the appearance of *Walden* (1854), which Hawthorne read and recommended to Monckton Milnes in the fall of 1854.[95] Yet Thoreau's abolitionist activities in that same year, which defended the attack on the Boston courthouse and the murder of the volunteer policeman Batchelder, revealed the angry and violent side of Thoreau's character.

The transformation that Donatello undergoes is foreshadowed early in *The Marble Faun,* when Miriam notices Donatello's anger at the appearance of the model and tells the others, "If you consider him well, you will observe an odd mixture of the bull-dog, or some other equally fierce brute, in our friend's composition; a trait of savageness hardly to be expected in such a gentle creature as he usually is" (4:18). Eighteen chapters later, Donatello has become Miriam's devoted protector, and in a moment of rage, he throws her persecutor from the Tarpeian Rock. This deed, the narrator tells us, "kindled him into a man; it had developed within him an intelligence which was no native characteristic of the Donatello whom we have heretofore known." In less explicit fashion, Hawthorne suggests the deed's demonic qualities.

"What have you done!" said Miriam, in a horrour-stricken whisper.

The glow of rage was still lurid on Donatello's face, and now flashed out again from his eyes.

"I did what ought to be done to a traitor!" he replied. "I did what your eyes bade me do, when I asked them with mine, as I held the wretch over the precipice!" (4:172)

Miriam does not deny her part in the murder. "We two slew yonder wretch," she tells him, adding, "The deed knots us together for time and eternity, like the coil of a serpent!" The narrator's comment on the bond reinforces this satanic image.

> Their deed—the crime which Donatello wrought, and Miriam accepted on the instant—had wreathed itself, as she said, like a serpent, in inextricable links about both their souls, and drew them into one, by its terrible contractile power. It was closer than a marriage-bond. So intimate, in those first moments, was the union, that it seemed as if their new sympathy annihilated all other ties, and that they were released from the chain of humanity; a new sphere, a special law, had been created for them alone. (4:174)

Readers familiar with the definition of the "Unpardonable Sin" in "Ethan Brand" and with Hester's claim "What we did had a consecration of its own" in *The Scarlet Letter* will recognize the moral deficiencies in Donatello's intelligence, especially since murder falls into a category beyond sin.

Miriam, like Hester, tries to rationalize their guilt away, but the consolation she offers rings hollow: "Surely, it is no crime that we have committed. One wretched and worthless life has been sacrificed, to cement two other lives forevermore" (4:175). Readers are meant to be suspicious of this claim, I believe, and also of the idea of the "Fortunate Fall" she later tries to purvey. As she and Kenyon stand admiring Donatello on the Campagna, she asks aloud, "Was the crime—in which he and I were wedded—was it a blessing in that strange disguise? . . . Was that very sin—into which Adam precipitated himself and all his race—was it the destined means by which, over a long pathway of toil and sorrow, we are to attain a higher, brighter, and profounder happiness, than our lost birthright gave?" (4:434). The correct answer is no. This "theory," as Miriam calls it (using a loaded term in

Hawthorne's vocabulary), has been taken at face value by many commentators on the novel; however, it does not accord with Hawthorne's disbelief in righteous violence. It does serve, though, to highlight the idea so that its diabolism can be seen, at least by those who take another view of it and arrive at Hawthorne's conclusion. As Evan Carton has pointed out, the concept of the "Fortunate Fall" "is expressly rejected at the end of the novel by Hawthorne's American characters and, implicitly, by his narrator."[96] When Hilda hears Kenyon venture it, she shrinks from him "with an expression of horrour" and exclaims, "This is terrible; and I could weep for you, if you indeed believe it. Do not you perceive what a mockery your creed makes, not only of all religious sentiment, but of moral law, and how it annuls and obliterates whatever precepts of Heaven are written deepest within us?" (4:460–61). Hilda trusts her heart, and Hawthorne, though critical of her severity, appears to validate her reaction, to which Kenyon defers, calling her his spiritual guide.

Hawthorne provides almost no support for Miriam's "theory" that Donatello has gained more than guilt as a result of his deed; on the contrary, he suggests that the murder has made Donatello even more like the hated "model" he kills. Throughout the romance, the appearances, characters, and roles of the model and Donatello subtly converge.[97] For example, when the model emerges from the catacombs, he is wearing goatskin breeches, making him appear a "antique Satyr," and during the wild "Sylvan Dance" in the Borghese Gardens, the model shows up as "a shaggy man in goat-skin breeches, who looked like rustic Pan in person, and footed it as merrily as he" (4:87–88). Like Donatello, he prances before Miriam, "almost vying with the agility of Donatello himself," and the model thus evokes the faun's "animal rage" and hatred (4:89–90). Donatello's murder of this double in response to Miriam's glance, places him in the same relationship to Miriam as that the model once held, for apparently the model committed some crime in concert with Miriam, possibly a political assassination, and Donatello does the same, eventually taking his place at Miriam's side.

Hawthorne never provides the reader with the specifics regarding Miriam's prior crime or with the motives behind it. Readers of the romance, since its first appearance, have objected to this uncertainty or "haziness," which Hawthorne pretended to correct with the paragraphs he added to subsequent printings. Brodhead has seen this as a major weakness of the novel and has attributed it to Hawthorne's failing powers as a writer: "This is the work of an author for whom fiction's ground of motivation and transformative action has become inaccessible, unsusceptible to imaginative production or definition."[98] Yet Hawthorne's decision not to specify these matters raises them to the transhistorical level he wishes to address; moreover, here, as elsewhere, his primary interest lies in consequences, rather than the "ground of motivation," which becomes irrelevant when the "transformative action" is the killing of another human being.

Like his friend John O'Sullivan, Hawthorne opposed the death penalty for any crime, and he felt revulsion at those who took it upon themselves to play the part of executioners. In his *Report on the Abolition of Punishment by Death* (1841), O'Sullivan, while serving as New York State legislator, argued, as Robert Sampson explains, that the

> Mosaic code of the ancient Jews . . . might be suitable for a "semi-barbarian nation" in ancient times but not for a civilized democracy such as the United States. In his view, Jesus Christ's "radically democratic spirit and direction of his whole doctrine" replaced the Mosaic code and at the center of Christ's teachings stands a "great truth in its naked and sacred simplicity—absolute, unequivocal, universal—'Thou shall not *kill*.'"[99]

Hawthorne's views coincided with O'Sullivan's on this issue. (The legislation O'Sullivan introduced into the New York legislature never passed, due, ironically, to strong opposition from members of the clergy.) Even though Hawthorne would declare of John Brown that "[n]obody was ever more justly hanged," he qualified even this outburst by adding that although Virginia "had a right" to take Brown's life, "it would have been better for her, in the hour that is fast coming, if she could generously have forgotten the criminality of his attempt in its enormous folly" (23:428).

Throughout Hawthorne's career, the New Testament, rather than the Old, guided his attitude toward the sinful, though he certainly succumbed to the temptation to take revenge on Upham (albeit with a pen), and at the beginning of the Civil War, he found himself briefly caught up in the war fever that pervaded Concord and New England. In *The Marble Faun*, the most powerful way he critiques Old Testament justice and advocates New Testament forgiveness is by means of iconography. Chapter 5, "Miriam's Studio," features drawings of murderous women, in particular Jael, who drove a tent stake through the temple of the sleeping Sisera; Judith, who killed Holofernes; and Salome, the daughter of Herodias, who asked for the head of John the Baptist. In the drawings, the first two Old Testament women, engaged in resisting political subjugation, fail to maintain their traditional heroic status. Miriam's sketch of Jael initially showed "the stern Jewess" as a perfect woman with "a lovely form, and a high, heroic face of lofty beauty"; but "dissatisfied either with her own work or the terrible story itself, Miriam had added a certain wayward quirk of her pencil, which at once converted the heroine into a vulgar murderess" (4:43). Similarly, in the sketch of the story of Judith, the head of Holofernes mocks and startles Judith by displaying "a diabolical grin of triumphant malice." These alterations, as the narrator points out, "bring out the moral, that woman must strike through her own heart to reach a human life, whatever were the motive that impelled her" (4:44). Although this sentence is admittedly cryptic (perhaps intentionally so), Hawthorne seems to be implying that to kill even an oppressor, one (especially a woman) must first destroy one's humanity or at least deaden one's heart to feelings of compassion and sympathy.

With the sketch of Salome and the head of John the Baptist, Hawthorne clarifies his point somewhat. Based on Bernardo Luini's picture in the Uffizi Gallery at Florence, which shows John's head with its eyes closed, Miriam's sketch imparts "to the Saint's face a look of gentle and heavenly reproach, with sad and blessed eyes fixed upward at the maiden; by the force of which miraculous glance, her whole womanhood was at once awakened to love and endless remorse" (4:44). The remorse is certainly not surprising, but the love is. Unlike Jael and Judith and Salome's mother, Herodias, Salome feels no sense of righteous vengeance but a new spirit of Christian love. According to Mark's Gospel, when Jesus is told of the murder of John the Baptist, he displays no anger or hostility; rather, he merely says, "Come ye yourselves apart into a desert place, and rest a while."[100] A multitude follows, which he miraculously feeds with five loaves and two fishes.

This spirit of Christian love and forgiveness makes its climactic appearance in chapters 34 and 35 of *The Marble Faun*, when Kenyon arranges the reunion between Donatello and Miriam in Perugia, near the statue of Pope Julius, who extends his benediction to all. As an icon of ideal governance, this figure sits in a bronze chair, elevated high above the pavement, and seemed to take kindly, yet authoritative cognizance of the busy scene which was, at that moment, passing before his eyes. His right hand was raised and spread abroad, as if in the act of shedding forth a benediction, which every man (so broad, so wise, and so serenely affectionate, was the bronze Pope's regard) might hope to feel quietly descending upon the need, or the distress, that he had closest at his heart. The statue had life and observation in it, as well as patriarchal majesty. An imaginative spectator could not but be impressed with the idea, that this benignly awful representative of Divine and human authority might rise from his brazen chair, should any great public exigency demand his interposition, and encourage or restrain the people by his gesture, or even by prophetic utterances worthy of so grand a presence. (4:313–14)[101]

Donatello feels "the blessing upon [his] spirit" as he looks upward at the statue, and Miriam, as she bows her head before it, feels its "benign and awe-inspiring influence." Hawthorne frees this ideal "representative of Divine and human authority" from its sectarian orthodoxy (but not its gender) by adding, "No matter though it were modeled for a Catholic Chief-Priest; the desolate heart, whatever be its religion, recognizes in that image the likeness of a Father!" (4:316). (The search for an absent loving father is a recurrent theme in Hawthorne's works, as well as Melville's, for obvious biographical reasons.)

Hawthorne must have been tempted, as Baym has observed, to conclude his romance with this moving scene in Perugia, but he added fifteen more chapters, and Baym speculates that he did so to explore Kenyon's "sympathetic participation in Donatello's 'crime' and to question whether it was a crime 'in an absolute sense.'"[102] She points out that the model "is a maniac and a specter of evil" and that because he "is characterized as a living phantom, his murder does not strike one as the taking of a life."[103] While I agree that Hawthorne wishes to explore the morality of the "crime," the model, despite Miriam's arguments, is not a demon or phantom but a human being who bleeds real blood and dies a real death, before their eyes. The use of the term "spectre" to refer to him surely signals Hawthorne's remembrance of "the saddest and most humiliating passage in our history" (6:79), when the battle against Satan and the use of specter evidence resulted in the deaths of so many innocent people in Salem. Moreover, Hawthorne's recurrent insight that to battle against evil in the world seldom achieves its desired results has to inform any interpretation of *The Marble Faun*. The mythological battle against evil, represented in the sketch of Guido's painting of the archangel Michael and Satan (where the model appears as Satan), thus stands as an unrealistic binary "model" of human behavior.

In contrast, Giovanni Sodoma's fresco of Christ bound to a pillar offers an alternative vision of heroism that Hawthorne obviously admires. As Hilda seeks spiritual revelation unsuccessfully in the galleries of Rome, she recalls this "inexpressibly touching" picture at Siena.

> The great and reverent painter has not suffered the Son of God to be merely an object of pity, though depicting him in a state so profoundly pitiful. He is rescued from it, we know not how—by nothing less than miracle—by a celestial majesty and beauty, and some quality of which these are the outward garniture. He is as much, and as visibly, our Redeemer, there bound, there fainting, and bleeding from the scourge, with the Cross in view, as if he sat on his throne of glory in the heavens! Sodoma, in this matchless picture, has done more towards reconciling the incongruity of Divine Omnipotence and outraged, suffering Humanity, combined in one person, than the theologians ever did. (4:340)

As we know from his notebooks, such imagery moved Hawthorne as well as his character Hilda, and his response was surely affected by the personal anguish he suffered while writing *The Marble Faun*. As is well known, his daughter Una's bout with malaria at this time made her seriously ill, to Hawthorne's deep distress. "I was fearfully anxious about him," Sophia wrote to her sister Elizabeth, explaining, "He never knew what suffering was before. . . . Mrs. Ward said his face surpassed any face she ever looked upon for infinite expression of sorrow too deep for tears—beautiful in endless woe—as if looking always on death."[104] Compassion, not anger, infused Hawthorne's writing during this dark time.

Jenny Franchot has argued that *The Marble Faun* suffers from a decadent atmosphere associated with Roman Catholicism. "Hawthorne," she writes, "images Rome as a monolithic corpse being slowly buried by time, as Capuchin cemeteries disgustingly crowded with monkish skeletons, as the sexualized interiors of confessionals and convents."[105] For her, the romance thus becomes an aesthetic failure, debilitated by a lack of representational vitality and by conventional anti-Catholicism. While not denying these aspects of the romance, I would point out, as Franchot does not, that Hawthorne's alternative images located outside of Rome—in particular, in Peruga, the statue of Pope Julius; in Siena, Sodoma's painting of the bound Christ—make powerful arguments on behalf of Christian heroism versus Old Testament vengeance.[106] These images offer the reader, as they may have offered Hawthorne, a sense of relief, hope, and renewal. Some five months after completing the novel, he wrote Ticknor from England, "If I have written anything well, it should be this Romance; for I have never thought or felt more deeply or taken more pains" (18:262).

Last Months in England

Hawthorne wrote the final words of *The Marble Faun* on November 8, 1859. John Brown's raid on Harpers Ferry occurred on October 16, 1859, and Brown was hanged on December 2, 1859. Soon afterward, Hawthorne learned that Emerson had compared Brown's hanging to Christ's death on the cross. Given Hawthorne's heightened sensitivity at the time to Christian iconography (acquired not through church attendance, which he disdained, but through Italian art), it is not surprising that he found the transcendentalist's statement offensive. He later told a correspondent,

> If Emerson chooses to plant John Brown's gallows on Mount Calvary, the moral and religious sense of mankind will insist on its being placed between the crosses of the two thieves, and not side by side with that of the Savior. I wish he would not say such things, and deem him less excusable than other men; for his apophthegms (though they often have strange life in them) do not so burn and sting his mouth that he is compelled to drop them out of it. (18:463)

In Hawthorne's view, Emerson's deliberate comparisons imply a forethought that should make the linking of Brown and Christ untenable for an eminent scholar like Emerson. (This is the same distinction, by the way, that Hawthorne makes with regard to Arthur's first and second liaisons with Hester in *The Scarlet Letter:* the first was an act of thoughtless passion; the second a matter of free will and therefore less excusable.)

As *The Marble Faun* shows, the larger issue Hawthorne found offensive about the transcendentalists' approach to political behavior was the egotism that encouraged them to deem unlawful behavior beneficent through appeals to a "higher law" than that established by their fellow man. Hawthorne was particularly sensitive to rationalizations of killing—even killing so-called evil persons—in response to a "higher law." When Sophia learned about the transcendentalists' support of John Brown several months after Hawthorne completed his romance, she laid out where she and her husband stood with regard to the rationalization of murder on behalf of the oppressed: "When you get so far out of my idea of right as to talk of its being proper to violate laws sometimes, because we 'can obey higher laws than we break'—this, dear Elizabeth, I used to hear in days past and I consider it a very dangerous and demoralizing doctrine and have always called it 'transcendental slang.' . . . I am just on the point of declaring that I hate transcendentalism because it is full of such immoderate dicta."[107] We do not know for sure whether Hawthorne agreed with Sophia (who served as one model for the severe Hilda), but he did tell a correspondent, in a letter of April 1, 1860, that Sophia "speaks so near me that I cannot tell her voice from my own" (18:256).

During the months before they returned to the United States, the Hawthornes kept up with events at home through a number of American and English newspapers. Hawthorne, in his letters home, indicated his knowledge that political tensions had increased. He wrote to his friend Hillard, "it is now more than six years since the eddies bore me out of the Republican Whirlpool. However, I suppose I must needs plunge in again, next year" (18:184). From the American papers, Hawthorne learned that the Democratic Party had split over slavery and that conventions were held in both Baltimore, Maryland, and Charleston, South Carolina, with each choosing candidates favorable to its position on slavery. In a letter to her sister Elizabeth, Sophia said that she and Hawthorne preferred to read the *Morning Star* of London because it "is on the side of freedom in all senses and is the most sensible, moderate, wise, paper."[108] This newspaper, now a rare text, advocated the principles of the "Manchester School" of politics: free trade, separation of church and state, and extended suffrage. More important, it supported the

"Peace Party" and carried articles and editorials congenial to Hawthorne's political pacifism. An article from April 7, 1860, shows the strength of its pacifism in terms that seem as relevant today as they did then: "Better to be the maimed soldier, the ruined peasant, the bayoneted child, the dishonoured mother—better endure the whole misery of a disastrous campaign collected and heaped upon one person, if such a thing could be—than have the fatal responsibility which lies upon that man who, in wantonness, or selfishness, or even from reckless miscalculation, has been the main promoter of a war that might have been avoided."[109]

During the insurrection in southern Italy in the spring of 1860, the paper advised the British government not to send ships of war to the area, declaring, "we have all a strong sympathy for a suffering people, contending against a brutal despotism; and the most effectual way to show that sympathy is to let the Southern Italians and their Government alone: the end will be the victory of the people."[110] In addition to opposing all forms of British imperialism, the *Morning Star* argued against growing military expenditures, against the London *Times* (which "falsifies facts, perpetuates aristocratic power, and tells readers that bribery is universal"), against slavery in the United States, against cruelty to animals, and against prizefighting (which has "all the popular attraction of a public execution").[111] It reported on political developments in the United States, including an account of a tumultuous scene in the House of Representatives on April 5, 1860, when Owen Lovejoy, Republican congressman of Illinois, gave a speech attacking Southern slaveholders and praising John Brown. "The principle of enslaving human beings because they are inferior," Lovejoy declared," is the doctrine of Democrats, and the doctrine of devils as well, and there is no place in the universe outside of the five points of hell and the Democratic party where the practice and prevalence of such doctrines would not be a disgrace."[112] These remarks and the mention of John Brown brought Southern Democrats to their feet, threatening to hang Lovejoy as they had Brown. Such was the threatening political scene Hawthorne knew awaited him upon his return to the United States.[113]

CHAPTER 7

The Stationary "Fall" of a Public Intellectual

When I hear their drums beating, and see their banners flying, and witness
their steady marching, I declare, were it not for certain silvery monitors hanging by my temples, suggesting prudence, I feel as if I could catch the infection,
shoulder a musket, and be off to the war myself!

—Hawthorne, letter to Francis Bennoch, ca. July 1861

Oh, high, heroic, tremulous juncture, when man felt himself almost an angel,
on the verge of doing deeds that outwardly look so fiendish; oh, strange rapture of the coming battle. We know something of that time now.

—Hawthorne, "Septimius Felton"

During the last five years of Hawthorne's life, most of which he spent in Concord, the gulf between him and his transcendentalist neighbors widened, and
as my introduction pointed out, most of the New England intelligentsia grew
hostile toward him. A number of factors contributed to what was called his
"fall," including his seven-year absence from Concord, his inherent pacifism,
his loyalty to Franklin Pierce, his publishing "Chiefly about War-Matters" in
the *Atlantic Monthly* (an ardently antislavery publication), and his dedication of *Our Old Home* (1863) to Pierce, who had recently—and falsely—been
accused of treason. As the preceding six chapters of this study have tried to
show, Hawthorne's politics did not change appreciably over the course of his

career, though he did become more concerned about the rise of political violence in the United States and more committed to a value system emphasizing peace and compassion. Thus, his "fall" can more accurately be described
as his standing his ground while others succumbed to the "strange rapture of
the coming battle" (13:17). The morality of his pacifism during a time of social injustice and political change is problematic, as he well knew, and his last
writings, both fiction and nonfiction, struggle to justify his politics to himself
and others.

Radicalized Concord

When Hawthorne returned to Concord following his years abroad, his political views seemed especially unwelcome and conspicuous, because Concord,
more than any other place in the country, teemed with a political radicalism
that sanctioned the insurrectionary activities of John Brown. These activities
played a key role in initiating the Civil War, because Brown's collusion with
his Northern supporters, when discovered, confirmed the South's worst fears
about the abolitionists' terrorist methods. Thanks to the moral and financial
support of Emerson and others, especially the "Secret Six"—Sanborn,
Parker, Higginson, Samuel Gridley Howe, Gerrit Smith, and George Luther
Stearns—Brown took with him to Harpers Ferry twenty-one men, 950 pikes,
two hundred revolvers, and 198 Sharps repeating rifles. The pikes were purchased to arm the slaves he expected to join him in an insurrection, though
he did little to organize or lead such an effort. Once in the arsenal at Harpers
Ferry, he procrastinated until captured, and the pikes went unused.

The Sharps rifles, however, served immediate purposes. The first person
Brown and his men killed at Harpers Ferry was Hayward Shepard, a free
black who worked as the porter at the Harpers Ferry train station. He was
shot in the back, the bullet "going through his body and coming out the nip-
ple of his left breast," according to the train conductor.[1] He died a lingering
and agonizing death after being taken inside the station. Thoreau later declared of the raid and the rifles,

> I know that the mass of my countrymen think that the only righteous use
> that can be made of Sharps' rifles and revolvers is to fight duels with
> them, when we are insulted by other nations, or to hunt Indians, or shoot

fugitive slaves with them, or the like. I think that for once the Sharps' rifles and the revolvers were employed in a righteous cause. The tools were in the hands of one who could use them.[2]

Perhaps not. Due to poor planning and bad decisions (e.g., letting a passing B&O train leave the area to alert authorities down the line), Brown's raid soon became a military failure. Not a single slave chose to join his band, and within thirty-six hours, federal troops, under the leadership of Robert E. Lee, put down the rebellion. In the fighting, Brown was wounded and captured; ten of his men were killed, as well as three townsmen, two slaves, one slave-holder, and one marine.[3]

Despite its apparent failure, the Harpers Ferry raid was a success in terms of provoking fear, confusion, and civil war. As historian James McPherson has pointed out, Brown's raid alarmed the South: "Thousands joined military companies; state legislatures appropriated funds for the purchase of arms."[4] The attack on Fort Sumter soon followed. Brown's famous last message suggests he welcomed and prophesied this result: "I John Brown am now quite *certain* that the crimes of this *guilty, land: will* never be purged *away;* but with Blood."[5] As Bertram Wyatt-Brown has speculated, Brown's blunders at Harpers Ferry may have been intentional.

> Warfare is always messy, and the unforeseen often determines victory or defeat. But suppose another motive was at work: a mysterious desire not to succeed in the ordinary sense but to sow sectional discord by making the whole enterprise, and himself in particular, a human sacrifice to the cause of freedom. Viewed in these terms, the outward failure of the raid becomes an inner triumph in the cause of Christ and bleeding humanity.[6]

Although Brown indeed sowed sectional discord, the issue of whether the raid represented a triumph "in the cause of Christ" is debatable. From the perspective of those opposed to righteous violence, including the author of *The Marble Faun,* Brown's actions were not only unlawful but retrograde, re-viving a dated Puritanism. Brown persuaded a number of those in the anti-slavery movement to abandon their adherence to New Testament pacifism and to return to Old Testament notions of a vengeful God. James Redpath, in his 1860 biography of Brown, celebrated this turn, comparing Brown to

Moses, Joshua, and Gideon and declaring that Brown followed a God that "had ordered His enemies to be smitten hip and thigh."[7] As John Seelye has pointed out, Redpath's assertion "is tantamount to saying that in Brown's eyes the New Testament was never written, a form of illiteracy of which the 'old Puritan' was often guilty as well."[8]

Initially, black abolitionists and only a handful of whites spoke out in support of the Harpers Ferry raid—or "invasion," as it was also called. Democrats and Republicans expressed outrage and disapproval, respectively, and blamed one another for Brown's actions, which were widely regarded as insane. The Democrats represented Brown as a tool of the fanatical Republicans, while the Republicans, as Betty Mitchell has argued, represented him as "an excellent citizen" "driven insane as a result of the violence committed by proslavery Democrats in Kansas."[9] Abraham Lincoln, in his Cooper Union Address, pointed out that "John Brown's effort was not a slavery insurrection. It was an attempt by white men to get up a revolt among slaves, in which the slaves refused to participate. In fact, it was so absurd that the slaves, with all their ignorance, saw plainly enough it could not succeed."[10] Among white abolitionists, the raid was similarly dismissed. Garrison called it "misguided, wild, and apparently insane." He pointed out, "The American Anti-Slavery Society and its organ the *Anti-Slavery Standard* and its ally, the *Liberator,* have always earnestly endeavored to dissuade the slaves and their helpers from this method of vindicating their rights."[11]

In the midst of such distancing, Thoreau, Phillips, Parker, Higginson, and Emerson came to Brown's early defense. As Betty Mitchell has pointed out, "the well-publicized words of New England Transcendentalists like Emerson and Thoreau who glorified Brown led traumatized southerners to mistakenly identify these individual sentiments with the main body of northern opinion."[12] Brown's image was also enhanced by his trial, the letters he wrote from prison, and the stoic manner in which he met his death. Denying the desire to kill anyone, he represented himself as a Christlike martyr. "Now, if it is deemed necessary," he famously declared at his trial, "that I should forfeit my life for the furtherance of the ends of justice, and mingle my blood further with the blood of my children and with the blood of millions in this slave country whose rights are disregarded by wicked, cruel, and unjust enactments—I submit: so let it be done."[13]

The transcendentalists were especially impressed by Brown's rhetoric. At first, Emerson was slightly ambivalent about Brown's raid, telling a correspondent in a letter of October 15, 1859, that Brown "is a true hero, but he lost his head there."[14] Yet on November 8, 1859, Emerson gave the address Hawthorne heard about in England, titled "Courage," in which he called Brown "that new saint . . . who, if he shall suffer, will make the gallows like the cross."[15] He quoted with approval what Brown said to him privately about the Golden Rule and the Declaration of Independence: "Better that a whole generation of men, women and children should pass away by a violent death than that one word of either should be violated in this country."[16]

For Thoreau, Brown was not only a Christ figure but also a Puritan warrior, an immortal avatar from the English Civil War, whose weapons and words were in service to his Lord. "It would be in vain to kill him," Thoreau declared, "He died lately in the time of Cromwell, but he reappeared here. Why should he not?"[17] Obviously identifying with Brown, Thoreau calls him "a transcendentalist above all, a man of ideas and principles,"[18] ignoring the bodily pain and death Brown inflicted on others to achieve his ends. When Thoreau spoke to William Dean Howells about his vision of John Brown, he recalled "a sort of John Brown type, a John Brown ideal, a John Brown principle,"[19] rather than John Brown himself. In "The Last Days of John Brown," Thoreau asserted that before Brown died, "he had taken up the sword of the spirit—the sword with which he has really won his greatest and most memorable victories. Now he has not laid aside the sword of the spirit, for he is pure spirit himself, and his sword is pure spirit also."[20] Brown's family, in gratitude for Thoreau's support, reportedly, as Walter Harding notes, presented him with "a huge knife that had belonged to Brown."[21]

By the time the Hawthornes returned to the United States, pacifism and nonresistance had been abandoned by all Brown's supporters in Concord and even by the Garrisonians. In a speech on December 9, 1859, in Boston, Garrison declared, "As a peace man, I am prepared to say, 'Success to every slave insurrection in the South,'" and, "Rather than see men wearing chains in cowardly and servile spirit, I would, as an advocate of peace, must rather see them breaking the head of the tyrant with their chains."[22] Brown's most avid supporter and publicist, James Redpath, an expatriate Scot who became friends with Brown in Kansas, had taken it upon himself, with the blessing of Brown's wife, Mary, to quickly write a biography of Brown, extolling his character and goals. The result was *The Public Life of Capt. John Brown*, published in January 1860 and dedicated "To Wendell Phillips, Ralph Waldo Emerson, and Henry D. Thoreau, Defenders of the Faithful, who, when the mob shouted, 'Madman!' said, 'Saint!'" The book was reviewed in the March issue of the *Atlantic Monthly,* which we know the Hawthornes read in England, because Sophia wrote to her sister Elizabeth that she found the review suitable for her daughter Una to read. According to the reviewer, "In seasons of excitement, and amid the struggles of political contention, the men who use the most extravagant and the most violent words have, for a time, the advantage; but, in the long run, they damage whatever cause they may adopt; and the truth, which their declamations have obscured or their falsehoods have violated, finally asserts itself."[23] These sentiments accorded with Hawthorne's, who consistently questioned the truth-value of "extravagant" and "violent" words.

Back in Concord in the summer of 1860, Hawthorne found himself surrounded by Brown supporters, including Emerson, Thoreau, the Alcotts, and Franklin Sanborn, all of whom were soon featured in Redpath's collection *Echoes of Harper's Ferry* (1860) published to preserve recent tributes to Brown and to assist the families of the black men killed as a result of the Harpers Ferry raid. The Hawthornes' home, the Wayside, they learned, had been implicated in the wake of Brown's raid, for Mary Peabody Mann, who had been living in the Wayside in the Hawthornes' absence, had hidden one of Brown's conspirators, Sanborn, in the house when he was being sought by federal agents. At the suggestion of Ellery Channing, the Hawthornes had enrolled their son Julian in Sanborn's school and soon learned that his classmates included two of Brown's daughters, Anne and Sarah, who boarded with the Emersons and then the Alcotts.[24] The Hawthornes' lives were thus involuntarily enmeshed with the man whose soul was marching on.

National Identity

Partly because of the radicalization that had occurred among Hawthorne's Concord friends and acquaintances during his seven-year absence, he experienced a sense of estrangement upon his return. In December 1860, he wrote his young friend Henry Bright, "I spend a monotonous life, seldom quitting my own hill-side, and trying earnestly to take root here. I find, however, that I staid abroad a little too long, and as a consequence, have lost my home-feelings for the present, if not forever" (18:356).[25] He tried to pursue his literary career by working on two romances (published in *The Centenary Edition of the Works of Nathaniel Hawthorne* under the volume titles *The American Claimant Manuscripts* and *The Elixir of Life Manuscripts*), which remained unfinished at his death. In both, he addresses the issues of warfare and violence that had long concerned him and that had acquired added urgency and complexity as the country approached civil war. In both romances, set aside in the summer of 1861 and the fall of 1862, respectively, he creates protagonists who seek to establish their identities within historical contexts marked by revolutionary violence—in the first case, the English Civil War; in the second, the American Revolution. Before he abandoned the "Elixir of Life" materials, he declared that he found it "impossible to possess one's mind in the midst of a civil war to such a degree as to make thoughts assume life. I hear the cannon and smell the gunpowder through everything" (18:501). In his last book publication, *Our Old Home* (1863), he identifies his "abortive project" with the United States itself and says he is "sadly content to scatter a thousand peaceful fantasies upon the hurricane that is sweeping us all along with it, possibly, into a Limbo where our nation and its polity may be as literally the fragments of a shattered dream as my unwritten Romance" (5:4). War, he realized, rendered his "peaceful" fantasies even more slight and inconsequential than he usually regarded them.

He apparently began working on the first unfinished romance, about an American claimant, during the winter of 1860–61, soon after Lincoln's election and amid widespread anxiety about Southern secession. On December 17, 1860, he wrote to Francis Bennoch in London, "I have been very idle since my return to America, but am now meditating a new Romance, which ought to be the most elevated of my productions, since I shall write it in the sky-parlour of my new tower" (18:352). He had written the first draft of this romance in Italy in 1858, calling it "The Ancestral Footstep." Based on his own genealogical interests, it features a young American who travels to England in search of his ancestral home and a lost inheritance.[26] The second and third versions, known as "Etherege" and "Grimshawe," he drafted in Concord during the first half of 1861. As Rita Gollin points out, "in each variant, the footstep signifies 'brotherly hatred and attempted murder.' All are glosses on America's ties to and severance from England, the archetypal fratricide of Cain, and the inherent fratricide of all civil wars."[27]

A central problem Hawthorne faced with these materials was what role to assign the "original emigrant" who had come to America from England in the 1630s and established a line of descendants, one of whom would someday return to England as his heir apparent. Given Hawthorne's comments (both public and in his notebooks) about his own patrilineal line, he took this problem personally, for its solution would help him determine his own political identity and perhaps explain why he felt so out of place in his own native land. Even from a distance, Alcott, surprisingly, noticed Hawthorne's struggle with this problem, recording in his journal on February 17,

> I hear he is writing a book on England where he spent his four years' consulate. . . . He seems not at home here in his temperament and tendencies. His English name, I suspect, designates but in part the stock he springs from. I am sure of his coming into Britain with William the Conqueror, and that there runs a drop of dingy Roman life in his veins, exclusive of the Saxon and the sunnier qualities of the British race. See how he behaves, as if he were the foreigner still, though installed in his stolen castle and its keeper, his moats wide and deep, his drawbridges all up on all sides, and he secure from invasion. Nobody gets a chance to speak with him unless by accident.[28]

While working on his "book on England" in his "stolen castle" (Alcott apparently thought Hawthorne bought Hillside from him at an unfair price),[29] Hawthorne mulled over a number of possibilities as he sought to determine the character of his "original emigrant."

One of his ideas was to make this character, who left a bloody footprint wherever he trod, one of Cromwell's Puritan rebels, a regicide, like the Gray Champion, who helped behead King Charles I on the scaffold then had to flee England. Another possibility, which became more attractive to Hawthorne as the American Civil War approached, was to make him an early Quaker, devoted to peace and love, yet persecuted for his faith. In the ruminations Hawthorne wrote to himself within his manuscripts, he thought for a time about combining the two figures—a startling idea. "Family tradition," he writes, shall have made this "first ancestor" seem a "dark and fierce Puritan—with his own hand a king killer, going into the darkness with a track of blood behind him, . . . with all sorts of terrible myths gathering about his memory," but he will turn out to be "a man of peace, and a follower and friend of George Fox" (12:203). The track of blood would thus signify not some secret guilt but, instead, persecution. "The original emigrant," Hawthorne tells himself, "must have been the model of a Christian, and therefore misunderstood by everybody—therefore maligned—therefore bitterly hated always. . . . He was on the scaffold to support and comfort the dying monarch, to die for him if possible; everywhere, he was sacrificing himself" (12:204). Such an incredible scenario could convert an aggressive and cruel Puritan progenitor into a peaceable man, long misunderstood. It would also take the burden of guilt off his present-day descendants. Small wonder, then, that this fantasy appealed to Hawthorne, whose "first ancestor" was known as "a bitter persecutor" of the Quakers" (1:9).[30]

The second and third versions of the "American Claimant" materials reveal Hawthorne mulling over additional Christian themes, which had been emergent in *The Marble Faun*. As Hawthorne's protagonist, the young Etherege, goes to England in quest of his birthplace and ancestry, he encounters there the oldest living descendant of the "original emigrant," and Hawthorne presents him as the emigrant's double, a humble man of peace. Hawthorne plans that the boy will be told ahead of time that this person is "the highest and noblest of men." Thus, the boy

> with this idea of him in his mind, shall expect to see somebody in high station, and of noble aspect;—the same mistake which the Jews made about the Savior. Then, at the Hospital, introduce this humble, lowly, unpretending man, much battered with the rebuffs he has received in this world, but still loving, hoping, working, for his fellow men. An enthusiast but now tamed, yet sweet to the last. The original shall have been a founder of a sect of one, himself his only disciple, teaching himself and growing better all his life. (12:204)

Hawthorne imagines creating a deathbed scene for the old man, whereby "something high, noble, courageous, sublime, must break out of all the feeblenesses which have hitherto made the reader despise him." With some wishful thinking, Hawthorne tells himself, "A good effect is capable of being produced, by the revelation that the humble pauper is the lord of Brathwaite and representative of this proud family" (12:208). Although Hawthorne abandoned these improbable scenarios, they provide insight into his struggle to give artistic expression to his rather unusual Christian democratic elitism.

War Matters

Like many in the nation, Hawthorne realized that the election of the controversial Republican Abraham Lincoln was an ominous event, bringing civil war close at hand. On December 17, 1860, he asked Francis Bennoch, "What do you think is going to become of us?—of our Republic, I mean. For my part, I am ready for anything that may happen, knowing that, if the worst comes to the worst, New England will still have her rocks and ice" (18:353). On the same day, he wrote to Henry Bright that if Bright came to the United States, he would have the pleasure "of seeing the Union in its death-throes," adding, "I am ashamed to say how little I care about the matter. . . . As to the South, I never loved it. We do not belong together; the Union is unnatural" (18:355). (Hawthorne also referred to an unnatural union when discussing amalgamation, which became one of the key issues in the "Elixir of Life" manuscripts. For him, hybridity, whether in persons or nations, created internal distress and a shortened life.)

To no one's surprise, South Carolina seceded from the Union on December 20, 1860, and six more Southern states soon followed. On February 16, 1861, Hawthorne told Ticknor of his hope that New England would become "a separate nation" (18:363). On April 12, Fort Sumter was fired upon, beginning the Civil War. In a letter of April 16, Hawthorne's friend Sumner wrote to him, "At last Freedom and Slavery are to stand face to face in battle; a united North against a united South. Alas! That it should be so. But I am always for Freedom. God bless you!"[31] One doubts that Hawthorne shared his elation. Whereas Sumner celebrated the binary of good and evil, which his political rhetoric had long featured, Hawthorne recognized the destructive consequences such rhetoric could produce. He resisted the demonization of others, even Southerners (with the one exception being his short essay "Northern Volunteers," which he published in the *Concord Monitor* on June 7, 1862).[32]

Concord's young volunteers went off to war on April 19 (a historic date in the town's history) in 1861. Their departure stirred everyone, including Hawthorne. As Emerson wrote to his daughter Edith the next day, "You have heard that our village was all alive yesterday with the departure of our braves. Judge Hoar made a speech to them at the Depot, Mr Reynolds made a prayer in the ring. . . . And when the whistle of the train was heard . . . grief & pride ruled the hour. All the families were there."[33] Lidian Emerson's letter to Edith is even more effusive. She writes, "Is it not a wonderful and most auspicious omen that our Soldiers went forth to fight for liberty and right on the Nineteenth of April. It means something, be sure. Oh what an exciting day! The bells & guns the cloudy day and the brilliant sunset the departure the enthusiastic meeting in the evening. There has not been such a day for 86 years."[34] With the beginning of the Civil War in Concord, Emerson completed his transformation from transcendental pacifist to political activist. Hawthorne would soon observe, accurately, that Emerson had become "merciless as a steel bayonet" (18:544). Emerson's son Edward confirmed this. In his notes to his father's essay "War," he recalls, "In the early days of the War of the Rebellion he visited Charlestown Navy-Yard to see the preparations, and said, 'Ah! sometimes gunpowder smells good.' In the opening of his address at Tufts College, in July, 1861, he said, 'The brute noise of cannon has a most poetic echo in these days, as instrument of the primal sentiments of humanity.'"[35]

Even Hawthorne, when he witnessed the spirit of the Concord volunteers, felt aroused: "When I hear their drums beating, and see their banners flying, and witness their steady marching, I declare . . . I feel as if I could catch the infection, shoulder a musket, and be off to the war myself!" (18:387–88). His use of the term "infection," however, indicates his reservations about his response. Only six weeks after the start of the war, he started losing his enthusiasm and facetiously wrote to William Ticknor, "I wish they would push on the war a little more briskly. The excitement had an invigorating effect on me for a time, but it begins to lose its influence. But it is rather unreasonable to wish my countrymen to kill one another for the sake of refreshing my palled spirits; so I shall pray for peace" (18:382). In July, he told Bennoch, "we seem to have little, or, at least, a very misty idea of what we are fighting for" (18:387). Earlier, he had declared to Bridge, "If we are fighting for the annihilation of slavery, to be sure, it may be a wise object, and offers a tangible result, and the only one which is consistent with a future Union between North and South" (18:381). Obviously, Hawthorne was neither proslavery nor a copperhead sympathizer with the South. Yet by late July, like almost everyone in the North, he became depressed after the rout of the Union army at the First Battle of Bull Run, and in August, in poor health, he wrote to his daughter Una from the seashore near Beverly, "On the whole, I enjoy this respite from the daily repetition and contradiction of telegraphs about skirmishes, victories, and defeats, and could almost be content to remain in the same ignorance till the war is over" (18:400).

The romance he began writing during 1861, "Septimius Felton," captures Hawthorne's conflicted responses to the war fever around him. It was based on a story Thoreau had told him about a former inhabitant of the Wayside (perhaps Alcott himself) who had resolved never to die. As Hawthorne explained it in his first memorandum to himself, this inhabitant "would sit there while oaks grew up and decayed; he would be always here. This was all that Thoreau communicated; and that was many years ago, when I first came to live at the old cottage. . . . I staid here but a little while; but often times, afar off, this singular idea occurred to me, in foreign lands, when my thoughts returned to this place which seemed to be the point by which I was attached to my native land" (13:499). Hawthorne planned to introduce the romance with a biographical sketch of Thoreau, who died in 1862, but neither the romance nor the sketch was ever completed. The various drafts of the book, however, are marked by Thoreau's invisible presence, especially in the protagonist's contemplative habits that belie an Indian-like savagery he has inherited.

As I tried to make clear in chapter 4 of this study, "Accord in Concord," Thoreau, along with Emerson, envisioned the scholar-artist much as did Hawthorne in the early 1840s; however, what I have yet to point out is that Thoreau's turn toward political activism in the 1850s—that is, his endorsement of John Brown and righteous violence—was accompanied by a doubt about whether such attention dealt with the illusory or the real, the trivial or the sacred. As Robert Richardson has observed, "Thoreau's absorption in John Brown ceased almost as suddenly as it began."[36] By the summer of 1860, when asked about giving a lecture, he declared that his subjects were "Transcendentalist & aesthetic. I devote myself to the absorption of nature generally,"[37] and in April 1861, he wrote to Parker Pillsbury, "As for my prospective reader, I hope that he *ignores* Fort Sumpter, & Old Abe, & all that, for that is just the most fatal and indeed the only fatal, weapon you can direct against evil ever; for as long as you *know of* it, you are *particeps criminis*.

. . . I do not so much regret the present condition of things in this country (provided I regret it at all) as I do that I ever heard of it. . . . Blessed are they who never read a newspaper, for they shall see Nature, and through her, God."[38] In the struggle between contemplation and action, the former attained dominance as Thoreau's life neared its close. In Hawthorne's apparent return to his old reclusive habits in Concord as the Civil War approached, there is a similar, though opposing, doubt about the virtue of emotional detachment. In many ways, Thoreau's exemplification of the contemplative way, with its overlay of romantic pastoralism, held great appeal for Hawthorne, and one can see him struggling to assert its value in the midst of violent political upheaval that made it seem trivial and inconsequential. In other words, Thoreau worried that his political activism took him away from more important spiritual work; Hawthorne worried that his creative activities counted for little in a country at war with itself.[39]

"Septimius Felton," set in Concord at the beginning of the American Revolution, April 19, 1775, provides a final example of how Hawthorne's imaginative thought drew upon images of revolutionary violence and witchcraft hysteria to shape and explore contemporary political issues. His protagonist, a scholar with Indian blood in his veins, tries to resist the pull of popular unrest but experiences a sense of isolation for doing so. As his neighbors array for battle with the British, Septimius goes

> into his house, and [sits] there, in his study, for some hours, in that unpleasant state of feeling, which a man of brooding thought is apt to experience when the world around him is in a state of intense motion, which he finds it impossible to chord with. There seemed to be a stream rushing past him, which, even if he plunged into the midst of it, he could not be wet by it. He felt himself strangely ajar with the human race, and would have given much, either to be in full accord with it, or to be separated from it forever. (13:22–23)

In this description of Septimius's plight, Hawthorne draws on his own sense of discomfort in 1861 but also reveals his knowledge of mob psychology and his belief that "patriotism" is a dangerous sentiment and revolution a morally dubious action. (Septimius subsequently kills a British soldier himself, the key event in the romance.) As always for Hawthorne, the unreasoning impulse to join any religious, political, or social group, due to the stimulus of the moment, could, if acted upon, lead to lifelong guilt, but to resist such an impulse would be, as he puts it in "Chiefly about War-Matters," "a kind of treason" (23:403).

Hawthorne's protagonist Septimius lives in a house modeled on the Wayside, and when the farmers and neighbors start assembling for battle, he, like his creator, finds that his meditative cast of mind sets him apart from their excited patriotism. In "The Old Manse" (1846), Hawthorne had contrasted his "circle of repose" at the Manse with the social activism at the other end of Concord, centered on Emerson. In "Septimius" he sets up a similar polarity by creating the character of Robert Hagburn, an activist eager to join the fight. Hagburn's name connects him, I believe, to witch-hunting and the kinds of men willing to forsake reason and moderation in order to rid the land of what they consider evil. When Septimius hears the beat of the drum and the assemblage of farmers, neighbors, with their weapons, he asks himself, "What matters a little tyranny in so short a life" (13:16). The narrator responds by declaring,

> Oh, high, heroic, tremulous juncture; when man felt himself almost an angel, on the verge of doing deeds that outwardly look so fiendish; oh strange rapture of the coming battle. We know something of that time now; we that have seen the muster of the village soldiery on meeting-house greens, and at railway stations; and heard the drum and fife, . . . felt how a great impulse lifts up a people, and every cold, passionless, indifferent spectator, lifts him up into religion, and makes him join in what becomes an act of devotion, a prayer, when perhaps he but half approves. (13:17)

Such a passage reveals the degree to which Hawthorne's pacifism was contingent, on the one hand, yet a matter of principle, on the other. His emphasis on the principle emerges soon after the rapture, for as the British troops retreat from Concord, the trailing colonists shoot at them from hiding, which appears criminal. As one redcoat staggers and falls, Septimius shudders because "it was so like murder that he really could not tell the difference." Drawing on his lifelong disapproval of violence and warfare, Hawthorne writes, "How strange, how strange it is, this deep, wild passion that nature has implanted in us, to be the death of our fellow-creatures and which co-exists at the same time with horror" (13:24). He then generalizes as his narrator declares,

> In times of Revolution and public disturbance, all absurdities are more unrestrained; the measure of calm sense, the habits, the orderly decency, are in a measure lost. More people become insane, I should suppose; offenses against public morality, female license, are more numerous; suicides, murders, all ungovernable outbreaks of men's thoughts, embodying themselves in wild acts, take place more frequently, and with less horror to the lookers-on.

This is Hawthorne's nightmare world, which had been a part of his imagination for years, and he describes what is needed to dispel it: "there was not, as there would have been at an ordinary time, the same calmness and truth in the public observation, scrutinizing everything with its keen criticism, in that time of seething opinions and overturned principles" (13:67).

One example of such calmness that does appear in "Septimius Felton" is when Hawthorne's character Rose looks closely at the British troops as they march into Concord. "Why should we shoot these men, or they us?" she asks. "They look kind of homely and natural! Each of them has a mother and sisters, I suppose, just like our men." Septimius replies, "It is the strangest thing in the world that we can think of killing them" (13:21). But like his fellow villagers, he does kill one of them, a handsome young officer. He does so not by shooting at him from hiding but in a face-to-face confrontation on the hillside behind his house. The officer detects Septimius concealed in a thicket and calls him out. When Septimius steps into the open, his "fierce Indian blood stirs in him, and gives him bloody incitements" (13:26). Seeing that Septimius holds a gun, the officer declares, "'Let us fight it out. Stand where you are, and I will give the word of command. Now! Ready, aim! Fire!'" After they fire, Septimius is grazed in the temple by the officer's shot, but he finds he has inflicted a mortal wound on the other.

> "Good God!" said Septimius. "I had no thought of this—no malice towards you in the least."
>
> "Nor I towards you," said the young man. "It was boy's play, and the end of it is, that I die a boy, instead of living forever, as perhaps I otherwise might." (13:27)

The duel draws on Hawthorne's interest in the fate of the farm boy at the Manse who killed a British soldier with an ax at the beginning of the Revolution; like him, Septimius transforms into a guilt-ridden killer.[40] Although Septimius obviously kills in self-defense, he nevertheless is tormented by what he has done. Hawthorne, by failing to complete "Septimius," never sorted out the attitude he expected the reader to have toward its protagonist. Unlike Donatello, Septimius does not kill a defenseless man or one that is putatively "evil," yet he does kill, and there is something "fiendish" about it. The complexity and significance of the romance makes one regret that Hawthorne could not complete it, especially since, as Nina Baym has pointed out, it "promised to be the best thing of its kind Hawthorne had ever done."[41] Though dismissed by most Hawthorne scholars, the "Elixir of Life" manuscripts, which include "Septimius," represent Hawthorne's most sustained, direct, and tortured effort to work through the issues of popular violence, mass hysteria, and partisan politics, especially with regard to natural, ethnic, and racial differences. With great effort and intermittent confidence, he sought to resolve fears about the dissolution of his life and that of his nation, especially the latter's bloody way of addressing the problem of variegated racial identities within the house divided.

The Question of Patriotism

The issue of disunion versus union came between Hawthorne and Pierce in 1862 and also split the abolitionist ranks. Garrison, Phillips, and other abolitionist leaders, who had previously argued for disunion, supported the war effort on behalf of the Union, seeing the opportunity to impose emancipation on the South. On February 13, 1862, Hawthorne, in a letter to Bridge, tells about a visit from their mutual friend Pierce.

> We drank a bottle of arrack together, and mingled our tears and condolements [sic] for the state of the country. Pierce is truly patriotic, and thinks there is nothing left for us but to fight it out; but I should be sorry to take his opinion implicitly as regards our chances in the future. He is bigoted to the Union, and sees nothing but ruin without it; whereas, I, (if we can only put the boundary far enough south) should not much regret an ultimate separation. A few weeks will decide how this is to be; for, unless a

powerful Union feeling shall be developed by the military successes that seem to be setting in, we ought to turn our attention to the best mode of resolving ourselves into two nations. . . . If we do hold them, I should think Sumner's territorial plan the best way. (18:427–28).

Sumner had proposed reducing the Confederate states to territories of the United States and abolishing slavery in those territories, and this plan appealed to Hawthorne because of his contempt for the South.

Between Lincoln's two emancipation proclamations, given on March 6 and September 23, 1862, Hawthorne met the president and wrote a satirical, yet admiring, description of him. At the invitation of Bridge, now a commodore working in Washington, D.C., Hawthorne and Ticknor visited that city and spent a month touring the area and learning about the progress of the war. He visited Alexandria, Fort Ellsworth, Harpers Ferry, Fortress Monroe, and Manassas. He saw General McClellan reviewing the troops and encountered refugee Negro slaves making their way north. Within weeks after his return, he wrote of his impressions for the *Atlantic Monthly,* signing himself "A Peaceable Man." He knew full well that he would be identified as the author and that his remarks would provoke hostility.

In "Chiefly about War-Matters," Hawthorne returns to the view of war as juvenile and barbaric: "Set men face to face, with weapons in their hands, and they are as ready to slaughter one another now, after playing at peace and good will for so many years, as in the rudest ages, that never heard of peace societies. . . . It is so odd, when we measure our advances from barbarism, and find ourselves just here" (23:421). Such a statement obviously impugns the militancy of both North and South at the time, but even more outrageous to the *Atlantic*'s readers was his sympathy for the captured rebel soldiers—"simple, bumpkin-like fellows," Hawthorne calls them, who lacked "the remotest comprehension of what they had been fighting for" (23:429). In an attempt to anticipate criticism of his expressed willingness to let portions of the South secede if the North did not win the war, he includes a final footnote written by his fictional "Editor."

We regret the innuendo in the concluding sentence. The war can never be allowed to terminate, except in the complete triumph of Northern principles. . . . We should be sorry to cast a doubt on the Peaceable Man's loyalty, but he will allow us to say that we consider him premature in his kindly feelings toward traitors, and sympathizers with treason. . . . There are some degrees of absurdity that put Reason herself into a rage, and affect us like an intolerable crime—which this Rebellion is, into the bargain. (23:442)

Ironically, Hawthorne had expressed some of this criticism himself, so both text and opposing notes are shaped by a political vision made up of multiple perspectives.

A key feature of "Chiefly about War-Matters" is the excursion to Harpers Ferry and Hawthorne's visit to an old engine house—"rusty and shabby like every other work of man's hands in this God-forsaken town"—that John Brown had seized as his fortress and that had been converted into a prison holding captured rebels. By calling Brown a "blood-stained fanatic" and publicly expressing his disagreement with Emerson's sanctification of him, he surely irritated his Concord neighbors. In the process, he also entered into an ongoing debate between Whittier, the popular Quaker poet, and Brown's ardent abolitionist admirers. Hawthorne writes, "I shall not pretend to be an admirer of old John Brown, any further than sympathy with Whittier's excellent ballad about him may go" (23:427). This ballad, as Hawthorne surely knew, had been criticized by Brown's newfound admirers, particularly Garrison.

Whittier, an acquaintance of Hawthorne's, had been active in the abolitionist cause for decades, and his credentials could not have been more unassailable. Yet he was resolute in his Quaker pacifism. Thus, in his poem titled "Brown of Osawatomie," he tried to strike a balance between admiration for Brown's heart and revulsion at his deed, especially as he described Brown's encounter with a slave mother and child on his walk to the gallows.

> Then the bold, blue eye grew tender,
> And the old, harsh face grew mild,
> As he stooped between the jeering ranks
> And kissed the negro's child!
>
> The shadows of his stormy life
> That moment fell apart:
> Without, the rash and bloody hand,

Within, the loving heart.
That kiss, from all its guilty means,
Redeemed the good intent,
And round the grisly fighter's hair
The Martyr's aureole bent![42]

Although this passage presents Brown as compassionate, Whittier's reference to Brown's "bloody hand" upset Brown's admirers. In the *Liberator*, Garrison complained,

> we think there is not the same magnanimous recognition of the liberty-loving heroism of John Brown, which is found in many of the poet's effusions relating to the war-like struggle of 1776, and our revolutionary fathers. . . . Let such of us as are believers in the doctrines of peace be careful to award to John Brown at least as much credit as we do to a Joshua or Gideon, a Washington or Warren, and especially not to do him the slightest injustice. Though he was far from being a non-resistant, yet he was not a man of violence and blood, in a lawless sense, any more than those Jewish and American heroes; and if no reproachful epithets ought to be cast upon their memories, none ought to be cast upon his.[43]

In various poems, Whittier had seemed to advocate violence, and Garrison quotes these to make his point. However, Whittier, in his reply to Garrison, calls attention to "the fact, that in almost every instance, the articles from which thou hast quoted passages containing warlike allusions and figures, contain distinct and emphatic declarations of the entirely peaceful character of the Anti-slavery enterprise; and equally emphatic denunciations of war and violence in its behalf."[44] Garrison's rejoinder points out that he did not mean to question Whittier's peace principles but intended only to object to his recognizing the nobility of "our revolutionary fathers, without passing any condemnation upon them," while not doing so in the case of John Brown. Of course, to hold such a position regarding Brown, Garrison had to recast the raid at Harpers Ferry and ignore Brown's participation in the Pottawatomie Massacre.

By signing himself "A Peaceable Man," Hawthorne aligned himself not only with Whittier but with most Quakers at the time and added to the hostility directed at his politics. The opposition to war and the sympathy accorded rebel soldiers, however, were not the only objectionable features of the essay. Its lighthearted, flippant tone also offended, and it has struck even modern critics as off-putting and inappropriate.[45] I suspect that this tone originated from an attempt to imitate James Russell Lowell's humor in the influential *The Biglow Papers, Second Series,* appearing in the *Atlantic* during this time. Hawthorne's "editorial" notes to his own essay are analogous to Lowell's use of Parson Wilbur as the earnest and condescending editor of Hosea Biglow's poetry. Hawthorne's notes, however, take the form of political protest. After mentioning a visit to the Capitol, for example, the "Editor" writes, "We omit several paragraphs here, in which the author speaks of some prominent Members of Congress with a freedom that seems to have been not unkindly meant, but might be liable to misconstruction" (23:408). Hawthorne, having thus craftily censored himself, told the *Atlantic*'s publisher Ticknor, "I don't think it will bear any more castration," but the firm's editor, James T. Fields, indeed stepped in and cut the essay more, removing a satirical portrait of President Lincoln.

The parodic silencing Hawthorne did of himself apparently fell short of that required by the patriotic *Atlantic.* At least one reader objected to the silencing, though. The author Donald Mitchell misinterpreted the notes and defended Hawthorne by declaring, "a man's opinions can take no catholic or philosophic range nowadays, but they call out some shrewish accusation of disloyalty."[46] Henry James, many years later, misinterpreted the persona of the editor, objecting to the "numerous editorial ejaculations and protests appended," which he found in "questionable taste."[47] When shown the article and notes, Emerson, who knew Hawthorne better, immediately observed, "Of course he wrote the footnotes himself."[48]

When Rebecca Harding Davis visited Concord in the spring of 1862, after Hawthorne's tour of the front lines, she recorded a scene that reveals Hawthorne's growing distance from the transcendentalists due to divergent attitudes toward the war. Davis indicates that she was shocked by a conversation between Bronson Alcott, Emerson, and Hawthorne in the parlor at the Wayside. Alcott apparently held forth about the beneficial results of the war, which he characterized as "an armed angel . . . wakening the nation to a lofty life unknown before." Emerson bowed his head in approval, and Hawthorne looked on with "laughing, sagacious eyes" that were "full of mockery."[49] Davis apparently identified with Hawthorne, whom she calls "an alien among these men, not of their kind." In her memoirs, she asserts, "I had just come up from the border where I had seen the actual war, the filthy spewing of it; the political jobbery in Union and Confederate camps, the malignant personal hatreds wearing patriotic masks, and glutted by burning homes and outraged women. . . . This would-be seer [Alcott] who was talking of [the war], and the real seer [Emerson] who listened, knew no more of war as it was, than I had done in my cherry-tree when I dreamed of bannered legions of crusaders debouching in the misty fields."[50] As an informed skeptic, Hawthorne struck Davis as more in touch with the realities of war, more reluctant to celebrate it, than were his Concord neighbors.

As the war drug on during the remainder of 1862 and the beginning of 1863, more people in the North lost their enthusiasm for it, and Hawthorne experienced poor health. The Army of the Potomac suffered great losses at Fredericksburg and Chancellorsville, and Grant's initial assaults at Vicksburg failed. At the time, Hawthorne abandoned his attempts at fiction and began to edit entries from his English notebooks for publication in the *Atlantic Monthly.* He also consolidated them for publication in the volume *Our Old Home,* published in the fall of 1863. In the summer of 1863, Hawthorne visited Pierce in New Hampshire and sat on the stage as Pierce delivered a fiery Fourth of July speech criticizing the war and the Lincoln administration's handling of it.

> And now, war! War, in its direst shape—war, such as it makes the blood run cold to read of in the history of other nations and of other times—war on a scale of a million men in arms—war, horrid as that of the barbaric ages, rages in several States of the Union, as its more immediate field, and casts the lurid shadow of its death and lamentation athwart the whole expanse, and into every nook and corner of our vast domains.

Pierce reminded the crowd of what he had told another audience in the spring of 1861: "I did not believe aggression by arms was either a suitable or positive solution to existing evils. All that occurred since then has but strengthened and confirmed my convictions in this regard."[51] As Pierce was speaking, news arrived of Union victories in Gettysburg and elsewhere, undermining all that he had been saying.

Because of his speech, Pierce was widely viewed as unpatriotic, if not treasonous. He suffered the abuse frequently heaped on those that criticize a current administration during wartime, when a president or his loyal party members insist on conflating the president with the nation. Although Pierce despised Lincoln and considered his decisions unconstitutional, he loved the United States. Hawthorne knew this, and even before he attended the July 4 meeting in New Hampshire, he had determined to dedicate *Our Old Home* to Pierce and to commend his patriotism. Before he did so, Elizabeth Peabody got wind of it and wrote Hawthorne advising him not to do it. His letter of response on July 20, 1863, is a fascinating political document, revealing not only his loyalty to Pierce but also his understanding of various undesirable consequences of the Civil War, including his conviction that the one thing worse than war was slavery.

Given that this entire study up to this point has emphasized Hawthorne's pacifism, let me here declare in stark terms that Hawthorne objected to slavery even more than he did to war. This is not to say he developed any sympathy for abolitionists or new compassion for slaves; he did not. However, he viewed slavery as an immoral stain upon the nation. He agreed with Pierce that the war could and should have been avoided, but since it began, he supported it and did not object to Lincoln's unconstitutional measures. He wrote, "I do not care a fig what powers the President assumes, at such a crisis as this, if he only used them effectually" (18:592). With some irritation, he told Peabody, "You do not in the least shake me by telling me that I shall be supposed to disapprove of the war; for I always thought that it should have been avoided, although, since it has broken out, I have longed for military success as much as any man or woman of the North." In his response, Hawthorne points out to Peabody that unless the South is totally defeated, slavery will persist. Recent Northern successes, he explains,

> will suggest to the rebels that their best hope lies in the succor of the Peace Democrats of the North, whom they have heretofore scorned, and by amalgamation with whom I really think that the old Union might be restored, and slavery prolonged for another hundred years, with new bulwarks; while the people of the North would fancy that they had got the victory, and never know that they had shed their blood in vain, and so would become peace Democrats to a man. In that case, woe to the Abolitionists! I offer you in advance the shelter of the nook in our garret, which Mary contrived as a hiding-place for Mr. Sanborn.

Clearly no "peace Democrat," Hawthorne here demonstrates he opposed slavery so strongly that he felt no peace should be made with the South unless slavery were abolished. He warns Peabody that she "cannot possibly conceive (looking through spectacles of the tint which yours have acquired) how little the North really cares for the negro-question, and how eagerly it would grasp at peace if recommended by a delusive show of victory." Thus, he concludes, "Free soil was never in so great danger as now" (18:591).[52]

In the dedication to *Our Old Home,* Hawthorne addresses Pierce as "my dear friend" and says he "shall defer a colloquy with the Statesman till some calmer and sunnier hour." In an attempt to defend Pierce's politics, Hawthorne adds that he needs "no assurance that you continue faithful forever to that grand idea of an irrevocable Union" and that "it rests among my certainties that no man's loyalty is more stedfast, no man's hopes or apprehensions on behalf of our national existence more deeply heartfelt" (5:5). This section of his dedication replaced an earlier one in which Hawthorne ventured his own political views of the war, his own willingness "to be content with half the soil that was once our broad inheritance" (5:360). Even though he thus depoliticized the dedication somewhat, it still brought disgust Hawthorne's way from Emerson, Stowe, and others, as I have detailed earlier. Hawthorne's fellow Saturday Club member Charles Eliot Norton wrote to George Curtis that he was "half annoyed, half amused at Hawthorne. . . . His dedication to F. Pierce reads like the bitterest of satires; and in that I have my satisfaction. The public will laugh."[53] In a small notice in *Harper's Weekly,* probably written by Curtis, the author concludes by remarking, "that one of the most gifted and fascinating of American writers should fail to see, or to care for, the very point of our contest [the War] is monstrous."[54] The publication in the New York papers of a letter from Pierce to Jefferson Davis, found by Union troops in Davis's study after he had fled, brought additional abuse to Pierce and Hawthorne.

In a letter she wrote to Horatio Bridge long after Hawthorne's death (June 4, 1887), Elizabeth Peabody inaccurately characterizes Pierce's disclosed correspondence with Davis, which appeared in the *New York Evening Post.* The letter, she insists, "showed under Pierce's hand that he had encouraged Davis *to secede* & trust that the war would at once be transferred to the streets of the north where the Democrats would fight on the

Southern Side" (18:593). This was just not true. Pierce would never encourage secession, given his love of the Union. The letter itself was taken out of context by Emerson, Peabody, and other readers of it. As the account in *Record of a Month* (1864) shows, the letter found by Union troops was written to Davis three years before, on December 7, 1859, shortly after the attack on Harpers Ferry, and its purpose was to prevent secession by reassuring Davis and other Southerners that many Northerners disapproved of Brown's actions and were sympathetic to the distress in the South. The key passage in Pierce's letter to Davis, which was misinterpreted, reads: "Without discussing the question of right—of abstract power to secede, I have never believed that actual disruption of the Union can occur without blood. And if, through the madness of northern abolitionism, that dire calamity must come, the fighting will not be along Mason and Dixon's line merely. It will be within our own borders, in our own streets."[55] Several other letters Pierce wrote at about the same time—in response to invitations to speak at meetings in Boston, Massachusetts; New York City; and Bangor, Maine—convey the same warning. He laments the "exhibition of an insurrectionary spirit" in the North and the "actual invasion of a sister State by an armed organization," which is "openly justified and applauded at large meetings of men and women in your midst."[56] In other words, Pierce could not have been a stronger advocate of national unity, and he labored to preserve the Union, not hasten its breakup.

This fact gives the charge of "traitor" leveled at him and, by extension, at Hawthorne an irony that Hawthorne could appreciate. In an insightful posthumous review of Hawthorne, Edward Dicey points out that Hawthorne loved the North but could not hate the South: "Unjustly, but yet not unreasonably, he was looked upon as a pro-slavery man, and suspected of Southern sympathies. . . . He sympathized with the war in principle; but its inevitable accessories—the bloodshed, the bustle, and above all perhaps, the bunkum which accompanied it—were to him absolutely hateful."[57] Dicey adds, "That he was not in harmony with the tone of his countrymen was to him a real trouble, and he envied keenly the undoubting faith in the justice of their cause, which was possessed by the brother men-of-letters among whom he lived. . . . It was curious to me at that time to see how universal this conviction of the justice of the war was amongst the American people."[58]

Politics of Quiet Imagination

Though certainly out of step with his times, Hawthorne was not as unfeeling or detached as Curtis and others have portrayed him. Rather, he was reserved—or as he put it, not "one of those supremely hospitable people, who serve up their own hearts delicately fried, with brain-sauce, as a tidbit for their beloved public" (10:33). Like Emerson, he suppressed his feelings and tried to hide or displace them. His imaginative writings reveal his considerable powers of human understanding and sympathy, yet his letters are brusque, severe, and sometimes mean-spirited—intentionally so, as if to assert his masculinity. In a well-known letter to Bridge in February 1850, he joked about reading *The Scarlet Letter* to his wife, who then went to bed with a headache; this he considered a sign of "triumphant success," like "what bowlers call a 'ten-strike'" (16:311). Five years later, however, as I mentioned in chapter 5, he revisited this scene in his *English Notebooks* and recalled being overcome with emotion reading the novel to Sophia. Such glimpses into Hawthorne's method of denying his feelings should caution readers not to take his more callous and flippant remarks at face value.

Although Hawthorne can easily be viewed as someone who abdicated his moral responsibilities during a time of crisis, he was constitutionally unable to ignore the needs of his fellow human beings, try as he might. In his *English Notebooks,* he tells about a "wretched, pale, half-torpid" child that asks to be held by him as he tours the West Derby workhouse. After holding the child, he says, "I wish I had not touched the imp; and yet I never should have forgiven myself if I had repelled its advances" (21:412–13). In *Our Old Home,* in a long, detailed passage, he relates and elaborates on this experience, yet he keeps his social conscience to himself by putting all into the third person. He creates a fictional gentleman of their party, "a person burthened with more than an Englishman's customary reserve, shy of actual contact with human beings, afflicted with a peculiar distaste for whatever was ugly, and, furthermore, accustomed to that habit of observation from an insulated stand-point which is said (but, I hope, erroneously) to have the tendency of putting ice into the blood" (5:300–301). The child, "sickly, wretched, humor-eaten," followed the man everywhere "and, at last, exerting all the speed that his poor limbs were capable of, got directly before him and held forth its arms, mutely insisting on being taken up" (5:300). Hawthorne claims he watched the struggle in the gentleman's mind "with a good deal of interest" and arrived at the opinion that he "effected more than he dreamed of towards his final salvation, when he took up the loathsome child and caressed it as tenderly as if he had been its father." "No doubt, the child's mission in reference to our friend," he adds, "was to remind him that he was responsible, in his degree, for all the sufferings and misdemeanors of the world in which he lived, and was not entitled to look upon a particle of its dark calamity as if it were none of his concern" (5:301). There is a moving self-knowledge revealed in Hawthorne's account, which sheds both negative and positive light on his character. Try as he might to remain detached from the lives of others, he recognized his social responsibility and reluctantly acted on it, in his own fashion.

If Hawthorne had extended his imagination to take in the plight of the slaves, few could fault him as a public intellectual. In *The Life of Franklin Pierce,* he credited his subject with "the liberal, generous, catholic sympathy, that embraces all who are worthy of it. Few men possess any thing like it" (23:282). As a democratic elitist, he surely knew the description applied more to himself than to his friend. One wishes, of course, that he had condemned slavery, as he wanted Kossuth to do, or that he had at least acquired more knowledge and understanding of the practice. Yet even with this now glaring limitation in his vision, shared by more of his contemporaries than is usually acknowledged, its scope could impress a nonpartisan observer. The young Dicey, who spent some days with Hawthorne at the Wayside while the rest of the family was away in 1862, equaled Melville in his appreciation of Hawthorne's acuity. The two men went rowing on Walden Pond, visited neighbors, and chatted in the evenings over cigars and whiskey. After Hawthorne's death, Dicey related,

> It is difficult to analyze the charm of anything which pleases you; but if I were obliged to try to explain the attraction of Hawthorne's talk, I should say it lay in the odd combination of clear, hard-headed sense and dreamy fancy. Cynical he was not; his mind was too large a one for anything small or mean; but he was tolerant of everything to a marvelous degree; catholic in all his judgments; skeptical because he saw any question from so many points of view. In truth, at the time I often fancied that Shaks-

peare's conversation in private life must have been akin to that I heard on those evenings spent in Hawthorne's study.[59]

At a time when most of Hawthorne's neighbors found him reserved and "perverse," Dicey gained his trust. Consequently, Hawthorne, who had a strong sense of how estranged he was from almost all of his contemporaries, found in this young Englishman a sympathetic audience, one who could discern the rarity, depth, and integrity of his political thought.

Notes

Preface

1. Henry David Thoreau, *Journal,* vol. 8, *1854,* ed. Sandra Harbert Petrulionis (Princeton, NJ: Princeton University Press, 2002), 165.

2. See, for example, Lawrence Sargent Hall, *Hawthorne, Critic of Society* (1944; reprint, Gloucester, MA, Peter Smith, 1966), 147; Edwin Haviland Miller, *Salem Is My Dwelling Place: A Life of Nathaniel Hawthorne* (Iowa City: University of Iowa Press, 1991), 474; Sacvan Bercovitch, *The Rites of Assent: Transformations in the Symbolic Construction of America* (New York: Routledge, 1993), 236.

3. For the most severe judgments, see Eric Cheyfitz, "The Irresistibleness of Great Literature: Reconstructing Hawthorne's Politics," *American Literary History* 6 (1994): 539–58; Jean Fagan Yellin, "Hawthorne and the Slavery Question," in *Historical Guide to Nathaniel Hawthorne,* ed. Larry J. Reynolds (New York: Oxford University Press, 2001), 135–64.

4. James R. Mellow, *Nathaniel Hawthorne in His Times* (Boston: Houghton Mifflin, 1980), 540; Brenda Wineapple, *Hawthorne: A Life* (New York: Knopf, 2003).

5. Henry James, *Hawthorne* (1879; reprint, New York: Collier-Macmillan, 1966), 105.

Introduction

1. Richard Hold Hutton, *Essays Theological and Literary,* 2 vols. (London: Strahan, 1871), 2:416.

2. *Congressional Globe,* 31st Cong., 1st sess., 1850, 22, pt. 1:263–69, quoted in

Ferenc M. Szasz, "Antebellum Appeals to the 'Higher Law,' 1830–1860," *Essex Institute Historical Collections* 10 (1974): 46. As Szasz points out, "although the Higher Law argument in the North did not become widespread until sometime after 1850, there had been a few scattered appeals to it before that time" (44), most notably Thoreau in his famous 1849 essay "Civil Disobedience."

3. Ralph Waldo Emerson, *The Journals and Miscellaneous Notebooks of Ralph Waldo Emerson,* ed. William H. Gilman, Ralph H. Orth, et al., 16 vols. (Cambridge, MA: Harvard University Press, Belknap, 1960–82), 15:60.

4. Philip R. Ammidon, "Hawthorne's Last Sketch," *New England Magazine and Bay State Monthly* 4 (June 1886): 516.

5. "The Thorn That Bears Haws," *Liberator,* June 27, 1862.

6. Moncure Daniel Conway, *Life of Nathaniel Hawthorne* (1890; reprint, New York: Haskell House, 1968), 203.

7. Whitman went on to say, "but aside from that, all my tendencies about Hawthorne are towards him—even affectionate, I may say—for his work, what he represented" (Horace Traubel and William White, *With Walt Whitman in Camden,* vol. 6, ed. Gertrude Traubel [Carbondale: Southern Illinois University Press, 1982], 123).

8. See David J. Potter, *The Impending Crisis, 1848–1861* (New York: Harper and Row, 1976), 30–33.

9. *Harper's Weekly* 7 (November 21, 1863): 739.

10. Harriet Beecher Stowe, quoted in Annie Fields, *Authors and Friends* (Boston: Houghton Mifflin, 1896), 184.

11. [George W. Curtis], "The Works of Nathaniel Hawthorne," *North American Review* 99 (October 1864): 542, 543, 551, 540, 547, 554, 555.

12. Franklin Sanborn, *Hawthorne and His Friends: Reminiscence and Tribute* (Cedar Rapids, IA: Torch, 1908), 51.

13. Quoted in Roy Franklin Nichols, *Franklin Pierce: Young Hickory of the Granite Hills,* rev. ed. (Philadelphia: University of Pennsylvania Press, 1958), 522.

14. Sanborn, *Hawthorne,* 61, 64. To his credit, Sanborn, in a summary statement, offers one of the most accurate explanations of Hawthorne's political positions: "Forgiveness was the key to his moral nature, and friendliness was at the bottom of his silent and seemingly unsocial habit. Sympathy with many various phases of human life explains much that he favored, or, endured with no protest" (82).

15. Merle Curti, *The Growth of American Thought,* 3rd ed. (New Brunswick, NJ: Transaction, 1982), 457, 464.

16. George M. Frederickson, *The Inner Civil War: Northern Intellectuals and the Crisis of the Union* (New York: Harper and Row, 1965), 2.

17. Mellow, 536.

18. Miller, 474.

19. Wineapple, 264, 263.

20. Jonathan Arac, "The Politics of *The Scarlet Letter*," in *Ideology and Classic American Literature*, ed. Sacvan Bercovitch and Myra Jehlen (New York: Cambridge University Press, 1986), 254.

21. Bercovitch, *Rites of Assent*, 235.

22. Cheyfitz, 540, 545.

23. Yellin, 153.

24. Clark Davis, *Hawthorne's Shyness: Ethics, Politics, and the Question of Engagement* (Baltimore: Johns Hopkins University Press, 2005), 31, 99.

25. Richard Brodhead, "Hawthorne and the Fate of Politics," *Essays in Literature* 11 (Spring 1984): 95.

26. Ibid., 95–96.

27. Sacvan Bercovitch, *The Office of "The Scarlet Letter"* (Baltimore: Johns Hopkins University Press, 1991), 27.

28. Brook Thomas, "Citizen Hester: *The Scarlet Letter* as Civic Myth," *American Literary History* 13, no. 2 (2001): 202.

29. Richard Hofstadter, *The American Political Tradition and the Men Who Made It* (New York: Vintage, 1948), 145.

30. Quoted in Hofstadter, 145.

31. See James M. McPherson, *Battle Cry of Freedom: The Civil War Era* (New York: Oxford University Press, 1988), 500, 563–65.

32. Quoted in Rose Hawthorne Lathrop, *Memories of Hawthorne* (1897; reprint, New York: AMS, 1969), 438.

33. H. James, 151.

Chapter 1

1. See Arac; Bercovitch, *Office of "The Scarlet Letter."*

2. As Roy Harvey Pearce has shown, Hawthorne sought not to suppress the novel itself, as the recollections of Elizabeth Hawthorne and Horatio Bridge have led many scholars to believe, but to keep his authorship of it a secret. See Pearce's "Introduction to *Fanshawe*" (3:308–9).

3. Nina Baym, "Hawthorne's Gothic Discards: *Fanshawe* and 'Alice Doane,'" *Nathaniel Hawthorne Journal* 4 (1974): 110.

4. In an illuminating statement, Hawthorne's daughter Rose recalled of her father, "He hated failure, dependence, and disorder, broken rules and weariness of discipline, as he hated cowardice. I cannot express how brave he seemed to me" (Lathrop, 478).

5. Austin Warren, *Nathaniel Hawthorne: Representative Selections* (New York: American Book, 1934), 1.

6. Frederick C. Crews, *The Sins of the Fathers: Hawthorne's Psychological Themes* (New York: Oxford University Press, 1966), 37.

7. Elizabeth Hawthorne to James T. Fields, December 12, 1870, Boston Public Library, quoted in Wineapple, 89.

8. For the classic study of the mythic Jackson, see John William Ward, *Andrew Jackson: Symbol for an Age* (London: Oxford University Press, 1962).

9. T. Walter Herbert, *Dearest Beloved: The Hawthornes and the Making of the Middle-Class Family* (Berkeley: University of California Press, 1993), 73.

10. For a fine discussion of the internal contradictions of Hawthorne's Jacksonianism, see Herbert, 88–112.

11. F. O. Matthiessen, *American Renaissance: Art and Expression in the Age of Emerson and Whitman* (New York: Oxford University Press, 1941), 318–19.

12. Michael Davitt Bell makes the excellent point that though hostile toward "the radical ideal of revolution," Hawthorne "saw the essential connection between the unleashing of fantasy and the unleashing of revolutionary violence" (*Hawthorne and the Historical Romance of New England* [Princeton, NJ: Princeton University Press, 1971], 170–71).

13. See chapter 5, "*The Scarlet Letter* and Revolutions Abroad," in Larry J. Reynolds, *European Revolutions and the American Literary Renaissance* (New Haven, CT: Yale University Press, 1988), 79–96.

14. Quoted in Ammidon, 526.

15. Herman Melville, "Hawthorne and His Mosses, by a Virginian Spending July in Vermont" (1850), in *Nathaniel Hawthorne, Critical Assessments,* ed. Brian Harding (Mountfield, East Sussex: Helm, n.d.), 1:219.

16. Frederick Newberry, *Hawthorne's Divided Loyalties: England and America in His Works* (Rutherford, NJ: Associated University Presses, 1987), 23–24.

17. As Margaret Reid has shown, the Old World Puritan revolution of 1642 to 1649, with its climactic regicide, attained cultural currency in the antebellum years and was reimagined in contemporary historical narratives (see *Cultural Secrets as Narrative Form: Storytelling in Nineteenth-Century America* [Columbus: Ohio State University Press, 2004], 81–97).

18. Newberry has noted, "The prayer for a champion ironically evokes the darkest side of the Puritan character and should properly be associated with the 'master-stroke' of Satan" (55).

19. Michael Colacurcio has pointed out that this account of early colonial history calls into question "the flagrant idolatries of America's pseudo-Puritan civil religion." In its place, Hawthorne offers "a Tory view" emphasizing "provincial unruliness, a mob scene" (*The Province of Piety: Moral History in Hawthorne's Early Tales* [Durham, NC: Duke University Press, 1995], 136–38). See also John P. McWilliams Jr., "'Thorough-Going Democrat' and 'Modern Tory': Hawthorne and the Puritan Revolution of 1776," *Studies in Romanticism* 15 (1976): 549–71.

20. Peter Shaw, "Fathers, Sons, and the Ambiguities of Revolution in 'My Kinsman, Major Molineux,'" *New England Quarterly* 49 (December 1976): 559–76.

21. Ralph Waldo Emerson, "Hymn: Sung at the Completion of the Concord Monument, April 19, 1836," in *Collected Poems and Translations* (New York: Library of America, 1994), 125.

22. Edward Dicey, *Six Months in the Federal States* (1863), reprinted as *Spec-

tator of America, ed. Herbert Mitgang (Athens: University of Georgia Press, 1989), 269.

23. Ibid.

24. See Harold Murdock, *The Nineteenth of April, 1775* (Boston: Houghton Mifflin, 1923), 72. Murdock also cites an 1835 deposition given by Charles Handley, who states that the young man "told me in 1807, that it had worried him very much; but that he thought he was doing right, at the time" (73n). See also Robert A. Gross, *The Minutemen and Their World* (New York: Hill and Wang, 1976), 126–27. Gross suggests the young man may have been trying to put the British soldier out of his misery.

25. Quoted in Mary Beth Norton, *In the Devil's Snare: The Salem Witchcraft Crisis of 1692* (New York: Vintage, 2002), 58.

26. Ibid., 59.

27. Quoted in ibid., 144.

28. Quoted in Junius P. Rodriguez, *Chronology of World Slavery* (Santa Barbara, CA: ABC-CLIO, 1999), 416.

29. See ibid., 221.

30. Colacurcio, *Province,* 121.

31. Cotton Mather, *Magnalia Christi Americana; or, The ecclesiastical history of New-England, from its first planting in the year 1620. unto the year of our Lord, 1698. In seven books. . . . By . . . Cotton Mather, . . .* (London: T. Parkhurst, 1702), 91.

32. Nathaniel Hawthorne, *American Magazine* 2 (May 1836): 397. Hawthorne's sister Elizabeth wrote some pieces for the magazine, but this is her brother's work, as she acknowledged in a letter to James T. Fields on December 26, 1870, printed in *Hawthorne in His Own Time,* ed. Ronald A. Bosco and Jillmarie Murphy (Iowa City: University of Iowa Press, 2007), 6–10.

33. John O'Sullivan, "Introduction," *United States Magazine and Democratic Review* 1 (October 1837), 15.

34. For strong expressions of O'Sullivan's pacifism, see O'Sullivan, "The Peace Movement," *United States Magazine and Democratic Review* 10 (February 1842): 107–21; "The Late William Ladd, the Apostle of Peace," *United States Magazine and Democratic Review* 10 (March 1842): 211–23.

35. See Neal Frank Doubleday, *Hawthorne's Early Tales: A Critical Study* (Durham, NC: Duke University Press, 1972), 117–37; Sohui Lee, "Hawthorne's Politics of Storytelling: Two 'Tales of the Province House' and the Specter of Anglomania in the *Democratic Review,*" *American Periodicals* 41, no. 1 (2004): 35–62. Both Doubleday and Lee argue that Hawthorne sought to advance O'Sullivan's political agenda.

36. John O'Sullivan, "Annexation," *United States Magazine and Democratic Review* 17 (July–August 1845): 8, 7, 5.

37. John O'Sullivan, "The Texas Question," *United States Magazine and Democratic Review* 14 (April 1844), 424.

38. See Robert D. Sampson, *John L. O'Sullivan and His Times* (Kent, OH: Kent State University Press, 2003), 155–57.

39. O'Sullivan failed at any number of political schemes, most notably his filibustering in Cuba, which earned him censure by the U.S. government. In a letter to Sophia when she was staying with the O'Sullivans in Lisbon, Hawthorne described O'Sullivan as "not the man in whom I see my ideal of a friend. . . . he never stirs me to any depth beneath my surface; I like him, and enjoy his society, and he calls up, I think, whatever small part of me is elegant and agreeable; but neither of my best nor of my worst has he ever, or could he ever, have a glimpse" (17:438).

40. For a penetrating comparison of Bancroft's *History* and Hawthorne's "Legends," see Colacurcio, *Province*, 453–57.

41. John P. McWilliams Jr. has pointed out, "Although Hawthorne's old Tories are engagingly humane and sympathetic in their victimization, they are never allowed to be models of political behavior" (*Hawthorne, Melville, and the American Character: A Looking-Glass Business* [New York: Cambridge University Press, 1984], 79).

42. John W. Crowley has argued that although *Grandfather's Chair* was a children's book, it was informed by "the weight of adult ideas and impressions he had been gathering for over ten years." Crowley makes the important point that "Hawthorne was writing not just for children but for the adults they would become" ("Hawthorne's New England Epochs," *ESQ: A Journal of the American Renaissance* 25 [1979]: 60).

43. Harrison died of pneumonia after only a month in office. Wishing to demonstrate his vigor, he wore neither hat nor coat during his inauguration on a cold March day. Vice President John Tyler, a former Democrat turned Whig, assumed the presidency upon Harrison's death.

44. Quoted in Samuel Carter III, *Cherokee Sunset: A Nation Betrayed; A Narrative of Travail and Triumph, Persecution and Exile* (New York: Doubleday, 1976), 258.

45. Quoted in ibid., 259.

46. Quoted in ibid., 262.

47. Ralph Waldo Emerson to Martin Van Buren, 1838, in *Emerson's Antislavery Writings,* ed. Len Gougeon and Joel Myerson (New Haven, CT: Yale University Press, 1995), 3.

48. My discussion of Hawthorne's ironic perspective on the concept of manifest destiny, as used to justify the supplanting of the native population of New England, is indebted to Michael Colacurcio's " 'Red Man's Grave': Art and Destiny in Hawthorne's 'Main-street,' " *Nathaniel Hawthorne Review* 31 (Fall 2005): 1–18.

49. In a letter from England on March 2, 1855, Hawthorne told William Tick-

nor, "I do love old Massachusetts, in spite of its ten thousand varieties of nonsense" (17:315).

50. Eric J. Sundquist, *To Wake the Nations: Race in the Making of American Literature* (Cambridge, MA: Harvard University Press, Belknap, 1993), 31.

51. Major studies in English include Laurent Dubois's *Avengers of the New World: The Story of the Haitian Revolution* (Cambridge, MA: Harvard University Press, Belknap, 2004), Joan Dayan's *Haiti, History, and the Gods* (Berkeley: University of California Press, 1995), and Carolyn Fick's *The Making of Haiti: The Saint-Domingue Revolution from Below* (Knoxville: University of Tennessee Press, 1990).

52. Jeremy D. Popkin, "Facing Racial Revolution: Captivity Narratives and Identity in the Saint-Domingue Insurrection," *Eighteenth-Century Studies* 36, no. 4 (2003): 512.

53. Quoted in Dayan, 217.

54. Ibid.

55. [William Drayton], *The South Vindicated from the Treason and Fanaticism of the Northern Abolitionists* (1836; reprint, New York: Negro Universities Press, 1969), 263.

56. See Bryan Edwards, *An Historical Survey of the French Colony in the Island of St. Domingo* (London: printed for J. Stockdale, 1797). Edwards reported, "This unfortunate woman (my hand trembles while I write!) was far advanced in her pregnancy. The monsters, whose prisoner she was, having first murdered her husband in her presence, ripped her up alive and threw the infant to the hogs— They then (how shall I relate it!) sewed up the head of the murdered husband in— —!!!" (quoted in Robert Debs Heinl Jr. and Nancy Gordon Heinl, *Written in Blood: The Story of the Haitian People, 1492–1971* [Boston: Houghton Mifflin, 1978], 53).

57. Virginia newspapers of 1803 detail the brutality during the last days of the conflict, including blacks taking corkscrews to the eyes of women and "ripping up the bellies of those with child, and exposing the unborn infants to the eyes of their expiring mothers" (quoted in Alfred N. Hunt, *Haiti's Influence on Antebellum America: Slumbering Volcano in the Caribbean* [Baton Rouge: Louisiana State University Press, 1988], 39). The French, as Hunt points out, behaved no better, massacring prisoners and importing "two hundred bloodhounds from Cuba to ferret out and kill any black foolish or unfortunate enough not to flee to the hills surrounding the white stronghold at le Cap" (39). Dessalines's final slaughter of whites began at Port-au-Prince in January. According to a Frenchman who escaped, "on 17 and 18 March, they were finished off en masse. All, without exception, have been massacred, down to the women and children. A young mulâtresse, named Fifi Pariset, ranged the town like a madwoman, searching the houses to slay the little children. Many men and women were chopped

down by sappers, who hacked off their limbs and smashed in their chests. Some were stabbed, others mutilated, others *passes par la baionette,* others disemboweled, still others stuck like pigs" (quoted in Heinl and Heinl, 126). Such reports provided Americans with images of the "Santo Domingo Hour," as it was called, and made them fearful of black emancipation.

58. C. L. R. James, *The Black Jacobins: Toussaint L'Ouverture and the San Domingo Revolution,* 2nd ed. (New York: Random House, 1963), ix.

59. See Corporation of Charleston, *An Account of the Late Intended Insurrection among a Portion of the Blacks of This City* (Charleston: A. E. Miller, 1822), reprinted in *Slave Insurrections: Selected Documents* (Westport, CT: Negro Universities Press, 1970), 34–39.

60. Matt D. Childs, " 'A Black French General Arrived to Conquer the Island': Images of the Haitian Revolution in Cuba's 1812 Aponte Rebellion," in *The Impact of the Haitian Revolution in the Atlantic World,* ed. David P. Geggus (Columbia: University of South Carolina Press, 2001): 137.

61. Ibid., 150.

62. Patricia Dunlavy Valenti, *Sophia Peabody Hawthorne: A Life,* vol. 1, *1809–1847* (Columbia: University of Missouri Press, 2004), 53.

63. Ibid., 122.

64. Sophia Peabody Hawthorne, " 'The Cuba Journal' of Sophia Peabody Hawthorne," ed. Claire Badaracco (PhD diss., Rutgers University, 1978), 319.

65. Ibid., 616.

66. Ibid., 61.

67. Quoted in Nathaniel Hawthorne, *The Centenary Edition of the Works of Nathaniel Hawthorne,* ed. William Charvat et al., 23 vols. (Columbus: Ohio State University Press, 1962–97), 23:534 n. 197.3.

68. Quoted in Julian Hawthorne, *Nathaniel Hawthorne and His Wife: A Biography,* 2 vols. (Boston: Houghton Mifflin, 1884), 1:185.

69. For an account of Sophia's cleaning of the painting, see Valenti, 125.

70. Robert Cantwell, *Nathaniel Hawthorne: The American Years* (New York: Rinehart, 1948), 254.

71. Ibid., 257.

72. Despite Garrison's visibility within the abolitionist movement, he was anticipated by a group of Northern black leaders—including Hawthorne's Bowdoin classmate John Russwurm—who agitated for the end to Southern slavery and Northern oppression through their own "newspapers, conventions, tracts, orations, and legislative petitions." Leon F. Litwack notes that "four years before the publication of the first issue of *The Liberator,*" Russwurm and Samuel E. Cornish "launched the first Negro newspaper—*Freedom's Journal*—in an effort to disseminate useful ideas and information and to attract public attention to the plight of those still in bondage" (*North of Slavery: The Negro in the Free States, 1790–1860* [Chicago: University of Chicago Press, 1961], 230–32).

73. Quoted in Herbert Aptheker, *Nat Turner's Slave Rebellion: Together with the Full Text of the So-Called "Confessions" of Nat Turner Made in Prison in 1831* (New York: Humanities, 1966), 61. In an 1861 *Atlantic Monthly* essay, Thomas Wentworth Higginson, one of John Brown's "Secret Six," explains that Turner and his followers (sixty to eighty Negroes) mistakenly believed that the British would aid them, but they suffered from poor arms and a total lack of ammunition. Higginson also notes that though the rebellion failed, Turner and Cinque became John Brown's heroes ("Nat Turner's Insurrection," *Atlantic Monthly* 8 [August 1861]: 173–87).

74. See Henry Mayer, *All on Fire: William Lloyd Garrison and the Abolition of Slavery* (New York: St. Martin's Press, 1998), 120–21.

75. William Lloyd Garrison, "The Dangers of the Nation" (1832), reprinted in *Selections from the Writings and Speeches of William Lloyd Garrison* (1852; reprint, New York: Negro Universities Press, 1968), 59.

76. *Salem Gazette*, October 23, 1835.

77. Quoted in ibid.

78. See Wineapple, 251.

79. *New York Evening Post*, August 7, 1833, quoted in Lorman Ratner, *Powder Keg: Northern Opposition to the Antislavery Movement, 1831–1840* (New York: Basic, 1968), 44.

80. See William H. Pease and Jane H. Pease, "Antislavery Ambivalence: Immediatism, Expediency, Race," *American Quarterly* 17 (Winter 1965): 682–95.

81. See Ratner, 131–41.

82. James Fenimore Cooper, *The American Democrat, and Other Political Writings*, ed. Bradley J. Birzer and John Wilson (Washington, DC: Regnery, 2000), 483.

83. Harriet Beecher Stowe, *Uncle Tom's Cabin*, ed. Elizabeth Ammons, Norton Critical Edition (New York: Norton, 1994), 386.

84. See Patrick Brancaccio, "'The Black Man's Paradise': Hawthorne's Editing of the *Journal of an African Cruiser*," *New England Quarterly* 53 (March 1980): 23–41. Brancaccio points out that the American Colonization Society listed the *Journal* in its annual report for 1846 as "one of the most prominent events in the history of colonization for the past year" (39).

Chapter 2

1. Although Hawthorne acknowledged the cruelty of John and William Hathorne, he suppressed the sexual transgressions of his maternal Manning ancestors, as Gloria Erlich has shown. In 1680, his great-great-grandfather Nicholas Manning was accused by his wife of incest with his two sisters, Anstiss and Margaret. Apparently guilty as charged, Nicholas fled Salem, but his sisters were tried, convicted, and sentenced "to be imprisoned a night, whipped, or pay £5, and to sit, during the services of next lecture day, on a high stool, in the middle

ally of Salem meeting-house, having a paper on their heads with their crime writ-ten in capital letters" (Joseph B. Felt, *Annals of Salem,* 2nd ed. [Salem: Ives, 1845], 1:459–60, quoted in Gloria C. Erlich, *Family Themes and Hawthorne's Fiction: The Tenacious Web* [New Brunswick, NJ: Rutgers University Press, 1984], 35–36).

Hawthorne never mentioned this instance of male cowardice and female dis-grace in his family's history, but he re-created versions of both in *The Scarlet Let-ter,* using Arthur Dimmesdale and Hester Pyrnne to do so. The character flaws of Nicholas Manning, along with those of John Hathorne, probably confirmed the theory of Puritan declension Hawthorne arrived at sometime early in his career. His sympathetic attitude toward Indians may also have been inspired by ancestral guilt, for in 1676, John Hathorne's younger brother, Captain William Hathorne Jr., tricked some 350 friendly Wabanaki Indians in Maine and took them as pris-oners to Boston, where seven or eight were executed and some two hundred, mostly women and children, were sold into slavery. See Norton, 89–90.

2. The literature on the Salem witchcraft crisis is vast, of course, but for the best discussions of its causes, see Paul Boyer and Stephen Nissenbaum, *Salem Possessed: The Social Origins of Witchcraft* (Cambridge, MA: Harvard Univer-sity Press, 1974); James E. Kenes, "Some Unexplored Relationships of Essex County Witchcraft to the Indian Wars of 1675 and 1689," *Essex Institute Histor-ical Collections* 120 (1984): 179–212; Carol F. Karlsen, *The Devil in the Shape of a Woman: Witchcraft in Colonial New England* (New York: Norton, 1987); Jane Kamensky, "Words, Witches, and Woman Trouble: Witchcraft, Disorderly Speech, and Gender Boundaries in Puritan New England," *Essex Institute His-torical Collections* 128 (1992): 286–309; Larry Gragg, *The Salem Witch Crisis* (New York: Praeger, 1992); Peter Charles Hoffer, *The Salem Witchcraft Trials: A Legal History* (Lawrence: University Press of Kansas, 1997); Norton.

3. Two important exceptions are Peter Charles Hoffer's *The Devil's Disciples: Makers of the Salem Witchcraft Trials* (Baltimore: Johns Hopkins University Press, 1996) and Bernard Rosenthal's *Salem Story: Reading the Witch Trials of 1692* (Cambridge: Cambridge University Press, 1993), which argue that the Puri-tan authorities encouraged the lies of the "afflicted," resulting in the deaths of the innocent.

4. Samuel Parris, "27 March, Sab. 1692, Sacrament day," in Francis Hill, *The Salem Witch Trials Reader* (New York: Da Capo, 2000), 123.

5. Paul Boyer and Stephen Nissenbaum, eds., *The Salem Witchcraft Papers: Verbatim Transcripts of the Legal Documents of the Salem Witchcraft Outbreak of 1692,* 3 vols. (New York: Da Capo, 1977), 3:746–47.

6. Ibid., 3:753–55.

7. Thomas Hutchinson, *The History of the Province of Massachusetts-Bay, from the Charter of King William and Queen Mary, in 1691, until the Year 1750* (Boston: Thomas and John Fleet, 1767), 26.

8. Robert Calef, *More Wonders of the Invisible World* (1700), reprinted in

George Lincoln Burr, ed., *Narratives of the Witchcraft Cases, 1648–1706* (New York: Scribner's, 1914), 343.

9. John Hale, *A Modest Enquiry into the Nature of Witchcraft* (1702), reprinted in Burr, 415. As Elaine G. Breslaw has pointed out, "Tituba supplied the evidence of a satanic presence legally necessary to launch a witch-hunt. Had she remained silent, the trials might not have occurred or, at the least, would have followed a different course" ("Tituba's Confession: The Multicultural Dimensions of the 1692 Salem Witch-Hunt," *Ethnohistory* 44, no. 3 [1997]: 536).

10. Boyer and Nissenbaum, *Salem Witchcraft Papers,* 1:248–54.

11. On Corey's mulatto son, see Vernon Loggins, *The Hawthornes: The Story of Seven Generations of an American Family* (New York: Columbia University Press, 1951), 136.

12. This is evident in a letter written by Elizabeth Cary's husband, Nathaniel, telling of his wife's treatment at the hands of Hathorne and Corwin on May 24.

> Being brought before the Justices, her chief accusers were two Girls; my Wife declared to the Justices, that she never had any knowledge of them before that day; she was forced to stand with her Arms stretched out. I did request that I might hold one of her hands, but it was denied me; then she desired me to wipe the Tears from her Eyes, and the Sweat from her Face, which I did; then she desired she might lean her self on me, saying, she should faint.
>
> Justice Hathorn replied, she had strength enough to torment those persons, and she should have strength enough to stand. I speaking something against their cruel proceedings, they commanded me to be silent, or else I should be turned out of the Room. . . . I being extreamly troubled at their Inhumane dealings, uttered a hasty Speech (That God would take vengeance on them, and desired that God would deliver us out of the hands of unmerciful men). (Quoted in Calef, 351)

13. Boyer and Nissenbaum, *Salem Witchcraft Papers,* 2:475.

14. See ibid., 1:166–67.

15. See Calef, 361.

16. Increase Mather, *Cases of conscience concerning evil spirits personating men, witchcrafts, infallible proofs of guilt in such as are accused with that crime* (Boston: Benjamin Harris, 1693), 1.

17. Thomas Brattle, letter, October 8, 1692, in Burr, 188–89.

18. Cotton Mather, *The Wonders of the Invisible World* (1693; reprint, Mount Vernon, NY: Peter Pauper, 1950), 6.

19. Calef, 305–6.

20. Hutchinson, 20–21.

21. Charles Upham, *Lectures on Witchcraft, Comprising a History of the Delusion in Salem, in 1692* (Boston: Carter, Hendee, and Babcock, 1831), 113–14.

22. George Bancroft, *History of the United States from the Discovery of the American Continent,* vol. 3, *History of the Colonization of the United States* (Boston: Little and Brown, 1840), 84.

23. Ibid., 86.

24. Ibid., 85.

25. Ibid.

26. Ibid., 84.

27. Ibid., 88.

28. In a letter of February 10, 1840, Hawthorne exclaims to his friend W. B. Pike, "What an astounding liar our venerated chief [Bancroft] turns out to be!" (15:410). (Hawthorne is sympathizing with Pike's frustrated office seeking.) Arlin Turner observes, "In the Hawthorne household, George Bancroft was called the Blatant Beast, after the many-tongued slanderer of *The Faerie Queene*" (*Nathaniel Hawthorne: A Biography* [New York: Oxford University Press, 1980], 170).

29. David Anthony, in an astute discussion of *The House of the Seven Gables* and "Alice Doane's Appeal," has made the important point that "for Hawthorne, the debased aesthetic of mass-culture sensationalism is seen as a threat to bodily integrity, one that disturbingly carries with it an often seductive and always dangerous erotics" ("Class, Culture, and the Trouble with White Skin in Hawthorne's *The House of the Seven Gables*," *Yale Journal of Criticism* 12, no. 2 [1999]: 265 n. 6). The accusations of the young girls of Salem in 1692, although not mentioned by Anthony, surely contributed to this perspective of Hawthorne's.

30. Nina Baym, *The Shape of Hawthorne's Career* (Ithaca, NY: Cornell University Press, 1976), 38.

31. Ibid., 39.

32. Ibid.

33. See Colacurcio, *Province,* 283–313; David Levin, "Shadows of Doubt: Specter Evidence in Hawthorne's 'Young Goodman Brown,'" *American Literature* 34 (November 1962): 344–52.

34. C. Mather, *Wonders,* 105.

35. Margaret Fuller, *"These Sad but Glorious Days": Dispatches from Europe, 1846–1850,* ed. Larry J. Reynolds and Susan Belasco Smith (New Haven, CT: Yale University Press, 1991), 76.

36. Henry David Thoreau, *"Walden" and "Resistance to Civil Government,"* ed. William Rossi, 2nd ed., Norton Critical Edition (New York: Norton, 1996), 58.

37. "Sophia Peabody Hawthorne's *American Notebooks,*" ed. Patricia Dunlavy Valenti, in *Studies in the American Renaissance, 1996,* ed. Joel Myerson (Charlottesville: University Press of Virginia, 1996), 146.

38. Cotton Mather, *Memorable Providences, Relating to Witchcrafts and Possessions* (1689), reprinted in Burr, 99.

39. I. Mather, 3.

40. Hale, 426–27.

41. Curtis, 552.

42. Ibid., 544.

43. As Emily Budick has pointed out, "Young Goodman Brown" not only explores the power and nature of spectral evidence but also reveals Hawthorne's appreciation of moral relativity, by dramatizing "Brown's failure to question the sweeping and unsubstantiated claim that his ancestors willingly accepted the devil's help, that they performed deeds that they (and not a subsequent generation) considered evil" ("The World as Specter: Hawthorne's Historical Art," *PMLA* 101 [1986]: 221).

44. Joanne Pope Melish, *Disowning Slavery: Gradual Emancipation and "Race" in New England, 1780–1860* (Ithaca, NY: Cornell University Press, 1998), 224. Michael Colacurcio points out that Hawthorne "had the critical intelligence to discern how much of the familiar politics of mission and destiny was but the public face of a piety that flourished in America distinctively." Colacurcio observes that "eventually, especially in the 1840s," Hawthorne "acquired the perspective to notice how much of the morale of his own generation of intellectuals was suitably understood as neo-Puritan, despite their vigorous rejection of the theological idioms of the older orthodoxy" (introduction to *Selected Tales and Sketches,* by Nathaniel Hawthorne [New York: Penguin, 1987], viii).

45. Elizabeth B. Clark, "Sacred Rights of the Weak: Pain and Sympathy in Antebellum America," *Journal of American History* 82 (September 1995): 471.

46. Moncure Daniel Conway, *Emerson, at Home and Abroad* (1883; reprint, New York: Haskell House, 1968), 303.

47. Boyer and Nissenbaum, *Salem Witchcraft Papers,* 3:753.

48. Calef, 343.

49. Bancroft, 86.

50. Quoted in Charles Upham, *Salem Witchcraft, with an Account of Salem Village, and a History of Opinions on Witchcraft and Kindred Subjects,* 2 vols. (1867; reprint, Williamstown, MA: Corner House, 1971), 2:82.

51. Quoted in Kenneth Silverman, *The Life and Times of Cotton Mather* (New York: Harper and Row, 1984), 127.

52. Cotton Mather, "A Brand Pluck'd Out of the Burning" (1693), reprinted in Burr, 267.

53. Michael Rogin, *"Ronald Reagan," the Movie: And Other Episodes in Political Demonology* (Berkeley: University of California Press, 1987), xiii.

54. Cheyfitz, 545.

55. Moncure Daniel Conway, *Autobiography: Memories and Experiences,* 2 vols. (New York: Cassell, 1904), 2:185.

56. Thoreau, *Journal,* 8:165.

57. C. Mather, *Wonders,* 67–68.

58. Garrison, 180.

59. Quoted in Leonard L. Richards, *"Gentlemen of Property and Standing":
Anti-Abolition Mobs in Jacksonian America* (New York: Oxford University
Press, 1970), 56–57.

60. Bertram Wyatt-Brown. *Yankee Saints and Southern Sinners* (Baton Rouge:
Louisiana State University Press, 1985), 23.

61. In his narratives of the witchcraft trials, Calef describes Cotton Mather's
treatment of Margaret Rule on September 13, 1793, recording that when she fell
into a fit, he "brush'ed her on the Face with his Glove, and rubb'd her Stomach
(her breast not covered with the Bed-cloaths) and bid others do so too" (325).
Mather, outraged at the insinuation of lewdness, charged Calef with slander (see
Silverman, 131).

62. Thomas Jefferson, *Notes on the State of Virginia* (New York: printed by
M. L. and W. A. Davis for Furman and Loudon, 1801), 240.

63. As Ronald G. Walters has shown, antebellum abolitionists created an image of the South as filled with licentiousness, where both female slaves and their
masters degraded one another without check. Walters quotes one abolitionist
who declares, "women who have been drawn into licentiousness by wicked men,
if they retain their vicious habits, almost invariably display their revenge for their
own debasement, by ensnaring others into the same corruption and moral ruin"
("The Erotic South: Civilization and Sexuality in American Abolitionism," in
History of the American Abolitionist Movement, vol. 1, *Abolitionism and American Reform,* ed. John R. McKivigan [New York: Garland, 1999], 360).

64. Donald M. Scott, "Abolition as a Sacred Vocation," in *Antislavery Reconsidered: New Perspectives on the Abolitionists,* ed. Lewis Perry and Michael Fellman (Baton Rouge: Louisiana University Press, 1979), 67, quoting Samuel
Crothers, *An Address to the Churches on the Subject of Slavery* (1831).

65. Wendell Phillips, *The Philosophy of the Abolitionist Movement,* Anti-Slavery Tract no. 8 (New York, 1860), II, quoted in Hunt, 6.

66. Horace Mann, "Speech on the Institution of Slavery" (1852), in *Against
Slavery: An Abolitionist Reader,* ed. Mason Lowance (New York: Penguin, 2000),
267.

67. For a detailed discussion of how this linkage developed in the nineteenth-
century, see Sander Gilman, *Difference and Pathology: Stereotypes of Sexuality,
Race, and Madness* (Ithaca, NY: Cornell University Press, 1985).

68. The timing of Arthur's death makes it coincide with the beheading of
Charles I, defeated enemy of Cromwell, and his roundhead rebels. See L.
Reynolds, *European Revolutions,* 84; Reid, *Cultural Secrets,* 81.

69. See Simon P. Newman, "American Political Culture and the French and
Haitian Revolutions: Nathaniel Cutting and the Jeffersonian Republicans," in
The Impact of the Haitian Revolution in the Atlantic World, ed. David P. Geggus
(Columbia: University of South Carolina Press, 2001), 72–89.

70. Hunt, 80. For a detailed account of the place of religion in the slave insurrection, see Dubois, 99–102.

71. See Hunt, 81.

72. *New Orleans Bee,* July 25, 1851.

73. *New Orleans Bee,* October 15, 1860.

74. Chadwick Hansen, "The Metamorphosis of Tituba, or Why American Intellectuals Can't Tell an Indian Witch from a Negro," *New England Quarterly* 47 (March 1974): 3–12.

75. Upham, *Salem Witchcraft,* 2:2.

76. In the antebellum United States, Haiti, like Cuba, became a screen on which Americans projected their political fears and desires. As the spirit of American expansionism gained momentum with the Mexican War and the clandestine foreign policies of Presidents Polk, Pierce, and Buchanan, Haiti became an inviting target of annexation. As it did, the voodoo religion gained attention due to its practice by Haiti's president Faustin Soulouque, who made himself emperor in 1849. Anna Brickhouse points out, "Figured as 'an abominable African despot' and a frightening practitioner of religious 'barbarism' who kept a 'fetish serpent' for 'Wodoo' hidden in his throne, Soulouque provided a continuous reminder of potential slave revolts for 'planter[s] of the south,' recalling 'the trouble and sorrow that conjured servants have caused . . . from time to time'" (*Transamerican Literary Relations and the Nineteenth-Century Public Sphere* [New York: Cambridge University Press, 2004], 224).

Demonizing Soulouque was the first step in justifying a military invasion of Haiti, which was ardently advocated by O'Sullivan's *Democratic Review.* Such a demonization served, as it did with Mexicans before the Mexican War, to cast white Americans as potential victims of a savage menace that needed to be removed, by violence if necessary. Throughout the nineteenth century, as Brickhouse points out, American writers and editors "repeatedly invent a Franco-Africanist figure to crystallize the ambiguities confounding an Anglo-Saxonist national ideology seeking paradoxically to solidify the imaginary racial borders of the nation even as its proponents debated the future of expansionism in the Americas" (249).

77. For Yellin, the novel ends up repudiating the ideology of the antislavery feminists, by having Hester accept "the patriarchy's paradigm of true womanhood, the Angel in the House" (654). For Leland Person, however, Hawthorne's identification of Hester with a slave mother is ironic and intended to critique "the presumptions of white female abolitionists like Margaret Fuller and his sister-in-law, Elizabeth Peabody," who commandeer the subject position of slave women for their own political purposes ("The Dark Labyrinth of Mind: Hawthorne, Hester, and the Ironies of Racial Mothering." *Studies in American Fiction* 29 [Spring 2001]: 664, 662. Ultimately, Hawthorne's use of antislavery iconography, I

believe, goes beyond such specific purposes, to develop his larger political critique of self-righteous individuals and groups. He addresses not only representations of slavery, in other words, but also the kind of impassioned behavior generated by such provocative imagery.

78. Yellin, 154–55.

Chapter 3

1. There would have been ample contemporary evidence of the abuses of slavery from less suspect sources than abolitionist writings. Advertisements for the return of runaway slaves, written by slave owners themselves, described scars from whippings, beatings, mutilations, branding, and other forms of severe violence, testifying to the brutal realities of slavery (see John Hope Franklin and Loren Schweninger, *Runaway Slaves: Rebels on the Plantation* [New York: Oxford University Press, 1999]). Moreover, the census figures for mulatto slaves speak to the sexual exploitation of female slaves by their masters. In 1850, there were 246,000 mulatto slaves out of a slave population of 3.2 million; by 1860, the number rose to 411,000 mulatto slaves out of a total slave population of 3.9 million (John Hope Franklin, *From Slavery to Freedom: A History of Negro Americans* [1956; reprint, New York: Knopf, 1968], 158). As for the obvious question of whether Hawthorne could have learned of such facts, the answer is yes.

2. Wyatt-Brown, *Yankee Saints,* 28.

3. Litwack, vii.

4. John M. Werner, *Reaping the Bloody Harvest: Race Riots in the United States during the Age of Jackson, 1824–1849* (New York: Garland, 1986), 298; Richards, 40, 157.

5. Melish, 199.

6. Richards, 5.

7. Quoted in Louis Rochames, ed., *Racial Thought in America from the Puritans to Abraham Lincoln* (Amherst: University of Massachusetts Press, 1963), 380–81.

8. Pease and Pease, "Antislavery Ambivalence," 685–86.

9. Child, Grimké, and Parker, quoted in Pease and Pease, "Antislavery Ambivalence," 692, 686.

10. Walt Whitman, "Prohibition of Colored Persons," *Brooklyn Daily Times,* May 6, 1858, reprinted in *Race and the American Romantics,* ed. Vincent Freimark and Bernard Rosenthal (New York: Schocken, 1971), 46–47.

11. Bertram Wyatt-Brown, *Lewis Tappan and the Evangelical War against Slavery* (Cleveland: Press of Case Western Reserve, 1969), 179.

12. Ibid.

13. Litwack, 229–30.

14. Louis Menand, *The Metaphysical Club* (New York: Farrar, Straus and Giroux, 2001), 103.

15. Quoted in George M. Frederickson, *The Black Image in the White Mind: The Debate on Afro-American Character and Destiny, 1817–1914* (Hanover, NH: Wesleyan University Press, 1987), 78.

16. Josiah Clark Nott, *Types of Mankind: or, Ethnological Researches, Based upon the Ancient Monuments, Paintings, Sculptures, and Crania of Races, and upon Their Natural, Geographical, Philological and Biblical History* (Philadelphia: Lippincott Gramoo; London: Trubner, 1855), 461.

17. Oliver Wendell Holmes, "Oration, Semi-centennial Celebration of the New England Society in the City of New York" (1855), in *The Autocrat's Miscellanies,* ed. Albert Mordell (New York: Twayne, 1959), 80.

18. George R. Gliddon to Samuel George Morton, January 9, 1848, Samuel Morton Papers, Historical Society of Pennsylvania, quoted in Menand, 109.

19. Lawrence Buell, *Emerson* (Cambridge, MA: Harvard University Press, Belknap, 2003), 4–5.

20. See Martin Duberman, *James Russell Lowell* (Boston: Houghton Mifflin, 1966), 185; Thomas Wortham, "Did Emerson Blackball Frederick Douglass from Membership in the Town and Country Club?" *New England Quarterly* 65 (June 1992): 295–98. Wortham argues that Lowell was misinformed.

21. R. Emerson, *Journals,* 2:48.

22. R. Emerson, *Journals,* 9:125. For a strong account of Emerson's racism, see Kun Jong Lee, "Ellison's Invisible Man: Emersonianism Revisited," *PMLA* 107 (March 1992): 331–44.

23. R. Emerson, *Journals,* 10:357.

24. R. Emerson, *Journals,* 13:35.

25. R. Emerson, *Journals,* 13:198.

26. R. Emerson, *Journals,* 13:286.

27. Bronson Alcott, *The Journals of Bronson Alcott,* ed. Odell Shepard (Boston: Little, Brown, 1938), 496.

28. Madelon Bedell, *The Alcotts: Biography of a Family* (New York: Clarkson N. Potter, 1980), 15.

29. Frederickson, *Black Image,* 156–57.

30. See Bedell, 24.

31. Sarah Elbert, *Louisa May Alcott: On Race, Sex, and Slavery* (Boston: Northeastern University Press, 1997), xv–xvi.

32. Henry David Thoreau, *The Journal of Henry D. Thoreau,* ed. Bradford Torrey and Francis H. Allen (1906; reprint, 14 vols. in two, New York: Dover, 1962), 1:130. This quotation is not included in the second volume of the Princeton University Press edition of Thoreau's journals, because it appears on loose leaves of paper laid within the manuscript journal but not a material part of it. I am grateful to Sandra Petrulionis and Robert Sattelmeyer for this information.

33. Quoted in Sandra Harbert Petrulionis, *To Set This World Right: The Anti-*

slavery Movement in Thoreau's Concord (Ithaca, NY: Cornell University Press, 2006), 65.

34. See Michael Meyer, "Thoreau and Black Emigration," *American Literature* 53 (November 1981): 386. Meyer emphasizes that "though Thoreau shared some nineteenth-century racial views about blacks, few of his contemporaries shared his intense passion for justice" (390).

35. Margaret Fuller, *Summer on the Lakes, in 1843*, with an introduction by Susan Belasco Smith (1844; reprint, Urbana: University of Illinois Press, 1991), 120.

36. [Elizabeth A. Peabody], "Slavery in the United States: Its Evils, Alleviations, and Remedies," *North American Review* 73 (October 1851): 363.

37. Elizabeth Peabody to Horatio Bridge, June 4, 1887, quoted in N. Hawthorne, 18:593 n. 6.

38. Quoted in Samuel T. Pickard, "Postscript," in *Hawthorne's First Diary, with an Account of its Discovery and Loss* (Boston: Houghton Mifflin, 1897), 102. This diary, not included in *The Centenary Edition of the Works of Nathaniel Hawthorne,* is a copy, not the original, and questions have surrounded its authenticity since entries were first provided by Symmes to Pickard, who published them in the *Portland Transcript* (1870–73). However, as Arlin Turner has pointed out, "the circumstances and the events reported in the diary square fully with information from other sources, and in outlook and interests the diarist is enough like the Hawthorne of the later works to argue that he was the diarist" (20–21). Wineapple points out that "most scholars consider the diary a hoax. . . . Yet we, like Ebe [Hawthorne's sister Elizabeth], can't discard it out of hand. If not by Hawthorne himself, the passages were written by someone who knew him and his family" (36). Symmes's own recollections, which Pickard included with the diary and from which I have quoted, probably deserve the same amount of skepticism as the diary itself.

39. Quoted in Samuel T. Pickard, "The Story of William Symmes," in *Hawthorne's First Diary, with an Account of Its Discovery and Loss* (Boston: Houghton Mifflin, 1897), 28–29.

40. Quoted in ibid., 31.

41. Sanborn, *Hawthorne*, 16.

42. Edward Dicey, "Nathaniel Hawthorne," *Macmillan's Magazine* 10 (July 1864): 244.

43. Conway, *Emerson, at Home and Abroad*, 224.

44. For the importance of racialism to Emerson's thought, see Philip L. Nicoloff, *Emerson on Race and History: An Examination of "English Traits,"* (New York: Columbia University Press, 1961); Cornel West, *The American Evasion of Philosophy: A Genealogy of Pragmatism* (Madison: University of Wisconsin Press, 1989), 28–35.

45. [Horatio Bridge], *Journal of an African Cruiser, by an Officer of the U.S.*

Navy, ed. Nathaniel Hawthorne (New York: Wiley and Putnam, 1845), 164 (hereafter cited parenthetically in text as *JAC*).

46. Teresa Goddu, *Gothic America: Narrative, History, and Nation* (New York: Columbia University Press, 1997), 137. Goddu has pointed out, "Slavery was a significant part of the historical context that produced the gothic and against which it responded" (133). Joan Dayan, in her powerful *Haiti, History, and the Gods,* observes, "One has only to read the 1685 *Code Noir* (Black Code) to understand how what first seems phantasmagoric is locked into a nature mangled and relived as a spectacle of servitude" (192).

47. Clark, 467.

48. Thomas Rankin, *Letters on American Slavery Addressed to Mr. Thomas Rankin* (Boston: Garrison and Knapp, 1833), 62–65.

49. For a well documented account of this gruesome murder, committed by Lilburne Lewis with the help of his brother Isham, see Boynton Merrill, Jr., *Jefferson's Nephews: A Frontier Tragedy* (Princeton, N.J.: Princeton University Press, 1976).

50. Frances Smith Foster, *Witnessing Slavery: The Development of Ante-Bellum Slave Narratives* (Westport, CT: Greenwood, 1979), 20.

51. Clark, 469.

52. See John W. Blassingame, introduction to *Slave Testimony: Two Centuries of Letters, Speeches, Interviews, and Autobiographies,* ed. John W. Blassingame (Baton Rouge: Louisiana State University Press, 1977), xxiii.

53. William Lloyd Garrison, Preface to *Narrative of the Life of Frederick Douglass, an American Slave, Written by Himself,* by Frederick Douglass, ed. William L. Andrews and William S. McFeely (1845; reprint, New York: Norton, 1997), 7.

54. Blassingame, xxvii.

55. Quoted in Goddu, *Gothic America,* 135.

56. Other studies of antislavery discourse, in addition to Goddu's *Gothic America,* have examined its complex relation to slavery itself, though they credit the horrors of the actual institution more than Hawthorne was willing to do. In *Touching Liberty: Abolition, Feminism, and the Politics of the Body* (Berkeley: University of California Press, 1993), a study of the intersecting rhetorics of feminism and abolition, Karen Sanchez Eppler has shown that domestic and sentimental antislavery writings tend to appropriate the pain of the suffering victim and to displace or obscure the particularity of the victim's experience. Similarly, in *Scenes of Subjection: Terror, Slavery, and Self-Making in Nineteenth-Century America* (New York: Oxford University Press, 1997), Saidiya V. Hartman focuses on the "convergence of terror and enjoyment" (23) with regard to slavery and asks, "Can the moral embrace of pain extricate itself from pleasures borne by subjection? . . . Is the act of 'witnessing' a kind of looking no less entangled with the wielding of power and the extraction of enjoyment?" (22).

57. Garrison, preface, 8.

58. *Liberator,* February 27, 1846.

59. Frederick Douglass, "Letters to His Old Master," published as "Appendix" in *My Bondage and My Freedom,* by Frederick Douglass, ed. William L. Andrews (1855; reprint, Urbana: University of Illinois Press, 1987), 270.

60. Douglass does not apologize but relates that "information concerning you and your household, lately received, makes it unjust and unkind for me to continue the style of remark, in regard to your character, which I primarily adopted. I have been told by a person intimately acquainted with your affairs . . . that you have ceased to be a slaveholder, and have emancipated all your slaves, except my poor old grandmother, who is now too old to sustain herself in freedom; and that you have taken her from the desolate hut in which she formerly lived, into your own kitchen, and are now providing for her in a manner becoming a man and a Christian" ("To Captain Thomas Auld, formerly my Master," *The North Star,* September 7, 1849).

61. See Audrey A. Fisch, *American Slaves in Victorian England: Abolitionist Politics in Popular Literature and Culture* (Cambridge: Cambridge University Press, 2000), 70.

62. "Celebration of W.I. Emancipation at Manchester, England," *Manchester Examiner and Times,* August 5, 1854, reprinted in the *Liberator,* September 1, 1854.

63. In 1846, for example, out of the nineteen fugitives that the committee helped, two were suspected imposters. See Irving H. Barlett, "Abolitionists, Fugitives, and Imposters in Boston, 1846–1847," *New England Quarterly* 55 (March 1982): 97–101.

64. Quoted in Fisch, 96.

65. Fisch, 124 n. 4. Hawthorne never mentions fugitive slave imposters during his stay in England, but in his account of the beggars and supplicants who approached him in England, he declares, "England is full of such people, and a hundred other varieties of peripatetic tricksters, higher than these, and lower, who act their parts tolerably well, but seldom with an absolutely illusive effect. I knew at once, raw Yankee as I was, that they were humbugs, almost without an exception—rats that nibble at the honest bread and cheese of the community, and grow fat by their petty pilferings—yet often gave them what they asked, and privately owned myself a simpleton" (5:292).

66. See N. Hawthorne, 19:297 n. 3.

67. In perhaps the most thorough discussion of Hawthorne's reform efforts as consul, Hall has concluded that Hawthorne participated "more frankly and efficiently than most of the other New England writers of his day in the actual business of reformation" (25).

68. See Mason Lowance, introduction to *Against Slavery: An Abolitionist Reader,* ed. Mason Lowance (New York: Penguin, 2000), xxx.

69. Deodat Lawson, *A Brief and True Narrative of Some Remarkable Passages Relating to Sundry Persons Afflicted by Witchcraft* (1692), reprinted in Burr, 156.

70. Quoted in Julian Hawthorne, 2:166.

71. See N. Hawthorne, 18:186–87.

72. *London Times*, August 3, 1859.

73. Bill Ellis, introduction to *The Consular Letters, 1853–1855*, by Nathaniel Hawthorne, vol. 19 of *The Centenary Edition of the Works of Nathaniel Hawthorne*, ed. Bill Ellis (Columbus: Ohio State University Press, 1988), 52.

Chapter 4

1. E. Hawthorne, 10.

2. John O'Sullivan, "The Martyrdom of Cilley," *United States Magazine and Democratic Review* 1 (March 1838): 493.

3. For an account of Clay's behind-the-scenes contribution, see John O'Sullivan, "Mr. Henry A. Wise and the Cilley Duel," *United States Magazine and Democratic Review* 10 (May 1842): 482–87; Sampson, 137.

4. In his early novel *Fanshawe*, Hawthorne hints at his moral estimate of dueling when he describes his protagonist's thoughts the morning after he has received a challenge from his arch enemy Butler: "More than once, during the progress of dressing, he was inclined to believe, that the duel had actually taken place, and been fatal to him, and that he was now in those regions, to which, his conscience told him, such an event would be likely to send him" (3:407–8).

5. Ralph L. Rusk, *The Life of Ralph Waldo Emerson* (New York: Columbia University Press, 1949), 302.

6. For a summary of Emerson's finances, see Ronald A. Bosco and Joel Myerson, *The Emerson Brothers: A Fraternal Biography in Letters* (New York: Oxford University Press, 2006), 327. For the conversion, see http://www.measuring worth.com/.

7. James Russell Lowell, *A Fable for Critics* (1848; reprint, London: Gay and Bird, 1890), 43.

8. Ralph Waldo Emerson, *The Letters of Ralph Waldo Emerson*, ed. Ralph L. Rusk and Eleanor M. Tilton, 10 vols. (New York: Columbia University Press, 1939–95): 8:44.

9. Julian Hawthorne, 1:287.

10. Perhaps the most telling evidence supporting this impression appears in a private travel diary that the young Englishman Henry Arthur Bright kept when he toured America in 1852. He visited with Emerson and Hawthorne in Concord after learning that the travel writer Fredrika Bremer, who spent an evening with Hawthorne in September 1850, planned to express her displeasure with him in her *The Homes of the New World: Impressions of America* (1853). Bright and a

friend named Burder were dining with Emerson, who had invited Hawthorne to join them. Here is Bright's account of what then transpired:

> Hawthorne arrived, and seemed in decent spirits and all right. Unluckily, a moment or two before dinner Emerson maliciously said "I hear Hawthorne that Miss Bremer makes honourable mention of you." "Where?" asked Hawthorne; Emerson appealed to Burder who had mentioned to Emerson the story I had told him about Miss Bremer: Burder threw the onus of it all on me, and I had to blurt out that I didn't know that anything was printed, Miss B. had mentioned Mr. H. in private conversation. "My interview with Miss Bremer was not a very successful one," said Hawthorne, and, dinner being announced, he said he could not stay, and vanished, to my annoyance and Emerson's amusement. (*Happy Country This America: The Travel Diary of Henry Arthur Bright,* ed. Anne Henry Ehrenpreis [Columbus: Ohio State University Press, 1978], 399–400)

11. Ralph Waldo Emerson, *Lectures and Biographical Sketches,* ed. James Eliot Cabot (Boston: Houghton Mifflin, 1884), 352–53.

12. For excellent studies of Hawthorne's responses to contemporary social experiments, see Taylor Stoehr, *Hawthorne's Mad Scientists: Pseudoscience and Social Science in Nineteenth-Century Life and Letters* (Hamden, CT: Archon, 1978); Joel Pfister, *The Production of Personal Life: Class, Gender, and the Psychological in Hawthorne's Fiction* (Stanford: Stanford University Press, 1991). For specifics of these experiments, see Carl J. Guarneri, *The Utopian Alternative: Fourierism in Nineteenth-Century America* (Ithaca, NY: Cornell University Press, 1991).

13. See Buford Jones, "'The Hall of Fantasy' and the Early Hawthorne-Thoreau Relationship," *PMLA* 83 (1968): 1429–38.

14. Ellery Channing, "The Selected Letters of William Ellery Channing the Younger (Part One)," ed. Francis B. Dedmond, in *Studies in the American Renaissance, 1989,* ed. Joel Myerson (Charlottesville: University Press of Virginia, 1989), 192.

15. For an extension of this interpretation of the Hawthorne-Emerson relationship, see Larry J. Reynolds, "Hawthorne and Emerson in 'The Old Manse.'" *Studies in the Novel* 23 (Spring 1991): 403–24; Larry J. Reynolds, "Hawthorne's Labors in Concord," in *The Cambridge Companion to Nathaniel Hawthorne,* ed. Richard H. Millington (New York: Cambridge University Press, 2004), 10–34.

16. Margaret Fuller, "'The Impulses of Human Nature': Margaret Fuller's Journal from June through October 1844," ed. Martha L. Berg and Alice de V. Perry, *Massachusetts Historical Society Proceedings* 102 (1990): 92.

17. Ralph Waldo Emerson, *Emerson's "Nature": Origin, Growth, Meaning,*

ed. Merton M. Sealts Jr. and Alfred R. Ferguson, 2nd ed. (Carbondale: Southern Illinois University Press, 1979), 35.

18. The only exception was Emerson's complaint that Hawthorne revealed too much of himself to his readers. What probably bothered Emerson more than the autobiographical elements in Hawthorne's works, his prefaces especially, were references to Emerson himself, by name. As Emerson's dialogue with Caroline Sturgis about the proper content of poetry reveals, he preferred that the personal be transformed into the general when put into print (see Andrew Jenkins, " 'O Sister of my Song!': Caroline Sturgis, Ralph Waldo Emerson, and 'Poems' (1847)," master's thesis, Texas A&M University, 1999). Emerson's poems "Uriel" and "Thenody"—about the uproar over his address to Harvard Divinity School and the death of his son Waldo, respectively—are examples of his treatments of intense personal experiences.

19. R. Emerson, *The Letters of Ralph Waldo Emerson,* 7:454–47.

20. See Anthony; Nancy Bentley, "Slaves and Fauns: Hawthorne and the Uses of Primitivism," *ELH* 57 (1990): 901–37; Anna Brickhouse, "Hawthorne in the Americas: Frances Calderón de la Barca, Octavio Paz, and the Mexican Genealogy of 'Rappaccini's Daughter,' " *PMLA* 113, no. 2 (1998): 227–42; Brickhouse, *Transamerican Literary Relations;* Goddu; Jay Grossman, " 'A' is for Abolition?: Race, Authorship, *The Scarlet Letter,*" *Textual Practice* 7, no. 1 (spring 1993): 13–30; Person; Yellin.

21. Brickhouse has pointed out that Hawthorne borrows ideas about racial mixing from Calderón's *Life in Mexico.* His "appropriation of Calderón was not simply an isolated act of inspired revision but, rather, a more general symptom of what Robert Young has called an 'obsession and paranoia about hybridity' that was, despite global imperialism in the mid-nineteenth century, most pronounced in the United States ("Hawthorne in the Americas," 231).

22. The issue of Hawthorne's attitude toward women has been the topic of a vast amount of commentary, most of it critical and charging him with various forms of sexism and misogyny. The most persuasive and sustained case for Hawthorne as a feminist has been made by Nina Baym, most recently in "Revisiting Hawthorne's Feminism," in *Hawthorne and the Real: Bicentennial Essays,* ed. Millicent Bell (Columbus: Ohio State University Press, 2005), 107–24.

23. Ralph Waldo Emerson, "American Civilization" (1862), in *The Political Emerson: Essential Writings on Politics and Social Reform,* ed. David M. Robinson (Boston: Beacon, 2004), 168.

24. Nancy Bentley, "White Slaves: The Mulatto Hero in Antebellum Fiction," *American Literature* 65 (September 1993): 504. For an in-depth exploration of the effects of racial hybridity and racial mixing on the writings of a number of nineteenth-century American authors (though not Hawthorne), see Betsy Erkkila, *Mixed Bloods and Other Crosses: Rethinking American Literature from the Rev-*

olution to the Culture Wars (Philadelphia: University of Pennsylvania Press, 2005).

25. Lathrop, 161–62.

26. Petrulionis, 391.

27. The group formed in October 1837, after a one-week visit by the abolitionist lecturers Angelina and Sarah Grimké, and grew to about one hundred members. Petrulionis explains that they "sponsored speakers, disseminated periodicals and other propaganda, circulated and signed petitions, raised money, traveled to national conventions, and worked to improve the lives of the few African Americans in their community" (387).

28. See Phyllis Cole, "Pain and Protest in the Emerson Family," in *The Emerson Dilemma: Essays on Emerson and Social Reform,* ed. T. Gregory Garvey (Athens: University of Georgia Press, 2001), 67–92. Cole explains, "Waldo remained both open to the words of women and capable of refusing or transforming their meanings. Mary was a deep, long-term source of his idealist principles, while Lidian established his daily context as one of sentimental feeling. . . . Male surrogates were the necessary vehicle of female ambition under circumstances of societal constraint" (68).

29. R. Emerson, *Journals,* 5:382.

30. See Joseph Slater, "Two Sources for Emerson's First Address on West Indian Emancipation," *ESQ: A Journal of the American Renaissance* 44 (1966): 97–100; Len Gougeon, *Virtue's Hero: Emerson, Antislavery, and Reform* (Athens: University of Georgia Press, 1990), 73–77.

31. R. Emerson, *Journals,* 8:119.

32. Ralph Waldo Emerson, *The Correspondence of Emerson and Carlyle,* ed. Joseph Slater (New York: Columbia University Press, 1964), 373; R. Emerson, *Journals,* 9:120.

33. Margaret Fuller, *The Letters of Margaret Fuller,* vol. 2, *1839–1841,* ed. Robert N. Hudspeth (Ithaca, NY: Cornell University Press, 1983): 197.

34. Fuller, *"These Sad but Glorious Days,"* 166. Fuller added, "But, after all, they had a high motive, something eternal in their desire and life; and, if it was not the only thing worth thinking of it was really something worth living and dying for to free a great nation from such a terrible blot, such a threatening plague. God strengthen them and make the wise to achieve their purpose!" (166).

35. Linck C. Johnson, "Reforming the Reformers: Emerson, Thoreau, and the Sunday Lectures at Amory Hall, Boston," *ESQ: A Journal of the American Renaissance* 37 (1991): 258, 274.

36. Ralph Waldo Emerson, "New England Reformers," in *Essays: First and Second Series,* Library of America Edition (New York: Vintage, 1990), 366.

37. Ibid., 372–73.

38. Ibid., 369.

39. Ibid., 379.

40. Thoreau, *"Walden,"* 53.

41. B. Alcott, 225.

42. Ibid., 230.

43. See Louisa May Alcott's "M.L.," "An Hour," and "My Contraband," in *Louisa May Alcott on Race, Sex, and Slavery,* ed. Sarah Elbert (Boston: Northeastern University Press, 1997), 3–28, 47–68, 69–86.

44. R. Emerson, *Journals,* 9:126–27.

45. Thoreau, *"Walden,"* 4.

46. Henry David Thoreau, *Journal,* vol. 2, *1842–1848,* ed. Robert Sattelmeyer (Princeton, NJ: Princeton University Press, 1984), 156.

47. Margaret Fuller, *Margaret Fuller, Critic: Writings from the "New-York Tribune," 1844–1846,* ed. Judith Mattson Bean and Joel Myerson (New York: Columbia University Press, 2000), 150.

48. Emerson's most famous articulation of this idea appears in *Nature:* "A correspondent revolution in things will attend the influx of the spirit. So fast will disagreeable appearances, swine, spiders, snakes, pests, mad-houses, prisons, enemies, vanish" (*Emerson's "Nature,"* 35).

49. For an excellent discussion of the pattern of escape and reengagement with regard to Hawthorne's ethical vision, see C. Davis, especially 77–104.

50. Randall Stewart, introduction to *The American Notebooks* by Nathaniel Hawthorne, ed. Randall Stewart (New Haven, CT: Yale University Press, 1932), xliv. See also Millicent Bell's classic study *Hawthorne's View of the Artist* (Albany: State University of New York Press, 1962). For a fine reading of how Hawthorne as artist engaged his contemporary culture as his career unfolded, see Richard H. Millington, *Practicing Romance: Narrative Form and Cultural Engagement in Hawthorne's Fiction* (Princeton, NJ: Princeton University Press, 1992).

51. Sacvan Bercovitch's persuasive argument in *Rites of Assent* suggests that Hawthorne's self-conception is a delusion and that such artists as Leutze and Hawthorne, rather than shaping future "national existence," are actually participants in an ideological process that shapes their art in ways that advance a set of dominant social practices and cultural values. For a theoretically sophisticated study of Hawthorne's relation to the nation (i.e., to an imagined "America"), see Lauren Berlant, *The Anatomy of National Fantasy: Hawthorne, Utopia, and Everyday Life* (Chicago: University of Chicago Press, 1991).

52. For recent studies emphasizing the social and political activism of Emerson and Thoreau, see Barbara Packer, "The Transcendentalists," in *Cambridge History of American Literature,* vol. 2, *1820–1865,* ed. Sacvan Bercovitch (Cambridge: Cambridge University Press, 1995), 329–604; Gougeon; Richard F. Teichgraeber III, *Sublime Thoughts/Penny Wisdom: Situating Emerson and Thoreau in the American Market* (Baltimore: Johns Hopkins University Press, 1995); Albert J. von Frank, *The Trials of Anthony Burns: Freedom and Slavery in Emerson's*

Boston (Cambridge, MA: Harvard University Press, 1998); Albert J. von Frank, "Mrs. Brackett's Verdict: Magic and Means in Transcendental Antislavery Work," in *Transient and Permanent: The Transcendentalist Movement and Its Contexts,* ed. Charles Capper and Conrad Edick Wright (Boston: Massachusetts Historical Society, 1999), 385–407; T. Gregory Garvey, ed., *The Emerson Dilemma: Essays on Emerson and Social Reform* (Athens: University of Georgia Press, 2001), especially the essays by Linck C. Johnson, Michael Strysick, Len Gougeon, Harold K. Bush, and David M. Robinson; David S. Reynolds, *John Brown, Abolitionist: The Man Who Killed Slavery, Sparked the Civil War, and Seeded Civil Rights* (New York: Knopf, 2005); Maurice S. Lee, *Slavery, Philosophy, and American Literature, 1830–1860* (New York: Cambridge University Press, 2005), 165–209.

Gougeon has been the most vigorous proponent of Emerson as "a committed social reformer" (337) and has asserted "there can be no doubt that in August 1844 Emerson made the transition from antislavery to abolition, and his association with organized abolitionists would continue to grow from this point forward" (85). As my discussion shows, I doubt the first part of this assertion. For excellent analyses of Emerson's 1844 address and his ambivalence toward organized abolitionism in the 1840s, see Teichgraeber, 90–112.

53. Thoreau, *"Walden,"* 50.

54. Henry David Thoreau, *Reform Papers,* ed. Wendell Glick (Princeton, NJ: Princeton University Press, 1973), 50.

55. Thoreau, *The Correspondence of Henry David Thoreau,* ed. Walter Harding and Carl Bode (New York: New York University Press, 1958), 165. The only criticism Thoreau includes in the letter is that Phillips "stands so distinctly, so firmly, and so effectively, alone, and one honest man is so much more than a host, that we cannot but feel that he does himself injustice when he reminds us of 'the American Society, which he represents'" (164).

56. Fuller, *Margaret Fuller, Critic,* 150.

57. Von Frank, "Mrs. Brackett's Verdict," 393.

58. See Wendell P. Glick, "Thoreau and the 'Herald of Freedom,'" *New England Quarterly* 22 (June 1949): 193–204; Petrulionis, 42–44.

59. Ralph Waldo Emerson, "An Address . . . on . . . the Emancipation of the Negroes in the British West Indies" (1844), in *Emerson's Antislavery Writings,* 9.

60. Ibid., 31.

61. Ibid., 30.

62. Ibid., 31.

63. Emerson's essay "Character," with its hypothetical example, indicates the extent to which he saw Toussaint as atypical: "Suppose a slaver on the coast of Guinea should take on board a gang of negroes, which should contain persons of the stamp of Toussaint L'Ouverture: or, let us fancy, under these swarthy masks he has a gang of Washingtons in chains. When they arrive at Cuba, will the rela-

tive order of the ship's company be the same?" (*Essays: First and Second Series,* 268).

64. See L. Reynolds, *European Revolutions,* 27–28.

65. Ralph Waldo Emerson, "Ode, Inscribed to W. H. Channing," in *Collected Poems and Translations,* 63–64.

66. R. Emerson, *Emerson's Antislavery Writings,* 33.

67. The same occurred with other audiences who wished to see Emerson as agreeing with them, such as members of the American Peace Society in 1838 and the organizers of Brook Farm in 1840.

68. Von Frank, "Mrs. Brackett's Verdict," 393.

69. By the 1860s, Sophia Hawthorne, a disaffected devotee of Emerson's, perceived this trait, and she observed that her sister Mary had misunderstood Emerson with regard to a retaliatory policy toward the South: "Mr. Emerson has used so many *ifs* in talking to my sister [Mary], that in effect he differs from her, while she is deceived by the *ifs*" (quoted in N. Hawthorne, 18:464 n. 2).

70. Ralph Waldo Emerson, "Uriel," in *Collected Poems and Translations,* 15–16.

71. Leonard Neufeldt, "Emerson and the Civil War," *Journal of English and Germanic Philology* 61 (October 1972): 506.

72. R. Emerson, *Emerson's Antislavery Writings,* 22.

73. In many ways, the *Journal* anticipates and confirms Eric Williams's classic study *Captalism and Slavery* (1944; reprint, Chapel Hill: University of North Carolina Press, 1994), which points out that the removal of Negroes from Africa to the sugar plantations of Cuba and Brazil continued for some twenty-five years after 1833. "Consistency alone," Williams argues, "demanded that the British abolitionists oppose this trade. But that would retard Brazillian and Cuban development and consequently hamper British trade. The desire for cheap sugar after 1833 overcame all abhorrence of slavery" (192). David Brion Davis, among others, has refuted Williams's indictment of British abolitionists and instead, like Emerson, credited them with humanitarian efforts that succeeded. "Capitalist self-interest," Davis writes, "as a source of human exploitation and suffering in the early industrial era, *could* have been even worse than it proved to be! If Britain had not outlawed its slave trade, emancipated nearly eight hundred thousand slaves, and then promoted abolitionism throughout the world, the Western world's economic growth might well have increased at a faster rate—but with even more appalling human costs" (*In Human Bondage: The Rise and Fall of Slavery in the New World* [New York: Oxford University Press, 2006], 244). For multiple perspectives on this issue, featuring essays by John Ashworth, Davis, and Thomas L. Haskell, see Thomas Bender, ed., *The Antislavery Debate: Capitalism and Abolitionism as a Problem in Historical Interpretation* (Berkeley: University of California Press, 1992).

74. Brancaccio, 24.

75. Wineapple, 186–87.

76. See Frederickson, *Black Image*, 19.

77. When King Peter deeded Cape Mesurado to the Colonization Society, he received goods—muskets, tobacco, gunpowder, rum, and so on—worth less than three hundred dollars. See P. J. Staudenraus, *The African Colonization Movement, 1816–1865* (New York: Columbia University Press, 1961), 65.

78. Lamin Sanneh, *Abolitionists Abroad: American Blacks and the Making of Modern West Africa* (Cambridge, MA: Harvard University Press, 1999), 221.

79. Quoted in ibid., 220.

80. Frederickson, *Black Image*, 27.

81. Litwack cites the many injustices Negroes faced in the 1850s that led to the "dismal conclusion" that emigration constituted the "the sole alternative to continued repression" (29).

82. See Brancaccio, 36; Wineapple, 188–89; Teresa Goddu, "Letters Turned to Gold: Hawthorne, Authorship, and Slavery," *Studies in American Fiction* 29 (Spring 2001): 56–57.

83. The compliment does not appear in Bridge's manuscript, which is why I attribute it to Hawthorne. Hawthorne wrote of meeting Roberts personally in Liverpool at the consulate in 1856: "I was rather favorably impressed with him; for his deportment was very simple, without any of the flourish and embroidery which a negro might be likely to assume, on finding himself elevated from slavery to power" (22:35).

84. Horatio Bridge, *Personal Recollections of Nathaniel Hawthorne* (New York: Harper and Brothers, 1893), 30.

85. *Freeman's Journal*, February 14, 1829, quoted in Sandra Sandiford Young, "A Different Journey: John Brown Russwurm, 1799–1851," PhD diss., Boston College, 2004.

86. Ibid., 222.

87. Brancaccio, 33.

88. [Horatio Bridge], holograph journal, June 1843–January 19, 1844, Berg Collection, New York Public Library, 19–20.

89. After first meeting Bridge, Longfellow wrote in his journal, "Bridge is gigantic; and stands and looks plumb-down onto the top of my head" (March 17, 1838, MS, Harvard, quoted in N. Hawthorne, 15:39 n. 71).

90. [Bridge], holograph journal, 75–76.

91. In the 1850 elections, this opposition would lead to the alliance that emerged in Massachusetts between Free-Soilers and Democrats.

Chapter 5

1. Quoted in Mellow, 627 n. 255.

2. Lilian Handlin, *George Bancroft: The Intellectual as Democrat* (New York: Harper and Row, 1984), 193.

3. Quoted in J. Hawthorne, 1:284–85.

4. See N. Hawthorne, 16:140 n. 1.

5. Quoted in J. Hawthorne, 1:284–85.

6. Quoted in M. A. DeWolfe Howe, *The Life and Letters of George Bancroft,* 2 vols. (1908; reprint, New York: Kennikat, 1971), 1:264–65.

7. Ibid., 1:287.

8. Franklin Pierce to George Bancroft, May 12, 1846, manuscript, Massachusetts Historical Society.

9. Martin Van Buren to W. H. Hammet, April 20, 1844, in *History of American Presidential Elections, 1789–1968,* ed. Arthur M. Schlesinger Jr. et al., vol. 1, *1789–1844* (New York: Chelsea House, 1971), 825.

10. See Russell B. Nye, *George Bancroft: Brahmin Rebel* (New York: Knopf, 1945), 146–47.

11. O'Sullivan, "Annexation," 5.

12. See chapter 9, "The Pinnacle," in Sampson, 163–92.

13. Ibid., 192.

14. Sophia Hawthorne to her mother Elizabeth Peabody, March 6, 1845, Berg Collection, New York Public Library.

15. Wineapple (187) points out that Sophia probably tailored the letter to mollify her mother, who was staunchly antislavery.

16. Fuller, *"These Sad but Glorious Days,"* 165.

17. Theodore Parker, "A Sermon of War," in Robert E. Collins, *Theodore Parker: American Transcendentalist; A Critical Essay and a Collection of His Writings* (Metuchen, NJ: Scarecrow, 1973), 251–52.

18. R. Emerson, *Journals,* 9:74.

19. Ralph Waldo Emerson, *The Conduct of Life,* ed. Edward Waldo Emerson (1904; reprint, New York: AMS Press, 1968), 256.

20. Colacurcio, " 'Red Man's Grave,' " 9.

21. See Robert W. Johannsen, *To the Halls of the Montezumas: The Mexican War in the American Imagination* (New York: Oxford University Press, 1985), 204–40.

22. Some sincerity apparently adheres in Hawthorne's praise. While in England, during the Crimean War, he recorded in the privacy of his notebook, "It is rather agreeable . . . to observe how all Englishmen pull together; how each man comes forward with his little scheme for helping on the war—feeling themselves members of one family, and talking together about their common interest, as if they were gathered about one fireside. And then what a hearty meed of honor they award to their soldiers. It is worth facing death for! Whereas, in America, when our soldiers fought as good battles in the Mexican war, with as great proportionate loss, and far more valuable triumphs, the country seemed rather ashamed than proud of them" (21:147). Given the importance Hawthorne attaches to a sense of community in this entry, it is not surprising that he, among the Concord authors, was the only one to join Brook Farm.

23. Quoted in Carey McWilliams, *North from Mexico: The Spanish-Speaking People of the United States* (New York: Greenwood, 1948), 101.

24. Quoted in ibid., 101.

25. Quoted in Rodolfo Acuña, *Occupied America: The Chicano's Struggle toward Liberation* (San Francisco: Canfield, 1972), 37.

26. James Russell Lowell, *The Biglow Papers, First Series: A Critical Edition,* ed. Thomas Wortham (DeKalb: Northern Illinois University Press, 1977), 51.

27. "Memorial of the Whigs of Salem, (Mass.)," sent to Hon. William M. Meredith, secretary of the treasury of the United States, signed by Nathaniel Silsbee Jr., chairman, and Joseph B. F. Osgood, secretary, Nathaniel Hawthorne file, Fiscal Section, National Archives, Washington, DC, 10.

28. See Stephen Nissenbaum, "The Firing of Nathaniel Hawthorne," *Essex Institute Historical Collections* 114 (1978): 57–86.

29. Quoted in Lathrop, 100.

30. "Memorial of the Whigs of Salem, (Mass.)," 8.

31. Ibid., 12.

32. Ibid., 15, 12.

33. See Potter, 237.

34. See David Donald, "Toward a Reconsideration of Abolitionists," in *Lincoln Reconsidered,* 2nd ed. (1956; reprint, New York: Knopf, 1965).

35. Ibid., 32.

36. See Michael F. Holt, *The Rise and Fall of the American Whig Party: Jacksonian Politics and the Onset of the Civil War* (New York: Oxford University Press, 1999), 580.

37. Ibid., 581.

38. Ibid., 583.

39. Melville, 219.

40. L. Reynolds, *European Revolutions,* 94.

41. Hawthorne was familiar with such sermons. While at Bowdoin, he wrote to his sister Elizabeth about the college rules: "the worst of all is to be compelled to go to meeting every Sunday, and to hear a red hot Calvinist Sermon from the President, or some other dealer in fire and brimstone" (15:159).

42. This is not to say that Hawthorne viewed all Puritan leaders as manipulative fanatics (John Wilson, for example, he calls "a man of kind and genial spirit" [1:65]) or the people as mere dupes (their intuitive conclusions, he claims in chapter 9, "The Leech," are often profound and unerring, even though when they attempt to see with their eyes, they are "exceedingly apt to be deceived" [1:127]). He thus gives Puritan society the benefit of historical relativism by representing leaders, as well as followers, as victims of delusion.

43. Jonathan H. Earle, *Jacksonian Antislavery and the Politics of Free Soil, 1824–1854* (Chapel Hill: University of North Carolina Press, 2004), 121.

44. Anthony, 263–64.

45. Walter Benn Michaels, "Romance and Real Estate," in *The American Renaissance Reconsidered,* ed. Walter Benn Michaels and Donald E. Pease (Baltimore: Johns Hopkins University Press, 1985), 160.

46. Nina Baym, "Hawthorne's Holgrave: The Failure of the Artist-Hero," *Journal of English and German Philology* 69 (1970): 587.

Chapter 6

1. "The Impending Crisis—the Irrepressible Conflict between Freedom and Slavery" was the title of a speech delivered by Congressman Alfred Wells of New York in the House of Representatives on April 6, 1860. Compare also the title of David M. Potter's classic study of this period, *The Impending Crisis, 1848–1861* (New York: Harper and Row, 1976).

2. John Demos, "The Antislavery Movement and the Problem of Violent 'Means,'" *New England Quarterly* 37 (December 1964): 501–26. See also William H. Pease and Jane H. Pease, *They Who Would Be Free: Blacks' Search for Freedom, 1830–1861* (New York: Atheneum, 1974). The Peases point out that Black abolitionists saw in the European revolutions of 1848 "models for their own future" (236).

3. For an account of Fuller's influence, see Larry J. Reynolds, "Righteous Violence: The Roman Republic and Margaret Fuller's Revolutionary Example," in *Margaret Fuller: Transatlantic Crossings in a Revolutionary Age,* ed. Charles Capper and Cristina Giorcelli (Madison: University of Wisconsin Press, 2008), 172–91. The following three paragraphs in text are drawn from this account.

4. Fuller, *"These Sad but Glorious Days,"* 240.

5. Margaret Fuller, *The Letters of Margaret Fuller,* vol. 5, *1848–49,* ed. Robert N. Hudspeth (Ithaca, NY: Cornell University Press, 1988), 147.

6. See L. Reynolds, *European Revolutions,* 79–96.

7. Thomas R. Mitchell, *Hawthorne's Fuller Mystery* (Amherst: University of Massachusetts Press, 1998), 208.

8. I interpret as a curse (and thus an act of rebellion not unlike that of a Salem witch or Matthew Maul) the message Zenobia gives Coverdale for Hollingsworth: "'Tell him he has murdered me! Tell him that I'll haunt him!'— she spoke these words with the wildest energy" (3:226).

9. Thoreau, *Reform Papers,* 77.

10. For an account of Thoreau's knowledge of Brown's past, see Michael Meyer, "Thoreau's Rescue of John Brown from History," in *Studies in the American Renaissance, 1980,* ed. Joel Myerson (Charlottesville: University Press of Virginia, 1980), 301–16.

11. Peter P. Hinks discusses this speculation in his introduction to *David Walker's "Appeal to the Coloured Citizens of the World,"* ed. Peter P. Hinks (University Park: Pennsylvania State University Press, 2000), xli.

12. Quoted in Litwack, 244.

13. See ibid., 145.

14. *Liberator,* June 8, 1849.

15. As Lawrence J. Friedman has shown, the movement from moral suasion in the 1830s to acceptance of violent means in the 1850s among abolitionists "was neither clear nor direct. . . . Whereas violence became more attractive as time passed, most immediatists never relinquished their peace principles" (*Gregarious Saints: Self and Community in American Abolitionism, 1830–1870* [Cambridge: Cambridge University Press, 1982], 196–97). For a close examination of the embrace of violence by the radical abolitionists, specifically John Brown, Gerrit Smith, McCune Smith, and Frederick Douglass, see John Stauffer, *The Black Hearts of Men: Radical Abolitionists and the Transformation of Race* (Cambridge, MA: Harvard University Press, 2002).

16. Quoted in Demos, 523.

17. R. Emerson, *Journals,* 11:352, 412.

18. Theodore Parker, "From *The Function and Place of Conscience in Relation to the Laws of Men* (1850)," in *Against Slavery: An Abolitionist Reader,* ed. Mason Lowance (New York: Penguin, 2000), 277–78.

19. See Theodore Parker, *The Rights of Man in America,* ed. F. B. Sanborn (1911; reprint, New York: Negro Universities Press, 1969), 151.

20. See Potter, 134.

21. See Earle, 185–86.

22. Potter, 138.

23. See Earle, 188.

24. Ibid., 192.

25. See T. Mitchell, 204–19.

26. Sophia Hawthorne, letter of April 6, 1845, quoted in William E. Cain, "Prospects for Change," in *The Blithedale Romance,* by Nathaniel Hawthorne, ed. William E. Cain (Boston: St. Martin's, Bedford, 1996), 224.

27. Mary Mann to Horace Mann, August 15, 1852, Massachusetts Historical Society, quoted in Wineapple, 251.

28. Brodhead, "Hawthorne," 98.

29. *New-York Weekly Tribune,* May 22, 1852.

30. In a letter of August 20, 1862, to her husband, Sophia Hawthorne wrote, "I went to see Mr Bull's garden yesterday, and his vineyards are loaded with grapes[.] On one twig, no longer than this paper, often hang six heavy bunches, side by side. His first old seedling of twenty years ago was as full of clusters as the younger plants. There was not a weed in the garden!!!" (Morgan Library and Museum [formerly The Pierpont Morgan Library], New York).

31. *History of American Presidential Elections, 1789–1968,* ed. Arthur M. Schlesinger Jr. et al., vol. 2, *1848–1896* (New York: Chelsea House, 1971), 954.

32. Mann would lose, with 27 percent of the vote. See Jonathan Messerli, *Horace Mann: A Biography* (New York: Knopf, 1972), 538.

33. See Bercovitch, *Office of "The Scarlet Letter,"* 88–102. Hawthorne's praise of Daniel Webster is also used by Bercovitch to support his argument about Hawthorne's commitment to the Compromise and to compromise, but this praise can also be traced to Webster's support (at mutual friend George Hillard's urging) of Hawthorne's retaining the Salem surveyorship and of the Democrat Pierce during the 1852 campaign.

See also Hall's *Hawthorne, Critic of Society*, which mistakenly asserts that Hawthorne "clung at times feebly to the old idea of the Union, and to the men like Pierce who stood for it. 'Is there not a prospect of a compromise,' he inquired of his friend Burchmore in 1851, 'between the Whigs and Freesoilers in favor of the Union?'" (151). Hall is quoting from Hawthorne's letter as published in the *Saturday Evening Gazette* of August 12, 1883, but the editors of *The Centenary Edition of the Works of Nathaniel Hawthorne* point out that the phrase "in favor of the Union" should read "in favor of Upham" (16:730–31 n. 449). The correction yields an entirely different meaning.

34. Peter A. Wallner, *Franklin Pierce: New Hampshire's Favorite Son* (Concord, NH: Plaidswede, 2004), 203.

35. Charles Sumner, *The Selected Letters of Charles Sumner*, 2 vols., ed Beverly Wilson Palmer (Boston: Northeastern University Press, 1990), 1:386.

36. *New York Times*, June 5, 1854.

37. *National Era*, February 2, 1854.

38. Horace Greeley, *Recollections of a Busy Life* (1868; reprint, New York: Confucian, 1981), 294.

39. Potter, 164–65.

40. Sophia Peabody to Mary Mann, July 3, 1854, Berg Collection, New York Public Library.

41. *Boston slave riot, and trial of Anthony Burns: Containing the report of the Faneuil hall meeting; the murder of Batchelder; Theodore Parker's lesson of the day; speeches of counsel on both sides, corrected by themselves; a verbatim report of Judge Loring's decision; and detailed account of the embarkation* (Boston: Fetridge, 1854), 19.

42. Parker's thought and rhetoric had been influenced by the ardent fugitive slave William Wells Brown, whose book *Santo Domingo: Its Revolution and Its Patriots* (1855) warned slave owners that the Haitian revolution would soon be reenacted in the South. See Jeffery Rossbach, *Ambivalent Conspirators: John Brown, the Secret Six, and a Theory of Slave Violence* (Philadelphia: University of Pennsylvania Press, 1982), 154.

43. Quoted in the *Liberator*, June 9, 1854.

44. Quoted in the *Liberator*, June 16, 1854.

45. Quoted in ibid.

46. Quoted in Harold Schwartz, "Fugitive Slave Days in Boston," *New England Quarterly* 27 (June 1954): 210.

47. *National Era,* June 8, 1854.

48. James Freeman Clarke, *The Rendition of Anthony Burns: Its Causes and Consequences; A Discourse on Christian Politics* (Boston: Prentiss and Sawyer, 1854), 7, 19, 27.

49. Sophia Hawthorne to Nathaniel Peabody (father), July 4, 1854, Berg Collection, New York Public Library.

50. Thoreau, *Journal,* 8:165–66.

51. Thoreau, *Reform Papers,* 102.

52. Thoreau, *Journal,* 8:175.

53. Quoted in von Frank, *Trials of Anthony Burns,* 111.

54. Thoreau, *Reform Papers,* 104.

55. Thoreau, *Journal,* 8:185

56. Thoreau, *Reform Papers,* 108.

57. See Rossbach; Edward J. Renehan Jr., *The Secret Six: The True Tale of the Men Who Conspired with John Brown* (New York: Crown, 1995).

58. Thomas Wentworth Higginson, *Margaret Fuller Ossoli* (1898; reprint, New York: Confucian, 1980), 2.

59. Thomas Wentworth Higginson, "Massachusetts in Mourning! A Sermon," *National Anti-Slavery Standard,* June 24, 1854.

60. Higginson's dispatch of September 25, 1856, to the *Tribune,* for example, describes antislavery settlers fleeing federal troops and concludes, "As Hungary, having successfully resisted her natural enemy, Austria, yielded at length to the added strength of Russia; so the Kossuths of Kanzas, just as they had cleared her borders of Missourians, are subdued by the troops of the United States at last" (reprinted in *The Magnificent Activist: The Writings of Thomas Wentworth Higginson,* ed. Howard N. Meyer (n.p.: Da Capo, 2000), 80.

61. Potter, 219.

62. See ibid., 220.

63. *New York Tribune,* May 30, 1856.

64. *National Anti-Slavery Standard,* May 1, 1856.

65. *New York Herald,* June 8, 1856, quoted in John Stauffer, "Advent among the Indians: The Revolutionary Ethos of Gerrit Smith, James McCune Smith, Frederick Douglass, and John Brown," in *Antislavery Violence: Sectional, Racial, and Cultural Conflict in Antebellum America,* ed. John R. McKivigan and Stanley Harrold (Knoxville: University of Tennessee Press, 1999), 253.

66. Ralph Waldo Emerson, "Assault on Charles Sumner," in *Emerson's Antislavery Writings,* 108.

67. Charles Sumner, "The Crime against Kansas" (1856), in T. Lloyd Benson, *The Caning of Senator Sumner* (Belmont, CA: Wadsworth/Thomson, 2004), 117.

68. Ibid., 97, 99.

69. Ibid., 130.

70. See Benson, 184.

71. Quoted in David Donald, *Charles Sumner and the Coming of the Civil War* (New York: Knopf, 1961), 320.

72. Quoted in ibid., 303.

73. Ralph Waldo Emerson, "Lecture on Slavery," in *Emerson's Antislavery Writings,* 103, 105.

74. Ralph Waldo Emerson, "Kansas Relief Meeting," in *Emerson's Antislavery Writings,* 111.

75. Donald, *Charles Sumner,* 350.

76. Franklin Sanborn, *Recollections of Seventy Years,* 2 vols. (Boston: Gorham, 1909), 1:104.

77. D. Reynolds, 222.

78. Petrulionis, 122–23.

79. Robert D. Richardson Jr., *Emerson: The Mind on Fire* (Berkeley: University of California Press, 1995), 498.

80. Gay Wilson Allen, *Waldo Emerson* (New York: Penguin, 1981), 588.

81. R. Emerson, *Journals,* 14:125.

82. Edward Emerson, "Notes," in *Miscellanies* by Ralph Waldo Emerson, ed. Edward Emerson (1904; reprint, New York: AMS Press, 1968), 579.

83. In her Roman diary, in an entry for February 1849, Fuller commented on the assassination, agreeing with a "young Frenchman" that "the act would have been heroic, if the murderer had stood firm and avowed it. It would indeed then have been the act of Brutus" (Leona Rostenberg, "Margaret Fuller's Roman Diary," *Journal of Modern History* 12 [June 1940]: 217–18). From her perspective, such a violent act could be justified as an act of civic duty, or obedience to a "higher law," comparable to the assassination of the tyrant Caesar in the Roman Forum in 44 BC.

84. T. Mitchell, 235.

85. See Bentley, "Slaves and Fauns."

86. When Hawthorne met with James Buchanan in Liverpool in January 1855, he accurately perceived the political machinations of that future president (who beat out Pierce and Douglass for the Democratic presidential nomination in 1856). The Kansas-Nebraska furor undermined Pierce altogether, and he had no chance of gaining his party's nomination for a second term. Buchanan, who had been overseas during the recent controversy, had few enemies.

87. In the early 1850s, Hawthorne identified his politics with those of Bryant's *New York Evening Post,* at least according to Charles Sumner, who passed the information along to John Bigelow. See John Bigelow, *Retrospections of an Active Life,* vol. 1 (New York: Baker and Taylor, 1909), 122.

88. In a letter of January 31, 1857, to William Ticknor, Hawthorne commented that Sumner should have helped him with the cause of abused seamen: "Had he busied himself about this, instead of Abolitionism, he would have done good service to his country and have escaped Brooks's cudgel. I offered to

supply him with any amount of horrible facts; but he never noticed my letter" (18:13).

89. Robert S. Levine, "'Antebellum Rome' in *The Marble Faun*," *American Literary History* 2, no. 1 (1990): 25.

90. Levine, 26. In Levine's reading, Hawthorne evidences "anxiety" in the face of revolutionary violence, which he wishes to dispel, as he does through his account of the Carnival. Although I appreciate the argument that Hawthorne's politics involved escaping from radical impulses through sublimation or the imposition of a liberal ideology emphasizing return and reconciliation, I now believe Hawthorne's position was more independent and bold than this. For persuasive interpretations that see Kenyon's and Hilda's return to the United States as integral to a consensus ideology, see Bercovitch, *Office of "The Scarlet Letter,"* 104, and Mark A. R. Kemp, "*The Marble Faun* and Postcolonial Ambivalence," *Modern Fiction Studies* 43, no. 1 (1997): 214–15.

91. Levine, 28.

92. John Carlos Rowe, "Nathaniel Hawthorne and Transnationality," in *Hawthorne and the Real,* ed. Millicent Bell (Columbus: Ohio State University Press, 2005), 101.

93. A number of scholars, beginning in the 1870s, have suggested that Thoreau served as a model for Hawthorne's Donatello. The most thorough exploration of the link between the two appears in Edward Cronin Peple Jr.'s 1970 University of Virginia dissertation titled "The Personal and Literary Relationship of Hawthorne and Thoreau." Peple presents a number of *Marble Faun* passages referring to Donatello that appear to be echoes of passages in Hawthorne's notebooks and letters referring to Thoreau. Peple does not observe that Thoreau's turn to violence in the 1850s may have influenced Hawthorne's depiction of Donatello's murderous behavior.

94. Lathrop, 53.

95. See N. Hawthorne, 17:277–80.

96. Evan Carton, *The Marble Faun: Hawthorne's Transformations* (New York: Twayne, 1992), 37.

97. For an excellent discussion of this doubling, see Carton, 103–4.

98. Richard H. Brodhead, *The School of Hawthorne* (New York: Oxford University Press, 1986), 69.

99. Sampson, 97–98.

100. Mark 6:31.

101. As Levine has pointed out, the pontiff bears resemblance to Hawthorne's Gray Champion, who reappears in the people's hour of need (33).

102. Baym, *Shape of Hawthorne's Career,* 233–34.

103. Ibid., 234.

104. Sophia Hawthorne to Elizabeth Palmer Peabody, July 3, 1859, quoted in

Herbert, 256. For an insightful discussion of the effects of Hawthorne's personal crises in Italy on his writing of *The Marble Faun,* see Herbert, 256–72.

105. Jenny Franchot, *Roads to Rome: The Antebellum Protestant Encounter with Catholicism* (Berkeley: University of California Press, 1994), 353.

106. James T. Fields in his *Yesterdays with Authors* recalls Hawthorne's knowledge of and sensitivity to scripture: "his voice would be tremulous with feeling, as he sometimes quoted a touching passage from the New Testament ([Boston: Houghton Mifflin, 1900], 95).

107. Quoted in Louisa Hall Tharp, *The Peabody Sisters of Salem* (Boston: McIntosh and Otis, 1950), 288–89.

108. Quoted in ibid., 288.

109. "Responsibility of Deciding on War," from *Friends in Council—Second Series,* reprinted in the *Morning Star* (London), April 7, 1860.

110. *Morning Star* (London), April 13, 1860.

111. *Morning Star* (London), May 9, 1860.

112. "Slavery Question—Mr. Lovejoy," *Appendix to the Congressional Globe,* House of Representatives, 36th Cong., 1st sess., April 5,1860, 203.

113. For a thorough account of Hawthorne's response to John Brown, see Margaret Moore, "Nathaniel Hawthorne and 'Old John Brown,'" *Nathaniel Hawthorne Review* 26 (Spring 2000): 25–32.

Chapter 7

1. See Benjamin Quarles, *Allies for Freedom: Blacks on John Brown* (New York: Oxford University Press, 1974), 94, 212 n. 3.

2. Thoreau, *Reform Papers,* 133.

3. See Stephen B. Oates, *To Purge This Land with Blood: A Biography of John Brown* (Amherst: University of Massachusetts Press, 1984), 302.

4. McPherson, 213.

5. Quoted in Oates, 351.

6. Bertram Wyatt-Brown, "'A Volcano beneath a Mountain of Snow': John Brown and the Problem of Interpretation," in *His Soul Goes Marching On: Responses to John Brown and the Harpers Ferry Raid,* ed. Paul Finkelman (Charlottesville and London: University Press of Virginia, 1995), 27.

7. James Redpath, *The Public Life of Capt. John Brown* (Boston: Thayer and Eldridge, 1860), 82.

8. John Seelye, *Memory's Nation: The Place of Plymouth Rock* (Chapel Hill: University of North Carolina Press, 1998), 333.

9. Betty L. Mitchell, "Massachusetts Reacts to John Brown's Raid," *Civil War History* 19 (March 1973): 65–79.

10. Abraham Lincoln, *Selected Speeches and Writings* (New York: Library of America, 1992), 246.

11. William Lloyd Garrison, *Liberator,* October 28, 1859, quoted in B. Mitchell, "Massachusetts Reacts," 66.

12. B. Mitchell, "Massachusetts Reacts," 65.

13. Quoted in Redpath, 341–42.

14. R. Emerson, *The Letters of Ralph Waldo Emerson,* 5:178.

15. Ralph Waldo Emerson, "Courage," in *The Complete Works of Ralph Waldo Emerson,* ed. Edward Waldo Emerson, 12 vols. (1903–4; reprint, New York: AMS Press, 1968), 7:427.

16. Ralph Waldo Emerson, "Remarks at a Meeting for the Relief of the Family of John Brown," in *Complete Works,* 11:268.

17. Thoreau, *Reform Papers,* 113.

18. Ibid., 115.

19. Quoted in Walter Harding, *The Days of Henry Thoreau* (New York: Knopf, 1970), 434.

20. Thoreau, *Reform Papers,* 152.

21. Harding, 423.

22. *Liberator,* December 9, 1859.

23. "Reviews and Literary Notices," *Atlantic Monthly* 5 (March 1860): 379.

24. Sophia took an immediate dislike to Sanborn, Julian's teacher. The apparent cause was his teaching methods, particularly his letting boys and girls be in activities together. After Sanborn visited Sophia to talk about Julian's difficulties with school (he had trouble sleeping and eating), Sophia wrote to her husband, "I did not like Mr Sanborn. He has a face of Agrippina's type—sharply cut, small features, and the small head of a cruel person. . . . This much lauded angel [lauded because of his support of John Brown] is part—well,—the opposite of angel" (Sophia Hawthorne to Nathaniel Hawthorne, September 13, 1860, quoted in N. Hawthorne, 18:317–18).

25. Thoreau found Hawthorne unchanged. In a letter of July 8, 1860, to his sister Sophia, Thoreau writes, "I suppose that you have heard that Mr Hawthorne has come home. I went to meet him the other evening & found that he has not altered except that he was looking pretty brown after his voyage. He is as simple & child-like as ever" (*Correspondence,* 582).

26. The protagonist in the first version is named Middleton, a name resonant with political significance, given Hawthorne's concern about the "tumult and excitement, and bad blood" (17:188) that sickened him when he looked at America from England. As Rita K. Gollin has pointed out, this hero "is a lawyer who, like Franklin Pierce, had fought in the Mexican-American War and served in Congress, and who, like Hawthorne, had been scarred by party politics" ("Estranged Allegiances in Hawthorne's Unfinished Romances," in *Hawthorne and the Real,* ed. Millicent Bell [Columbus: Ohio State University Press, 2005], 163).

27. Gollin, 163.

28. B. Alcott, 336.

29. It does appear that Hawthorne was not above taking advantage of Alcott's financial incompetence. In a letter to Ticknor from England on November 1857, Hawthorne writes, "I understand that Mr. Alcott (of whom I bought the Wayside) has bought a piece of land adjacent to mine, and two old houses on it. . . . If he should swamp himself by his expenditures on this place, I should be very glad to take it off his hands; and it seems to me highly probable (judging from the character of the man) that he will ultimately be glad to have me do so" (18:127–28).

30. At times, Hawthorne identified with this ancestor. In an entry in his *English Notebooks,* he records, "My ancestor left England in 1630. I return in 1853. I sometimes feel as if I myself had been absent these two hundred and eighteen years—leaving England just emerging from the feudal system, and finding it on the verge of Republicanism" (21:138).

31. Quoted in N. Hawthorne, 18:373 n. 4.

32. In the piece, Hawthorne discusses the rebels using the skulls of Union dead "to hold their whiskey and water, and to be passed from lip to lip of man and maiden at their social and family gatherings. It seems possible (not now, but at some future time) to forgive our chivalrous antagonists almost anything save such atrocities as these, which show something so grotesquely hideous in the Southern character that our benevolent impulses are entirely non-plussed" (23:443).

33. Ralph Waldo Emerson, *The Selected Letters of Ralph Waldo Emerson,* ed. Joel Myerson (New York: Columbia University Press, 1997), 404–5.

34. Lidian Jackson Emerson, *The Selected Letters of Lidian Jackson Emerson,* ed. Delores Bird Carpenter (Columbia: University of Missouri Press, 1987), 209.

35. E. Emerson, 579.

36. Robert D. Richardson Jr., *Henry David Thoreau: A Life of the Mind* (Berkeley: University of California Press, 1986), 372.

37. Thoreau, *Correspondence,* 583.

38. Ibid., 611.

39. For a fuller discussion of this comparison, see Larry J. Reynolds, "The Cimeter's 'Sweet' Edge: Thoreau, Contemplation, and Violence," in *More Day to Dawn: Thoreau's "Walden" for the Twenty-first Century,* ed. Sandy Petrulionis and Laura Walls (Boston: University of Massachusetts Press, 2006), 75–78.

40. Dueling had been linked to guilt in Hawthorne's mind since the death of his friend Cilley in 1838. According to Julian, his father felt partly responsible for Cilley's death. Hawthorne had previously challenged their mutual friend John O'Sullivan to a duel at the instigation of the beautiful and manipulative Mary Silsbee. When Hawthorne learned that Silsbee had deceived him, he withdrew his challenge, but Cilley, a friend of both men and an intermediary between them, accepted a challenge he received several weeks later from a political opponent. According to Julian, Cilley overcame his hesitation about the duel when reminded of Hawthorne's bold example. Consequently, Hawthorne "felt as if he were al-

most as much responsible for his friend's death as was the man who shot him. He said little; but the remorse that came upon him was heavy, and did not pass away" (J. Hawthorne, 1:174).

41. Baym, *Shape of Hawthorne's Career,* 261.

42. Quoted in James Redpath, *Echoes of Harper's Ferry* (1860; reprint, Westport, CT: Negro Universities Press, 1970), 304.

43. Quoted in ibid., 305.

44. Quoted in ibid., 311.

45. Daniel Aaron, for example, in his insightful discussion of the essay, accuses Hawthorne of treating "sacred themes with a dangerous lightness" (*The Unwritten War: American Writers and the Civil War* [New York: Knopf, 1973], 50).

46. Donald Mitchell to Nathaniel Hawthorne, January 12, 1864, quoted in N. Hawthorne, 18:632 n. 1.

47. H. James, 151.

48. Conway, *Life of Nathaniel Hawthorne,* 204.

49. Rebecca Harding Davis, *Bits of Gossip* (1904), quoted in Janice Milner Lasseter, "Hawthorne's Legacy to Rebecca Harding Davis," in *Hawthorne and Women: Engendering and Expanding the Hawthorne Tradition,* ed. John L. Idol Jr. and Melinda M. Ponder (Amherst: University of Massachusetts Press, 1999), 173. This paragraph in the text is indebted to Lasseter's essay.

50. Ibid., 174.

51. Quoted in the *New York Times,* July 12, 1863. James R. Mellow points out that less than two weeks after Pierce's speech on July 4, 1863, the New York draft riots erupted, and "Pierce's speech, circulating in the newspapers, was considered one of the precipitating causes of the violence" (565). Mellow does not document this statement, and I have been unable to do so. I have doubts about its accuracy, for Pierce was not among those provoking hatred against blacks and the rich by his rhetoric, and the unscrupulous *New York Herald* treated the speech as trivial, declaring, "Ex-President Pierce made a silly peace speech in New Hampshire on the Fourth of July. . . . Poor Pierce ought to be forever silent, and either jump into Winnipiseogee Lake or call on the rocks of the White Mountains to cover him. He opened Pandora's box, whence issued the bitter sectional strifes and heartburnings and all the horrors of war that have afflicted the land for the last two years" (*New York Herald,* July 9, 1863).

52. Ironically, two years earlier, the pragmatic Lincoln had told two other abolitionists—Moncure Conway and William H. Channing—practically the same thing as they lobbied for emancipation: "In working in the anti-slavery movement you may naturally come in contact with a good many people who agree with you, and possibly may over-estimate the number in the country who hold such views. But the position in which I am placed brings me into some knowledge of opinions in all parts of the country and of many different kinds of people; and it appears to me that the great masses of this country care comparatively little

about the negro, and are anxious only for military successes." As they left his office, Lincoln, according to Conway, said gravely, "When the hour comes for dealing with slavery I trust I will be willing to do my duty, though it cost my life" (Conway, *Autobiography,* 1:307).

53. Quoted in Randall Stewart, *Nathaniel Hawthorne: A Biography* (1948; reprint, New York: Archon, 1970), 233.

54. *Harper's Weekly* 7 (November 21, 1863): 739.

55. Franklin Pierce, *Record of a Month: Four letters, Written December 7, 1859 through January 6, 1860* (n.p.: n.p., ca. 1864), 14.

56. Ibid., 8.

57. Dicey, "Nathaniel Hawthorne," 244.

58. Ibid., 245.

59. Ibid., 246.

Bibliography

Aaron, Daniel. *The Unwritten War: American Writers and the Civil War.* New York: Knopf, 1973.

Acuña, Rodolfo. *Occupied America: The Chicano's Struggle toward Liberation.* San Francisco: Canfield, 1972.

Alcott, Bronson. *The Journals of Bronson Alcott.* Ed. Odell Shepard. Boston: Little, Brown, 1938.

Alcott, Louisa May. *Louisa May Alcott on Race, Sex, and Slavery.* Ed. Sarah Elbert. Boston: Northeastern University Press, 1997.

Allen, Gay Wilson. *Waldo Emerson.* New York: Penguin, 1981.

Ammidon, Philip R. "Hawthorne's Last Sketch." *New England Magazine and Bay State Monthly* 4 (June 1886): 516–26.

Anthony, David. "Class, Culture, and the Trouble with White Skin in Hawthorne's *The House of the Seven Gables.*" *Yale Journal of Criticism* 12, no. 2 (1999): 249–68.

Aptheker, Herbert. *Nat Turner's Slave Rebellion: Together with the Full Text of the So-Called "Confessions" of Nat Turner Made in Prison in 1831.* New York: Humanities, 1966.

Arac, Jonathan. "The Politics of *The Scarlet Letter.*" In *Ideology and Classic American Literature,* ed. Sacvan Bercovitch and Myra Jehlen, 247–66. New York: Cambridge University Press, 1986.

Bancroft, George. *History of the United States from the Discovery of the American Continent.* Vol. 3, *History of the Colonization of the United States.* Boston: Little and Brown, 1840.

Barlett, Irving H. "Abolitionists, Fugitives, and Imposters in Boston, 1846–1847." *New England Quarterly* 55 (March 1982): 97–101.

Baym, Nina. "Hawthorne's Gothic Discards: *Fanshawe* and 'Alice Doane.'" *Nathaniel Hawthorne Journal* 4 (1974): 105–15.

Baym, Nina. "Hawthorne's Holgrave: The Failure of the Artist-Hero." *Journal of English and German Philology* 69 (1970): 584–98.

Baym, Nina. *The Shape of Hawthorne's Career.* Ithaca, NY: Cornell University Press, 1976.

Bedell, Madelon. *The Alcotts: Biography of a Family.* New York: Clarkson N. Potter, 1980.

Bell, Michael Davitt. *Hawthorne and the Historical Romance of New England.* Princeton, NJ: Princeton University Press, 1971.

Bell, Millicent. *Hawthorne's View of the Artist.* Albany: State University of New York Press, 1962.

Bender, Thomas, ed. *The Antislavery Debate: Capitalism and Abolitionism as a Problem in Historical Interpretation.* Berkeley: University of California Press, 1992.

Benson, T. Lloyd. *The Caning of Senator Sumner.* Belmont, CA: Wadsworth/ Thomson, 2004.

Bentley, Nancy. "Slaves and Fauns: Hawthorne and the Uses of Primitivism." *ELH* 57 (1990): 901–37.

Bentley, Nancy. "White Slaves: The Mulatto Hero in Antebellum Fiction." *American Literature* 65 (September 1993): 501–22.

Bercovitch, Sacvan. *The Office of "The Scarlet Letter."* Baltimore: Johns Hopkins University Press, 1991.

Bercovitch, Sacvan. *The Rites of Assent: Transformations in the Symbolic Construction of America.* New York: Routledge, 1993.

Berlant, Lauren. *The Anatomy of National Fantasy: Hawthorne, Utopia, and Everyday Life.* Chicago: University of Chicago Press, 1991.

Blassingame, John W. Introduction to *Slave Testimony: Two Centuries of Letters, Speeches, Interviews, and Autobiographies,* ed. John W. Blassingame. Baton Rouge: Louisiana State University Press, 1977.

Bosco, Ronald A., and Joel Myerson. *The Emerson Brothers: A Fraternal Biography in Letters.* New York: Oxford University Press, 2006.

Boston slave riot, and trial of Anthony Burns: Containing the report of the Faneuil hall meeting; the murder of Batchelder; Theodore Parker's lesson of the day; speeches of counsel on both sides, corrected by themselves; a verbatim report of Judge Loring's decision; and detailed account of the embarkation. Boston: Fetridge, 1854.

Boyer, Paul, and Stephen Nissenbaum. *Salem Possessed: The Social Origins of Witchcraft.* Cambridge, MA: Harvard University Press, 1974.

Boyer, Paul, and Stephen Nissenbaum, eds. *The Salem Witchcraft Papers: Verba-*

tim Transcripts of the Legal Documents of the Salem Witchcraft Outbreak of 1692. 3 vols. New York: Da Capo, 1977.

Brancaccio, Patrick. "'The Black Man's Paradise': Hawthorne's Editing of the *Journal of an African Cruiser.*" *New England Quarterly* 53 (March 1980): 23–41.

Brattle, Thomas. Letter, October 8, 1692. In Burr, 169–90.

Breslaw, Elaine G. "Tituba's Confession: The Multicultural Dimensions of the 1692 Salem Witch-Hunt." *Ethnohistory* 44, no. 3 (1997): 535–56.

Brickhouse, Anna. "Hawthorne in the Americas: Frances Calderón de la Barca, Octavio Paz, and the Mexican Genealogy of 'Rappaccini's Daughter.'" *PMLA* 113, no. 2 (1998): 227–42.

Brickhouse, Anna. *Transamerican Literary Relations and the Nineteenth-Century Public Sphere.* New York: Cambridge University Press, 2004.

[Bridge, Horatio]. Holograph journal, June 1843–January 19, 1844. Berg Collection. New York Public Library.

[Bridge, Horatio]. *Journal of an African Cruiser, by an Officer of the U.S. Navy.* Ed. Nathaniel Hawthorne. New York: Wiley and Putnam, 1845.

Bridge, Horatio. *Personal Recollections of Nathaniel Hawthorne.* New York: Harper and Brothers, 1893.

Bright, Henry Arthur. *Happy Country This America: The Travel Diary of Henry Arthur Bright.* Ed. Anne Henry Ehrenpreis. Columbus: Ohio State University Press, 1978.

Brodhead, Richard. "Hawthorne and the Fate of Politics." *Essays in Literature* 11 (Spring 1984): 95–103.

Brodhead, Richard. *The School of Hawthorne.* New York: Oxford University Press, 1986.

Budick, Emily Miller. "The World as Specter: Hawthorne's Historical Art." *PMLA* 101 (1986): 218–32.

Buell, Lawrence. *Emerson.* Cambridge, MA: Harvard University Press, Belknap, 2003.

Burr, George Lincoln, ed. *Narratives of the Witchcraft Cases, 1648–1706.* New York: Scribner's, 1914.

Cain, William E. "Prospects for Change." In *The Blithedale Romance,* by Nathaniel Hawthorne, ed. William E. Cain, 221–24. Boston: St. Martin's, Bedford, 1996.

Calef, Robert. *More Wonders of the Invisible World.* 1700. Reprinted in Burr, 296–393.

Cantwell, Robert. *Nathaniel Hawthorne: The American Years.* New York: Rinehart, 1948.

Carter, Samuel, III. *Cherokee Sunset: A Nation Betrayed; A Narrative of Travail and Triumph, Persecution and Exile.* New York: Doubleday, 1976.

Carton, Evan. *The Marble Faun: Hawthorne's Transformations.* New York: Twayne, 1992.

Channing, Ellery. "The Selected Letters of William Ellery Channing the Younger (Part One)." Ed. Francis B. Dedmond. In *Studies in the American Renaissance, 1989,* ed. Joel Myerson, 115–218. Charlottesville: University Press of Virginia, 1989.

Cheyfitz, Eric. "The Irresistibleness of Great Literature: Reconstructing Hawthorne's Politics." *American Literary History* 6 (1994): 539–58.

Childs, Matt D. "'A Black French General Arrived to Conquer the Island': Images of the Haitian Revolution in Cuba's 1812 Aponte Rebellion." In *The Impact of the Haitian Revolution in the Atlantic World,* ed. David P. Geggus, 135–56. (Columbia: University of South Carolina Press, 2001.

Clark, Elizabeth B. "Sacred Rights of the Weak: Pain and Sympathy in Antebellum America." *Journal of American History* 82 (September 1995): 463–93.

Clarke, James Freeman. *The Rendition of Anthony Burns: Its Causes and Consequences; A Discourse on Christian Politics.* Boston: Prentiss and Sawyer, 1854.

Colacurcio, Michael. Introduction to *Selected Tales and Sketches,* by Nathaniel Hawthorne. New York: Penguin, 1987.

Colacurcio, Michael. *The Province of Piety: Moral History in Hawthorne's Early Tales.* Durham, NC: Duke University Press, 1995.

Colacurcio, Michael. "'Red Man's Grave': Art and Destiny in Hawthorne's 'Main-street." *Nathaniel Hawthorne Review* 31 (Fall 2005): 1–18.

Collins, Robert E. *Theodore Parker: American Transcendentalist; A Critical Essay and a Collection of His Writings.* Metuchen, NJ: Scarecrow, 1973.

Conway, Moncure Daniel. *Autobiography: Memories and Experiences.* 2 vols. New York: Cassell, 1904.

Conway, Moncure Daniel. *Emerson, at Home and Abroad.* 1883. Reprint, New York: Haskell House, 1968.

Conway, Moncure Daniel. *Life of Nathaniel Hawthorne.* 1890. Reprint, New York: Haskell House, 1968.

Cooper, James Fenimore. *The American Democrat, and Other Political Writings.* Ed. Bradley J. Birzer and John Wilson. Washington, DC: Regnery, 2000.

Corporation of Charleston. *An Account of the Late Intended Insurrection among a Portion of the Blacks of This City.* Charleston: A. E. Miller, 1822. Reprinted in *Slave Insurrections: Selected Documents,* 34–39. Westport, CT: Negro Universities Press, 1970.

Crews, Frederick C. *The Sins of the Fathers: Hawthorne's Psychological Themes.* New York: Oxford University Press, 1966.

Crowley, John W. "Hawthorne's New England Epochs." *ESQ: A Journal of the American Renaissance* 25 (1979): 59–70.

Curti, Merle. *The Growth of American Thought.* 3rd ed. New Brunswick, NJ: Transaction, 1982.

[Curtis, George W.]. "The Works of Nathaniel Hawthorne." *North American Review* 99 (October 1864): 539–57.

Davis, David Brion. *In Human Bondage: The Rise and Fall of Slavery in the New World.* New York: Oxford University Press, 2006.

Davis, Clark. *Hawthorne's Shyness: Ethics, Politics, and the Question of Engagement.* Baltimore: Johns Hopkins University Press, 2005.

Dayan, Joan. *Haiti, History, and the Gods.* Berkeley: University of California Press, 1995.

Demos, John. "The Antislavery Movement and the Problem of Violent 'Means.'" *New England Quarterly* 37 (December 1964): 501–26.

Dicey, Edward. "Nathaniel Hawthorne." *Macmillan's Magazine* 10 (July 1864): 241–46.

Dicey, Edward. *Six Months in the Federal States.* 1863. Reprinted as *Spectator of America,* ed. Herbert Mitgang. Athens: University of Georgia Press, 1989.

Donald, David. *Charles Sumner and the Coming of the Civil War.* New York: Knopf, 1961.

Donald, David. *Lincoln Reconsidered.* 2nd ed. 1956. Reprint, New York: Knopf, 1965.

Doubleday, Neal Frank. *Hawthorne's Early Tales: A Critical Study.* Durham, NC: Duke University Press, 1972.

Douglass, Frederick. "Letters to His Old Master." Published as "Appendix" in *My Bondage and My Freedom,* by Frederick Douglass, ed. William L. Andrews, 264–71. 1855. Reprint, Urbana: University of Illinois Press, 1987.

[Drayton, William]. *The South Vindicated from the Treason and Fanaticism of the Northern Abolitionists.* 1836. Reprint, New York: Negro Universities Press, 1969.

Duberman, Martin. *James Russell Lowell.* Boston: Houghton Mifflin, 1966.

Dubois, Laurent. *Avengers of the New World: The Story of the Haitian Revolution.* Cambridge, MA: Harvard University Press, Belknap, 2004.

Earle, Jonathan H. *Jacksonian Antislavery and the Politics of Free Soil, 1824–1854.* Chapel Hill: University of North Carolina Press, 2004.

Edwards, Bryan. *An Historical Survey of the French Colony in the Island of St. Domingo.* London: printed for J. Stockdale, 1797.

Elbert, Sarah. *Louisa May Alcott: On Race, Sex, and Slavery.* Boston: Northeastern University Press, 1997.

Ellis, Bill. Introduction to *The Consular Letters, 1853–1855,* by Nathaniel Hawthorne, vol. 19 of *The Centenary Edition of the Works of Nathaniel Hawthorne,* ed. William Charvat et al., 3–53. Columbus: Ohio State University Press, 1988.

Emerson, Edward. "Notes." In *Miscellanies,* by Ralph Waldo Emerson, ed. Edward Emerson, 547–648. 1904. Reprint, New York: AMS Press, 1968.

Emerson, Lidian Jackson. *The Selected Letters of Lidian Jackson Emerson.* Ed. Delores Bird Carpenter. Columbia: University of Missouri Press, 1987.

Emerson, Ralph Waldo. *Collected Poems and Translations.* New York: Library of America, 1994.

Emerson, Ralph Waldo. *The Complete Works of Ralph Waldo Emerson.* Ed. Edward Waldo Emerson. 12 vols. 1903–4. Reprint, New York: AMS Press, 1968.

Emerson, Ralph Waldo. *The Conduct of Life.* Ed. Edward Waldo Emerson. 1904. Reprint, New York: AMS Press, 1968.

Emerson, Ralph Waldo. *The Correspondence of Emerson and Carlyle.* Ed. Joseph Slater. New York: Columbia University Press, 1964.

Emerson, Ralph Waldo. *Emerson's Antislavery Writings.* Ed. Len Gougeon and Joel Myerson. New Haven, CT: Yale University Press, 1995.

Emerson, Ralph Waldo. *Emerson's "Nature": Origin, Growth, Meaning.* Ed. Merton M. Sealts Jr. and Alfred R. Ferguson. 2nd ed. Carbondale: Southern Illinois University Press, 1979.

Emerson, Ralph Waldo. *Essays: First and Second Series.* Library of America Edition. New York: Vintage, 1990.

Emerson, Ralph Waldo. *The Journals and Miscellaneous Notebooks of Ralph Waldo Emerson.* Ed. William H. Gilman, Ralph H. Orth, et al. 16 vols. Cambridge, MA: Harvard University Press, Belknap, 1960–82.

Emerson, Ralph Waldo. *Lectures and Biographical Sketches.* Ed. James Eliot Cabot. Boston: Houghton Mifflin, 1884.

Emerson, Ralph Waldo. *The Letters of Ralph Waldo Emerson.* Ed. Ralph L. Rusk and Eleanor M. Tilton. 10 vols. New York: Columbia University Press, 1939–95.

Emerson, Ralph Waldo. *The Political Emerson: Essential Writings on Politics and Social Reform.* Ed. David M. Robinson. Boston: Beacon, 2004.

Emerson, Ralph Waldo. *The Selected Letters of Ralph Waldo Emerson.* Ed. Joel Myerson. New York: Columbia University Press, 1997.

Eppler, Karen Sanchez. *Touching Liberty: Abolition, Feminism, and the Politics of the Body.* Berkeley: University of California Press, 1993.

Erkkila, Betsy. *Mixed Bloods and Other Crosses: Rethinking American Literature from the Revolution to the Culture Wars.* Philadelphia: University of Pennsylvania Press, 2005.

Erlich, Gloria C. *Family Themes and Hawthorne's Fiction: The Tenacious Web.* New Brunswick, NJ: Rutgers University Press, 1984.

Fick, Carolyn. *The Making of Haiti: The Saint-Domingue Revolution from Below.* Knoxville: University of Tennessee Press, 1990.

Fields, Annie. *Authors and Friends.* Boston: Houghton Mifflin, 1896.

Fields, James T. *Yesterdays with Authors.* Boston: Houghton Mifflin, 1900.

Fisch, Audrey A. *American Slaves in Victorian England: Abolitionist Politics in Popular Literature and Culture.* Cambridge: Cambridge University Press, 2000.

Foster, Frances Smith. *Witnessing Slavery: The Development of Ante-Bellum Slave Narratives.* Westport, CT: Greenwood, 1979.

Franchot, Jenny. *Roads to Rome: The Antebellum Protestant Encounter with Catholicism.* Berkeley: University of California Press, 1994.

Franklin, John Hope. *From Slavery to Freedom: A History of Negro Americans.* 1956. Reprint, New York: Knopf, 1968.

Franklin, John Hope, and Loren Schweninger. *Runaway Slaves: Rebels on the Plantation.* New York: Oxford University Press, 1999.

Frederickson, George M. *The Black Image in the White Mind: The Debate on Afro-American Character and Destiny, 1817–1914.* Hanover, NH: Wesleyan University Press, 1987.

Frederickson, George M. *The Inner Civil War: Northern Intellectuals and the Crisis of the Union.* New York: Harper and Row, 1965.

Friedman, Lawrence J. *Gregarious Saints: Self and Community in American Abolitionism, 1830–1870.* Cambridge: Cambridge University Press, 1982.

Fuller, Margaret. "'The Impulses of Human Nature': Margaret Fuller's Journal from June through October 1844." Ed. Martha L. Berg and Alice de V. Perry. *Massachusetts Historical Society Proceedings* 102 (1990): 38–126.

Fuller, Margaret. *The Letters of Margaret Fuller.* Vol. 5, *1848–49.* Ed. Robert N. Hudspeth. Ithaca, NY: Cornell University Press, 1988.

Fuller, Margaret. *Margaret Fuller, Critic: Writings from the "New-York Tribune," 1844–1846.* Ed. Judith Mattson Bean and Joel Myerson. New York: Columbia University Press, 2000.

Fuller, Margaret. *Summer on the Lakes, in 1843.* With an introduction by Susan Belasco Smith. 1844. Reprint, Urbana: University of Illinois Press, 1991.

Fuller, Margaret. *"These Sad but Glorious Days": Dispatches from Europe, 1846–1850.* Ed. Larry J. Reynolds and Susan Belasco Smith. New Haven, CT: Yale University Press, 1991.

Garrison, William Lloyd. "The Dangers of the Nation." 1832. Reprinted in *Selections from the Writings and Speeches of William Lloyd Garrison,* 44–61. 1852. Reprint, New York: Negro Universities Press, 1968.

Garrison, William Lloyd. Preface to *Narrative of the Life of Frederick Douglass, an American Slave, Written by Himself,* by Frederick Douglass. Ed. William L. Andrews and William S. McFeely. 1845. Reprint, New York: Norton, 1997.

Garvey, T. Gregory, ed. *The Emerson Dilemma: Essays on Emerson and Social Reform.* Athens: University of Georgia Press, 2001.

Glick, Wendell P. "Thoreau and the 'Herald of Freedom.'" *New England Quarterly* 22 (June 1949): 193–204.

Goddu, Teresa. *Gothic America: Narrative, History, and Nation*. New York: Columbia University Press, 1997.

Goddu, Teresa. "Letters Turned to Gold: Hawthorne, Authorship, and Slavery." *Studies in American Fiction* 29 (Spring 2001): 49–76.

Gollin, Rita K. "Estranged Allegiances in Hawthorne's Unfinished Romances." In *Hawthorne and the Real: Bicentennial Essays*, ed. Millicent Bell, 159–80. Columbus: Ohio State University Press, 2005.

Gougeon, Len. *Virtue's Hero: Emerson, Antislavery, and Reform*. Athens: University of Georgia Press, 1990.

Gragg, Larry. *The Salem Witch Crisis*. New York: Praeger, 1992.

Greeley, Horace. *Recollections of a Busy Life*. 1868. Reprint, New York: Confucian, 1981.

Gross, Robert A. *The Minutemen and Their World*. New York: Hill and Wang, 1976.

Grossman, Jay. "'A' Is for Abolition? Race, Authorship, *The Scarlet Letter*." *Textual Practice* 7, no. 1 (Spring 1993): 13–30.

Guarneri, Carl J. *The Utopian Alternative: Fourierism in Nineteenth-Century America*. Ithaca, NY: Cornell University Press, 1991.

Hale, John Hale. *A Modest Enquiry into the Nature of Witchcraft*. 1702. Reprinted in Burr, 399–432.

Hall, Lawrence Sargent. *Hawthorne, Critic of Society*. 1944. Reprint, Gloucester, MA: Peter Smith, 1966.

Handlin, Lilian. *George Bancroft: The Intellectual as Democrat*. New York: Harper and Row, 1984.

Hansen, Chadwick. "The Metamorphosis of Tituba, or Why American Intellectuals Can't Tell an Indian Witch from a Negro." *New England Quarterly* 47 (March 1974): 3–12.

Harding, Walter. *The Days of Henry Thoreau*. New York: Knopf, 1970.

Hartman, Saidiya V. *Scenes of Subjection: Terror, Slavery, and Self-Making in Nineteenth-Century America*. New York: Oxford University Press, 1997.

Hawthorne, Elizabeth Manning. Letter to James T. Fields, December 26, 1870. In *Hawthorne in His Own Time*, ed. Ronald A. Bosco and Jillmarie Murphy, 6–10. Iowa City: University of Iowa Press, 2007.

Hawthorne, Julian. *Nathaniel Hawthorne and His Wife: A Biography*. 2 vols. Boston: Houghton Mifflin, 1884.

Hawthorne, Nathaniel. *The Centenary Edition of the Works of Nathaniel Hawthorne*. Ed. William Charvat et al. 23 vols. Columbus: Ohio State University Press, 1962–97.

Hawthorne, Sophia Peabody. "'The Cuba Journal' of Sophia Peabody Hawthorne." Ed. Claire Badaracco. PhD diss., Rutgers University, 1978.

Heinl, Robert Debs, Jr., and Nancy Gordon Heinl. *Written in Blood: The Story of the Haitian People, 1492–1971*. Boston: Houghton Mifflin, 1978.

Herbert, T. Walter. *Dearest Beloved: The Hawthornes and the Making of the Middle-Class Family*. Berkeley: University of California Press, 1993.

Higginson, Thomas Wentworth. *Margaret Fuller Ossoli*. 1898. Reprint, New York: Confucian, 1980.

Higginson, Thomas Wentworth. "Massachusetts in Mourning! A Sermon." *National Anti-Slavery Standard,* June 24, 1854.

Higginson, Thomas Wentworth. "Nat Turner's Insurrection." *Atlantic Monthly* 8 (August 1861): 173–87.

Hill, Francis. *The Salem Witch Trials Reader*. New York: Da Capo, 2000.

Hinks, Peter P. Introduction to *David Walker's "Appeal to the Coloured Citizens of the World,"* ed. Peter P. Hinks. University Park: Pennsylvania State University Press, 2000.

History of American Presidential Elections, 1789–1968. Ed. Arthur M. Schlesinger Jr. et al. Vol. 1, *1789–1844*. New York: Chelsea House, 1971.

History of American Presidential Elections, 1789–1968. Ed. Arthur M. Schlesinger Jr. et al. Vol. 2, *1848–1896*. New York: Chelsea House, 1971.

Hoffer, Peter Charles. *The Devil's Disciples: Makers of the Salem Witchcraft Trials*. Baltimore: Johns Hopkins University Press, 1996.

Hoffer, Peter Charles. *The Salem Witchcraft Trials: A Legal History*. Lawrence: University Press of Kansas, 1997.

Hofstadter, Richard. *The American Political Tradition and the Men Who Made It*. New York: Vintage, 1948.

Holmes, Oliver Wendell. "Oration, Semi-centennial Celebration of the New England Society in the City of New York." 1855. In *The Autocrat's Miscellanies,* ed. Albert Mordell, 58–82. New York: Twayne, 1959.

Holt, Michael F. *The Rise and Fall of the American Whig Party: Jacksonian Politics and the Onset of the Civil War*. (New York: Oxford University Press, 1999.

Howe, M. A. DeWolfe. *The Life and Letters of George Bancroft*. 2 vols. 1908. Reprint, New York: Kennikat, 1971.

Hunt, Alfred N. *Haiti's Influence on Antebellum America: Slumbering Volcano in the Caribbean*. Baton Rouge: Louisiana State University Press, 1988.

Hutchinson, Thomas. *The History of the Province of Massachusetts-Bay, from the Charter of King William and Queen Mary, in 1691, until the Year 1750*. Boston: Thomas and John Fleet, 1767.

Hutton, Richard Hold. *Essays Theological and Literary*. 2 vols. London: Strahan, 1871.

James, C. L. R. *The Black Jacobins: Toussaint L'Ouverture and the San Domingo Revolution*. 2nd ed. New York: Random House, 1963.

James, Henry. *Hawthorne*. 1879. Reprint, New York: Collier-Macmillan, 1966.

Jefferson, Thomas. *Notes on the State of Virginia*. New York: printed by M. L. and W. A. Davis for Furman and Loudon, 1801.

Johnson, Linck C. "Reforming the Reformers: Emerson, Thoreau, and the Sunday Lectures at Amory Hall, Boston." *ESQ: A Journal of the American Renaissance* 37 (1991): 235–89.

Jones, Buford. "'The Hall of Fantasy' and the Early Hawthorne-Thoreau Relationship." *PMLA* 83 (1968): 1429–38.

Kamensky, Jane. "Words, Witches, and Woman Trouble: Witchcraft, Disorderly Speech, and Gender Boundaries in Puritan New England." *Essex Institute Historical Collections* 128 (1992): 286–309.

Karlsen, Carol F. *The Devil in the Shape of a Woman: Witchcraft in Colonial New England.* New York: Norton, 1987.

Kenes, James E. "Some Unexplored Relationships of Essex County Witchcraft to the Indian Wars of 1675 and 1689." *Essex Institute Historical Collections* 120 (1984): 179–212.

Lasseter, Janice Milner. "Hawthorne's Legacy to Rebecca Harding Davis." In *Hawthorne and Women: Engendering and Expanding the Hawthorne Tradition,* ed. John L. Idol Jr. and Melinda M. Ponder, 168–78. Amherst: University of Massachusetts Press, 1999.

Lathrop, Rose Hawthorne. *Memories of Hawthorne.* 1897. Reprint, New York: AMS Press, 1969.

Lawson, Deodat. *A Brief and True Narrative of Some Remarkable Passages Relating to Sundry Persons Afflicted by Witchcraft.* 1692. Reprinted in Burr, 152–64.

Lee, Kun Jong. "Ellison's Invisible Man: Emersonianism Revisited." *PMLA* 107 (March 1992): 331–44.

Lee, Maurice S. *Slavery, Philosophy, and American Literature, 1830–1860.* (New York: Cambridge University Press, 2005.

Lee, Sohui. "Hawthorne's Politics of Storytelling: Two 'Tales of the Province House' and the Specter of Anglomania in the *Democratic Review.*" *American Periodicals* 41, no. 1 (2004): 35–62.

Levin, David. "Shadows of Doubt: Specter Evidence in Hawthorne's 'Young Goodman Brown.'" *American Literature* 34 (November 1962): 344–52.

Levine, Robert S. "'Antebellum Rome' in *The Marble Faun.*" *American Literary History* 2, no. 1 (1990): 19–38.

Lincoln, Abraham. *Selected Speeches and Writings.* New York: Library of America, 1992.

Litwack, Leon F. *North of Slavery: The Negro in the Free States, 1790–1860.* Chicago: University of Chicago Press, 1961.

Loggins, Vernon. *The Hawthornes: The Story of Seven Generations of an American Family.* New York: Columbia University Press, 1951.

Lowance, Mason. Introduction to *Against Slavery: An Abolitionist Reader,* ed. Mason Lowance. New York: Penguin, 2000.

Lowell, James Russell. *The Biglow Papers, First Series: A Critical Edition.* Ed. Thomas Wortham. DeKalb: Northern Illinois University Press, 1977.

Lowell, James Russell. *A Fable for Critics.* 1848. Reprint, London: Gay and Bird, 1890.

Mann, Horace. "Speech on the Institution of Slavery." 1852. In *Against Slavery: An Abolitionist Reader,* ed. Mason Lowance, 266–72. New York: Penguin, 2000.

Mather, Cotton. "A Brand Pluck'd Out of the Burning." 1693. Reprinted in Burr, 203–88.

Mather, Cotton. *Magnalia Christi Americana; or, The ecclesiastical history of New-England, from its first planting in the year 1620. unto the year of our Lord, 1698. In seven books. . . . By . . . Cotton Mather, . . .* London: T. Parkhurst, 1702.

Mather, Cotton. *Memorable Providences, Relating to Witchcrafts and Possessions.* 1689. Reprinted in Burr, 93–143.

Mather, Cotton. *The Wonders of the Invisible World.* 1693. Reprint, Mount Vernon, NY: Peter Pauper, 1950.

Mather, Increase. *Cases of conscience concerning evil spirits personating men, witchcrafts, infallible proofs of guilt in such as are accused with that crime.* Boston: Benjamin Harris, 1693.

Matthiessen, F. O. *American Renaissance: Art and Expression in the Age of Emerson and Whitman.* New York: Oxford University Press, 1941.

Mayer, Henry. *All on Fire: William Lloyd Garrison and the Abolition of Slavery.* New York. St. Martin's, 1998.

McPherson, James M. *Battle Cry of Freedom: The Civil War Era.* New York: Oxford University Press, 1988.

McWilliams, Carey. *North from Mexico: The Spanish-Speaking People of the United States.* New York: Greenwood, 1948.

McWilliams, John P., Jr. *Hawthorne, Melville, and the American Character: A Looking-Glass Business.* New York: Cambridge University Press, 1984.

McWilliams, John P., Jr. "'Thorough-Going Democrat' and 'Modern Tory': Hawthorne and the Puritan Revolution of 1776." *Studies in Romanticism* 15 (1976): 549–71.

Melish, Joanne Pope. *Disowning Slavery: Gradual Emancipation and "Race" in New England, 1780–1860.* Ithaca, NY: Cornell University Press, 1998.

Mellow, James R. *Nathaniel Hawthorne in His Times.* Boston: Houghton Mifflin, 1980.

Melville, Herman. "Hawthorne and His Mosses, by a Virginian Spending July in Vermont." 1850. In *Nathaniel Hawthorne, Critical Assessments,* ed. Brian Harding, 1:215–28. Mountfield, East Sussex: Helm, n.d.

"Memorial of the Whigs of Salem, (Mass.)." Sent to Hon. William M. Meredith, secretary of the treasury of the United States, signed by Nathaniel Silsbee Jr., chairman, and Joseph B. F. Osgood, secretary. Nathaniel Hawthorne file. Fiscal Section. National Archives, Washington, DC.

Menand, Louis. *The Metaphysical Club*. New York: Farrar, Straus and Giroux, 2001.

Merrill, Boynton, Jr. *Jefferson's Nephews: A Frontier Tragedy*. Princeton, NJ: Princeton University Press, 1976.

Messerli, Jonathan. *Horace Mann: A Biography*. New York: Knopf, 1972.

Meyer, Michael. "Thoreau's Rescue of John Brown from History." In *Studies in the American Renaissance, 1980,* ed. Joel Myerson, 301–16. Charlottesville: University Press of Virginia, 1980.

Michaels, Walter Benn. "Romance and Real Estate." In *The American Renaissance Reconsidered,* ed. Walter Benn Michaels and Donald E. Pease, 156–82. Baltimore: Johns Hopkins University Press, 1985.

Miller, Edwin Haviland. *Salem Is My Dwelling Place: A Life of Nathaniel Hawthorne*. Iowa City: University of Iowa Press, 1991.

Millington, Richard H. *Practicing Romance: Narrative Form and Cultural Engagement in Hawthorne's Fiction*. Princeton, NJ: Princeton University Press, 1992.

Mitchell, Betty L. "Massachusetts Reacts to John Brown's Raid." *Civil War History* 19 (March 1973): 65–79.

Mitchell, Thomas R. *Hawthorne's Fuller Mystery*. Amherst: University of Massachusetts Press, 1998.

Moore, Margaret. "Nathaniel Hawthorne and 'Old John Brown.' " *Nathaniel Hawthorne Review* 26 (Spring 2000): 25–32.

Murdock, Harold. *The Nineteenth of April, 1775*. Boston: Houghton Mifflin, 1923.

Neufeldt, Leonard. "Emerson and the Civil War." *Journal of English and Germanic Philology* 61 (October 1972): 502–13.

Newberry, Frederick. *Hawthorne's Divided Loyalties: England and America in His Works*. Rutherford, NJ: Associated University Presses, 1987.

Newman, Simon P. "American Political Culture and the French and Haitian Revolutions: Nathaniel Cutting and the Jeffersonian Republicans." In *The Impact of the Haitian Revolution in the Atlantic World,* ed. David P. Geggus, 72–89. Columbia: University of South Carolina Press, 2001.

Nichols, Roy Franklin. *Franklin Pierce: Young Hickory of the Granite Hills*. Rev. ed. Philadelphia: University of Pennsylvania Press, 1958.

Nissenbaum, Stephen. "The Firing of Nathaniel Hawthorne." *Essex Institute Historical Collections* 114 (1978): 57–86.

Norton, Mary Beth. *In the Devil's Snare: The Salem Witchcraft Crisis of 1692*. New York: Vintage, 2002.

Nott, Josiah Clark. *Types of Mankind; or, Ethnological Researches, Based upon the Ancient Monuments, Paintings, Sculptures, and Crania of Races, and upon Their Natural, Geographical, Philological and Biblical History.* Philadelphia: Lippincott Gramoo; London: Trubner, 1855.

Nye, Russell B. *George Bancroft: Brahmin Rebel.* New York: Knopf, 1945.

Oates, Stephen B. *To Purge This Land with Blood: A Biography of John Brown.* Amherst: University of Massachusetts Press, 1984.

O'Sullivan, John. "The Abolitionists." *United States Magazine and Democratic Review* 16 (January 1845): 3–10.

O'Sullivan, John. "Annexation." *United States Magazine and Democratic Review* 17 (July–August 1845): 5–10.

O'Sullivan, John. "Introduction." *United States Magazine and Democratic Review* 1 (October 1837): 1–15.

O'Sullivan, John. "The Late William Ladd, the Apostle of Peace." *United States Magazine and Democratic Review* 10 (March 1842): 211–23.

O'Sullivan, John. "The Martyrdom of Cilley." *United States Magazine and Democratic Review* 1 (March 1838): 493–508.

O'Sullivan, John. "Mr. Henry A. Wise and the Cilley Duel." *United States Magazine and Democratic Review* 10 (May 1842): 482–87.

O'Sullivan, John."The Peace Movement." *United States Magazine and Democratic Review* 10 (February 1842): 107–21.

O'Sullivan, John. "The Texas Question." *United States Magazine and Democratic Review* 14 (April 1844): 423–30.

Packer, Barbara. "The Transcendentalists." In *Cambridge History of American Literature,* vol. 2, *1820–1865,* ed. Sacvan Bercovitch, 329–604. Cambridge: Cambridge University Press, 1995.

Parker, Theodore. "From *The Function and Place of Conscience in Relation to the Laws of Men* (1850)." In *Against Slavery: An Abolitionist Reader,* ed. Mason Lowance, 275–84. New York: Penguin, 2000.

Parker, Theodore. *The Rights of Man in America.* Ed. F. B. Sanborn. 1911. Reprint, New York: Negro Universities Press, 1969.

[Peabody, Elizabeth A.]. "Slavery in the United States: Its Evils, Alleviations, and Remedies." *North American Review* 73 (October 1851): 347–86.

Pearce, Roy Harvey. "Introduction to *Fanshawe.*" In *"The Blithedale Romance" and "Fanshawe,"* by Nathaniel Hawthorne, vol. 3 of *The Centenary Edition of the Works of Nathaniel Hawthorne,* ed. William Charvat et al., 301–16. Columbus: Ohio State University Press, 1964.

Pease, William H., and Jane H. Pease. "Antislavery Ambivalence: Immediatism, Expediency, Race." *American Quarterly* 17 (Winter 1965): 682–95.

Pease, William H., and Jane H. Pease. *They Who Would Be Free: Blacks' Search for Freedom, 1830–1861.* New York: Atheneum, 1974.

Peple, Edward Cronin, Jr. "The Personal and Literary Relationship of Hawthorne and Thoreau." PhD diss., University of Virginia, 1970.

Person, Leland S. "The Dark Labyrinth of Mind: Hawthorne, Hester, and the

Ironies of Racial Mothering." *Studies in American Fiction* 29 (Spring 2001): 33–47.

Petrulionis, Sandra Harbert. *To Set This World Right: The Antislavery Movement in Thoreau's Concord.* Ithaca, NY: Cornell University Press, 2006.

Pfister, Joel. *The Production of Personal Life: Class, Gender, and the Psychological in Hawthorne's Fiction.* Stanford: Stanford University Press, 1991.

Pickard, Samuel T. "Postscript." In *Hawthorne's First Diary, with an Account of Its Discovery and Loss,* 100–111. Boston: Houghton Mifflin, 1897.

Pickard, Samuel T. "The Story of William Symmes." In *Hawthorne's First Diary, with an Account of Its Discovery and Loss,* 22–48. Boston: Houghton Mifflin, 1897.

Pierce, Franklin. *Record of a Month: Four Letters, Written December 7, 1859 through January 6, 1860.* N.p.: n.p., ca. 1864.

Popkin, Jeremy D. "Facing Racial Revolution: Captivity Narratives and Identity in the Saint-Domingue Insurrection." *Eighteenth-Century Studies* 36, no. 4 (2003): 511–33.

Potter, David J. *The Impending Crisis, 1848–1861.* New York: Harper and Row, 1976.

Quarles, Benjamin. *Allies for Freedom: Blacks on John Brown.* New York: Oxford University Press, 1974.

Rankin, Thomas. *Letters on American Slavery Addressed to Mr. Thomas Rankin.* Boston: Garrison and Knapp, 1833.

Ratner, Lorman. *Powder Keg: Northern Opposition to the Antislavery Movement, 1831–1840.* New York: Basic, 1968.

Redpath, James. *Echoes of Harper's Ferry.* 1860. Reprint, Westport, CT: Negro Universities Press, 1970.

Redpath, James. *The Public Life of Capt. John Brown.* Boston: Thayer and Eldridge, 1860.

Reid, Margaret. *Cultural Secrets as Narrative Form: Storytelling in Nineteenth-Century America.* Columbus: Ohio State University Press, 2004.

Renehan, Edward J., Jr. *The Secret Six: The True Tale of the Men Who Conspired with John Brown.* New York: Crown, 1995.

Reynolds, David S. *John Brown, Abolitionist: The Man Who Killed Slavery, Sparked the Civil War, and Seeded Civil Rights.* New York: Knopf, 2005.

Reynolds, Larry J. "The Cimeter's 'Sweet' Edge: Thoreau, Contemplation, and Violence." In *More Day to Dawn: Thoreau's "Walden" for the Twenty-first Century,* ed. Sandy Petrulionis and Laura Walls, 60–81. Boston: University of Massachusetts Press, 2006.

Reynolds, Larry J. *European Revolutions and the American Literary Renaissance.* New Haven, CT: Yale University Press, 1988.

Reynolds, Larry J. "Hawthorne and Emerson in 'The Old Manse.'" *Studies in the Novel* 23 (Spring 1991): 403–24.

Reynolds, Larry J. "Hawthorne's Labors in Concord." In *The Cambridge Companion to Nathaniel Hawthorne,* ed. Richard H. Millington, 10–34. New York: Cambridge University Press, 2004.

Reynolds, Larry J. "Righteous Violence: The Roman Republic and Margaret Fuller's Revolutionary Example." In *Margaret Fuller: Transatlantic Crossings in a Revolutionary Age,* ed. Charles Capper and Cristina Giorcelli, 172–91. Madison: University of Wisconsin Press, 2008.

Richards, Leonard L. *"Gentlemen of Property and Standing": Anti-Abolition Mobs in Jacksonian America.* New York: Oxford University Press, 1970.

Richardson, Robert D., Jr. *Emerson: The Mind on Fire.* Berkeley: University of California Press, 1995.

Richardson, Robert D., Jr. *Henry David Thoreau: A Life of the Mind.* Berkeley: University of California Press, 1986.

Rodriguez, Junius P. *Chronology of World Slavery.* Santa Barbara, CA: ABC-CLIO, 1999.

Rogin, Michael. *"Ronald Reagan," the Movie: And Other Episodes in Political Demonology.* Berkeley: University of California Press, 1987.

Rosenthal, Bernard. *Salem Story: Reading the Witch Trials of 1692.* Cambridge: Cambridge University Press, 1993.

Rossbach, Jeffery. *Ambivalent Conspirators: John Brown, the Secret Six, and a Theory of Slave Violence.* Philadelphia: University of Pennsylvania Press, 1982.

Rostenberg, Leona. "Margaret Fuller's Roman Diary." *Journal of Modern History* 12 (June 1940): 209–20.

Rowe, John Carlos. "Nathaniel Hawthorne and Transnationality." In *Hawthorne and the Real: Bicentennial Essays,* ed. Millicent Bell, 88–106. Columbus: Ohio State University Press, 2005.

Rusk, Ralph L. *The Life of Ralph Waldo Emerson.* New York: Columbia University Press, 1949.

Sampson, Robert D. *John L. O'Sullivan and His Times.* Kent, OH: Kent State University Press, 2003.

Sanborn, Franklin. *Hawthorne and His Friends: Reminiscence and Tribute.* Cedar Rapids, IA: Torch, 1908.

Sanborn, Franklin. *Recollections of Seventy Years.* 2 vols. Boston: Gorham, 1909.

Sanneh, Lamin. *Abolitionists Abroad: American Blacks and the Making of Modern West Africa.* Cambridge, MA: Harvard University Press, 1999.

Schwartz, Harold. "Fugitive Slave Days in Boston." *New England Quarterly* 27 (June 1954): 192–212.

Scott, Donald M. "Abolition as a Sacred Vocation." In *Antislavery Reconsidered: New Perspectives on the Abolitionists,* ed. Lewis Perry and Michael Fellman, 51–74. Baton Rouge: Louisiana University Press, 1979.

Seelye, John. *Memory's Nation: The Place of Plymouth Rock.* Chapel Hill: University of North Carolina Press, 1998.

Shaw, Peter. "Fathers, Sons, and the Ambiguities of Revolution in 'My Kinsman, Major Molineux.'" *New England Quarterly* 49 (December 1976): 559–76.

Silverman, Kenneth. *The Life and Times of Cotton Mather.* New York: Harper and Row, 1984.

Slater, Joseph. "Two Sources for Emerson's First Address on West Indian Emancipation." *ESQ: A Journal of the American Renaissance* 44 (1966): 97–100.

Staudenraus, P. J. *The African Colonization Movement, 1816–1865.* (New York: Columbia University Press, 1961.

Stauffer, John. "Advent among the Indians: The Revolutionary Ethos of Gerrit Smith, James McCune Smith, Frederick Douglass, and John Brown." In *Antislavery Violence: Sectional, Racial, and Cultural Conflict in Antebellum America,* ed. John R. McKivigan and Stanley Harrold, 236–73. Knoxville: University of Tennessee Press, 1999.

Stauffer, John. *The Black Hearts of Men: Radical Abolitionists and the Transformation of Race.* Cambridge, MA: Harvard University Press, 2002.

Stewart, Randall. Introduction to *The American Notebooks,* by Nathaniel Hawthorne, ed. Randall Stewart. New Haven, CT: Yale University Press, 1932.

Stewart, Randall. *Nathaniel Hawthorne: A Biography.* 1948. Reprint, New York: Archon, 1970.

Stoehr, Taylor. *Hawthorne's Mad Scientists: Pseudoscience and Social Science in Nineteenth-Century Life and Letters.* Hamden, CT: Archon, 1978.

Stowe, Harriet Beecher. *Uncle Tom's Cabin.* Ed. Elizabeth Ammons. Norton Critical Edition. New York: Norton, 1994.

Sumner, Charles. "The Crime against Kansas." 1856. In *The Caning of Senator Sumner,* by T. Lloyd Benson, 97–121. Belmont, CA: Wadsworth/Thomson, 2004.

Sumner, Charles. *The Selected Letters of Charles Sumner.* 2 vols. Ed. Beverly Wilson Palmer. Boston: Northeastern University Press, 1990.

Sundquist, Eric J. *To Wake the Nations: Race in the Making of American Literature.* Cambridge, MA: Harvard University Press, Belknap, 1993.

Szasz, Ferenc M. "Antebellum Appeals to the 'Higher Law,' 1830–1860." *Essex Institute Historical Collections* 10 (1974): 22–48.

Teichgraeber, Richard F., III. *Sublime Thoughts/Penny Wisdom: Situating Emerson and Thoreau in the American Market.* Baltimore: Johns Hopkins University Press, 1995.

Tharp, Louisa Hall. *The Peabody Sisters of Salem.* Boston: McIntosh and Otis, 1950.

Thomas, Brook. "Citizen Hester: *The Scarlet Letter* as Civic Myth." *American Literary History* 13, no. 2 (2001): 181–211.

Thoreau, Henry David. *The Correspondence of Henry David Thoreau.* Ed. Walter Harding and Carl Bode. New York: New York University Press, 1958.

Thoreau, Henry David. *Journal.* Vol. 2, *1842–1848.* Ed. Robert Sattelmeyer. Princeton, NJ: Princeton University Press, 1984.

Thoreau, Henry David. *Journal.* Vol. 8, *1854.* Ed. Sandra Harbert Petrulionis. Princeton, NJ: Princeton University Press, 2002.

Thoreau, Henry David. *The Journal of Henry D. Thoreau.* Ed. Bradford Torrey and Francis H. Allen. 1906. Reprint, 14 vols. in two, New York: Dover, 1962.

Thoreau, Henry David. *Reform Papers.* Ed. Wendell Glick. Princeton, NJ: Princeton University Press, 1973.

Thoreau, Henry David. *"Walden" and "Resistance to Civil Government."* Ed. William Rossi. 2nd ed. Norton Critical Edition. New York: Norton, 1996.

"The Thorn That Bears Haws." *Liberator,* June 27, 1862.

Traubel, Horace, and William White. *With Walt Whitman in Camden.* Vol. 6. Ed. Gertrude Traubel. Carbondale: Southern Illinois University Press, 1982.

Turner, Arlin. *Nathaniel Hawthorne: A Biography.* New York: Oxford University Press, 1980.

Upham, Charles. *Lectures on Witchcraft, Comprising a History of the Delusion in Salem, in 1692.* Boston: Carter, Hendee, and Babcock, 1831.

Upham, Charles. *Salem Witchcraft, with an Account of Salem Village, and a History of Opinions on Witchcraft and Kindred Subjects.* 2 vols. 1867. Reprint, Williamstown, MA: Corner House, 1971.

Valenti, Patricia Dunlavy. *Sophia Peabody Hawthorne: A Life.* Vol. 1, *1809–1847.* Columbia: University of Missouri Press, 2004.

Von Frank, Albert J. "Mrs. Brackett's Verdict: Magic and Means in Transcendental Antislavery Work." In *Transient and Permanent: The Transcendentalist Movement and Its Contexts,* ed. Charles Capper and Conrad Edick Wright, 385–507. Boston: Massachusetts Historical Society, 1999.

Von Frank, Albert J. *The Trials of Anthony Burns: Freedom and Slavery in Emerson's Boston.* Cambridge, MA: Harvard University Press, Belknap, 1998.

Wallner, Peter A. *Franklin Pierce: New Hampshire's Favorite Son.* Concord, NH: Plaidswede, 2004.

Walters, Ronald G. "The Erotic South: Civilization and Sexuality in American Abolitionism." In *History of the American Abolitionist Movement,* vol. 1, *Abolitionism and American Reform,* ed. John R. McKivigan, 355–79. New York: Garland, 1999.

Ward, John William. *Andrew Jackson: Symbol for an Age.* London: Oxford University Press, 1962.

Warren, Austin. *Nathaniel Hawthorne: Representative Selections.* New York: American Book, 1934.

Werner, John M. *Reaping the Bloody Harvest: Race Riots in the United States during the Age of Jackson, 1824–1849.* New York: Garland, 1986.

Whitman, Walt. "Prohibition of Colored Persons." *Brooklyn Daily Times*, May 6, 1858. Reprinted in *Race and the American Romantics*, ed. Vincent Freimark and Bernard Rosenthal, 46–47. New York: Schocken, 1971.

Williams, Eric. *Capitalism and Slavery*. 1944. Reprint, Chapel Hill: University of North Carolina Press, 1994.

Wineapple, Brenda. *Hawthorne: A Life*. New York: Knopf, 2003.

Wortham, Thomas. "Did Emerson Blackball Frederick Douglass from Membership in the Town and Country Club?" *New England Quarterly* 65 (June 1992): 295–98.

Wyatt-Brown, Bertram. *Lewis Tappan and the Evangelical War against Slavery*. Cleveland: Press of Case Western Reserve University, 1969.

Wyatt-Brown, Bertram. "'A Volcano beneath a Mountain of Snow': John Brown and the Problem of Interpretation." In *His Soul Goes Marching On: Responses to John Brown and the Harpers Ferry Raid*, ed. Paul Finkelman, 10–38. Charlottesville: University Press of Virginia, 1995.

Wyatt-Brown, Bertram. *Yankee Saints and Southern Sinners*. Baton Rouge: Louisiana State University Press, 1985.

Yellin, Jean Fagan. "Hawthorne and the Slavery Question." In *Historical Guide to Nathaniel Hawthorne*, ed. Larry J. Reynolds, 135–64. New York: Oxford University Press, 2001.

Young, Sandra Sandiford. "A Different Journey: John Brown Russwurm, 1799–1851." PhD diss., Boston College, 2004.

Index